PRAISE FOR BESTSELLING AUTHOR
STEPHEN LEATHER:

'A writer at the top of his game'
Sunday Express

'A brilliant read that stands out of the morass of so-so
military thrillers around nowadays'
News of the World on *Hot Blood*

'As tough as British thrillers get . . . gripping'
Irish Independent on *Hard Landing*

'A master of the thriller genre'
Irish Times

'An aggressively topical novel but a genuinely thrilling
one, too'
Daily Telegraph on *Cold Kill*

'The sheer impetus of his story-telling is damned hard
to resist'
Sunday Express

'Leather has the rare knack of writing in such a way that
you almost feel as if you are watching a film . . . I devoured
chapter after chapter late into the night'
www.crimesquad.com on *Fair Game*

'Explores complex contemporary issues while keeping
the action fast and bloody'
Economist on *Dead Men*

Also by Stephen Leather

About the author

Stephen Leather is one of the UK's most successful thriller writers. He was previously a journalist on newspapers including *The Times* and the *South China Morning Post* and his bestsellers have been translated into fifteen languages.

Find out more at www.stephenleather.com.

STEPHEN
LEATHER
TAKEDOWN

HODDER

First published in Great Britain in 2017 by Hodder & Stoughton
An Hachette UK company

First published in paperback 2017

2

Copyright © Stephen Leather 2017

A CIP catalogue record for this title is available from the British Library

ISBN 978 1 473 60555 8
Ebook ISBN 978 1 473 60554 1
A format ISBN 978 1 473 60556 5

Typeset in Plantin by Palimpsest Book Production Limited,
Falkirk, Stirlingshire

Printed and bound by Clays Ltd, St Ives plc

Hodder & Stoughton policy is to use papers that are natural, renewable
and recyclable products and made from wood grown in sustainable forests.
The logging and manufacturing processes are expected to conform to the
environmental regulations of the country of origin.

Hodder & Stoughton Ltd
Carmelite House
50 Victoria Embankment
London EC4Y 0DZ

www.hodder.co.uk

For Abby

I

Caleb McGovan sat back in his seat as the aircraft began its roll-back and the easyJet flight attendants went through the usual pre-flight rituals. He had heard airline safety drills so many times in his life that he could have recited the script word for word from memory, but it was less conspicuous to pretend to pay attention than to read a newspaper ostentatiously while it was going on. Around him there was the usual excited buzz of chatter from people setting off on vacation, one or two of whom were already well into the holiday spirit after a session at one of the airside bars in Departures. Apart from one particularly boisterous hen party, all in matching outfits including pink feather boas and 'Horny Hens on Tour' T-shirts, the other passengers were couples or families. McGovan might have been just another holidaymaker, except that he was travelling alone and did not have the air of a man with pleasure on his mind. One look at his closed and slightly forbidding expression was enough to stop the person in the next seat to him trying to strike up a conversation.

As soon as the flight safety briefing was over, he closed his eyes and cat-napped throughout the rest of the four-hour flight to Turkey.

* * *

Three other flights had just disgorged their passengers at Dalaman airport, and McGovan joined the seemingly endless queue of tourists snaking its slow way through Passport Control. The Turkish immigration official gave his passport no more than a cursory glance before waving him through. While the other passengers were spilling from the arrivals hall to hail taxis or were being picked up by their hotel and resort shuttle buses, McGovan walked straight past the taxi stands and out across the car park in front of the terminal. A four-by-four was parked at the far side and four men wearing Arab dress were waiting for him. They exchanged only a few words before they all climbed into the four-by-four and set off. McGovan was squashed into the back seat between two others as they drove east while the setting sun sank slowly over the Mediterranean behind them. It was a gruelling, all-night drive, heading away from the Turquoise Coast, then skirting the forbidding ranges of the Taurus Mountains, capped by the towering Mount Tahtali, which flanked the Mediterranean coast all the way to the Syrian border far to the east. There were other smaller airports much closer to the border but none with the anonymity that came from using a bustling tourist hub like Dalaman, where almost every passenger passing through it was a foreign holidaymaker.

As dawn broke they were still three hours' drive from the Syrian border. Apart from a few isolated tourist sites, almost the whole of south-east Turkey was a military zone, and as they drew closer to the border the driver of the four-by-four took a circuitous route, turning off the highway for the back roads, keeping well away from the Turkish army bases. They drove through dense forests, where the scent of black pine, cedar and juniper filled the air, and crossed an arid plateau where shepherds and their scrawny flocks paused to watch them pass in a cloud of dust. Steering well clear of the border posts, they eventually took a rock-strewn dirt road, a smugglers' track leading up into the high mountains.

Eventually they crested a rise and McGovan saw the track running on ahead towards a steel-mesh and barbed-wire fence. Death's head warning signs in Turkish and Arabic hung from it at intervals, showing that the fence marked the Turko-Syrian border. The smugglers' track ended at the fence, but an even fainter, narrower path continued on the other side, zigzagging away down the far side of the ridge. The four-by-four ground to a halt beside the fence. There was silence broken only by the metallic ticking of the engine as it began to cool. McGovan looked at his companions. Although he had been travelling with them for hours, he was still not sure whether they were acting as his guides or his guards. They stared back at him in silence. 'What now?' he said at last, in Arabic.

'This is where you get out,' one said. 'Crawl under the wire and walk due south for a mile where, *inshallah*, another of our vehicles will be waiting in a *wadi* to collect you.'

McGovan paused a moment, in case they had anything to add, but they remained silent. One of the men next to him opened the door, got out and made a gesture with his hand, as if wafting away an irritating fly. McGovan shrugged his shoulders and followed him. The man climbed back into the vehicle, the engine roared into life and the four-by-four slewed around, spraying sand over him as the wheels slipped and skidded, then sped back the way it had come.

He watched it go, then took a careful look around. Satisfied that he was alone in the sweep of desert landscape, he drank some water from his flask and urinated against a rock, then moved towards the fence. From the fresh tyre tracks running parallel to the wire, Turkish Army vehicles patrolled this area frequently and he had no desire to be stopped and interrogated.

When he reached the wire, he lay flat in the dust and wormed under the lowest strand at the point where the smugglers' track intersected with the fence. The compacted earth, scored by the marks left by the elbows and feet of countless others as they had wriggled under the fence, showed that he was far from the first to cross the border there. He picked himself up on the far side, brushed down his clothes and took another careful look around him. Then he set off, moving away from the fence and heading due south.

The sun was high in the sky and the heat was pitiless. The mountains and the desert were shimmering in the heat-haze, but there was no other movement, apart from a pair of vultures circling on the thermals high above. The sun-bleached animal bones he saw at intervals as he picked his way among the rocks, suggested that they never had to wait too long in this unforgiving landscape for their next meal.

He walked for perhaps twenty minutes, picking his way along a narrow dry riverbed cutting through the steep scree slope that marked the Syrian side of the border. Further down he could see the riverbed broaden as it disappeared into the mouth of a *wadi* and, as he drew nearer, the glint of sunlight reflecting from the white metal roof of a Toyota

Landcruiser showed him that his escort for the next stage of his journey was waiting for him.

As he approached, four more men, who had been sheltering from the sun in the shade beneath an overhang of rock, stepped into the open and stared at him impassively. Once more all were dressed in black Arab robes. Two wore *keffiyeh*s but the others wore hoods with crude holes cut for their mouths and eyes. There were few words of greeting. One merely grunted and pointed to the back seat of the Landcruiser, where McGovan again found himself wedged between two burly, silent Arabs as the Toyota bounced and buffeted its way down the rough, rock-strewn bed of the *wadi*. The men on either side of him smelled as if neither they nor their robes had seen soap and water for many weeks, but his years serving in the British Army had inured McGovan to far worse.

They drove for more than an hour, coming to a halt at a checkpoint flying the Islamic State flag. 'The Black Standard' was claimed to date back to the time of Muhammad in the seventh century. It was inscribed with the Shahada – 'There is no god but Allah and Muhammad is the messenger of Allah' – above the seal of Muhammad, both etched in white Arabic script against the black background of the flag.

The ISIS men manning the checkpoint were armed to the teeth with what McGovan's well-trained eye immediately recognised as brand-new American M-16 assault rifles and M-203 grenade launchers. All were no doubt part of the endless shipments of US military equipment that had been poured into Iraq during Operation Iraqi Freedom and its aftermath. McGovan's weather-beaten face creased into a sour smile as he savoured the irony of the title. America's desire to lash out at someone, anyone, in the wake of 9/11 and its professed intention to replace Saddam Hussein's brutal dictatorship with an American-style democracy had, directly or indirectly, caused the deaths of an estimated half a million Iraqi citizens, most of them civilians. Now the country was dissolving into civil war, inflicting yet more misery on its long-suffering population.

Despite the unprecedented levels of manpower, equipment and resources devoted to the Iraqi Army since the American conquest, the Iraqi troops that the Americans had traincd in their thousands had evaporated, like water in the desert, on almost every occasion when the going had got even slightly tough. In addition, 90 per cent of their American-supplied military equipment – just like 90 per cent of the billions of dollars the US had poured into the country as military aid or bribes to buy the loyalty of Sunni tribesmen – had also disappeared. Some had gone into the pockets of corrupt American contractors and military personnel, while the rest had been funnelled through Iraqi middlemen to reappear in the hands of hostile Iraqi forces, and the jihadists who were now turning the weapons against the Americans and their Iraqi stooges. Bought or stolen from the American-trained Iraqi troops, or carried by deserters joining ISIS from the Iraqi Army, some of those weapons had now been brought across the border into Syria.

The guards manning the second ISIS checkpoint exchanged greetings with the Arab occupants of the Toyota but directed baleful, suspicious looks at McGovan. 'The *faranji* must be hooded and bound before you can go further,' one said in

Arabic, glaring at him. 'It is forbidden for all unbelievers to see the route or the houses we use.'

One of McGovan's escorts reached under his seat and pulled out a black cloth hood, which was placed over McGovan's head and tied with a cord around his neck. His wrists were secured behind him. The cloth sack was even more foul-smelling than his escorts' body odour and the thick cloth made the heat beneath it even more intense, but McGovan ignored the stench and the sweat trickling down his face, focusing only on what he would need to say to the ISIS commander whom he would soon be meeting. Before he had set out to travel to Syria, he had been left in no doubt that if he did not convince the commander of his bona fides, the journey he was now making would be the last he ever took.

The Landcruiser drove on for another twenty minutes, and McGovan felt the vehicle making frequent changes of direction, presumably in an attempt to disorient him. Eventually it pulled up and the engine was switched off. He heard more challenges and greetings in guttural Arabic, then the car doors were opened. He was hustled out and taken inside a building, where the hood was removed and his wrists untied. He stood blinking for a couple of minutes, getting a sense of his surroundings. He was inside a low, mud-walled building, a goat-herder's hut from the smell, which was now evidently doubling as an ISIS safe-house. A few ISIS fighters, yet more anonymous bearded figures in long black robes, with black hoods or *keffiyeh*s, kept watch over the surrounding desert from the narrow windows, while others leaned against the wall, directing malevolent stares at him. The look in their eyes told him that if their commander was not satisfied with any of the answers McGovan gave in response to his questions he would not leave the building alive.

After a few minutes' silence, broken only by the buzzing of the flies that swarmed around him, a door at the rear of the building opened and the ISIS commander swept into the room, flanked by two massive bodyguards. The commander, who looked to be in his late forties or early fifties, was dressed like his men, in flowing black robes, but he was bare-headed and the fringes of his greying beard were dyed with henna – McGovan knew that was usually the mark of a *hajji* of South Asian origins. However, whatever his origins might have been, he spoke to McGovan in flawless Arabic, first making the traditional greeting, '*As salam aleykum.*'

'*Wa aleykum as salam,*' McGovan said. His accent was nowhere near as good, but it was passable.

'We already know your name and much about you,' the commander said. 'I am known as Saif al-Islam.'

'The Sword of Islam,' McGovan said, nodding. 'A good name for a warrior.'

'Indeed so, and one whose blade will not be sheathed until, inshallah, the Caliphate has been established and history will turn again, overthrowing the empire of the United States and the world Jewish government.'

McGovan said nothing in reply, and after a few moments, Saif al-Islam gestured towards a low table at the side of the room. The two men sat cross-legged on the floor, facing each other across the table. They sat in silence at first, scrutinising each other, while the commander's men brought them cups of bitter cardamom-scented coffee and fresh dates.

'So, Englishman,' Saif al-Islam said at last, 'you claim to have come to join our jihad.'

McGovan nodded. 'I can help you in your fight, I'm sure of that.'

'We have many foreign fighters here,' said Saif al-Islam, 'many from England, but also from around the world.'

McGovan nodded again. 'It's good that so many Muslims are prepared to help their brothers where help is needed,' he said.

'You realise that we do not pay our foreign fighters? We can give you food and arms but we are not interested in mercenaries.'

'I am not doing this for money, Saif al-Islam. In fact I don't want to take part in the fighting here. I've come to seek your help to stage a high-profile attack inside the UK.'

'You do us too much honour,' the ISIS commander said, with what might have been a mocking smile. 'We are only simple fighters. We are used to waging a guerrilla war in the desert, but we have no experience –' again the mirthless smile '– or, at least, very little, of waging war on the streets of Western cities. Tell me, what or who would be the target of such a high-profile attack?'

McGovan shot a glance towards the circle of ISIS men standing around the walls, all well within earshot of their conversation. He took a piece of paper and a pen from his pocket, wrote a few words on it and slid it across the table.

Saif al-Islam regarded him with amusement. 'You do not

trust my men, Englishman? Yet I would trust any of them with my life.'

McGovan inclined his head. 'But you know them, Saif al-Islam, whereas I do not. And I am a cautious man. The fewer people who know of my plans, the less chance there is of them being compromised.'

As if to reinforce his words, as soon as Saif al-Islam had glanced at the note, McGovan took it back and burned it with his cigarette lighter. The commander's expression did not change. 'Before we can talk further about this,' he said, 'I need to know more about you. As the Prophet has ordered us, we fight in the name of Allah and in the way of Allah. Why would you, a *faranji*, a Westerner, and a Christian,' his lip curled, 'wish to join our jihad against your own people?'

'I no longer consider myself a Christian,' said McGovan. 'I fought for the British in Iraq and in Afghanistan.' He saw the ISIS fighters stir and the hatred on their faces. One spat on the ground and began to stride towards him, fists clenched, but was stopped in his tracks as Saif al-Islam held up a warning hand.

'Let the *faranji* speak first,' he said, 'and then we will decide what to do with him.' He turned back to McGovan. 'Most of my fighters have lost friends and family,' he said, 'brothers and fathers on the battlefield, of course, but also wives, mothers and children killed by bombs, shells and bullets. No one who fought for the Americans and their friends in those countries can expect any sympathy or forgiveness from us.' He paused for a few seconds, holding McGovan's gaze. 'And no mercy either.'

McGovan nodded in acknowledgement. 'I fought there

because at first I believed what I was told, that we were there to protect the people from their brutal rulers, end the torture and the killings, and give them the chance of the peace, prosperity and freedom that we in the West enjoy.' He gave a bitter laugh. 'It was all a lie, of course. It was never about helping the people. It was about oil. Sure enough, we removed one set of brutal rulers, but those the Americans installed to replace them were little if any better than those we had deposed. And, worst of all, we Westerners, British and American alike, showed ourselves to be no less capable of brutality, torture and killing. For that I hang my head in shame.'

'As you should,' said Saif al-Islam.

'I lost all faith in my religion, and in my country,' said McGovan. 'As you know only too well, hundreds of thousands of Iraqi people have died, not because they were fighting against us, though some were, but because they happened to be in the wrong place at the wrong time. Some were killed by their own countrymen because they were Sunni, or because they were Shia, or because they were Kurds, but many more were killed because they chose the wrong moment to walk down the street, drive in their car or even attend a wedding when American and British bombs, missiles, drones or heavy weapons were raining destruction on our supposed enemies. And the dead were always described as "terrorists", of course, even when they were women, older people or tiny children. The officers and politicians never admitted their errors. Never apologised for the civilians they killed.'

Saif al-Islam stared at McGovan with unblinking eyes.

'Even after most of the forces were pulled out, when

they realised that they were fighting a battle they could never win, still the pain and suffering continued. Thousands crippled and poisoned, an economy that cannot support its people.'

'We are aware of the damage that your country did to ours,' said Saif al-Islam. 'But what has turned you against your own people?'

'Shame,' said McGovan. 'I am ashamed of what they made me do. The men and boys we captured were held in military prisons of which the very existence was denied, and many of those held there were tortured over and over again, for months and even years. Some were water-boarded, taken to the point of drowning, then revived, at least a hundred times. Others were beaten to a pulp, abused, sodomised, and some were murdered. Or they were handed over to different torturers – Iraqis who had last practised their skills on behalf of Saddam Hussein, and Afghanis every bit as cruel as the Taliban we were supposed to be fighting. Some victims, hooded and manacled like prisoners from the Middle Ages, were flown out of the country for even more extreme interrogation and torture by short- or long-term allies, like the Jordanians and Libyans, whose brutalities in the infamous secret prisons they operated were not restrained by even the faintest pretence of Western values.'

'You were there?' asked Saif al-Islam. 'You took part in the torture?'

McGovan held Saif al-Islam's gaze. 'Yes. I was at Abu Ghraib.' He saw the ISIS commander's eyes narrow in recognition of the name. Abu Ghraib – Arabic for the 'Place of Ravens' – was also known as Baghdad Central Prison even though it was twenty miles west of the Iraqi capital. The American military had controlled it from 2003, after the invasion of Iraq, until they handed it back to Iraqi forces in 2006. When Saddam Hussein ran Iraq, the prison kept as many as fifty thousand men and women jammed into its twelve-by-twelve-foot cells, with torture a daily occurrence and weekly executions. When the Americans took over, they retiled the floors, cleaned the cells, repaired the toilets and filled it with suspected terrorists, mainly civilians scooped up in random sweeps and at military checkpoints, or on the word of often anonymous tipsters. And while the executions stopped, killings and torture were again a regular occurrence at Abu Ghraib.

'I saw innocent people tortured and killed there,' said McGovan, quietly. 'I looked the other way while these atrocities were taking place and then I helped to sanitise the prisons and torture chambers. I hid the evidence, cleaned up the blood and even buried some of the victims. I have not had an undisturbed night's sleep ever since. It has burned into my conscience and it has changed me as a man, to my very core. I owe it to those people to take revenge, to force my fellow Britons to understand what has been done in their name and what the consequences will be.'

'And you are now, what?' asked Saif al-Islam. 'Now you are no longer a Christian. Now you say you have stopped being a crusader.'

'I am a Muslim. I converted while I was in Iraq.'

'You were allowed to become a Muslim?' Disbelief was written across his face.

'I did it in secret. I was schooled by an imam who was

held there for two years. I watched as the Americans tortured him and the British stood by and did nothing. I saw them beat him and humiliate him, and all the time he just smiled. I used to speak to him afterwards, to see if there was anything he wanted, and he said he already had everything he needed because he was serving Allah and that was all that mattered. He taught me about Islam and about Allah, and now I'm a Muslim and will be until the day I die.'

There was a long silence. 'Very well, Englishman,' Saif al-Islam said. 'If what you say is true, then we fight on the same side and for the same cause. But the attack you seek to make will be at the risk of your life. Even if you succeed, you are unlikely to emerge alive. Does that not concern you?'

McGovan shrugged. 'The thought of death doesn't frighten me. And it won't deter me from doing what I believe to be right.'

The ISIS commander gave him one last searching look, then turned to his men, many of whom were still regarding McGovan with intense suspicion or hatred. 'The *faranji* is a true believer in our cause,' he said. 'He is willing to atone for the wrongs he did to our brethren in Iraq and Afghanistan, even at the risk of his own life. While he remains under our protection, you are to guard him as you would guard me.' He turned back to McGovan. 'So if your attack is to take place,' he said, 'what do you need from us?'

'Money, arms and at least a dozen jihadists within the UK from whom I can select a group to support the attack. They must all be men whose loyalty and obedience to you are absolute, and men who would rather be martyred than betray our plans.'

'All such things might be possible,' Saif al-Islam said, 'providing you can convince me that it is the best use of our men and resources.' He allowed himself a brief smile. 'Our Arab friends are generous, but even their generosity has its limits. If the targets you have described can be successfully attacked, that would, of course, be a great blessing to us and the cause we serve. But many men before you must have dreamed of such a thing and none has ever been successful, or even come close.'

McGovan could tell the ISIS commander was tempted but was still more than a little suspicious of him. 'That is undoubtedly true,' he said, 'but perhaps they did not possess the resources or manpower you can command, and lacked the skills that I possess. Skills I am prepared to put at your disposal.'

Again there was the briefest flicker of a smile from Saif al-Islam. 'And yet, for all the particular skills you may possess, your most valuable asset in such an attack might be the colour of your skin. You may be able to pass without challenge in places where men such as we . . .' he waved a hand languidly around the circle of his men watching them '. . . would be subject to instant suspicion.'

He studied McGovan from beneath his eyebrows. 'However, there remains the question of trust. We know who you are and what you may be capable of,' he said, 'and your words seemed to be spoken from the heart, but that does not mean we can be certain that we can trust you.' He thought for a few more moments. 'My men will now take you back to the Turkish border, where others will be waiting to escort you. Return with them a week from today and I will tell you my decision.' He turned his back and strode out of the room as McGovan's escorts replaced the foul-smelling hood over his head, tied his wrists behind him and hustled him outside to the Landcruiser.

M cGovan spent the next week maintaining his cover as a tourist. He stayed at a modest hotel in a small resort town two hours east of Dalaman on Turkey's Turquoise Coast. Unlike his fellow guests, he did not use the swimming pool during the day or frequent the bar in the evenings, and those other guests who had noticed him at all would have been hard put to describe him other than as an aloof, monosyllabic Englishman who had spent most of the week sitting on the terrace with his nose in a book or running up a viciously steep track through the pine forests cloaking the hills that fringed the sea.

At the end of the week, he checked out of the hotel and rendezvoused with his escort in a supermarket car park on the outskirts of the town. He was taken back to the Syrian border by the same route as before, but this time, having once more slipped under the border fence and made his way down to the *wadi*, he was driven to a different safe-house, much deeper inside Syria and very close to the border with Iraq. The same ISIS commander, Saif al-Islam, was waiting for him. 'I never sleep more than one night under the same roof,' he said, in explanation for the change of safe-house. 'The *faranji* have spies and informers everywhere, and the skies are full of their aircraft and drones. So we move by night and go to earth before the dawn.'

'Infrared surveillance cameras can still see you in the dark,' McGovan said.

'Indeed so, and many martyrs are already in Paradise as a result, but as you see, may Allah be praised for His mercy, I have been spared for the great task, the holy jihad we pursue.' His eyes had been raised Heavenwards as he spoke, but he now switched his shrewd gaze to McGovan's face. 'Now, to the point. In order for us to be sure we can trust you, you must carry out a trial task for us.'

'You want to test me?'

'Of course. You wouldn't be the first spy who has tried to infiltrate our ranks with stories of conversion. We need to separate the wheat from the chaff.'

'And if I refuse your test?'

'Then you will be treated as chaff. Are you refusing?'

McGovan smiled easily. 'I had expected to be tested, and I will carry out any task you ask of me. I am more than happy to prove my commitment, and my worth. What's the task?'

'The US Army training team,' Saif al-Islam said, watching him closely, 'is based at an Iraqi Army base near Mosul. You are to kill the leader of that team. If you succeed, we will give you the help you seek.'

McGovan thought for a few moments, then nodded. 'First I will need all the intelligence information you have on the target and the base where he is operating. I'll need mapping of the area, aerial photography of the compound, if possible, details of which forces, Iraqis, Americans or

British, are mounting the guard on the base, the ORBAT – the Order of Battle – of the training team on the base, and the VRN. Sorry,' he said, as he saw the ISIS commander's blank expression. 'Acronyms are an occupational hazard in the armed forces and it is a habit I've found hard to shake, I meant the registration number of the vehicle he uses. Once all that is assembled, I'll need three or four days to prepare. I'm assuming you can obtain weapons, plastic explosives, timers and so on.'

'We have already assembled everything you need,' Saif al-Islam said. 'But you will not be making the attack in three or four days, you will attack the base tomorrow night.'

McGovan frowned. 'I'll study the intel and mapping, then tell you if that schedule is possible.'

'No,' Saif al-Islam said. 'You will not. I will tell you what is possible, not the other way round. And I'm telling you that you will do it tomorrow night. That is your test. Accept or decline.'

McGovan glanced round the room at the dozen ISIS men, who still stared unblinkingly back at him, each with an M-16 or M-203 slung over their shoulders, and then he spread his hands in a gesture of surrender. 'Very well. It shall be tomorrow night. Inshallah.'

He spent the next twenty-four hours studying every scrap of information they could put in front of him. To an untrained eye, the Iraqi Army base appeared a daunting target. The outer compound of the sprawling site was surrounded by a barbed-wire fence, punctuated by four watchtowers. Each was manned by armed guards, and at intervals between the watchtowers arc lights illuminated the fence at night. At the heart of the base was an inner compound, with a steel-mesh fence topped with coils of razor wire. The outer fence was patrolled by Iraqi guards, but the inner one was guarded by American troops. American and British soldiers both operated from within that compound.

'Not easy, is it?' one of the ISIS soldiers said to McGovan, peering over his shoulder at the surveillance images of the compound he was studying. One of ISIS's British Asian jihadists, the man had a strong Black Country accent, which sounded utterly incongruous in the heart of the Syrian desert.

McGovan turned to him. 'It's easy if you know how,' he said.

'What – even though there are two barbed-wire fences and all those armed guards to get past?'

McGovan gave him a cold smile. 'You're not a trained soldier, are you, my friend? The base may look daunting with all those watchtowers, barbed wire and guards patrolling it, but if you think about it, who will be guarding those fences? It won't be crack troops, will it? And you can be certain they won't be dedicated to the task they've been given. The men on guard duty will be the ones who happen to have pissed off their commanders recently. They won't want to be there either, because it's dark and it's cold, and they'd rather be in bed asleep, or playing Warcraft on their PCs. They'll be staying under cover as much as they can. And because there's a barbed-wire fence, they'll be relying on that to keep out intruders. If we fire a rocket into the base, all hell will break loose, of course, but I guarantee that I can be in and out through both those fences without any of the guards hearing a sound or seeing anything but dust blowing over the desert.'

Just before sunset the following night, once more escorted by four ISIS fighters, McGovan climbed into one of their four-by-fours and was driven towards the Iraqi border. The only weapon he carried was a pistol, though he was as effective with that in close-quarters combat as any less well-trained soldier armed with an automatic rifle. He wore a light pack on his back, containing two sophisticated IEDs. A trained demolitions expert in the special forces, he had put the devices together himself, moulding the plastic explosive into pieces of right-angled steel section to create devastating shaped charges that would concentrate the force of the blast in one direction. Both devices were triggered by pressure release switches, designed to activate if pressure was placed upon them or if existing pressure was taken away. He then checked the detonators, tested the firing circuits and loaded everything into his pack.

Night had fallen before they reached the frontier and they crossed into Iraq without incident, once more using one of the many smugglers' tracks on which everything, from food and drugs to explosives and heavy weapons, was traded across the porous borders.

The Iraqi Army base they were targeting was another three-hour drive beyond the border. They reached the area just after midnight and left the four-by-four in dead ground, a dip in the desert floor that hid it from view unless you were standing almost directly on top of it, then made their way onwards on foot. The arc-lights around the fence were illuminated, but they cast small, intense pools of light directly below them, which made the areas of fence between them seem even darker by comparison. The guards in the watch-towers were motionless, bored and inattentive. Some appeared to be dozing or were perhaps even fast asleep. The only creatures patrolling the fence were not soldiers, but the prowling feral dogs that were as ubiquitous in Arab countries as crows in an English cornfield.

McGovan lay in cover, assessing the guards and estab-lishing the routine of their patrols – or at least the routine of those who ventured beyond their shelters – but he spent as much time watching the movements of the wild dogs around the fence line. Well inside the outer fence, close to the inner one surrounding the American and British area of the base, he could see refuse bins overflowing with garbage. If he could see them and smell the stench on the breeze, the feral dogs would certainly be well aware of them. As he watched, he saw a steady stream of the braver animals, bellies to the ground, squirming under the barbed-wire fence, then padding across the compound towards the bins.

McGovan nudged one of the ISIS fighters in the ribs and breathed in his ear, 'Those animal tracks are going to be our way in as well.'

While two of the fighters remained outside the compound to give them cover, the other two belly-crawled forward with McGovan and slid under the wire after him as the prowling dogs backed away, eyeing them suspiciously. One emitted a low growl, resenting the interruption to its evening routine, which caused one of the guards to glance in that direction and sweep the beam of his torch across the compound. McGovan and the ISIS fighters had already flattened themselves to the ground and lay motionless, almost invisible. After a moment, the guard, convinced that whatever he had seen or heard was only the dogs arguing over a choice bit of refuse, turned away.

A moment later, McGovan saw a flare of light and the red glow as the guard lit a cigarette. If he needed any additional sign of the guards' carelessness and unpreparedness, the cigarette had provided it. The flare of flame from the soldier's lighter would ruin his night vision for some minutes and smoking the cigarette would distract him from his duty. If the guard heard a noise, he was as likely to think it was his sergeant out on an inspection as an intruder breaking in, and would be more concerned with getting rid of his cigarette end before he was put on a charge than anything else.

McGovan waited for five more minutes, then continued to creep forward, belly-crawling across the outer compound, the two ISIS fighters at his heels. They paused again in the deeper shadow cast by a Portakabin while McGovan studied the ground ahead. Two American soldiers were patrolling the inner fence, but their body language showed their boredom and disinterest. They clearly thought their sentry duty was a pointless waste of time and stayed close to the warm yellow light from the guard post at the entrance gates to the inner compound, patrolling no more than ten or twenty yards away from it before turning back towards their shelter.

The two ISIS fighters who had slipped under the wire with him now remained by the Portakabin, covering the American guards, while McGovan crawled forward alone. The steel mesh of the inner fence was tight to the ground and there were no animal tracks leading beneath it to aid him, but he pulled a pair of wire clippers from his belt and began cutting through the wire next to one of the stanchions supporting the fence. Each strand snapped with a faint click, but it was virtually inaudible even to the two ISIS men watching from close behind him, let alone to the Americans near the gates.

He eased the clippers into his belt, folded back the section of wire he had cut, then wriggled through the gap. He paused to rearrange the wire so that, to a casual glance, it appeared to be untouched, then crept across the compound to the vehicle park. It was the work of a moment to identify his target's Land Rover and he went to work at once. He fixed one of the IEDs, activated by a pressure-release switch, under the driver's seat, then coupled it to another IED, which he installed on the underside of the petrol tank. As an insurance policy, it would guarantee that anyone travelling in the Land Rover when the IEDs were detonated would be killed. If anyone now put weight on the switch or lifted the seat away from it, the IED would activate with devastating effect.

He took one last look around, making sure he had left no visible traces that would trigger an alarm, then crept back into the shadows. He made his way back through the inner fence, once more carefully replacing the cut wire behind him. With the ISIS fighters again at his heels, he wriggled under the outer fence. They linked up with the other two fighters, who were waiting in cover a few yards outside the compound. They stole into the darkness, and within half an hour, they were back in the four-by-four and driving fast across the desert towards the Syrian border.

The four-hour return drive meant that the sun was already climbing the sky well before they reached the border. They followed a track up a rough incline, and emerged onto the plateau of rock, gravel and coarse, gritty sand that stretched all the way to the border. As they scanned the plateau, they saw a plume of dust to the south-west ahead of them: a vehicle driving a course that would intersect with theirs. McGovan's escort exchanged worried looks and a few words of muttered Arabic, but they could see no option other than to carry on. To turn back would place them in greater danger from Iraqi patrols. The driver changed direction, taking a side-track running further to the north of their previous route, but almost at once they saw the other vehicle change its course too.

As the minutes ticked by, the outline of the other vehicle became clearer. It was a squat, broad-based vehicle with a jagged black outline projecting above its roof. 'It's a Humvee,' McGovan said, 'an American armoured vehicle, though the chances are that it's being driven by an Iraqi Army patrol, not the Yanks.' He pointed. 'Drive to that low ridge ahead of us and stop,' he said to the driver. 'It'll give us the advantage of the ground overlooking them, if nothing else.' The man scowled at him but did as McGovan had suggested. McGovan had spotted a shallow dip just to the right of the place on the ridge-line he had indicated, which would provide enough cover to protect a man lying prone. The four-by-four came to a halt and they waited in an atmosphere of rising tension as the other vehicle closed with them. They could now see it clearly and, as McGovan had said, it was indeed a Humvee, with Iraqi Army insignia. The jagged shape mounted on the back had resolved itself into an M-2 Browning .50 calibre heavy machine-gun, the operator sitting behind it, keeping its barrel pointing straight at them.

Still as stone, McGovan watched it approach, willing it to move closer and closer before stopping. Their training required SAS men to know the range and capabilities of every weapon they were likely to encounter, whether in the hands of their allies or their enemies. He knew that the M-2 had an effective range of 1800 metres, over twice the range of the M-16s that the ISIS fighters were carrying, and more than eight times the range of the M-203 grenade-launcher fitted to one of the M-16s. Had the Humvee been driven by an American patrol, they would have stopped no closer than 800 metres away and used a loudhailer to order the occupants to get out of the four-by-four and flatten themselves in the dirt, or be cut apart by machine-gun fire. The Iraqi patrol in it, though, were less circumspect, and whether through overconfidence or incompetence, they did not pull up until they were just a couple of hundred metres from the four-by-four.

McGovan's keen gaze missed no detail. He saw that the machine-gunner manning the M-2 was only partly hidden by the armoured shield in front of him, which covered his body from the breastbone downwards, but left his upper chest and his face below his steel helmet exposed. The Iraqi commander had climbed out but remained standing close to the side of the Humvee, shielded behind its open armoured door, with only his lower legs exposed. The rest of his team were still inside the Humvee.

'Let me handle this,' McGovan said, turning to the ISIS fighter sitting next to him. 'Give me your rifle.'

The ISIS fighter glared at him. 'Why should I give you my weapon?'

'Because if you don't, we'll all die. That heavy machine-gun you see on the back can fire over five hundred rounds a minute and each one will slice through this vehicle's soft metal skin like a knife through paper. It will shred everyone inside it to pieces, whereas your rifle rounds won't even penetrate the Humvee's armour. So I'll get out and talk to them. When they see I'm a Westerner, they'll hesitate, thinking I might be special forces on a secret op. That hesitation is all I'll need to take out the machine-gunner. But if you keep me arguing any longer, they're likely to shoot first and ask questions afterwards. Then we're all finished. Okay?'

The fighter hesitated a fraction of a second longer, then handed over his weapon. McGovan clambered past him, opened the door and jumped out, holding his rifle at the vertical in one hand, wide of his body. At once, the Iraqi commander shouted in Arabic, 'Drop your weapon! Get down on the ground!'

'We are British special forces,' McGovan shouted, lowering his arm to bring the rifle down by his side. 'SAS! We're on the same side! Don't shoot!' He stepped away from the vehicle into the open, and saw the barrel of the machine-gun move to cover him again.

'Drop your weapon! Get down on the ground or we fire!'

McGovan spread his arms wide in a what-the-hell gesture, then fell to his knees at the edge of the shallow dip in the ground. He saw the machine-gun barrel swing back momentarily to cover the occupants of the four-by-four. At that moment, he dived forward, bringing up the rifle in one fluid movement and fired a short, unaimed burst at the machine-gunner. As the man swung the barrel round and his weapon began to erupt in rapid fire, the deafening rattle was echoed by the *thwock-thwock* sound as some of its rounds buried themselves in the sand, and the crack and whine as others ricocheted from the rocks to howl away.

McGovan barrel-rolled sideways, then brought up the rifle again, firing from a point several metres away and this time stilling his breathing with a slow exhale and squeezing off two carefully aimed shots. The first hit the machine-gunner dead centre in the chest, an inch or so above the armoured shield, and the next struck him under the chin as he was thrown backwards by the first. He was stone dead even before his body had tumbled from the back of the Humvee to the ground. His fingers, clamped to the trigger in his death agony, caused his weapon to stitch a tracer line of rounds across the sky before it jammed and fell silent.

McGovan had already rolled and fired again. The Iraqi Army commander's body was still protected by the armoured door of the Humvee, but his legs from the knee down were visible beneath it. McGovan again inhaled deeply as he took up the first pressure on the trigger, squinting down the sight, then released the breath in a slow exhale and squeezed the trigger home. He felt the recoil into his shoulder and saw the man's right knee blown apart by the impact of the round. He slumped to the ground at the side of the Humvee, lying fully exposed in the open. He was now disabled, incapable of walking and in agonising pain, but McGovan knew that none of that could be guaranteed to prevent him firing his weapon. He squinted through the sight again, aiming at the bridge of the man's nose, and drilled a single shot through his brain.

McGovan switched targets again as the other Iraqi soldiers jumped from their vehicle and opened fire. Their shooting was nervy and inaccurate, their months of American and British training forgotten in the nervous terror of real combat in which one error might be their last. By now the ISIS fighters had leaped out of the four-by-four, and added their own weight of fire to McGovan's, including rockets from an RPG-7 and grenades from an M-203. One of the ISIS men was hit, gut-shot by return fire, and slumped to the ground, but by then two more Iraqi soldiers already lay dead.

Their last man, the driver, panic-stricken by the sight of his comrades being wiped out, made a frantic attempt to save himself, flooring the accelerator, slewing his vehicle around in a storm of dust and debris, then roaring off across the desert as a fresh torrent of rounds from the ISIS fighters rattled against the armoured bodywork.

McGovan was already on his feet and sprinting for the four-by-four. 'After him!' he shouted at the ISIS driver, as he dived into the back seat. 'If he escapes, we're all dead.'

One of the other fighters, still clutching the RPG-7, threw himself into the four-by-four as the driver hit the accelerator, but his other comrade, tending the wounded man, was left staring after them as they sped away. The Iraqi Humvee had a minute's start on them. In other types of desert terrain its weight and power would have seen it pull away from them, but the four-by-four was a lighter and faster vehicle over the rocky ground they were traversing and was soon rapidly overhauling it. McGovan snatched the RPG from the ISIS fighter, loaded a high-explosive, dual-purpose round, capable of penetrating five centimetres of steel armour-plating, then snarled at the driver, 'When I say stop, hit the brakes as hard as you can. Got it?'

He met the driver's eyes in the rear-view mirror and waited for his nod of agreement, then knelt on the seat and leaned out of the open rear window, bracing his arms against the frame and locking his knee against the back of the driver's seat, as the four-by-four bounced and jolted over the desert floor.

The grey shape of the Humvee, half hidden by the dust cloud it was raising as it stormed along the rough desert road, was now no more than a quarter of a mile ahead and the distance between them was still shrinking. It was impossible to shoot accurately from such an unstable, bouncing platform, and McGovan raised his gaze from the sight to scan the terrain ahead, searching for a straight, level section where he would have the best chance of a clean shot. He saw what he was looking for some way ahead and waited, counting down the distance as they approached it.

'Ready . . . ready . . . STOP!' he shouted. The driver hit the brakes hard, sending the four-by-four slithering and sliding to a halt. Even as it was still rocking on its suspension, McGovan was taking aim at the Humvee's front offside tyre, clearly visible in half-profile as the vehicle swerved around a bend in the track ahead. He wasn't confident that the RPG round would penetrate the Humvee's armoured bodywork or bulletproof glass windows unless fired at right angles to them, so the tyre and wheel were the percentage target. He squeezed the trigger and the RPG round launched with a soft pop, a flash of flame and smoke. Despite the size of the projectile he barely felt the recoil against his shoulder.

The round armed itself automatically after flying for twenty yards or so, then sped to its target. It detonated right on the aiming point, blasting into the front wheel of the Humvee. The explosion ripped the wheel from the vehicle and sent the Humvee careering across the track, where it smashed into a boulder on the far side with a sickening impact. Despite its two-ton weight, it was thrown into the air for a few seconds before it crashed down into a ditch running alongside the track. It hung on its side for a moment, then toppled slowly on to its roof.

As the four-by-four slewed to a halt alongside, McGovan leaped out and sprinted towards it. The Iraqi Army driver was semi-conscious, hanging upside down from his seat belt, blood dripping from his head where he had been thrown against the side window. There was no pity in McGovan's eyes, only an icy determination that there would be no witnesses to tell the tale of what had happened. His expression blank, McGovan jerked open the door on the other side of the cab, slid his rifle barrel in through the opening and put two rounds into the man's head at point-blank range. He reached into the cab and ripped off the sleeve of the man's army shirt and walked to the back of the Humvee, where he forced open the fuel cap and soaked the cloth in the diesel spilling from the upside-down fuel tank. He retreated a few yards, held his gas lighter to the sleeve and waited while the flame heated the diesel to its combustion point. When it burst into flame, he tossed the burning sleeve into the spreading pool of spilled diesel and ran back to the four-by-four as the fuel ignited and the Humvee was engulfed in flames.

McGovan got into the four-by-four and they drove back across the desert to pick up the other two fighters. The wounded man was by now grey-faced and probably beyond help as they drove flat-out, aiming to have crossed the Syrian border before the inevitable Iraqi Army sweep for the killers of their comrades began. McGovan was a trained patrol medic and could have treated the ISIS fighter's wounds, but he ignored his groans and the spreading stain from the blood pulsing out of his stomach wound, keeping his gaze fixed on the terrain around them, searching for any sign of further army patrols. His wounds left untreated, the injured man was continually jolted and thrown around in the back of the four-by-four as it bucketed over the rocky ground that stretched for miles on either side of the frontier. He had bled to death long before they reached the safe-house inside Syria. He was carried off for a martyr's burial while his comrades were debriefed by their commander.

When they had given him their account of the firefight with the Iraqi soldiers and McGovan's role in killing them, the commander embraced him. 'You have shown yourself a worthy brother to us,' he said. 'You shall have everything that it is in my power to give you to help you achieve your own aims.'

McGovan remained in the safe-house with the ISIS fighters throughout the next day. An hour before sunset, the commander received a radio message. He listened in silence, removed the headphones and smiled. '*Allahu Akbar,*' he said. 'The *faranji* unbeliever, the American officer, is dead. His vehicle blew up while he was climbing into it in the compound this morning. Two of his traitorous Iraqi guards died with him. There will be much fear among the training teams from now on. They will not feel safe anywhere. We move to a different safe-house after dark, and tomorrow we begin planning your attack in Britain.'

McGovan spent much of the next day with Saif al-Islam, as he laid out his requirements for cash, weapons and equipment. They discussed the potential fighters the ISIS commander could offer him. After hearing Saif al-Islam give details of each man, including how they had come to join ISIS and what skills and experience they had, if any, McGovan rejected most, but eventually he had a list of a dozen names. Some were already based in Britain and others were UK passport holders who, although now fighting as jihadists in Syria, could return to Britain with few questions asked, entering the country through the Channel Tunnel on Eurostar trains where immigration controls and passport checks were likely to be less stringent than at UK airports.

The following night McGovan began his journey back to Britain through Turkey. As soon as he arrived in London, he booked a room in a military club north of Oxford Street for an indefinite period. As he reflected to himself, after he had finished checking in and was moving away from the desk towards the stairs, there could be no better cover for what he was planning than to be an ex-military man, staying in a military club, surrounded by other serving and former soldiers. It was the last place that any agency searching for terrorists would be likely to look.

As soon as he was settled in his room, he searched the

internet for news reports of the American soldier's death in Iraq but, as he had predicted to Saif al-Islam, the incident had made barely a ripple in the British press. There was only a tiny paragraph on an inside page of the *Daily Telegraph*. The deaths of all four members of an Iraqi Army patrol did not rate a mention.

The robbery had been planned to perfection, but not by the men who carried it out. They were hired hands, brought in for the job with no idea of the big picture. They were being paid a flat fee, plus a share of the proceeds, and were all happy with the arrangement. There were four in the initial group. They gained access through the next-door building, easy enough because it was a regular office block with no special security arrangements and deserted at weekends.

They opened one of the lifts on the ground floor and pressed the button to send it up to the top of the building. One had a key he used to open the doors. Once it was open the lift was automatically locked in place, a safety feature they were using to their advantage. They had ropes and abseiling equipment with them and two of the men lowered themselves to the basement, where they unhitched themselves. The men on the ground floor took a Hilti DD350 industrial power drill from a large black nylon kit bag and carefully lowered it to the men below. It was a big drill for a big job: they had to bore through half a metre of reinforced concrete.

The first hole took just under an hour. The men took it

in turns to operate the equipment, wearing masks to keep the dust from their mouths and noses, and heavy-duty earmuffs against the noise. The drill made quick progress through the concrete but slowed markedly each time it hit the reinforced steel bars that threaded through the wall. Eventually it burst through into the vault. The man operating the drill switched it off and pulled it out. He knelt down, peered through the hole and grinned as he saw the rows of metal safe-deposit boxes. The man with him patted him on the back. 'Let the dog see the rabbit,' he said, slipping his mask over his mouth and nose. He took over the drilling, starting a second hole that overlapped slightly with the first. It took just forty-five minutes to break through, and the third another forty minutes. By the time they had finished, the three holes formed a gap twelve inches deep and two and a half feet wide. The four men who had carried out the task were carrying a few more pounds than was good for them and weren't anywhere near slim enough to squeeze through. They packed up the drill and cabling and two climbed back up the ropes, hauling the equipment after them.

As they left the building, their kitbags hidden in a wheelie-bin, two more men arrived, wearing grey backpacks. They were smaller than the first four, wiry and shorter than average. Their small stature belied their strength: they were both former SAS and as hard as nails. They abseiled down the lift shaft and examined the hole that had been drilled into the vault. 'Tight fit, but it'll do,' said one. He took off his backpack and went through head first. He had to breathe in and wriggle a bit but he managed it. His colleague passed through the two backpacks and followed him.

They stood up and surveyed the 999 safe-deposit boxes. They were graded in size, the larger ones at the bottom, the topmost ones only a couple of inches deep. Each had a number, and two locks. The owner of each safe-deposit box held one key, the company the other. Both keys were necessary to open the box. That was the idea, anyway, but the drills the men had in their backpacks meant that it was a matter of seconds to open any of them. Unlike the massive drill that had been used to bore through the wall, the smaller models came with their own power supply. One man took a folded piece of paper from the pocket of his overalls. 'Seven six two,' he read out. It was on the right of the room, a medium-sized box at about waist-height. The other man pressed the trigger of his drill and pushed the bit against one of the locks. It ripped through it in seconds. He did the second lock, then opened the flap. His colleague pulled out a slim metal box, placed it on the floor and opened the top. Inside were three men's watches, several small red boxes, a stack of notebooks and a black thumbdrive. The man took out the notebooks and the thumbdrive and put them into his backpack. As an afterthought he took out one of the watches – a gold Rolex GMT Master – and slipped it onto his wrist. 'What do you think?' he asked.

'I think with what you're being paid for this, you could buy your own fucking watch.'

The man grinned. 'I like this one.' He waved his arm around the strong room. 'Make it look good.'

'How good?'

'Fifty, at least.'

The other gunned the drill. 'And we get to keep the ill-gotten gains, right?'

'The guys outside take the gear and sell it. We'll get our cut down the line. The important thing is that it looks like the jewellery and cash were the prizes. Catch you later.'

'Not if I catch you first.' He began on another lock as his colleague threw his backpack through the hole and wriggled after it.

4

Charlotte Button poured Pinot Grigio into a large glass and carried it with a plate of spinach risotto to the sofa. She flopped down, took a long drink of wine, and pressed the remote to watch Sky News. She ate her risotto as a pretty blonde girl with augmented breasts and a too-perfect pixie nose went through the events of the day in an annoying sing-song voice more suited to a primary-school teacher addressing a class of eight-year-olds.

The raid on the Manchester safe-deposit company was the third item. The fork froze in the air on its way to Button's mouth. Fifty-eight boxes opened: no idea yet how much money and jewellery had been stolen but several Premier League footballers were thought to have had boxes in the vault. And allegations were flying that the Manchester police hadn't been doing their job properly. Next a grey-haired security expert described the robbery as a 'good old-fashioned caper', which bore an astonishing number of similarities to the break-in at the Hatton Garden safe-deposit company earlier in the year.

Button put down her fork, drained her glass and walked over to the burglar alarm console in the hallway. She activated the perimeter system but kept the motion-sensors and infrared detectors on standby. She opened the cupboard under the stairs and took out a black North Face backpack and placed it by the front door. It contained a change of clothes, a torch, a first-aid kit, five thousand pounds and five thousand dollars in cash, and two passports, one Irish and one British, both with her photograph but neither using her real name. The Americans called them bug-out bags, but at MI5 they had always referred to them as go-bags. Every officer on overseas assignment had to have their go-bag close by so that they could leave at a moment's notice, and even though she no longer worked for the security service, keeping an up-to-date go-bag was second nature to Button.

She took her plate and glass to the kitchen, washed them and put them on the rack. The kitchen door was locked but she flicked the bolts across, top and bottom. She switched off the lights and went back to the hallway. She killed the lights there, too, and in the sitting room, then went to the window and looked outside. Her car was parked in front of the garage, a two-seater Audi. The driveway was gravelled so she'd have heard anyone walking across it, but there was plenty of grass around the house.

She went back to the burglar alarm. The outside lights were normally linked up to motion detectors but she pressed a button to switch them on. She went into the sitting room and looked out. No unusual shadows that she could see. No movement.

She picked up her black Chanel handbag and took out her car keys, slung the backpack over her shoulder and set the alarm. She closed the front door behind her as it was bleeping, jogged over to her car and climbed in, heart pounding. She started the engine, put the car in gear with a shaking hand and drove away, the tyres of the Audi kicking up a spray of gravel behind her.

Less than three hours after Sky News had reported on the robbery, Barbara Reynolds left Heathrow Airport on a flight bound for JFK. Her only luggage was a black North Face backpack and a Chanel handbag.

5

Button had arranged to meet Richard Yokely at midday in Central Park. Specifically Sheep Meadow, the fifteen-acre field on the west side of the park, between 66 and 69 Streets. It was a popular spot for dog-walkers and picnickers, and a favourite site for demonstrators to gather and protest. It was also the perfect place to spot watchers and followers. At eleven o'clock Button found herself a seat in a coffee shop on 67th Street overlooking the meadow, sipped a latte and nibbled a croissant as she read that day's *New York Times*. She saw Richard Yokely arrive at exactly midday. He seemed to be alone, but Richard Yokely was a pro with decades of experience in surveillance and counter-surveillance working for agencies that preferred to identify themselves by initials, including the CIA, NSA and DIA. He was wearing a long black coat over a grey suit, a gleaming white shirt and a yellow tie with pale blue stripes. He was too far away for her to see his footwear but she was sure he'd be wearing his trademark tasselled loafers.

Button left the coffee shop, crossed the road and entered the park. He saw her the second she stepped onto the grass, smiled and waved as if he was an old friend. Yokely was in his very early fifties with short grey hair, thin lips and teeth so white they were either veneers or chemically treated. He air-kissed her on both cheeks and she caught the scent of sandalwood.

'I didn't know you were visiting the US, Charlotte,' he said. 'You should have let me know you were coming.'

'It wasn't planned,' she said. 'All a bit rushed, actually.'

'What's interesting is that the INS doesn't seem to be aware of you arriving on our shores either. But an Irish lady named Barbara Reynolds seems to bear an uncanny resemblance to you and has identical fingerprints.'

'Ah, yes, sorry about that.'

'False papers aren't the asset they used to be, not now we take the fingerprints of any foreigner who flies in.'

'I've been a very naughty girl,' said Button, fluttering her eyelashes theatrically. 'Please don't arrest me.'

'Why the fake passport, Charlotte?'

'It's genuine, issued by the Irish authorities.'

'You know what I mean.'

She smiled tightly. 'I know, I'm sorry. It was more about leaving the UK discreetly,' she said.

'Are you in trouble, my dear?'

She nodded. 'I'm afraid so.'

'And that's why you wanted to meet here instead of at a perfectly good restaurant?'

'I thought it might be more appropriate, yes.'

'Don't you trust me? After all we've been through?'

'I'm not sure who I can trust just now. I'm sorry.'

'You might at least have chosen somewhere I could smoke,' he said. 'Smoking is illegal in Central Park. Pure madness. It's outside, but you can't smoke. Cross the street to the sidewalk and you can smoke there. The wind will blow the smoke into the park, but that's the rule.'

'Health Nazis,' said Button. 'What can you do?'

'What about the UK?' asked Yokely. 'Can you smoke in Hyde Park still?'

'I think so. But I'm not a smoker.' She started walking across the field and Yokely kept pace with her. 'How much do you know, Richard?'

'I know everything. It's my job.'

'About my position?'

He smiled, like a kindly uncle. 'I know you left MI5 under a cloud. I know you've been accused of using government resources to resolve personal issues.'

'I used the Pool to kill the men who were responsible for the death of my husband,' said Button. 'Shame on me.'

'Charlotte, I would have done the same, trust me. You have my sympathy. But what you did . . .' He shrugged.

'You were never one to shy away from an off-the-books operation, Richard.'

'It wasn't what you did that was the problem,' said Yokely. 'It was the fact you got caught. But that's water under the bridge. What's happened to get you over here under a false name, looking over your shoulder, like a fox who can hear the hounds on her tail?'

'I'm in shit, Richard. Deep, deep shit.' The wind tugged at her hair. 'I kept records of everything I was asked to do, obviously.'

'Obviously.'

'After what I did, they couldn't keep me on, but they could hardly drag me through the courts. Not with what I know.'

Yokely chuckled. 'You know where all the bodies are buried. Figuratively and literally.'

'So, basically, they had two choices. Lose me, or use me. And my insurance policy against anything bad happening to me was a file. A very big file. I made three copies of that file, and stored those copies in safe places.' She smiled thinly and corrected herself. 'In what I assumed were safe places. Did you read about the safe-deposit robbery in Manchester?'

'Sure. A professional job, perfectly executed.' Realisation dawned. 'Ah. You had a box there.' It was a statement, not a question.

'There were nine hundred and ninety-nine boxes in that vault. They broke in without being discovered, they had all weekend to work, and they opened fifty-odd.'

'Because they were interested in just one? Yours?'

'That's what I'm assuming,' said Button.

'It could be a coincidence,' said Yokely. 'Have you been told officially that yours was one of those opened?'

'I don't need to hear officially,' she said. 'It's the second of my boxes to have been raided. Mine was one of those that was broken into when they raided the Hatton Garden Safe Deposit Company earlier this year. That time they broke open seventy-two boxes and one was definitely mine.'

'But didn't they arrest the men responsible?'

'They did indeed. But I'm pretty sure they were just the fall guys. I doubt they did the planning. Hired hands, I'm guessing.'

'And you think, what? The government?'

'Possibly.'

'I'm sure they wouldn't be stupid enough to try to hurt you, Charlotte.'

'There are some very stupid people in our intelligence services,' said Button. 'A lot of very bright people, but we have more than our fair share of idiots. And one of them might well have decided to have a go at me.'

'Your nemesis, Jeremy Willoughby-Brown?'

'I'd hardly call him my nemesis, Richard.'

'He did get your job at Five. And he was responsible for you leaving.' He sighed. 'Charlotte, I really need a smoke. Can we please go to the sidewalk? I give you my word we're not being followed.'

She nodded, and they walked across the grass towards 68th Street. 'I don't think it's Jeremy. He got what he wanted, my job. He wouldn't gain anything by killing me.'

'So who would?'

'A dozen people whose careers would come to an abrupt end if the file were ever made public,' said Button. 'Politicians and civil servants. The Pool was always acting in the interest of the greater good, but things were done that . . .' She sighed. 'Well, you know what I mean.'

'I do indeed, Charlotte. Sometimes the ends justify the means.'

'Morally, yes. But not legally. And a number of people would sleep easier if the file and my good self were laid to rest. I could go to the papers with the file I have left. But I'm reluctant to pull that trigger, obviously.'

They crossed the road and Yokely took a small cigar case from his coat pocket. He selected a cigar and lit it, taking care to blow the smoke away from her. 'You were never a smoker?'

She shook her head. 'My father smoked a pipe and I hated it. Hated the smell. It's funny – sometimes I forget what he looked like but if I walk past a pipe-smoker it hits me.'

'Smells can be like that. They're a direct link to memories.' He held up the cigar. 'I'm fairly sure that within my lifetime possession of one of these will be a criminal offence. At least, it will be here in the US.'

'So long as I can still get a decent bottle of wine, I'm happy,' said Button.

Yokely took another drag on his cigar as they walked south, the park to their left.

'I need protection, Richard. I need someone to watch my back. Just for a while until I get a grip on what's happening.'

'I thought you were in the protection business, these days. Your company, what's it called?'

'It's called Executive Solutions but it's still known as the Pool.'

'Because you're in at the deep end?'

She laughed softly. 'It was always called the Pool. Partly because we had people we could call on as and when required, but partly because so many of them seemed to come from Liverpool. The thing is, yes, I could get a couple of my guys to follow me around. But that's not the sort of protection I need. I need government-standard surveillance. I need to know the chatter, Richard. I need to know what's being said about me. I need to know if I'm being watched as I move through an airport. I need to know if I'm in danger.'

'You want the NSA looking out for you?'

'That would be nice. And I'd like it known that I'm being watched over.'

Yokely nodded. 'The idea being that if the world knows Charlotte Button is under the NSA microscope it's likely to leave her alone?'

'Just for a short time, until I get my ducks in a row.'

'Those ducks being?'

'I have one more copy of the file in what I consider to be a safe place. In view of what's happened at Hatton Garden and in Manchester, I need to make sure it isn't compromised, and I have to put other copies in other places. Clearly safe-deposit boxes aren't safe, despite the name.'

'There is an alternative, Charlotte. You could give me a copy.'

'I did think about that, Richard, but it's perilously close to treason.'

'We're on the same side.'

'Of course we are. But the information in that file is classified. And passing it to another government, even an ally, could be taken the wrong way.'

'You could give it to me personally.'

'To be opened in the event of my death?' She laughed again. 'No, I'll handle it. But until then, I need someone watching my back. Will you help?'

'Of course I'll help.' He put a bear-like arm around her and hugged her. 'You think I'd let anything happen to my favourite ex-spook?'

'Thank you, Richard. You're a sweetheart.'

He released his grip on her. 'Actually, it's fortuitous that you turned up when you did. I have a favour to ask of you.'

'A favour?'

'Let's call it a quid pro quo.'

'I'm listening.'

6

Lex Harper studied the menu, unable to decide between *pad thai* or the *khao pad*. Noodles or rice. The menu was idiot-proof and consisted of a plastic photograph album into which had been slotted a couple of dozen pictures of the dishes on offer. Each had a sticker, with the description in English and Thai and the price. The waitress, a pretty teenager with her hair in plaits, stood patiently with her notepad. Her name was Som and she was the daughter of the owner, still at school but helping her mother in the evenings.

'What do you think, Som? *Khao pad* or *pad thai*?'

'I like *pad thai. Pad thai mu.*' Thai fried noodles with pork.

'You've sold me,' said Harper, handing her back the photograph album. 'And another bottle of Heineken.'

He was sitting in a beer bar in a side road off Walking Street, Pattaya's main red-light strip. It was just after six, the street was quiet and there were only two other customers in Noy's, playing pool, the loser buying tequila shots. The bar was open to the air but two large fans overhead gave enough of a breeze to make the evening bearable.

Som returned with a fresh beer, slotted into a foam

cylinder bearing the bar's logo – a bright red lipstick kiss superimposed on a cross of St George. Noy's second and fourth husbands had been English. No one was quite sure how many she had had over the years, but they had all contributed to the upkeep of the bar in one way or another. Harper was just about to take a sip when he recognised the young girl walking purposefully along the street towards him. Her name was Em. Dark-skinned and lanky, she was nineteen years old and one of the top-earning dancers at the Firehouse, one of the busier Walking Street go-go bars. She was in the off-duty bar-girl uniform of tight black top, cut-off denim shorts and impossibly high heels, with a thick gold chain around her neck and an even thicker one around her left wrist. A dragon tattoo wound down her left leg. She looked upset and got straight to the point. 'Khun Lek, Pear is in hospital.'

Thais tended to have trouble pronouncing Alex or Lex and most ended up saying 'Lek', which happened to be the Thai for 'small' and was a common nickname. Harper had long ago given up correcting anyone who mispronounced his name and simply answered to Lek.

'What happened?' he asked. Pear was a dancer in Em's bar, and came from the same village outside Surin, not far from the border with Cambodia. He had known her since she'd started working in Pattaya two years earlier, sent to dance in the bars by parents who were having trouble scraping a living as farmers. He'd met her on her second day on the job and she had been relieved to discover that Harper could speak Thai. She had spent the whole evening sitting next to him, telling stories about her life as a farm kid, then thrown up over him and passed out after her fifth tequila shot. Harper had assumed that the drinks he'd been buying her had been watered down, but there had been a miscommunication with the barman and Pear had been as drunk as a skunk. From that day on he had always felt responsible for the girl and had often helped her out at the end of the month if she wasn't able to pay her rent or didn't have enough to send back to her parents.

'A customer attacked her,' said Em. 'He raped her. She's very sick, Khun Lek.'

'Which hospital?'

'Pattaya International. ICU.'

Harper was already off his stool and heading for the door. If Pear was in the intensive care unit, it had to be serious. He handed Som a five-hundred-baht note and told her to eat his *pad thai*. His Triumph Bonneville motorcycle was parked outside the bar, his black full-face helmet sitting on one of the mirrors. He pulled on the helmet, fired up the bike and drove off.

Ten minutes later he was outside the ICU talking to a pretty Thai doctor with waist-length jet black hair and makeup that would have been more at home on a fashion model. Her nails were painted a glossy Barbie pink that matched her lipstick. 'She's been badly beaten,' said the doctor. 'She has lost two of her teeth, her kidneys are swollen and she's passing blood at the moment. We'll know in a day or two how bad her kidneys are, but it's not looking good.' Her English was perfect but with a slight American accent, probably the result of being educated at an international school and university.

'Is she in pain?' asked Harper.

'We've made her as comfortable as we can but if we give

her any more painkillers she'll be unconscious and we don't want that.' The doctor looked uncomfortable. 'Is she your girlfriend?'

'Just a friend,' said Harper.

'Because there is something else, Mr Harper. I'm afraid she was raped. With considerable violence. Both her vagina and rectum are quite badly damaged.'

Harper cursed under his breath.

'We have contacted the police and they will be sending an officer with a rape kit to gather evidence,' said the doctor.

'Can I see her?'

The doctor shook his head. 'I'm afraid not. She's too sick for visitors at the moment. She's in no immediate danger now, though, and we'll be moving her out of the ICU tomorrow.'

'That's good to hear,' said Harper.

'But there is something else, I'm afraid . . .'

He cursed again, wondering just how bad it was going to get. 'There's the matter of Khun Pear's bill,' said the doctor. 'That's why she gave us your name. She said you would settle her account.'

'No problem at all,' said Harper. He unzipped his hip-pack, counted out twenty thousand baht, then handed it with a Visa card to the doctor. 'Take that on account and put whatever you need on the card.'

The doctor smiled and handed it back with the money. 'That's all right, Mr Harper. You can pay when she checks out. But we'll need a copy of your passport.'

Harper took his passport out of the hip-pack and gave it to the doctor. The hip-pack was around his waist pretty much all the time. It contained two of his many mobile phones, his passport, two credit cards and money. Always money. The pack, with the heavy gold neck chain he always wore, was his guarantee of a fast exit from any country, at any time, should the need arise. He had a more substantial escape kit stashed under the bed in his Thai apartment and another bug-out bag in a specially made concealed compartment beneath the floor of his SUV, but the hip-pack had everything he needed for a high-speed escape.

The doctor took the passport and headed down the corridor, her white coat flapping behind her to reveal an extremely shapely pair of legs and the red soles of fake Christian Louboutin high heels. At least, Harper assumed they were fake – Thai doctors weren't as highly paid as their UK and US counterparts but she might have been from a wealthy family. Or maybe she had a rich husband.

Harper waited until she'd turned a corner, then slipped into the ICU. A machine was beeping quietly in time with Pear's heartbeat. There was a bandage across her forehead and a plaster across her nose. Her eyes were almost hidden by puffed-up skin. Her lips were cracked and swollen and there were bandages on her arms. A tube ran from a bandage on her wrist to a clear bag hanging from a metal stand.

Harper touched her arm gently. She flinched and groaned but didn't open her eyes. 'Pear, baby, it's me. Lek.'

Pear's eyes fluttered open and she tried to smile but the effort made her wince. 'Lek, I'm sorry.'

'Don't be silly, baby. There's nothing to be sorry about.'

'I have no money.'

He patted her arm. 'Don't worry, I've taken care of it.'

'I'll pay you back.'

'You bloody won't,' said Harper. 'Now, who did this to you? Em said it was a customer.'

'It was a Russian. Valentine. He owns a bar in Walking Street.'

'Tell me what happened.'

'I went with my friend Ying. She dances at the Cellblock. She wanted to see Russian girls dancing so we went to Red Oktober. They have pretty girls there. Valentine was giving us drinks and I got drunk very quickly. When I woke up I was upstairs in a room and there were two men with me. Valentine and another man.'

'What was his name?'

'I don't know, Lek. I'm sorry. I forgot. He was a friend of Valentine's. A Russian man.' She shuddered. 'They'd taken my clothes off and Valentine was taking pictures as the other man had sex with me. I shouted at them, told them not to take my picture. Valentine laughed and slapped me. I started screaming and then they . . .' She shuddered again. 'They did this to me.' She sniffed. 'I thought I was going to die, Lek.'

'This room, where was it? Above the bar?'

'I don't think so. I think it was a short-time hotel. I don't remember.'

'Don't you worry,' he said again. 'Just get better, okay? I'll take care of everything.'

She nodded and slowly closed her eyes. 'Thank you, Lek. You're a good friend.'

Harper leaned over and kissed her on the forehead, then hurried out, just in time to see the doctor coming down the corridor with his passport. If she'd seen Harper disobeying her instruction not to disturb the patient, she didn't show it, just smiled, thanked him and returned the passport. She also gave him a business card with her mobile phone number. 'You can call me anytime to ask how Pear is,' she said.

'She's going to be all right, though?'

'She needs a lot of rest. And I worry that she will always have the scars. But other than that . . .'

'If you think a plastic surgeon will help with the scars, get one in,' said Harper. 'I'll pay whatever it costs.'

'We'll see about that once she's out of ICU, but I will be able to recommend someone, yes.'

'Do you know where she was when this happened?'

'I don't.'

'Did she come here in an ambulance?'

'No, a taxi. One of her friends brought her, I think.'

Harper thanked her and headed out of the hospital.

7

The Cellblock didn't usually start to get going until ten at night and the best girls didn't bother turning up until eleven. They knew they'd be taken out by a customer within an hour or so of going on stage so there was little point in clocking in early even if not doing so meant the management docking a few hundred baht from their pay. Most of the girls didn't care about the salary the bar paid, anyway. They earned most of their income from customers in hotel rooms, anything from two thousand baht from a Pattaya regular to five or six thousand from a newbie who didn't know the going rate.

The Cellblock was done out as if it was a prison, with an upper area of barred cells in which girls would dance and a lower area like a concrete exercise yard. Harper didn't want to miss Ying so he got there at eight and sat in a corner nursing a Heineken. There were two other customers and half a dozen girls pretending to dance on concrete podiums, shifting their weight from foot to foot as they checked their smartphones. Over the next hour a dozen or so more arrived, mostly wearing crop tops and shorts, flip-flops slapping on the floor. They would disappear through a curtain into the changing room, emerging a few minutes later in high-heeled boots, thongs and little else.

Several of them eyed Harper as they walked by but his body language and blank eyes betrayed him as a local, which meant they didn't bother trying to hit him up for a drink. That was the third way the dancers made money: they earned commission on every drink a customer bought them. A girl who hustled could easily get twenty drinks a night – usually cola or water masquerading as tequila – which meant a thousand baht or so in her hand. Harper had enough mates in the Pattaya bar business to know that a hard-working girl with a sweet mouth could earn more than two hundred thousand baht a month – close to fifty thousand pounds a year.

He was on his second beer when Ying walked into the bar. He almost missed her – with no makeup, her hair tied back and her figure disguised in an oversized T-shirt, she looked more like a farm-girl than one of the Cellblock's top-earning dancers. 'Hey, Ying, over here,' he called.

Her eyes widened when she saw him. 'Lek, you know about Pear?'

'That's what I want to talk to you about.' He patted the seat next to him. She slid onto it and almost immediately a chubby waitress with bad skin appeared, nodding expectantly. Harper didn't bother arguing, just ordered a drink for Ying. He knew the rules: if a girl sat with a customer she had to have a drink. The waitress pointed at herself and smiled, showing uneven teeth. Harper shook his head. He didn't mind buying Ying a cola but the waitress was pushing her luck. She held out her right hand so that he could see her palm. On it was written in felt-tip pen – BUY ME A DRINK?

Harper shook his head. No.

She held out her left hand, fingers splayed. CHEAP CHARLIE. She waited until he had read it, then spun on her heels and flounced off with her nose in the air.

'What happened last night?' Harper asked Ying.

She had high cheekbones and skin the colour of mahogany, big almond eyes and full lips. With her large breasts and long legs she was the sort of girl Westerners flocked to, though most Thais wouldn't have considered her pretty. 'We went to Red Oktober,' she said, her lips just inches from his ear. 'We wanted to see Russian girls dancing, and a man started buying us drinks.'

'His name was Valentine, right?'

She shook her head. 'Valentine wasn't the man who bought the drinks. His name was Grigory. Valentine owns the bar.' Her hand was stroking his thigh as she talked, from habit rather than any wish to arouse him. It was her bar-girl instinct kicking in.

'You know him?'

She shook her head again. 'No, he told me he was the boss. I joked about working for him but he said he only has Russian girls in his club.'

'And who was this Grigory?'

'Just a customer.'

'And he was a friend of Valentine?'

Ying nodded. 'They were good friends, I think. They kept talking to each other in Russian, and laughing. We'd been there about an hour and my boyfriend rang. He wanted to see me. He was gambling and he needed money.'

'So you left her?'

The waitress returned with Ying's cola, then flashed her CHEAP CHARLIE hand and flounced off again.

'She was okay, Lek. She seemed happy. A bit drunk, but you know Pear. She drinks a lot.'

Like most of the girls in the industry, Pear used alcohol and drugs to get through the night, partly for energy and partly to numb the pain.

'If I'd known what was going to happen, I wouldn't have left her.'

Harper sipped his beer. 'Do you know where they took her? Pear said she was in a room somewhere.'

'I don't know,' she said. Tears were welling in her eyes. 'It's my fault, isn't it?'

'No. It's Valentine and Grigory who are responsible.'

He paid for the drinks, then headed down Walking Street and along a darkened side street to BJ's, one of Pattaya's seedier bars, with half a dozen scantily dressed girls sitting outside touting for customers. 'Is Ricky in?' he asked one.

She pulled open a stained curtain. Harper ducked and walked through, wrinkling his nose at the stale smell of God knew what inside. BJ's was called BJ's because that was the speciality of the house, the act taking place in one of a dozen small booths around the edge of the bar, while a few plump girls went through the motions of dancing on a podium in the centre. To the right there was a Jacuzzi in which two even plumper girls were lathering themselves as a couple of elderly men in matching Chang Beer vests ogled them.

Ricky was standing at the cash register. His face lit up when he saw Harper. 'Fuck me, Lex, long time no see.' He walked over and hugged Harper. He was a big guy, well over six feet, a former merchant seaman, who had retired to Pattaya three years earlier. He had a good pension and several property investments back in England. The bar was more of a hobby than a business, which was why he'd staffed it solely with the sort of girls he liked – short, plump and dark. He couldn't care less whether it was busy or not. It was his own personal playground and that was all that mattered.

'Beer?' asked Ricky. 'On the house?'

'Sure,' said Harper, slipping onto a stool. Ricky joined him, waved at the barman, mimed a beer and held up two fingers. The barman nodded. Ricky had never bothered learning Thai but his sign language was understood the world over.

'What can you tell me about Red Oktober?' asked Harper, as the beers arrived.

'Russian go-go on Walking Street,' said Ricky. 'Pretty girls. A lot of Russian and Latvian blondes. Teenagers most of them.'

'Underage?'

'Borderline, but they're paying off the cops big time to let non-Thais work so I don't think anyone's bothered about how old they are.'

'And who runs it? A guy called Valentine?'

'Valentin,' corrected Ricky. 'Valentin Rostov. But he's the figurehead. It's Russian Mafia money. Have you got a problem with him, Lex? If you have, you need to stay well clear. They're vicious bastards and they're protected.'

'He put a friend of mine in hospital.'

'A girl?'

'Yeah, why do you ask?'

Ricky looked pained. 'Because he's got a bit of a reputation for liking the nasty stuff. We've warned our girls not to go there. He knocked around a girl from Electric Blue a few months ago. And a girl from Dollshouse before that. He's got a thing for anal, especially if the girls don't like it.'

'For fuck's sake, Ricky.'

Ricky held up his hands. 'Don't shoot the messenger, mate,' he said. 'What do you expect me to do? Go to the cops? Then I'll be the one taking it up the arse. Valentin Rostov is protected. There's nothing can be done.'

'What's he look like?'

'Big. Probably former military. Crew-cut. Scar across his left cheek. Jagged like it was done with a bottle. Diamond earring.'

'The gay ear or the straight ear?'

Ricky laughed. 'An earring in any man's ear is fucking gay, mate. But this is a big diamond. Real, by all accounts. A couple of carats.'

'And he's got a friend called Grigory?'

'That I don't know. There's a lot of Russians drink there, obviously. And Indians. The Indians like the Russian birds and the Russian birds aren't fussy.'

'I doubt they're given much choice, right?'

Ricky nodded. 'Fair comment.'

It was an open secret that many of the Russian girls working in the go-go bars were little more than slaves, trafficked into the country, their passports held by their bosses until they had paid off the cost of their flight, visa and assorted bribes. The local girls could always choose whether or not to go with a customer, but the Russians had to do as their pimps told them. If a Thai girl was unhappy with her bar she could quit and find another place to work. That wasn't a luxury afforded the Russians.

'Be careful, Lex,' said Ricky.

Harper grinned. 'Careful is my middle name.'

'Yeah? I heard you were christened Alex Mad Fucking Bastard Harper, in which case Fucking would be your middle name. At least if you can't be careful, be lucky.'

'I always am, mate,' said Harper. He patted Ricky's shoulder and headed out into the night.

8

Harper waited until midnight before visiting Red Oktober. Two busty blondes in evening dresses were standing at the entrance and flashed him beaming smiles as he walked between them. The entrance led to a flight of red-carpeted stairs, a large Russian bouncer, with a shaved head and an earpiece in his left ear, at the top. Harper flashed him a smile and the Russian pulled open a glass door. Techno music blared and the temperature dropped a good ten degrees as Harper walked in. A dozen sofas were spread around the room and there was a bar with a dozen stools to the right. Stunning girls in evening dresses sat at tables with customers while others wearing thongs did some impressive pole work at three podiums. Unlike the Thai dancers, who rarely did more than shuffle around the poles, the Russians girls put their hearts and souls into it with gymnastic performances worthy of an Olympic medal.

Harper spotted Valentin immediately. Ricky had been right: the diamond in his left ear was huge and the scar on his cheek had obviously been done with a broken bottle. It made sense to use a bottle because Valentin was a big bastard, and hard with it: broad-shouldered and with a chin that looked as if it could shrug off a punch from anyone less than a world heavyweight champion. The Russian was pouring whisky from a bottle of Johnnie Walker Blue into a large glass with his right hand while he massaged the backside of a teenage blonde in a tight blue dress with his left. He was sitting next to a smaller man, and laughing at something he'd said.

A Thai waiter motioned for Harper to sit at an empty table but he went to the bar and took the stool one away from the man who was sitting next to Valentin. He ordered a Heineken, then swivelled around to get a better look at the bar. Most of the customers appeared to be Indian or Thai in contrast to the regular go-go bars, which tended to attract Westerners. They seemed to be big spenders too – the Russian dancers were drinking colourful cocktails and there were opened bottles of champagne on several tables.

'Hello,' said a voice to his side. Harper turned to find himself looking into the eyes of a stunning brunette. Almost immediately his eyes dropped to a gravity-defying cleavage threatening to burst out of a skin-tight white dress. 'What's your name?' she asked. His eyes clawed back to her face and he saw that she was smiling in a way that suggested she was used to her breasts getting most of the attention.

'Gerry,' said Harper. 'From Wales.'

'Wales?'

'Near England.'

'You are here on holiday?'

'Been here a week. Having a great time. Lovely place, innit?'

The girl nodded. 'But very hot.'

'You're on holiday?'

She laughed. 'No, I work here. Do you want to buy me a drink?'

'Sure.'

'A cocktail is six hundred baht.'

'Money no object, I'm on holiday.'

The girl ordered a drink from a waitress, then turned back to him. 'I'm Alena,' she said. She offered him her hand.

Harper kissed it. They chatted for the best part of half an hour, with Harper playing the part of the naïve tourist and Alena apparently hanging on his every word while she sipped her cocktail. He bought her another, and another, then asked her about Red Oktober. 'I've been thinking I could run a bar in Pattaya,' he said.

'It's not easy,' she said.

'Who runs this place?'

'Valentine,' she said, indicating the man with the diamond earring. 'He's the boss.'

'Let me buy him a drink,' said Harper, slurring his words.

'He only drinks Johnnie Walker Blue.'

'Then I'll buy him a Johnnie Walker Blue.' He slid off the stool, making it look as if he was a lot drunker than he actually was. He walked unsteadily to Valentin and tapped him on the shoulder. 'Hi, mate, my name's Gerry. From Cardiff. Have you heard of Cardiff?' He held out his hand.

Valentin shook it. 'Of course. Wales.'

'And where are you from, Valentin?'

'Moscow,' said the Russian.

'That Putin's a laugh, isn't he?' said Harper, slurring his words again. He let go of Valentin's hand and clapped the other man on the shoulder. 'What's your name, mate?'

'Grigory.'

'You from Moscow, too, mate?'

Grigory's eyes hardened. 'My friend and I are in the middle of a private conversation, if you don't mind.'

Harper stepped back and raised his hands. 'Sorry, right, sure, yes, no problem. Just wanted to say hello, that's all.' He flashed an exaggerated double thumbs-up. 'Great bar!' He backed away unsteadily, and knocked over his Heineken. He grinned lopsidedly at Alena. 'Better be getting back to the hotel. My wife will be wondering where I am.' He paid his bill and headed out. As he went through the door, Alena was already moving in on another customer.

9

Valentin and Grigory left the bar when it closed, at about four o'clock in the morning. Harper had waited for them in one of the beer bars on the opposite side of the street, drinking water but buying drinks for the girls and playing them at Connect 4, the children's game where the aim was to get four coloured discs in a row. The girls had played for years and were experts and Harper was lucky to win one game in ten.

The two Russians were clearly drunk and walked unsteadily down one of the side alleys that led to a car park. Harper paid his bill and followed them. The car park was mainly full of pick-up trucks but in the far corner there was a white Lamborghini and the Russians headed for that.

Harper jogged over to a line of waiting motorcycle taxis and gave the rider at the front of the queue five hundred baht. 'Follow that car,' he said, in Thai. Valentin and Grigory had climbed into the car and Valentin had started the engine. A uniformed security guard blew a whistle and waved instructions for Valentin to avoid scraping any of the other vehicles.

'The Lamborghini?'

'Sure.' Harper climbed onto the back of the bike. 'Just don't let him see you. Find out where he lives and there's another five hundred for you.' The Lamborghini edged carefully out of the car park.

'Yes, boss,' said the driver, gunning the engine. He was wearing a purple vest with the number 56 in Thai on the back. Motorcycle taxis were a quick and cheap means of getting around the city, especially at rush hour. They were also an efficient way of following other vehicles: no one ever paid attention to the motorcycle taxis or their customers.

The Lamborghini headed south, parallel to the sea. Valentin drove erratically. The fact he had senior cops on his payroll meant he wasn't worried about being stopped for drunk-driving. Twice he went through a red light and he didn't indicate before turns. Harper patted his driver on the shoulder. 'Don't get too close,' he said.

'No problem, boss.'

The car reached Jontiem and headed east, up a hill overlooking the bay. It stopped in front of a pair of large metal gates covered by a CCTV camera. The gates opened, the car drove through, and the gates closed again. There was security wire on top of the wall but the only camera he saw was the one at the gates.

Harper asked the driver to take him back to his apartment, in a high-rise block close to Beach Road. He had just walked into his sitting room overlooking the sea when he felt a vibration inside his hip-pack. He took out his phone and read the three-word text message from a UK number: *You have mail.*

Harper cursed under his breath. The message was from Charlotte Button and nine times out of ten a message from her meant him being on a plane within hours. If he were going to deal with the Russians it would have to be now. Either that or he'd have to walk away. He thought of Pear, battered and bruised in her hospital bed, and put his phone away. He walked through to the kitchen and took a pair of wire-cutters from the toolbox under the sink. He put them into a nylon kitbag along with three old towels from the bathroom.

The wall had been about ten feet high, and he had noticed several ladders belonging to his apartment building's maintenance staff in the underground car park. Harper figured they wouldn't miss one for a few hours. There was a false back to his underwear drawer in the wardrobe and he slid it back to reveal a Glock pistol with three filled magazines. He put the gun and clips into the holdall and went downstairs to his truck. He put one of the smaller ladders into the back, his holdall on the front passenger seat, then drove down to Beach Road. He parked outside an internet café owned by a middle-aged former go-go dancer called Rose. She was open pretty much twenty-four/ seven though when Harper walked in her brother was minding the shop. There were two customers, a drunken Scandinavian tourist on Skype and a bar-girl browsing through online photographs of Louis Vuitton handbags, presumably preparing to hit up a sponsor for a gift.

'Hi, Kung – okay if I use a terminal?' asked Harper.

Kung was engrossed in a Thai soap opera and waved a languid hand at the line of computers without looking up. 'Help yourself to a beer if you want one,' he said.

'I'm good,' said Harper. He sat down at a screen at the far end of the room. He went first to Google Earth and called up a satellite view of the house in Jontiem, then spent several minutes studying the layout. There was a main villa built in an L-shape around a large pool, plus two smaller houses that he reckoned were for the staff and possibly bodyguards. The rear wall faced the back of the house and was clearly the best way in.

He googled Valentin Rostov but all that came up were a couple of Facebook pages, neither of which belonged to the man he'd followed back to the villa.

He logged on to the Yahoo Mail account he used to contact Charlotte Button. She was the only person other than himself who knew the password and could access the email account they used to communicate with each other. They never actually emailed: they communicated by leaving messages in the draft folder. Deceptively simple, it was an almost foolproof system, far more secure than any phone or email link.

Using a chain of listening stations, like Yorkshire's Menwith Hill and GCHQ, both in the UK, and the National Security Agency in the US, the British and American intelligence agencies could intercept every single landline and mobile phone call, made anywhere in the world, and any email. Button and Harper's messages for each other in the drafts folder could not be monitored or recorded by anyone trying to eavesdrop on their communications. To increase security still more, their standard operating procedure was to delete each one as soon as it had been read. The technique had been developed by al-Qaeda terrorists to evade high-tech surveillance of their communications by Western intelligence agencies, but Button and Harper had adapted it for their own use.

When Harper logged in, he discovered that a single, two-word message had been added to the drafts folder: *Paris. ASAP.*

Harper deleted the message and wrote another: *En route, Madame.* He went online looking for flights to Paris and booked himself a business class seat on the 9.50 a.m. Air France flight that would get him into Charles de Gaulle airport at just before six o'clock in the evening.

He dropped a hundred-baht note in front of Kung, who waved his thanks without looking up, then went back outside to his pick-up truck. He drove out to Jontiem and parked off-road a hundred metres from the villa, switched off the engine and sat, gazing out over the sea, as he waited for his night vision to kick in.

It was just after six o'clock in the morning when he placed the lightweight ladder against the wall and used it to reach up to the security wire. He clipped away a section and let it fall to the ground. Broken glass was embedded in the concrete running along the top of the wall and he put the folded towels over it before climbing up and hauling the ladder after him. He slipped over and placed the ladder carefully on the ground, then shrugged off the backpack and took out the Glock. He crouched low, getting his bearings, then crept on the balls of his feet over the grass to the main building. The lights were on in the large room that overlooked the pool. Music was playing. Pitbull. Harper glanced at the two smaller buildings in the compound. Both were in darkness.

He worked his way along the villa to a back entrance. There was a roofed area with a Thai kitchen, a barbecue and a door that led inside. The rear of the house was in darkness and Harper padded over the marble floor, the Glock in his hand. He crept down a hallway that was wreathed in dim shadows. There were two closed doors on the left and the hall turned right, opening into the main living area, a double-height room with a huge chandelier hanging from a wooden arch. Two massive sofas were placed at a right angle to each other. Valentin was sitting with his back to Harper, who could see the diamond in the man's ear. Valentin was talking loudly in Russian and waving a glass above his head. Grigory was sitting on the other sofa, his feet on a large marble coffee-table, side on to Harper.

He stayed put for a couple of minutes until he was sure that there was no one else in the villa, before walking quickly to Valentin. Grigory saw him at the last minute but was slow to react. He hadn't even got to his feet by the time Harper had slammed the butt of his gun against the side of Valentin's head. There was a satisfying crunch and the Russian toppled sideways without a sound. Now Grigory jumped up but Harper already had the gun trained on him.

'What the fuck do you want?' the Russian snarled.

'To give you a taste of your own medicine.'

Grigory frowned. 'What the fuck do you mean?'

'I mean I'm going to hurt you so bad you'll wish you'd never been born.'

'Do you know who I am?'

'I know you're a Russian prick who enjoys beating up little girls and fucking them up the arse. Now get down on your knees.'

'Fuck you. You think I'm scared of your gun?'

Harper kept the gun trained on Grigory's face as he

slowly walked around the sofa. 'Scared or not, it can still blow your fucking brains out.'

'If you were going to shoot me, you'd have done it already.'

'Good point,' said Harper. His foot lashed out and caught the Russian in the groin. He yelped and bent double just in time for Harper to smash the gun into the side of the man's face, cracking his jaw and sending two teeth clattering across the polished wooden floor. Grigory straightened up, blood trickling from between his lips. He opened his mouth to speak but Harper transferred the gun to his left hand and punched him in the solar plexus with his right fist, putting all his weight behind the blow. Grigory fell back, arms flailing, his bloodied lips opening and closing, like those of a stranded fish. He hit the floor hard and lay still. Harper went over to him and kicked him in the side. 'Come on, you nasty Russian fuck. Wake up. You'll miss all the fun.'

10

Harper arrived at Bangkok's Suvarnabhumi airport at just before eight o'clock in the morning. He was travelling light, just a small backpack, and the hip-pack. He'd hired a taxi, a driver he regularly used, who could at least be relied on not to take drugs, drink whisky, or use his mobile phone behind the wheel, which was more than could be said for the majority of the city's taxi drivers. He walked up to the Air France desk and handed over his passport. The woman sitting there was less than five feet tall with glossy black hair and a mischievous smile, but the second she took his passport Harper realised something was wrong. She looked at it, then at a list on her desk, then back to the passport and back to him. She frowned and looked at the list a second time, then beckoned to a man in a grey suit. He came over and took the passport from her. He read the details inside and his eyes flicked to the list. He gave Harper a beaming smile. 'I'm so sorry, Mr Harper, we have a problem with our computer at the moment. I'll have to run this through the computer in our office. Please wait a moment.' He walked away with the passport while the check-in girl flashed Harper a comforting smile that suggested she was sorry for the delay and that she hoped everything would soon be sorted.

Harper smiled back. He had two choices. He could turn and walk away, but they already had his passport and he doubted he would get far. Or he could stand there, smile and see how it panned out.

'Khun Harper?'

He turned. A Thai policeman was standing behind him. Like all Thai cops he had a big gun on his hip and cold eyes that said he'd used it more than once in his career and would happily use it again. 'Yes?' Harper said.

There was another cop to his right, younger and taller, and three more not too far away.

'Please come with us.' The officer motioned with his hand for Harper to move away from the desk.

'Sure, no problem,' said Harper, shouldering his backpack.

'Please give me your bag,' said the officer.

Harper's jaw tightened but he knew there was no point in resisting so he forced a smile and handed it over. The officer gave it to the younger policeman, who went over to the check-in desk and retrieved Harper's passport. As the three of them left the check-in desks, the other three officers fell into step a few yards behind.

They took him to an escalator and up one floor, then along to a door with a keypad. The officer tapped in a four-digit code and pushed open the door. It led to a long corridor. He opened the third door along and motioned for Harper to go inside. A uniformed police colonel was sitting behind a table, smoking a cigarette in clear defiance of the NO SMOKING sign behind him. He wore a tight-fitting brown uniform, gleaming boots, and a scattering of colourful medals on his chest. Police Colonel Somchai Wattanakolwit. He grinned up at Harper and waved his cigarette at the empty chair opposite him. 'I gather you've been a naughty boy, Lek.'

Harper shrugged but sat down and didn't say anything. He had known the colonel for the best part of five years, and had got drunk with him several times, but the relationship was more one of symbiosis than friendship. Harper made regular contributions towards the colonel's retirement fund and in return the colonel didn't pay much attention to what Harper did or didn't do in the Land of Smiles.

The officer took the backpack and placed it on the table, then left and closed the door behind him.

Somchai smiled as he flicked idly through Harper's passport. 'Apparently a *farang* broke into a house in Jontiem and attacked two Russians. Attacked them so badly that they are both in hospital. One of them has lost his spleen and the other will be lucky if he ever eats solid food again. Both are black and blue. They were given a serious beating. Very serious.'

'Pattaya can be a dangerous place, if you're not careful,' said Harper.

'The attacker seems also to have forced beer bottles up their backsides, doing a considerable amount of damage in the process.'

Harper had to fight to stop himself grinning.

The colonel also seemed to be having trouble keeping a straight face. 'The description they give matches you, my friend. Especially the bit about the attacker being cruel, sadistic and probably psychopathic.'

Harper raised a quizzical eyebrow. 'I'd say that description would fit most of the expat population of Pattaya, wouldn't you?'

Somchai chuckled. 'A fair point, my friend.'

'So what's led you to stop me boarding my plane?' He looked at his watch. 'A plane that is due to leave in just over an hour and a half.'

'A young lady called Pear,' said Somchai. 'Who coincidentally happens to be in the same hospital as the two Russians. In the same condition too, more or less.'

Harper folded his arms but said nothing.

'It seems you played the good Samaritan and paid the young lady's hospital bill.'

'Let's get to the point, Somchai. Because I really need to be getting on that plane.'

Somchai smiled and leaned forward. 'The Russians don't know your name yet, Lek. In fact, at the moment they seem to think you're a Welshman called Gerry. But they're not stupid. Do you have any idea who they are?'

'They beat the shit out of young girls, I know that much.'

'Valentin Rostov and Grigory Lukin are very well protected, Lek.'

'I thought I was protected, Somchai.'

'You are, Lek. Which is why you and I are having this conversation and you're not dead in a ditch somewhere. You and I are friends. But these Russians, they pay a lot of money for protection. And they pay people much, much higher up the food chain than me. Money flows uphill, Lek, and shit flows down. That's the way of the world. At the moment I have been told to look for the man who put the Russians in hospital. I'm still looking. But if someone else puts a name to the face . . .' He shrugged.

'You won't be able to protect me?'

'The best thing might be for you to get on that plane and not come back, Lek.'

'Are you threatening me?'

The colonel chuckled. 'Of course not, my friend. It's just a warning. And you should be grateful for that.'

Harper nodded. 'Message received and understood. And thank you.'

'No problem. You have a safe trip.' He slid Harper's passport across the table. 'And, please, be careful. I don't have many *farang* friends and I'd hate to lose one.'

The plane touched down in Paris on a cool spring evening and Harper caught the city train to Châtelet – Les Halles and set off to walk to the hotel. He had checked the draft folder and Button wanted to meet him there at ten so he was in no hurry and strolled casually, enjoying the contrast of the cool air after the fierce heat and humidity of Thailand. He crossed the rue Saint-Honoré and cut down a narrow street leading to the rue de Rivoli. It was now almost eight o'clock and the streets were crowded with hordes of rubber-necking foreigners out for an evening stroll while being pestered by a retinue of tour guides, souvenir sellers, ticket touts, street hawkers, pickpockets and others who, in one way or another, earned their living from the tourist trade. As he moved through the streets, he was aware of the constant background chatter, a babel of different languages.

Relaxed though he was, Harper never completely switched off. Without being conscious that he was doing it, his eyes were constantly checking the streets, the buildings and the street furniture for potential danger-points or for cover if attacked, and assessing the body language of the people coming towards him. It had saved his life on more than one occasion, and had become such an ingrained habit during his time in the army and his subsequent off-the-books career that it was now as much a part of his routine as a shower and a shave in the morning.

Harper's normal practice whenever he was in England was to stay in cheap, anonymous hotels and pay cash for his room. Even in countries where the law required all foreign visitors to deposit their passports with the desk clerk when they checked into a hotel, there were always places operating on the fringes. They were the sort of hotels in the seedier quarters of big cities that catered to those who, for whatever reason, preferred to keep the law at arm's length and hired rooms by the night or even by the hour, depending on the particular requirements of their clientele. In such hotels, no ID was required before checking in, cash was the only acceptable form of payment and a blind eye was routinely turned to any laws that might affect business. But Harper was sure he wasn't on the radar of the French police so he had decided he could treat himself to a decent room for his meeting, especially as Charlotte Button would be picking up the tab. The hotel he had chosen, Le Meurice, was one of Paris's dozen or so elite, ultra-luxurious 'Palace Hotels'. It was a tourist's wet dream, on the rue de Rivoli between the Place de la Concorde and the Louvre, with views over the Tuileries Gardens, but Harper's mind was on his mission, Alert for any signs of surveillance or pursuit, he barely took in his surroundings. He was convinced that no one was following him, but as he stepped past the liveried doorman into the hotel's lobby, he drew back against the wall next to the doors, waiting and observing those entering behind him, to make absolutely sure he was secure before going to the desk and checking in.

The duty manager, a chic stick-thin Parisienne in her mid-forties, escorted him through the hotel, giving no more than a hint of a raised eyebrow at the small pack that was his only luggage and which he kept firmly in his hand, resisting a bellboy's attempts to carry it for him. He showed no interest in the Louis XVI furniture and the over-the-top nineteenth-century bling of the hotel's fixtures and fittings as she led him through the lobby and took the private lift to his seventh-floor Belle Etoile suite. He was still paying no more than cursory attention as she showed him the terrace with a spectacular view that encompassed almost every Paris landmark, from Notre Dame, the Musée d'Orsay, the Eiffel Tower, the Grand Palais, the Place de la Concorde and the Arc de Triomphe, to the Opéra and Sacré Coeur. If she was surprised at his lack of interest in a view that had many guests gasping with delight, she was professional enough not to let it show and her expression remained impassive.

When she had gone, Harper showered and changed into a clean shirt, then ordered a club sandwich from room service. He was just finishing it when his phone rang. It was the front desk, announcing that he had a visitor. Harper said they could send her up and he had the door open for her by the time she stepped out of the lift. As always, Charlotte Button was immaculately dressed in an understated but beautifully cut grey designer suit. She had pinned up her chestnut hair and the only jewellery she wore was the gold Cartier watch on her left wrist. 'A suite in Le Meurice,' she said, as she looked around the plush interior.

'What happened to your policy of always flying below the radar?'

'It's Fashion Week so everywhere's fully booked. And it was short notice.' He grinned. 'Come on, it's Paris. If you want to meet here we should at least do it in some style.'

'It's France, Alex. And, as I'm sure you must know, the French secret service have a long history of targeting people of interest, usually their industrial competitors. The information they collect is analysed and shared with French industry. It saves them a fortune in research and development and is one of the reasons why the French economy remains competitive even though their executives are more obsessed with their mistresses than their businesses, and a lot of their shop-floor workers are bone idle.'

'Borderline racist, Charlie,' said Harper.

'I love France, and the French, but their intelligence services tend to be a bit over the top. The Direction Générale de la Sécurité Intérieure was caught red-handed a few years ago bugging first-class seats on Air France flights and it's well known in the trade that they target people of interest who are staying in French hotels. So next time maybe go downmarket a bit, same as you do in England.'

'And I'm sure you know that the owners of Le Meurice are just about the only hoteliers in Paris who refuse to cooperate with the French secret service when they want to plant bugs in their guest rooms.' His smile broadened. 'Which is another reason I chose it. Walls might well have ears, Charlie, but not in Le Meurice.' He waved for her to sit down and waited for her to tell him why she had summoned him.

'I need you to do a job for me in the UK,' she said. 'We think a former SAS trooper has gone rogue and is planning something particularly nasty.'

'Do I know him?'

'He was a Para and the end of his time in the Paras overlapped with the start of yours. But he went off to do Selection and joined the SAS while you were out in Afghanistan. Caleb McGovan. Does that ring a bell?'

Harper shook his head.

'McGovan went to Turkey on a charter flight and spent a few days on the Turquoise Coast. He disappeared for a while before reappearing back on the coast. This happened a couple of times and we think in the interim he was making trips into Syria to link up with Islamic State.'

'You keep saying "we" but you don't work for Five any more.'

'It's not come from the British end,' said Button. 'It's the Americans who want it taken care of.'

'Now I'm confused,' said Harper. 'A former British soldier is threatening an attack on British soil, but the Yanks want him taken out?'

'So far as I'm led to believe, the Brits don't know what's going on.'

'So why don't the Yanks tell them, special relationship and all?'

'I gather they worry that the Brits won't handle it . . . correctly.'

'Correctly?'

'They want McGovan dead. And they don't see the Brits carrying out the execution of a British citizen on British soil. And they're a little wary of doing it themselves. Or, at least, of being caught doing it. By using my company, they stay one step removed.'

'So we're doing their dirty work?'

'That's one way of looking at it. The other is to consider that we'll be preventing a terrorist attack on UK soil.'

'That's not really the job of private enterprise, is it, though? That's why we have MI5, MI6 and all those other agencies that use initials. Why not just pass the intel on to them?'

'Because they'd want to know where it came from. And because they almost certainly wouldn't deal with it in the way that the Americans want it dealt with.'

'Sounds to me as if there's something you're not telling me.'

She smiled. 'Alex, if you'd let me finish you'd have the full picture. While McGovan was in the region – in other words, between his outward flight to Dalaman and his return flight to Britain – an American senior instructor working with the Iraqi Army at a base near Mosul was killed by an IED. One Captain Geoff Buckthorn. We – i.e. the Americans – think he was deliberately targeted. The device, with another fail-safe IED attached to the fuel tank, was fitted to his vehicle while it was parked inside a secure compound that was itself within an outer compound at the Iraqi base. The barbed-wire perimeter fence of the outer compound was guarded by Iraqi troops. The fence surrounding the inner compound – it was steel mesh, capped with coils of razor wire – was guarded by Americans. Someone went to an awful lot of trouble to kill Captain Buckthorn. Possibly because his father is a Republican congressman.'

'Ah,' said Harper. 'The plot thickens.'

'Congressman Buckthorn made a big thing about his son being in the military. About his family not just talking the talk but walking the walk. Many of the rich American families are prepared to send ghetto kids to fight their battles, but young Buckthorn was prepared to put his life on the line and so on. The right-wing media lapped it up.'

'And young Buckthorn paid the price. I get it. Now Congressman Buckthorn wants his revenge. But how sure are they that McGovan was behind it?'

'It was a very professional job. Like I said, the compound was being guarded by the Americans.'

'That proves nothing,' Harper said. 'The Yanks are even lazier than the Iraqi soldiers. They'd just be hanging around, shooting the breeze and praying for dawn so they could go to bed. They'd respond to a sniper or a mortar attack, of course, but they wouldn't be out there patrolling the fence line and watching for intruders. You don't need to go looking for rogue special forces to explain what happened there.'

Button made a gesture of annoyance. 'Prior to that attack, the Americans considered there was no group in the Iraqi opposition, or the Syrian for that matter, who had the capability to carry out that kind of attack. It was a complete surprise, Alex, not only to the Iraqis – and, let's face it, plenty of things come as a surprise to them – but also to the Americans. Then they picked up some SIGINT, more background chatter between a couple of ISIS high-ups, that suggested there was something unusual about the incident. It's not just that our target was almost certainly in country when it happened, but the way the attack was

carried out bears all the hallmarks of a special-forces operation. The Americans compiled a thorough after-action
report, and got Delta Force to replay the incident as a
TEWT – a tactical exercise without troops.'

'I know what a TEWT is, Charlie,' said Harper. 'I had
to do enough of them in the bloody Paras.'

'Then you shouldn't be too surprised to learn that, after
they'd analysed the results of the TEWT, they found enough
similarities to be pretty certain that it wasn't some goatherd
wandering in off the desert who managed to penetrate the
Iraqi base and planted those IEDs. Nor, as far as they
could tell, was it some random jihadi, or even an ISIS
fighter. It had special-forces input written all over it. And
since ISIS doesn't have special forces and since, for obvious
reasons, the British and Americans don't teach Iraqi troops
the most advanced SF techniques, their conclusion can
only be that the expertise was provided by a rogue British
or American special-forces soldier. And the Americans are
pointing the finger at McGovan. And McGovan is now
back in the UK.'

'And you – i.e. the Americans – want him taken out.'

'If we can show that he's been turned by IS, yes.'

'And how much intel do you have on McGovan?'

'He was abandoned at birth and brought up in care. He
pulled himself up by his bootstraps, joined the Paras and
ended up in the SAS. He got married and had a couple
of kids before getting dragged into Iraq and Afghanistan,
where in the gaps between ops he taught himself to speak
Arabic and Pashto. The consequences of too many trips
and too much active service ended with his wife leaving
him and taking the kids. It's a familiar story in the forces,

of course, but it completely gutted him. Seems as if he's a loner now and not good company. I did hear that he'd been involved in clearing up the mess at Abu Ghraib and other less publicised atrocities done in the name of Christianity by our born-again GIs and their British acolytes.' She leaned forward. 'I know this is messy, but it's no messier than jobs you've done before.'

'He's a Brit, and a former Para. It could be me, Charlie. In another world, it could be him sitting here and you two discussing taking me out.'

'But you're not a terrorist, Alex.'

'I know exactly what I am,' said Harper. 'And I have no problems looking at myself in the mirror each morning. But, yes, this is very fucking messy and at the end of the day you're asking me to kill a British soldier on British soil.'

'A former British soldier who has gone rogue,' said Button. 'And who might well be planning a major terrorist atrocity in a British city. I need to know you'll do this.'

Harper shrugged. 'I've never let you down before.'

'On a more positive note, the Americans have made it clear that money's no object.' She looked around the palatial suite. 'Which, considering how much this is costing, is probably for the best.'

She was fiddling with her wedding ring as she spoke. Even though her husband had died some years earlier, Harper had never seen her without it. 'Are you okay, Charlie?' he asked.

She forced a smile. 'I'm fine. Why do you ask?'

'You look tense.'

'That goes with the territory.'

'More tense than usual, then.'

She ran a hand through her hair. 'I've had a rough few days.'

'Is that why we're meeting here, in Paris?'

She didn't answer and looked away.

'Maybe I can help,' he said.

She flashed him another tight smile. 'That's sweet of you, Alex. But I'm not sure you'd be able to do anything.'

'A trouble shared is a trouble halved.'

'Or doubled,' she said. 'It could go either way.' She laughed uneasily. 'Do you think there's wine in the minibar?'

'The prices they charge, there'd better be,' he said. He went over to the fridge, bent down and opened it. 'There's champagne.'

'We're not really celebrating.'

'And white.' He pulled out a half-bottle. 'It's a Chardonnay, with a screw top.'

'In Le Meurice? Now that's a surprise. But I suppose beggars can't be choosers.'

He opened the bottle and emptied it into two glasses, gave one to her and sat down on the winged chair facing her. He raised his glass in salute. 'Cheers.'

She toasted him back. 'You never take life seriously, do you, Alex?'

He shrugged. 'When it matters, I do. But if you can't have a little fun along the way, then what's the point?'

She pulled a face, then drank some more wine. 'You know I left MI5. Obviously.'

'Because of that little shit Willoughby-Brown?' He made a gun with his hand and mimed firing a couple of shots. 'Anytime you want him taken care of, I'll do it for free.'

'This isn't about him,' she said. 'At least, I don't think it is.'

'So, what's the story?'

She took another sip of wine. 'When I left Five, I made it clear that I'd set up what you might call insurance. A file that in the event of my death, et cetera, et cetera.'

'You were scared they might kill you?'

'I know stuff, Alex, a lot of stuff that could embarrass a lot of people and end a lot of careers. Now, my lips are sealed, anyone who knows me knows that, but there are some people who'd rather not rely on my word. I had to make sure I was more dangerous to them dead than alive. That appeared to be working swimmingly until there was a break-in at a safe-deposit vault last week.'

'The Manchester job? I knew that was iffy.'

'Because they only opened fifty-odd boxes?'

'That and the fact that the cops didn't investigate when the alarm went off. And the fact that it was almost identical to the Hatton Garden robbery. And then there's the CCTV footage of the workmen arriving and leaving. I mean, come on, it's the robbery of the century and they couldn't disable one camera?'

'Why do you think that was?' asked Button.

'Red herrings,' said Harper. 'They were all middle-aged and overweight. There was no way any of them could have got through the twelve-inch hole produced by the drill they used. That means the guys who went through the hole into the vault weren't caught on CCTV. Why was one lot of men filmed and the others not? Because they were red herrings, that's why. I knew there was something off about the whole thing.'

'Well, now you know why. One of my insurance policies was in one of the boxes.'

'One of the fifty-odd?'

Button nodded and took another sip of wine. 'They took the thumbdrive and one of my husband's watches. A gold Rolex. To be honest, that's what annoys me more than anything, the fact that one of the bastards behind this is wearing my husband's watch. And just so you don't think I'm being paranoid, I had a similar thumbdrive in a box in the Hatton Garden vault. One of the seventy-two that got opened there. It was my files they were after, I'm sure of it.'

'And who do you think "they" are?'

Button sighed. 'Someone in government, maybe. Someone who doesn't want the file ever being made public. But you know what sort of work the Pool did. There are a lot of people whose careers would die if it was ever found out who did what to whom.'

'And what about me, Charlie? Am I in that file?'

'Redacted,' she said. 'Along with the names of most of the other operatives who were used. This isn't about you, it's about the people who gave the orders and paid the bills.'

'So do you want me to ask around?'

'I'm not sure that'll do any good, Alex. They're probably spooks.'

'The guys who went into the vaults to get the thumb-drives, almost certainly. But the drillers? They'd be good old-fashioned criminals, I'm sure. Like the guys who were pulled in for the Hatton Garden job. And, like criminals the world over, they'll talk eventually. I mean, where's the fun in pulling off the crime of the century if no one knows you did it?'

She smiled over the top of her wine glass. 'There's been no chatter. None at all. I've asked. Quiet as the grave.'

'We move in different circles, Charlie. Let me ask around.'

'If it's not too much trouble, I'd be grateful.'

He grinned. 'How grateful?'

'Not that grateful.'

They laughed.

'You don't know what I was going to say.'

'Yes, I do, Alex.'

A man in his late thirties or early forties was among the crowds of tourists emerging from Westminster Underground station on a drizzly London morning. His dark hair was tinged with grey, he was clean-shaven, with no particular distinguishing features, and wore drab clothing that was neither sharp enough nor scruffy enough to catch the eye. The only distinguishing feature about his outfit was the black trilby, tilted down over his forehead, so that the brim cast his upper features into shadow. To a casual glance, his face must have appeared almost as nondescript as his outfit, and only someone watching him closely would have detected his keen gaze as he glanced around him, taking in every detail.

He took a free newspaper from the person handing them out at the entrance to the station and stood with his back to one of the pillars, facing across the road towards Parliament. He stood there for some time, leafing idly through the paper, but his gaze was fixed on the people moving around him, not on the pages he was turning. After five minutes he moved off, but his concentration never wavered, continually alert for anything unusual, any person out of place or paying him too close attention.

The hat he was wearing served two purposes: to obscure his face from the ubiquitous CCTV cameras and also to provide a recognition mark for anyone following him. That might have seemed a perverse act for anyone trying to avoid detection, but he knew even the best-trained followers tended to use a distinguishing feature, like a hat, as a recognition point when tracking a suspect. In a crowded street, if the hat was suddenly removed, the person wearing it could apparently disappear. Also, his jacket was reversible, with a different-coloured lining. It would be the work of only seconds to change his outward appearance, to the potential confusion of any follower.

He walked along Bridge Street, and after strolling right around Parliament Square, he bought a ticket for a walking tour, joining a group of a dozen foreigners who had already gathered around the guide, a woman in her early thirties. Her world-weary, slightly pained expression suggested that of all the job opportunities a master's degree in history from Girton College, Cambridge, should have brought her, tour guide was not the first that came to mind.

She noticed the man at once as he joined the group. Most of her customers were families with children or older couples, and the vast majority were foreign: American, German, Japanese, Chinese, or a score of other nationalities. From the few words he had spoken when buying his ticket, his accent suggested he was English, and a man on his own, especially an English one, was a rarity on her tours. Also, he had no obvious tourist paraphernalia – no camera, guide book or Union flag carrier-bag, full of souvenirs. He was not the only unusual member of this particular party: there was also a group of three young men, foreign-looking, she thought, though she could not have done more than hazard a guess at their nationality. She thought that perhaps they were vaguely Middle Eastern or from one of the former Soviet republics with unpronounceable names, but whatever their origins, they were all serious, unsmiling and, she felt, slightly creepy. Like the other man, they did not attempt to engage with her and their slightly brooding presence had a noticeable effect on the others, who seemed inhibited by their silence and were much less vocal than she was used to.

However, no matter how silent and unsmiling its members might be, it was her job to lead the tour and explain the significance of the landmarks and buildings they would pass, so she began her standard housekeeping notices – 'Follow the orange and white umbrella. Watch out for pickpockets. Feel free to ask questions' – then launched into her introduction to the tour.

Their route took them the short distance to the Houses of Parliament, where they gathered around her for her usual 'Magna Carta and the Mother of Parliaments' mini-lecture, with a brief detour to take in Pugin and the Gothic Revival. She then led them along Whitehall, pausing near the steel gates manned by armed police guarding Downing Street while she explained the difference between a prime minister and a head of state, and fielded the inevitable questions about Winston Churchill and Margaret Thatcher, the only British prime ministers that 95 per cent of her audience could ever name.

As she walked along, she noticed that the lone man was ignoring her commentary and keeping well to the back of the group. He asked no questions, spoke not a word, didn't crack a smile at any of her jokes and appeared to be paying minimal attention to any of the historical sites and statues that she pointed out, though he seemed to take a much keener interest in the buildings flanking the streets they were passing along. They moved on as far as Admiralty Arch, turned back along Horse Guards Road, past Horse Guards Parade, the back of Downing Street and the elegant Portland-stone façade of the Foreign Office, then went along Birdcage Walk to Buckingham Palace. As she carried on with her spiel she saw, out of the corner of her eye, one of the three young men walk across to the man and, after a glance around, murmur something to him. The man silenced him with a ferocious look, turned his back and moved away from him. Clearly chastened, the other man returned to his two comrades and stayed well away from him throughout the rest of the tour.

Dispirited by her unenthusiastic audience, she cut short her usual closing speech about the role of the monarch and, after pausing to allow her group to take the traditional battery of photographs and selfies in front of the palace gates, she led them back down Buckingham Gate and past New Scotland Yard to their starting point. The man did not tip her at the end of the tour and, in fact, she wasn't even sure at what point he had left the group because he certainly wasn't with them when they had returned to Parliament Square. The three young men had also melted into the crowds thronging the square, without tipping her. She frowned as she picked over the modest assortment of coins and the one five-pound note that the rest of the tour group had donated. It didn't look as if she would be able to afford to take a year off to complete her doctorate any time soon. She gave a resigned shrug. It wasn't her job to ponder the motives of those who paid to join her tour, or wonder why so many were such stingy tippers. She glanced at her watch. If she was quick she'd have time for a coffee and a few minutes' rest before she set off again with the next group.

13

Charlotte Button checked in for her Delta flight to New York, using her Barbara Reynolds passport. She waited until she was in the Club Lounge with a glass of chilled Pinot Grigio in her hand before phoning Richard Yokely. 'Harper's in play,' she said. 'I'm on my way back.'

'Yes, I know,' said the American. 'How's the wine?'

'You've got someone here with me now?' She looked around the lounge. A dozen other travellers, mainly suited businessmen, were pecking away on laptops.

'I said I'd watch your back,' said Yokely. 'Your back is watched.'

'And?'

'Nothing so far. Clean as a whistle. Which means either you're not being followed, or you are and they're damn good at it. But my money's on the former.'

'It could just be that they only tail me in the UK, of course,' she said.

'We'll know soon enough,' said the American. 'Now, I have more intel on McGovan. Including an address in London. I'll put it in my dropbox and send you a link.'

'I'll forward it to Harper,' said Button. 'Just to confirm,

Richard, you're not going to have anyone following McGovan, are you?'

'Would that be a problem?'

'I'm afraid so. Harper can get a bit rough, I wouldn't want him crossing paths with your people.'

'My people are good, Charlotte.'

'Clearly. But in view of what you want done, I'd prefer that Harper was left with a clear field. And I'm sure he would, too, given the choice.'

'Message received and understood. I'll call off my dogs. Any news on your insurance?'

'I thought I'd fly back to the States and see how that looks. If I'm still in the clear I'll do a run to the UK and see what happens.'

'Interesting times,' said Yokely.

'Tell me about it,' said Button. She sipped her wine. 'I keep expecting to see you pop out in front of me.'

'Or maybe behind you . . .' said Yokely. He chuckled. 'Made you look, didn't I?'

Button laughed. He was right: she had taken a quick look over her shoulder.

14

The Gulfstream jet touched down at Bangkok's Don Mueang airport and taxied to the general aviation terminal to await the arrival of the immigration officers who would check the passports of those on board. Don Mueang was one of the world's oldest international airports but, since the opening of Suvarnabhumi, it had been rebranded as a regional commuter-flight hub and the airfield of choice for private planes. Half of the private jets using Don Mueang were Russian. Thailand was one of the few countries Russian citizens could visit without a visa and that, coupled with the fact that Russians could buy property and own bank accounts there, meant there was a constant stream of oligarchs flying in and out.

There was only one passenger on the plane: a heavy-set man with a shaved head and a nose that appeared to have been broken several times. His name was Yuri Lukin. He had a gun in an underarm holster and two metal suitcases containing a million dollars in cash. Two immigration officers arrived, did a perfunctory check of his passport and pocketed an envelope of money in exchange for not asking Lukin what the suitcases contained. If the immigration officers noticed the gun, they didn't mention it.

A black limousine and a white Toyota four-by-four had pulled up next to the jet as it had parked, but the passenger stayed in the limousine until the immigration officers had left. Mikhail Mirov climbed out of the vehicle as Lukin came down the steps. He was Lukin's money man in Thailand, a former KGB officer who had realised, as the former USSR fell apart, that there was more money to be made in crime than policing. He was a big man with steel grey hair wearing a pale blue safari suit with short sleeves. Lukin jerked a thumb at the door behind him. 'Two cases,' he said.

Two big men in T-shirts and baggy shorts had climbed out of the four-by-four. Mirov clicked his fingers and pointed at the plane, and as soon as Lukin had reached the tarmac they hurried up the steps. 'How is he?' asked Lukin, taking off his jacket. Sweat stains were already forming under his arms.

'Grigory is as well as can be expected, considering what was done to him,' said Mirov. He held the door open and Lukin climbed into the back of the limousine. Mirov closed the door, then hurried around to the other side of the car. He was already sweating, partly because of the forty-degree heat but mainly because his boss was angry, and when Yuri Lukin was angry people tended to get hurt, and worse.

The two men came down the steps with the cases and bundled them into the back of the four-by-four. 'Are they Valentin's men?' growled Lukin.

Mirov shook his head. 'They're mine. They'll go straight to the bank.'

The limousine drove away from the plane, heading for the exit. 'This hospital, it's good?' growled Lukin.

'World class,' said Mirov. 'As good as anything in Moscow.'

'If there's a better hospital, we move him there.'

'I think he's fine where he is.'

'And what about Valentin?'

'He's out of intensive care. But he was beaten up pretty badly.'

'He pays his own fucking hospital bill, make sure of that,' snapped Lukin. He snarled like a caged animal. 'How the fuck did this happen? Valentin was supposed to be taking care of my son. Fuck him. Why were there no bodyguards?'

'There were, but they were sleeping.'

Lukin's eyes blazed. 'Fucking sleeping? They were fucking sleeping?'

'It was early. Six in the morning. Valentin and Grigory were in the house. The gate was locked. The men assumed they were done for the night.'

'What sort of shit bodyguard assumes anything? They should sleep when their boss sleeps, and even then with one fucking eye open. These bodyguards, they are to be trusted?'

'Former Spetsnaz,' said Mirov. Russian special forces.

'Spetsnaz means fuck-all,' said Lukin. 'Any shithead can join Spetsnaz. They're not like the British SAS or the American Delta Force. If I find these bodyguards were involved, they're dead.'

'Understood,' said Mirov.

'Worse than fucking dead.' Lukin scowled. He wiped his hands over his face. 'Is it always this fucking hot here?'

'Pretty much,' said Mirov. He shouted at the driver to boost the air-conditioning.

Lukin pulled open the drinks cabinet. There were bottles

of Johnnie Walker Blue and vodka. He grabbed the vodka. Mirov reached for a glass but Lukin shook his head, untwisted the cap and drank from the bottle. 'He shoved a bottle up my son's arse,' spat Lukin. 'A fucking bottle up his arse. What sort of sick fuck does that?'

Mirov looked out of the window. There were times when it was best to say nothing.

15

Lukin looked down at his son and shook his head contemptuously. 'Who did this to you?' he snarled. Grigory's face was swollen and there was a plaster across his nose. His lips were puffy and cracked and several of his teeth were broken. His right arm was in plaster and his legs were suspended from a metal frame. He looked as if he had been hit by a train.

'Some fucking tourist,' replied Grigory, the damage to his mouth rendering his words almost unintelligible.

'This tourist followed you back to the villa and beat the crap out of you? For what?'

'I don't know. He tried to shake our hands in the bar. I told him to leave us alone. He was drunk.'

'So a drunk tourist you snubbed in a bar follows you home and does this? Does that make any sense to you? Because it doesn't to me.'

Grigory closed his eyes. 'He mentioned a girl.'

'What? Speak the fuck up. I can't hear you.'

'A girl. He talked about a girl.'

'What fucking girl? If you don't tell me what the fuck happened I swear to God I'll break your other arm.'

Grigory sighed. 'There was this girl. Valentin had some

fun with her. It got a bit rough. The tourist talked about her. Said I'd get a taste of my own medicine.'

'What did he mean by that? What did you do to the girl?'

'We had fun, that's all. Fucked her, got a bit rough with her. It was Valentin mainly. It's how he gets his kicks and he asked me to join in.'

'You and Valentin fucked a girl? Together?'

'I'd been drinking. And he'd had some coke. Good stuff.'

'So, drunk and doped up on coke you fucked a girl and beat her up.' He shook his head angrily. 'And you fucked her in the arse, did you?'

'No, why?'

'Don't fucking lie to me. You fucked her in the arse and that's why you had a bottle shoved up yours.'

Grigory closed his eyes. 'I'm sorry.'

'I bet you're fucking sorry but sorry doesn't fix this, does it? That tourist, he did this to you for revenge. And he did a fucking good job, too.'

'He had a gun. He could have shot me.'

'Might have been better if he had,' said Lukin. 'At least then you wouldn't look like such a fucking idiot.'

'He had a fucking gun,' repeated Grigory.

'Yes, a drunken tourist with a gun. What's wrong with that picture?'

'What do you mean?'

'Tourists don't carry guns, as a rule. Did he say what his name was?'

'Gerry. From Wales. He was drunk. He could hardly stand in the bar.'

'Well, he was sober enough to overpower the two of you.'

'He had a gun.'

'So you keep saying.' He shook his head. 'Have you any idea how stupid this makes me look? It says I can't protect my own family. If they can do it to you they can do it to me – that's the message it sends – and I'll tell you here and now that no one, fucking *no one*, is going to shove a bottle up my arse.'

He stormed out of the hospital – Mirov had to run to get to the limousine first and open the door for him. 'Take me to the villa,' snarled Lukin. 'I want to talk to those so-called bodyguards.'

16

Harper checked out of Le Meurice early the next morning and moved into accommodation that was considerably less grand: a dingy second-floor hotel room with peeling wallpaper and a damp-stained ceiling, rented from an Arab who was happy to be paid in crisp euro notes. The tenement building also housed a derelict bistro on the ground floor, its steel shutters buckled and blackened by fire. The surrounding quarter of Saint-Denis, about ten kilometres north of the centre of Paris, had also definitely seen better days. A few ageing Pieds-Noirs still lived in Saint-Denis, the dusty-footed last remnants of the expatriate French colonists who had run the North African territories then returned, like swarms of starlings flying in at dusk, to settle in Saint-Denis, part of a 'homeland' that many had not seen in three generations. It had not welcomed them with open arms. These days they were far outnumbered by the large North African immigrant population that had followed in their footsteps.

From his window Harper could see the Basilica of Saint-Denis across the rooftops. It had once been a place of pilgrimage, but few who visited it today cared to venture more than a few yards from the basilica for fear of what might befall them in the surrounding streets. The Saint-Denis area scored highly on every index of poverty and disadvantage. It had one of the highest crime rates in the country – fifteen recorded crimes for every hundred inhabitants – and one of the lowest detection rates by a police force widely seen as incompetent, corrupt and racist. As a result, Saint-Denis was regarded by most outsiders as a no-go area. It suited Harper perfectly. The narrow streets made it easy to detect strangers and conduct anti-surveillance drills, while its flourishing sex industry and thriving black market for all sorts of stolen goods made the locals very sensitive to a police presence. People kept themselves to themselves, asked no questions and gave no answers if questioned by anyone who smelled even slightly official.

He spent several hours crisscrossing the city on the Métro, visiting phone shops to buy throwaway mobiles and Sim cards, never more than two of each at one place. By midday he arrived back at his room with a half-dozen cheap handsets and a dozen Sim cards. He sat on the bed and over the next hour spoke to four people, all of whom agreed to drop everything to fly to Paris.

First on his list was the man they called Barry Whisper – a slight, softly spoken figure who also answered to 'Bravo Whisky'. He had been a 14 Int operative during the later years of 'The Troubles' in Northern Ireland and had also plied his specialised trade with the American intelligence agencies for a couple of years. A trained linguist, he spoke fluent Arabic, German, French, Russian, passable Farsi and Pushto as well. An insular, spiky character, he lived alone between jobs on a remote smallholding on the North Yorkshire moors, tending his pigs, goats and the few crops that would grow on his bleak, rainwashed land.

The second call was to another Barry. Barry Big was also from Yorkshire but was Barry Whisper's polar opposite in almost every other way. A loud, hulking figure, he had been a member of the Special Reconnaissance Regiment, based in Hereford and used by the SAS for intelligence gathering and surveillance of potential targets. He now lived in the Dominican Republic because he'd met and fallen in love with a Dominican beauty of half his age. He'd bought a beach bar, and the thought of her there surrounded by amorous customers while he was away for weeks on end drove him mad with jealousy, but he loved his intelligence-gathering work so much that he could never refuse the offer of another job for Harper.

Third on the list was technical and electronics genius Hansfree. In the black humour of the armed forces, he had earned himself his nickname after losing both of his own hands in Bosnia when an IED he had been examining was remotely detonated. He was an intense character in his mid-thirties, always dressed in black, like his hero, Johnny Cash, and wore black leather gloves over his prosthetic hands. He had shown a ferocious determination in rebuilding his life, developing an expertise in electronics that would have made him a fortune in Civvy Street, but Hansfree had loved the military too much to be entirely comfortable working with civilians or corporate career structures. Instead he made a good living working on the margins of society, often for Harper.

Last but not least, Maggie May was a pale, dark-eyed brunette in her thirties. She was a surveillance professional whose career at MI5 had been curtailed after an ill-advised affair with her departmental boss. It had proved to be ill-advised because, in a story as old as civilisation, she had become pregnant whereupon her knight in shining armour had made it very clear that their relationship, 'just a bit of fun between two consenting adults', didn't extend to him taking any responsibility for the child, if she chose to keep it. She did so, and he had her transferred to a dead-end job in a different department. Maggie had taken maternity leave, and when the time came for her to return to work, she quit her job. A single parent, she looked after her son with the aid of her parents, who had no idea of her real work: they thought she worked for a travel agency because she frequently travelled overseas.

All four were pleased to hear from him and all agreed to drop everything to fly to Paris. The fact that he was offering them each a hundred-thousand-dollar signing-on fee was an incentive but Harper knew they weren't just doing it for the money. All four lived for their work and the adrenalin rush that came with the jobs he provided. Life in Lex Harper's orbit was complicated and often dangerous, but it was never boring.

'You understand what a bodyguard's job is, don't you?' growled Lukin. 'The clue is in the fucking job description. Body. Guard. You guard the fucking body. You protect it. If necessary you stand between the body and a bullet. Is that so fucking hard to understand?'

The three men standing in front of Lukin were all staring at the floor. They were big men, broad-shouldered, with hands the size of shovels, each a good six inches taller than their boss, but all three were trembling. Lukin was holding a gun and it was clear from the look in his eyes that he was gearing up to using it. They were in Valentin's villa. The maids had cleared up so there was no evidence of what had happened, except for a small area of darkened wood that Lukin suspected was a bloodstain. His son's blood.

'Call yourself Spetsnaz. Special fucking forces? Well, there's nothing special about you.' He waved at the bodyguard on the right. 'You, you big prick. Why the fuck weren't you in the house with my son?'

'They told us we weren't needed,' said the man. His hair was close-cropped, revealing a thick rope-like scar above his right ear.

'What's your name, Shit-for-brains?'

'Peter,' mumbled the man.

'I don't need to know your first name, you fucking prick. I'm not asking you out on a fucking date. Your surname.'

'Volkov.'

'Why was my son unprotected in the bar?'

'There is security in the bar. And they offered to escort Valentin home but he wanted to drive your son. We were waiting for him when he arrived and they were alone. They drove in and said we could stand down.'

'And if Valentin had told you to jump off a fucking cliff, you'd have done that, would you?'

Volkov looked at the floor.

'You, in the middle. Your name?'

'Zharkov,' said the man. He was the shortest of the three but was still well over six feet tall. He was wearing a tight-fitting black T-shirt that showed off over-muscular arms, which suggested steroid use rather than hours in the gym.

'Can you explain how a man gets into the villa without anyone seeing or hearing him?'

Zharkov shrugged but didn't reply.

'He cuts the wire, gets over the wall and no one sees a thing. Is that what happened?'

'There is no CCTV at the back of the house,' said Zharkov.

'And why the fuck not?'

'The CCTV is to check on the vehicles.'

'And whose idea was it not to have CCTV covering the whole wall?'

Zharkov looked at the man to his right. 'Myshkin is head of security,' he mumbled.

'Fuck you,' said Myshkin. His jet black hair was tied back in a short ponytail and he had several days' stubble on his massive chin. 'I organise the rota, that's all.'

'Why is there no CCTV at the back?' pressed Lukin.

'It's not our system,' said Myshkin. 'It was installed when Valentin bought the villa.'

'And why no dogs? Dogs would have spotted the intruder.'

'Valentin doesn't like dogs.'

'Valentin doesn't like dogs or CCTV but he has my son sleeping with the Three Stooges as bodyguards. For fuck's sake.' He shook his head angrily. 'Right. This is what's going to happen,' he said. 'I need two of you fuckwits to help me get the bastard who attacked my son. Only two of you. That means one of you is surplus to requirements. You can decide among yourselves who that one is. Two of you work with me, one of you goes to hospital. And I don't give a fuck which is which.' He sat down and gestured with the gun. 'Get on with it. I don't have all day.'

Myshkin looked across at Volkov and nodded.

Volkov stared back at him impassively.

Zharkov looked at Volkov, then back at Myshkin. 'You were in charge,' said Zharkov, his massive hands bunching into fists.

'Like fuck I was,' snarled Myshkin.

'You said you were the boss,' said Volkov, sullenly.

Myshkin glared at him. 'And I fucking well am, so I'm telling you it's me and you against him.' He nodded at Volkov. 'Okay? You and me, we stand together. Zharkov's always been shit to you.'

Zharkov stepped back and put up his fists. 'You think you can take me, fucker?'

Myshkin nodded earnestly at Volkov. 'Come on, you and me. Zharkov has always hated you. And he fucked that girl you like in Lone Star.'

Volkov glared at Zharkov, who shook his head. 'He's lying.'

'Did you fuck her?'

'What if I did? She's a hooker. I paid her. It's not as if she was fucking me for free.'

Myshkin's fist lashed out and caught Zharkov under the chin. He staggered back and Myshkin followed through with two piston-like jabs to the man's chest, just below the heart. Zharkov's hands went up to defend himself but he was in pain and didn't see the kick until it was too late. Myshkin's foot caught the side of his knee and Zharkov howled as the cartilage snapped, like a dry twig. He fell to the ground, clutching his injured leg and moaning.

Myshkin stepped back, hands up, and stared at Volkov. 'Your call. I'm easy either way. But it won't be me going to hospital.'

Volkov breathed in, grimaced, then turned and kicked Zharkov in the ribs. Hard. Myshkin joined in and for the next thirty seconds the two men kicked and stamped on Zharkov until his arms and legs were broken and his face was a bloody pulp. Eventually they stepped back. Zharkov was face down, unconscious, breathing slowly and heavily.

Lukin waved his gun at the body. 'Take that piece of shit to the hospital,' he said to Mirov. 'Not the one my son's in. Now, you two fuckers need to work hard to get back on my right side or you'll be joining that piece of shit in intensive care. And your first order of business is to find that fucking tourist and bring him to me.'

18

Dr Chanika's clicking high heels echoed off the walls as she headed towards her car, a two-seater BMW Z4 that was her pride and joy. She was tired and looking forward to getting home for a long soak in the bath and a bottle of wine. Her shift was supposed to have ended at six but a woman who had swallowed a bottle of weedkiller, after discovering that her husband was preparing to leave her for his girlfriend, had been brought in. That had been five days earlier. The woman had expected to die immediately but weedkiller didn't work like that. Apart from a little nausea she had been fine, for a few days at least, but behind the scenes the poison was systematically destroying her liver and poisonous toxins were building up in her blood. Now it was too late and, barring a liver transplant, she would be dead within the week. All Dr Chanika could do was to try to minimise her pain, and that was easier said than done. Dr Chanika wasn't looking forward to the next few days and she knew she'd need the bath and the wine to stand any chance of getting to sleep that night.

Headlights on full beam almost blinded her. She froze. The car was directly ahead of her. She shielded her eyes with her hand and shuffled to the side.

As she blinked, she realised that a figure was standing between the lights. A man. A big man.

'Dr Chanika?' said the man.

'Yes?' she said hesitantly. 'Who are you?' He wasn't Thai, she was sure of that. He was far too big and his accent was foreign. Russian, maybe.

'I need to talk to you about one of your patients. Miss Pear. She's in intensive care.'

'I'm sorry, are you a relative?' Her eyes were watering in the light's intensity.

'No, I'm just a concerned citizen,' said the man. 'I need to know the name of the man who came to see her. I understand he's paying Miss Pear's bill.'

'I'm sorry, I really can't help you,' she said, turning towards her car. 'You can call the main office tomorrow.'

A large figure appeared to her right, blocking her way. She turned to her left but another man stood there, even bigger than the first. The blinding light meant she couldn't see their faces.

'I need the name, Dr Chanika.'

'I'll call security,' she said. 'Or the police.' She fumbled for her phone in her handbag.

'You could do that, but by the time they get here you'll be in a pool of blood and we'll be long gone. And even if they get here quickly, we'll be back in a day or two. Maybe we'll follow you home. Have you got kids, Dr Chanika? Or a family? Parents? Do you want to be responsible for them being hurt?'

Dr Chanika stopped reaching for her phone. Tears were stinging her eyes.

'I just want a name,' said the man. 'Then we'll leave you in peace. Just a name.'

She wiped away her tears with the back of her hand. 'You can't do this to me,' she whispered.

'Yes, I can,' said the man. 'I can do what the fuck I want. Now stop fucking around and give me the name.'

Dr Chanika felt the strength go from her legs and staggered back, leaning against her car to stop herself falling. She could barely breathe – it was as if there was a steel band around her chest. 'Lex Harper,' she said. 'His name is Lex Harper.'

19

All four of the people Harper had called were in Paris within twenty-four hours, and one by one they sent him a text to confirm their arrival. The last was from Barry Big, who had flown from the Dominican Republic – he had left for the airport within minutes of Harper phoning him. When he had heard from them all, Harper locked the flimsy door of his room, went down the stairs and out through an entrance lobby that was festooned with cobwebs and carpeted with wind-blown rubbish.

He was carrying an envelope containing a dozen or so sheets of photographs and intel that Charlie Button had left for him in the drafts folder. He had collected it from an internet café a short walk from his room on the way to an early breakfast of croissants and coffee. He walked slowly through the streets, carrying out his usual anti-surveillance drills. Once he was certain he was not being observed or followed, he entered a side-street café. He nodded to the Lebanese owner, who had received a cash sum equivalent to the whole of his normal day's takings in return for the use of a private room on the fourth floor of the building, then climbed the stairs.

His team were already there, sitting around a table

drinking mint tea or the café's fearsomely sweet and strong coffee. Barry Big grinned when Harper walked into the room. 'Hey, hey, the gang's all here,' he said, standing up and hugging Harper.

Hansfree was next in line for a hug. His prosthetics were steel claws with rubber bumpers for added grip, and Harper felt them press between his shoulder blades as Hansfree hugged him. He had driven to Saint-Denis in his specially adapted van, using the cross-Channel ferry service. The van allowed him to be independent and he could live in it, if necessary.

Maggie May was next, and kissed him lightly on both cheeks. He caught the scent of her perfume, Dior's Poison, a fragrance that never failed to remind him of her.

Finally Barry Whisper gave him a minimalist hug and a whispered comment close to his right ear that Harper missed. He smiled and took his seat at the table.

'Thanks for coming,' he said. He looked at the machine sitting in front of Hansfree at the centre of the table. It was about the size of an iPhone with a small telescopic aerial sticking out of the top. Several coloured lights on it flashed intermittently, and it emitted the occasional high-pitched bleep. 'What the fuck's that?' he asked.

'Bug detector. State-of-the-art.'

'Looks like something left over from an early *Doctor Who* episode. You sure it works?'

'Absolutely positive,' Hansfree said. 'Looks aren't everything, Lex, as you should know better than anyone. It's performance that counts. I picked it up from a very good friend of mine in London and he assures me it's absolutely foolproof. And if my mate says it works then, believe me, it works. It bloody well should do – it cost enough.'

'So we're in good hands,' Harper said. 'Or not in your case.' He winked at Hansfree, who responded with a gesture that, even with a prosthetic hand, was an unmistakable two-finger salute.

Harper began briefing the team on their task. 'The target is a former Para and SAS trooper called Caleb McGovan,' he said. He opened the envelope and took out three photographs of the man. Two were surveillance pictures and one had clearly been taken from his army file. 'From now on McGovan is Tango One. Anyone he meets whom we do not know will automatically become a Yankee. We'll refer to Tangos when they're positively ID'd, and use Yankees for people we've not yet identified. To go back to McGovan, although he's ex-special forces, that doesn't mean he can walk on water. I've checked with people who served with him and he's a good all-round steady guy but you can rest assured that he's no James Bond.' He gave the last few words the full Sean Connery treatment and was rewarded with a few smiles from his team. 'He's special forces but not a spook, so we're dealing with a specialised skill set. We'll have untraceable pay-as-you-go phones, which are to be used only to communicate with other team members during the surveillance phase.' He grinned at Billy Big. 'So no phoning girlfriends on my tab.'

'The thought never occurred to me,' said Barry Big.

'Just to summarise where we are with the task,' said Harper. 'On the positive side we have a one hundred per cent solid ID of Tango One. We also know where he's living. He's based himself in a military club just on the north side of London's Oxford Street. Tango One does not have a private car, but he obviously does have access to the full range of London transport. He is staying within yards of several bus stops, a couple of hundred yards of a tube station and a short walk from Paddington main-line station. There are also black cabs galore in that area, so he can go mobile with minimal advance warning at any time. So, we know the subject's age, sex, location, modes of transport and some of his habits. On the negative side, we don't know as yet the identity of his associates. And we're going to need an ops room somewhere to coordinate everything.'

'I might have somewhere close by,' said Hansfree. 'Let me check.'

Harper nodded. 'Barry Big will be team medic, Maggie will take charge of the admin for the op, setting out working hours, reliefs and downtime, and Hansfree will issue the radios, body sets, batteries and the frequencies. As usual, you'll be on generous expenses with no receipts required, and your fees at the end of the op will be paid cash in hand or into any bank account, anywhere in the world. Anything else, anyone?'

Maggie spoke up: 'I'd say that any pick-up of the subject shouldn't be too difficult, bearing in mind where he's living. There are masses of bits of street furniture, cafés and shops we can use as cover. The follow shouldn't present too many difficulties, providing he sticks to central London where there are always going to be crowds of people about to give us cover. The major problem is going to be housing any Yankees, the unidentified suspects we may move on to. If they're in an area they're not too familiar with, they're usually pretty easy game, but when they get close to home, in an area they know like the back of their hand, then it can be really difficult.'

Barry Whisper had been looking thoughtful for some time and now raised his voice. 'One thing's puzzling me about all this. Exactly what do you think Tango One is planning?'

'I wish I knew,' Harper said. 'And don't think the same thing hasn't been bugging me. He's made a couple of visits to Turkey, landing at Dalaman airport, which is one of the main tourist gateways. We presume he travelled on from there overland and eventually made a covert crossing of the border between Turkey and Syria, but on each occasion, allowing for the time taken to travel there, he's spent just a handful of days inside Syria. So he can't have been training ISIS soldiers while he was there. He simply wasn't in country long enough to be able to impart any useful training, and he can't have been fighting for them because once more, he wasn't there long enough.'

Barry Big cleared his throat. 'So he was either delivering something to them or collecting something from them.'

'Which can only have been money, information, weapons or men,' Maggie added.

'Well, it can't have been weapons or manpower,' Hansfree said, 'because from what you've told us, Lex, he was travelling solo on his way in and out, and probably crossed the border on foot. That leaves money or information.'

'Either is possible,' Harper said, 'but Tango One doesn't have any source of funds, as far as we know, and certainly none substantial enough to justify the risks he's apparently been taking.'

'And why would ISIS divert funds from the campaign they're waging in Syria and Iraq anyway,' Barry Big said, 'just to fund some freelance adventure by a renegade SAS man?'

'They would if he was planning something that would further their own aims as well,' Barry Whisper said. 'But it would have to be big, obviously. A spectacular.'

'I'm with Barry Whisper there,' said Harper. 'But, hopefully, our surveillance will answer that question. OK, we're good to go. Make your own way to London, fix yourselves up with accommodation, and we'll get down to business the day after tomorrow.'

He shook hands with each of them, including Hansfree, then kept watch from the window as they filed out one by one, leaving at five-minute intervals. Only when he was satisfied that they had not been observed did he leave the building himself.

He entered the hallway of his flea-bitten hotel and encountered a prostitute servicing her client in the litter-strewn alcove beneath the stairs. He checked out, strolled back through the streets to the station next to the Basilica of Saint-Denis and caught the Métro to the Gare du Nord. Just over three hours later he was stepping onto the platform at St Pancras station.

20

It was a large apartment, three bedrooms and a huge sitting room with a terrace that overlooked the bay. Mirov was on the terrace, smoking a cigarette. It was early morning but tourists were parascending, towed behind fast-moving speedboats. On the thin strip of beach below, groups of Chinese holidaymakers gathered to be taken on the fifteen-minute trip to the beaches of Koh Larn.

'He's a fucking ghost, this Harper,' said Volkov.

'What do you mean?' asked Mirov. Volkov had kicked down the door to Harper's apartment, then he and Myshkin had spent the past fifteen minutes tearing it apart.

'No paperwork, no photographs, a few bills but other than that there's nothing.' He waved at a bookcase against one wall. 'There's nothing personal. No family photographs, no pictures of him with a drugged-up tiger or friends in a bar. It's as if this was a hotel room.'

'What about his computer?'

'There isn't one.'

'He took it with him?'

'I don't think he has one. There's no printer. No wiring. No desk. If it wasn't for the clothes, you'd think no one lived here.'

'Who the fuck doesn't have a computer these days?'

Volkov didn't answer.

'Okay, we need a phone number for the man, then pay whoever we have to pay to get a list of his calls and texts.' He flicked the remains of his cigarette over the side of the terrace. 'Do you think he's done a runner?'

'I think he's just careful,' said Volkov. 'Whoever this fucker is, he isn't a tourist.'

Mirov walked back into the sitting room and through to the master bedroom. The sheets had been ripped off the king-sized bed and most of the drawers had been pulled out and overturned. Volkov and Myshkin had been thorough and Mirov was certain they had missed nothing. He unzipped his fly and pissed over the bed, playing the stream of urine back and forth as he cursed Lex Harper and the bitch that had given birth to him.

21

Harper checked himself into a small hotel in Bayswater, a short walk from Queensway tube station. An African on the desk was bent over an English language textbook. He flashed Harper a beaming smile and said there was absolutely no problem with him paying in cash – in fact, the owner preferred it. Harper went up a cramped flight of stairs to his room, which was at the rear of the building. There was a single bed, a dressing table next to a sash window, which was smeared with pigeon droppings, and a bathroom the size of a wardrobe with a tiny shower cubicle, a half-size washbasin and a toilet that wasn't much bigger than a bucket. 'Home, sweet home,' muttered Harper, but it was exactly what he wanted: a bolthole that would allow him to stay off the grid. He headed out and spent the next couple of hours having a late lunch. He took the Tube far out into London's dismal industrial hinterland where he walked through a maze of side streets to a panel-beater and accident-repair workshop occupying one of the smoke-blackened brick arches beneath a railway line. It was well into the evening by now, but yellow light still spilled from the half-open door and Capital Radio was playing on a tinny transistor. Harper swung the door open and winked at the balding, middle-aged mechanic swigging from a bottle of beer as he sat in an old leather car seat propped against the wall.

'Bugger me,' the man said. 'Now I do believe in ghosts.'

'It's not been that long, Wheels,' Harper said. 'Eighteen months at most.'

'If you say so, Lex, if you say so,' Tom Wheeler said, 'though I'd have sworn it was longer than that. You need a car?' Tom 'Wheels' Wheeler was a first-class mechanic, who had a sideline in renting out cars to people who were reluctant to use Avis or Hertz. Unlike the major companies, Wheels didn't require his clients to produce a driving licence or a credit card: an envelope full of cash would do just fine.

'What have you got?'

'I've got a brand spanking new Porsche Cayenne, if you fancy something flash,' said Wheeler.

'When have I ever wanted something flash?'

'I've got a ten-year-old Nissan that looks like shit but will do the ton in less than five seconds.'

Harper wrinkled his nose. 'Speed won't be an issue. Comfort's more important – I might be behind the wheel for quite a while.'

'Range Rover?'

'I don't want to be filling the tank every couple of hours, mate.'

Wheeler took another pull on his beer, then grinned. 'I know – I've got a BMW Five Series. She's got a fair number of miles on the clock but she's reliable.'

'Ready to go?'

'Got the money?'

Harper took out a brown envelope and tossed it at Wheeler, who stood up, slid it into the pocket of his over-alls without opening it, selected a bunch of keys from the sets hanging on a row of hooks by the door and headed out of the workshop. They crossed the scrap-infested waste-land beyond it to a row of concrete lock-up garages at the back of a block of crumbling flats. Wheeler checked the heavy padlock on the steel shutters of a garage, looking for any scratches or other signs that would show it had been tampered with or picked, then unlocked it and raised the shutters. The BMW was dusty but rust-free, and Harper didn't have to lift the bonnet to know that the engine would be in perfect order.

'Paperwork's in the glovebox,' said Wheeler, tossing him the keys. 'Oh, and there's a neat little secret compartment in the passenger footwell. The previous owner used to bring stuff in from the Continent.'

'Stuff?'

'Not drugs, mate. Guns and ammo from the former Yugoslavia. He was never caught so the plate's clean. Just thought you might be able to make use of it.'

Harper climbed in and pulled on a pair of driving gloves. The interior was clean enough but not too clean, and he didn't want to add any of his prints to the ones that were already there. The engine started first time and he nodded his approval.

'Told you,' said Wheeler. 'As reliable as clockwork.'

Harper flashed him a thumbs-up and drove slowly out of the lock-up, then headed north, away from London.

22

It was eight o'clock in the evening when Harper pulled off the M6 into a service station to the west of Manchester. He flashed his lights as he saw a car cruising around on the far side of the car park. By the time he had driven across, Jony Hasan's silver BMW was already parked in a poorly lit area, well away from the service-station entrance. Harper pulled up next to him.

'Now that's more like it,' Jony said, as Harper got into the car. 'It makes a nice change from those crap motors you're usually driving. You can't go wrong with a Beamer.'

Harper smiled. 'Did you get me the short?'

'Does the pope shit in the woods? Of course I did. Have I ever failed you?' British-born to parents of Bangladeshi origin, Jony was a wheeler-dealer, who operated on the margins of Manchester's sizeable criminal fraternity and, providing the price was right, could supply untraceable weapons. In some ways he was as dodgy as they came, but Harper knew he could trust him absolutely never to grass him up, no matter who was asking the questions, and never to let him down.

The two men climbed out of their vehicles and Jony handed him a Tupperware container. He pulled a packet of cigarettes from the pocket of his black leather jacket and lit one. 'You're usually after something a bit more heavy-duty than a short,' he said, blowing a smoke-ring towards the clouds overhead.

'I'm hoping I won't need to use it,' Harper said. 'It's purely a precaution – in any case, carrying something bigger than this around in Britain is too much of a risk. And you can guarantee it's never been fired, can you, or not in this country at least?'

'One hundred per cent certain,' Jony said. 'Do you want to see its birth certificate?'

Harper opened the container. Inside there was a pistol, with fifty rounds of ammunition in a Ziploc bag.

'Smith & Wesson SD9 VE,' Jony said. 'Nine mil, capacity sixteen rounds plus one up the spout, four-inch barrel, twenty-two-ounce weight. It'd cost you about three hundred and fifty dollars in the States but . . .' He grinned.

'I know, I know,' Harper said wearily. 'We're not in the States. So what's the SP on it in an M6 car park?' As he was speaking, he took the pistol out of the box, checked the action and sighted down it.

Jony pretended to think about it. 'I couldn't let it go for less than seven hundred and fifty.'

'Dollars?'

'Pounds.'

'Bloody hell, Jony! There's supposed to be a recession on. You must be the only retailer in Britain who keeps putting his prices up.'

'What can I say, bruv? It's just the laws of supply and demand at work,' Jony said, grinning.

'Well, in that case I can supply you with six hundred

and you're not getting any more than that,' said Harper.

'All right, then,' Jony said, with a show of resignation, 'but only because it's you.'

'Damn,' Harper said. 'You never agree that quick. I should have knocked you down another hundred.'

'Too late now, bruv,' Jonny said, with a huge grin. 'A deal's a deal, right?'

Harper put the Tupperware container on the front passenger seat, peeled the money off a wad of notes and handed it over. 'Thanks, Jony. Take care and watch out for the jealous husbands.'

'Those days are behind me now, bruv,' Jony said, as he started his engine. 'I'm strictly a one-girl guy now . . . well, one girl at a time.'

Harper watched him drive off, then got back into his own car. He slipped the Tupperware box under the seat and set off back down the motorway towards London. He pulled off at the first interchange, found a deserted lay-by at the side of the road and, after looking around and listening carefully, he peeled back the carpet in the passenger foot-well. He took a knife from his pocket and eased up the lid of a concealed compartment, so artfully hidden that only a very keen eye would have detected it. He put the pistol and the ammunition inside it, then replaced the carpet and drove back towards the motorway, heading south. While he didn't want his team carrying weapons in London, his personal safety was a different matter altogether.

23

Even with near-deserted roads in the dead hours of the night, Harper wasn't back in London until five in the morning, but he had the luxury of a lie-in until ten. He was woken by a call from Hansfree, who said he had something to show him. He arranged to meet him in a café close to the military club where McGovan was staying.

An hour later Harper sat down opposite Hansfree and nibbled a croissant as the technical wizard outlined his plan. 'I've stayed at the club a few times over the years,' said Hansfree, 'so I know the lay-out there reasonably well. I'm sure I'll be able to access his room easily enough because the security there is of the old-fashioned kind, that is to say virtually non-existent, and so are the locks. They still use physical keys rather than key cards, not that those are too much of an obstacle either, if you know what you're doing. So, I can install a camera in his room for you. I'll replace the LED stand-by light in his TV with a combined camera and microphone that will transmit through the club's communal aerial on the roof. That will give you coverage of any calls he makes or receives in his room as well as alerting you when he's getting ready to move, and will help to identify any visitors.'

'Sounds like a plan,' said Harper.

'I'm going to see about us using drones, too.'

'Seriously? Drones in London?'

'I've got access to some state-of-the-art kit,' said Hansfree. 'I wanted to check what was available before raising it with you.' He sipped his coffee. A woman at a neighbouring table stared at his claw, open-mouthed. Hansfree smiled at her and she looked away, embarrassed. 'The latest models have much longer operating times by building on solar power, and the camera resolution is improving every month. They have on-board high-resolution viewing devices and everything is gyroscopically controlled so we don't get any shiver or jumping. They can be launched from pretty much anywhere, and our radios can have automatic seeker devices installed, which the drones will find without guidance. If the subject leaves the London area, they can be carried by vehicle, launched from any piece of waste ground and monitored on any tablet. Everything they photograph is automatically recorded on-board and relayed back to the ops room for evidence purposes.'

'That's all very well in theory,' Harper said, 'but what about the cops? Won't a drone buzzing round over central London cause a few heart failures and trigger a full scale-terror alert?'

Hansfree shook his head. 'We're not talking missile-armed Reaper or Predator drones here. The ones I have access to are so tiny and quiet you wouldn't hear them above the birdsong in the countryside, let alone the traffic in a busy London street. And if anyone does happen to catch sight of one, they're likely to assume it's just some spoilt rich kid – God knows there's no shortage of those around here – playing with the latest toy.'

'What about radios?' asked Harper.

'Assuming money isn't a problem, I can supply you with the latest body-fit radios available, frequency hopping and automatically encoding, of course, and they work using redundant Home Office emergency services frequencies, which are off-limits to everybody else. They give literally countrywide coverage, just as you would expect from emergency services frequencies. None of this will stop you using your own codes, but belt and braces is best, I always think.'

'You needn't have any worries on that score,' Harper said. 'I've been told that money is no object on this one. I'll pay whatever's necessary for the kit we need.'

'Sounds good,' said Hansfree. 'I'll be right onto it.'

'How soon can you install the bug and get the rest of the kit together?'

'The equipment is no problem. I'll have it ready by tomorrow. Installing the bug depends on your subject's routine. It'll take just a few minutes to set it up. The problem is, we'll need more manpower. The two Barrys and Maggie are going to be full-time on watching Tango One and I'm going to need people to help me. Are you okay with me bringing in extra manpower?'

'Providing you trust them one thousand per cent, and providing they're not aware of the big picture, sure,' said Harper. 'Just let me know what you need in the way of money.'

'And I think I've got an ops room sorted,' said Hansfree. 'Not far from here.'

Harper finished his coffee and followed Hansfree outside.

Hansfree took him around the corner and along to a news-agent and off-licence. An elderly Sikh wearing a blue turban was standing behind the counter. 'Okay to go up, Mr Singh?' asked Hansfree.

Singh waved a hand at the stairs at the rear of the shop. 'It hasn't been cleaned in a while.'

'I'll take care of that,' said Hansfree.

Hansfree took Harper up the narrow flight of stairs, made even narrower by the stacks of beer cans crammed against the wall. 'Bit of a health-and-safety issue, but Mr Singh can be trusted, providing he gets paid enough,' said Hansfree. 'I've used this place before.'

There was a metal door at the top of the stairs and a large hasp but no padlock. Hansfree pushed the door open. The room was windowless, or if there had ever been a window, it was now bricked up. Hansfree flicked a switch and two fluorescent tubes flickered into life. There were more stacks of beer along one wall and cardboard boxes full of other stock, but the room was certainly large enough.

'Security won't be a problem because I'll get a camp bed brought in and be here twenty-four/seven, pretty much,' said Hansfree.

'And you're sure about Singh?'

'I've known him for years,' said Hansfree.

Harper nodded. 'Go for it,' he said. 'Tell the rest of the team we now have an ops room.'

Harper left Hansfree rearranging the stock and went back to Bayswater. He dropped into an internet café and left Charlie a short message in the Yahoo draft email file: *Up and running.*

24

Charlotte Button landed at Heathrow Airport using her own name and her genuine British passport. She'd flown business class overnight and had managed to get some half-decent sleep. She had breakfast airside and caught a late-morning flight to Glasgow. She had never been to the city when it hadn't been either raining or threatening rain and, true to form, the sky was grey and overcast as she walked out of the airport. She climbed into the back of a taxi and asked to be dropped at Queen Street railway station.

She had only just got out of the cab when her phone rang. The caller was withholding his number but she answered. 'You have a tail and not in a cat-like way,' said a southern American drawl.

Button cursed.

'Why, Charlotte, that's so unlike you,' said Yokely.

'You're sure?' she asked, and immediately regretted it. Richard Yokely was a professional and if he said she was being followed there was no doubt.

'You were clear at JFK and there was no one on the plane, but they picked you up at Heathrow. Airside.'

'Airside?' repeated Button. The fact that her followers

were able to move so easily through airport security suggested they were government-sanctioned.

'They went with you through Immigration and had three cars on your taxi. They're watching you now, Charlotte.'

'How many?'

'Four on foot that my people can see. Plus the three vehicles. This operation is seriously manpower-intensive. Money no object.'

'I'm glad you're watching over me, Richard.'

'I am, but I'm not sure there's anything I can do if they decide to take you.'

'I think they're just looking at me at the moment,' she said. 'If they were going to hurt or snatch me they'd have done it already.'

'Well, I do hope your third insurance policy isn't in Glasgow,' said Yokely.

'It isn't,' said Button. 'And now I know how desperate they are, I won't be going anywhere near it.'

'My offer is still open,' said Yokely. 'Let me know where it is and I'll collect it. I'd take good care of it.'

'I'm sure you would, Richard, but I need to handle this myself.' She ended the call, flagged down a passing cab and asked to be taken back to the airport.

25

Harper and the rest of the team fell quickly into operational mode. Early every morning they took up their positions around the club. Harper had purchased a second-hand Yamaha trail bike for cash and parked it in a bay around the corner from the entrance. They spent the day rotating their positions between the many coffee shops and snack bars in the area, while Hansfree monitored the images being transmitted from McGovan's room. Harper and his team used the ABC system, with A immediately behind the subject, B behind him on the same side of the street and C keeping pace with A, but on the opposite side of the street. Every time the subject approached a corner, C would move up almost level with him, so C could look down the side street and alert the other team members if the subject stopped, or made a U-turn back towards his close followers, or disappeared down an alley or into a shop. They rotated at irregular intervals, too, so the same person was never close behind the subject for long enough to be noticed by him, with B replacing A as lead, C and A swapping places.

McGovan was an easy target to follow, and on the few occasions he left the club, he didn't seem to employ anything in the way of counter-surveillance. Over two days he did nothing more than walk to local cafés and browse in second-hand bookshops. In the afternoons he would emerge from the club in shorts and a shirt and spend an hour jogging around Hyde Park.

Each morning at six the team would start the day with a briefing in the ops room. Not that there was much to be briefed about.

Maggie was running through the previous day's non-events when Harper's Thai phone rang. He took it out of his hip-pack. The number wasn't recognised but that was probably because he was overseas. He accepted the call. 'Lex, where the fuck are you?'

Harper recognised the East End accent immediately. Mickey Moore, East End boy made bad, an old-school villain who had made Pattaya his home along with his brother Mark and the rest of his crew of armed robbers. They funded their hedonistic Thai lifestyle by flying back to the UK on a regular basis to carry out major robberies, usually involving firearms and at least the threat of violence. 'Mickey, how's things? I'm out of the country at the moment, back in a week or so.' He walked out of the room to get some privacy on the stairs.

'Yeah, well, that might be the best place for you, mate,' said Moore. 'Now where the fuck are you?'

'Ducking and diving, mate. What's the problem?' He sat down and leaned against a case of cheap cider.

'You heard of a Russian called Lukin? Yuri Lukin?'

'No, should I?'

'He's Russian Mafia, Lex. Hard as nails. And he's pissed off at you, big time.'

'I don't know anyone called Lukin.'

'Apparently you shoved a bottle up his son's arse? Does that ring a bell?'

'Ah. That would have been me, yes.'

'Fuck me, Lex, you don't half pick them. You don't know who this Lukin is, then?'

'I'm guessing you're going to tell me.'

'Fucking former KGB, that's what. Soviet empire fell apart and it was every man for himself. Some went the economic route to make their fortunes, some went Darth Vader. I don't have to tell you which way Lukin went. Word is he grabbed a stack of KGB files and used it to extort and blackmail his way to the top of the Moscow crime tree.'

'So what the fuck's his son doing in Pattaya?'

'Grigory's got a thing for Thai birds and he persuaded his dad to let him set up a money-laundering operation here. They fly in money and wash it through bars and restaurants, all cash businesses. Millions a month, by all accounts. Grigory flies back and forth in a private jet full of cash. Except he's not flying anywhere at the moment. I mean, mate, a bottle up the arse, what the fuck was that about?'

'He did the same to a friend of mine. Damn near killed her. Sauce for the goose . . .'

'You always were the white knight, mate. But I've got to say, Lukin is one dragon you don't want to be fucking with.'

'Does he know who I am?'

'Your name? Yeah. A couple of Russian heavies were around at Ricky's bar, asking for you. And the word on the street is they're offering money to anyone who tells them where the fuck you are. Where the fuck are you, anyway?'

'Ha fucking ha. You looking for the reward money?'

'Yeah, because I'm a fucking grass. Seriously, you need to stay the hell out of Dodge until this blows over.'

'You think it will?'

'I can't see the father staying here for ever. He'll have to go back to Moscow eventually. But you're going to have to watch your back.'

'You got any suggestions, Mickey?'

'Like what?'

'Like how I can fix this?'

'You fancy going to war with the Russian Mafia?'

'Not unless I have to.'

'You fucked the guy's son with a bottle, Lex. He's not going to forgive and forget. Truth be told, you'd have been better off shooting the guy in the head. At least then there wouldn't have been any witnesses.'

'Yeah, well, no use crying over spilt milk. I'll buy you a beer when I get back.'

'Not in a Russian bar you won't. Be lucky, Lex.'

'Before you go, Mickey, have you heard anything about this heist in Manchester? The safe-deposit boxes.'

Moore chuckled. 'Fucking hell, that was a good one. The papers are saying twenty million or more, but who the fuck knows, right? Those bloody footballers are always trying to hide their money from the taxman. Serves them right.'

'What's the gossip?'

'Professional job, obviously,' said Moore. 'Same as Hatton Garden.'

'Different team, though, obviously.'

'You know how it works, Lex. Someone puts the plan together, someone else carries it out. I heard it was Poles behind the latest lot.'

'Poles, are you sure?'

'Mark's just back from London and he said he was talking to a guy in the Mayfair who said it was a Polish crew. A couple of them have been living it large in Marbella and were shooting their mouths off. You know how it is with some of them, they can't keep their fucking mouths shut.'

'Don't suppose you've got a name, have you?'

'Nah, it was just gossip from Mark. I'll ask him if he knows anything else, if you like.'

'Be handy, mate, thanks.'

Moore ended the call and Harper slid the phone into his hip-pack. He went back into the ops room. 'What do we think, guys?' he asked. 'Are we flogging a dead horse here?'

Hansfree shook his head. 'No, he's definitely up to something.'

'Specifically?'

'Day before yesterday, remember, when he turned into that street that led to the mosque? Full of Asians, it was. Okay, he didn't talk to anyone but it felt to me as if he was there for a reason. There was no brush contact, but he didn't make eye contact with anyone, and that in itself is a red flag. Especially for a soldier who's served out in Iraq. If anything, he'd be overdoing the eye contact. In fact, it made no sense to me that he went down the road he did.'

'Unless he wanted to be seen?' said Harper.

'That's how I read it.'

'And afterwards he just went back to the club, remember?'

said Maggie. 'Okay, he went the long way, as if he was out for a stroll, but it seemed to me that the whole point of the exercise had been the walk by the mosque.'

'Maybe he was trying to make any tail show out,' suggested Barry Big.

'Except he wasn't looking,' said Harper. 'And it didn't look to me as if anyone else was. Not that they would have seen us.' He grinned. 'Us being professional and all. Right, let's keep on him, then. If he has gone jihadist, I'm guessing he'll move sooner rather than later.' He explained that he had to leave London for a day or so. The team weren't thrilled at the idea of being a man short, but as Harper was paying the bills they kept any unhappiness to themselves.

26

Yuri Lukin had been waiting in the arrivals area for half an hour when Fedkin appeared, a small shoulder bag his only luggage. He was escorted by a uniformed immigration officer who saluted Lukin, then walked away. The officer had been paid to meet Fedkin off the plane and get him through Immigration, a procedure that on a bad day could take ninety minutes. Lukin hugged the man, then took him upstairs to a coffee shop.

'Our man is in France,' said Lukin, after they had bought coffee and sat down at a circular table. He spoke in Russian and kept his voice low. 'At least, he left Bangkok on a plane to Paris. His name is Lex Harper. Former soldier. The guy's got money – lots of money.' He took a photograph from his jacket pocket and slid it across the table. It had cost him five hundred dollars and had been taken when Harper had flown out of the country. All visitors were photographed entering and leaving Thailand and had to fill out a landing and leaving card. Lukin also had a copy of the card Harper had filled in when he left, including his name, date of birth and passport number. He gave it to Fedkin. 'I don't know if or when he's coming back,' said Lukin. 'We've searched his apartment in Pattaya and there's nothing personal there so he might have run away.'

'Running won't do him any good,' said Fedkin. 'I have good contacts in France. I'll find him.'

Lukin handed him an envelope. 'Here is money for your expenses. He also has a Thai mobile phone. He's only had it a few weeks – he appears to change his phone and Sim card on a regular basis. But if you can locate the phone, it might save you time.'

Fedkin nodded and pocketed the envelope.

Lukin smiled. 'I'll pay double your normal fee, plus any expenses incurred. But I'll double your fee again if you do something special for me.'

Fedkin grinned. 'What would that be?'

Lukin leaned closer to Fedkin. 'Before you kill him, I want you to shove a bottle up his arse, as far as it will go. And I want you to ask him how it feels to get a taste of his own medicine. Can you do that?'

'It will be a pleasure,' said Fedkin.

27

Harper knew that the cops and the intelligence agencies closely monitored all flights between London and Marbella as a matter of course, to the extent of running facial recognition on every passenger. He thought about flying to Belfast and driving to Dublin to fly from there, but a few minutes on the internet showed him that the quickest way was to catch the Eurostar and travel via Paris. He ended up flying in on Vueling, a low-cost Spanish airline that delivered him on time but with an aching back and sore knees. He wasn't a fan of Marbella – too much bling and Versace, too many wannabe gangsters and faded soap-opera stars, and so many undercover cops and grasses that any half-decent villain had to keep his mouth permanently shut. The tans might be real but most of the smiles were fake, as was the bonhomie. The vast majority of villains based on the Costa del Crime would have preferred to be in the UK. They pretended to like the sun, the sand and the sea but at the end of the day they were in exile, albeit self-imposed.

Harper had lived there for a few years but a spate of gangland assassinations and high-profile arrests had had him on the move and he'd settled on Thailand as a bolthole. He'd never looked back. The Thais were easier to deal with than the Spanish, the cops far more amenable to a brown envelope full of cash, and while there was an extra-dition treaty it was mainly for deporting paedophiles and rarely used for ordinary decent criminals.

Harper made one phone call from the airport, and Dave Brewer was already at the beachfront restaurant waiting for him, a bottle of Cristal champagne open and beading with sweat as it sat in the ice bucket.

'Fuck me, as I live and breathe, I never thought I'd see you back here,' said Brewer, standing up and giving Harper an enthusiastic bear hug.

'Flying visit,' said Harper. He sat down and looked at the multi-million-pound yachts and cruisers bobbing in the Mediterranean as Brewer poured the champagne. 'I never did get the attraction of boats,' he said. 'Too much moving about, crewed by strangers, what's the point?'

Brewer handed him the glass, then raised his own in salute. 'Good to see you, mate.'

'Good to be seen,' said Harper. The two men clinked glasses and drank.

'I've ordered lobsters,' said Brewer. 'The ones you get here are the best in Marbella.'

'They're fucking good in Thailand, too,' said Harper. 'You should come over some time.'

Brewer laughed. 'That's not going to happen,' he said. 'My missus has heard all the stories. There's no way in hell she'd let me go.'

'Bring her with you. Take her down to Phuket – great beaches and more golf courses than you can shake a club at.'

Brewer shook his head. 'Mate, if she came it'd be like

taking a dog into a butcher's and keeping it on a lead. Plus I'm too old to be led into temptation. Sixty this year.'

'Fuck me. Where did the years go?' Harper raised his glass in salute. 'Congratulations. When do you get your free bus pass?'

'Fuck off. I've still got the Roller.' He sipped his champagne and stretched out his legs. 'We did all right, didn't we?'

'So far, so good,' agreed Harper.

'You know what I mean. A lot of the guys we knocked around with fifteen years ago either ended up in jail or pissed it all away. You and me, we always had our heads screwed on. I'm pretty much legit now. Sally and I have got about fifty apartments along the coast now, with managers to handle the letting. All we do is count the cash.'

'So you're on the straight and narrow?'

'Have been for the last ten years, Lex. Haven't even dipped my toe in.'

'The temptation must be there, though?'

'I've too much to lose,' Brewer said. 'When you're twenty or thirty, the idea of a five-stretch or even a ten is no big deal. You do it and you pick up where you left off. But if I got sent down for a ten-stretch now, that'd be the end. I couldn't expect Sally to wait for me. The kids, well, I don't know what they'd do but I doubt they'd fly over every week for a prison visit. I wouldn't see the grandkids . . . Nah, Lex, it'd be game over. I'd top myself.' He grinned. 'But that ain't gonna happen because I'm now a respectable businessman and a leading light of the British Chamber of Commerce here.' He raised his glass and clinked it against Harper's again. They both drank.

Their lobsters arrived, each the size of a small puppy, along with industrial-sized claw crackers and various implements for removing all the meat. They tucked in, with relish.

'So what can I do you for, Lex?' said Brewer, as he dabbed at his chin with a napkin.

'Can't a guy just fly out to see a mate?'

'Don't try to kid a kidder,' said Brewer. 'We go back a long way, no question, but you calling me out of the blue and asking for lunch makes it more than a social call.' He put down the crackers and picked up his glass. 'Seriously, mate, I'm well happy to see you, and anything you need, just ask.'

'You're a star, mate. Thanks.' He sipped some Cristal and put down his glass. 'You know this robbery at the safe-deposit company in Manchester?'

Brewer nodded. 'Nice bit of work.'

'What's the gossip?'

Brewer's eyes narrowed. 'Why do you ask?'

Harper laughed. 'Don't worry, mate. I've not turned grass. Friend of mine had a box. There was stuff in it that's of no value to anyone else but means a lot to her.'

'Footballer's wife?' asked Brewer. 'I heard a lot of the City and Man U boys had boxes.'

'She's just a pal. I'd like to help her out.'

Brewer nodded. 'It was a professional job, no question. Similar to the Hatton Garden job.'

'Very similar,' said Harper.

'You spotted that? Same drill, same way of accessing the vault, not opening all the boxes?'

'But the Hatton Garden mob were pulled, right?'

'Weren't they just? While the cameras were there. Don't you hate that, the way the cops now work hand in hand with the press to make sure they get good coverage? They started with celebrities but now they're doing it with pretty much everyone. The filth have no shame.'

'None at all,' said Harper. 'The Hatton Garden mob, were they faces?'

'A couple of them were known, sure. We were bloody surprised to see them on the front page, I can tell you that much. I mean, none of them was in line for the Brain of Britain title.'

'So they were hired hands?'

'I guess so.'

'So if the Manchester job was a carbon copy, it could be the same brains behind it?'

'That's how I read it.'

Harper grinned. 'Any idea whose brains they might be?'

Brewer chuckled and waved a lobster claw in the air. 'Now that's the million-dollar question, isn't it?'

'Thirty million pounds, if you believe the papers. Military?'

'It had that feel, didn't it? Both of them. Both went off without a hitch, both took a hell of a lot of planning coupled with inside knowledge. My money would be on a mastermind who then brought in contractors.'

'And what about the latest job? Any gossip?'

'I heard it might be a Polish crew.'

'Where did you pick that up?'

'Guy I met in a bar the day before yesterday. Said a couple of Poles had flown in from London and were living it large. Cristal all round, and then they took half a dozen girls from one of the brothels in Puerto Banús.'

'They talked about the raid?'

'Talked about Manchester. And pissed themselves laughing when the story was on TV.'

'Don't suppose you know where I can find these Poles?'

Brewer shook his head. 'I got it second-hand. But he mentioned the brothel, if that's any help. The Pussycat.'

Harper laughed. 'Bloody hell, that's a name from the past. Still going?'

'On its last legs, I think. So is Porto Banús. Cheap drugs and cheap East European tourists, these days. All the decent gaffs shut down ages ago.'

'Fancy a run out?'

'To the Pussycat? You're having a laugh. Can you imagine what Sally would do to me if she found out I'd been to a brothel with you?'

'Fair point, mate. But back in the day you were a great wingman.'

'Those days are long gone, Lex,' laughed Brewer, refilling their glasses. 'But you go and knock yourself out.'

'Can you do me a favour?'

'Sure.'

'Lend me a motor. Just for the day. Anything will do.'

'Mate, you can borrow the Roller. Just be careful with it.'

28

Harper figured that late afternoon probably wasn't the best time to be visiting a brothel and his fears were confirmed when he walked into the Pussycat and found only four girls on duty. The woman who was in charge was probably in her fifties but had been under the plastic surgeon's knife so often it was difficult to know for sure. Her forehead was glass-smooth, her arched eyebrows gave her a look of perpetual surprise and her mouth was a duck-like pout. Her waist was unnaturally thin and her breasts were the size and shape of watermelons. When she had opened the door, her plumped-up lips curled back in what was supposed to be a smile. 'Come in, my love,' she had said, in a heavy accent. Not Russian but close. 'The early bird catches the worm.'

She had taken him into the main sitting area where three large sofas faced a floor-to-ceiling window that overlooked a large pool and barbecue area. The villa was on the outskirts of Puerto Banús, set behind a tall wall to keep the activities inside away from prying eyes. It had probably been seven or eight years since Harper had last visited but little had changed décor-wise. Terracotta tiled floors, white walls and low-backed sofas.

'You been here before, my darling?' purred the woman.

'A few years ago,' said Harper. 'What happened to Tracey?' She was the former top London escort who had set up the Pussycat in the late nineties, backed by a couple of East End gangsters. She had run a tight operation, everyone trusted her and she could smell a wrong 'un at fifty paces. The Pussycat had become the drinking den of choice for those gangsters who wanted to let their hair down away from their wives and kids. In its heyday, bowls of cocaine had been set out on the coffee-tables for anyone to use, compliments of the management, along with the best hashish ever to have come out of Morocco.

'She sold up two years ago,' said the woman. 'Married a Texan oilman of all things. She's as rich as God now, they say.'

'Good for Tracey,' he said, and extended his hand 'Jeremy,' he said. 'From London.' He decided to go the whole hog. 'Jeremy Willoughby-Brown.'

'Pleased to meet you, Jeremy,' she said, shaking his with a jewel-encrusted hand. Its discoloured patches of skin and raised veins betrayed her true age. 'I'm Sylvia. It's early yet but we do have these beautiful girls for you.' She waved at the four sitting on the sofas. Two were bottle-blondes, one was a brunette and the fourth a dyed redhead. They all smiled hopefully up at Harper, though they looked tired and a little worn.

'I can recommend Elsa,' said Sylvia, nodding at an anorexic blonde with skin the colour of porcelain. 'She's new. Well, relatively new.'

Elsa gave him a little wave. She was wearing a short black silk kimono and had painted her toenails to match the vibrant red of her fingernails. 'Actually, I was looking for someone in particular,' said Harper. 'I met a couple of Polish guys who said they'd had a great time a couple of days ago.'

'What were the names of the girls?'

Harper feigned embarrassment. 'To be honest, I don't think they asked for their names, just said they'd been to the Pussycat and had the best sex of their lives.'

'All our girls will give you the best sex of your life,' said Sylvia. She gestured at Elsa. 'There's nothing Elsa won't do. I'm told that being with her is like being in your own private porn movie. And if you take her with another girl, well, you'll be doubling your pleasure. Elsa loves the company of other women, don't you, Elsa?'

'I love it,' said Elsa, but the haunted look in her eyes suggested otherwise.

Sylvia gestured at the redhead. 'Natasha and Elsa work very well together. Wouldn't you like to be the filling in that sandwich, Jeremy?'

Natasha winked and licked her upper lip suggestively.

'I promised the guys I'd try their girls,' said Harper. 'Be rude not to.'

'Their names?'

'Ah, they were drinking buddies rather than pals,' said Harper. 'But you'll remember them. Polish. Quite loud. Big spenders.'

Sylvia spoke to Elsa in their own language. Latvian, maybe. Or Estonian. Elsa replied. Sylvia smiled at Harper. 'One of the girls is upstairs, sleeping. If you could wait, say, fifteen minutes?'

'Perfect,' said Harper, dropping down onto a sofa.

'Her name is Katrin. I'll tell her to get ready.'

As Sylvia went upstairs, Elsa curled up on the sofa next to Harper. Natasha asked him what he wanted to drink. He'd had half a bottle of Cristal with Brewer but figured a teetotal customer would raise suspicion so he asked for a beer. As she went off to get it, the other two began to play on their smartphones. Elsa ran a finger up and down his thigh. Harper realised that the nails were fake, stuck on top of the real ones.

'I can work with Katrin. It'll be fun.' She smiled at him but her eyes were flat. Harper had seen the look a thousand times in the bars of Pattaya. A lot of girls enjoyed working in the bars but a percentage had been forced into it, not at gunpoint but by family pressure. It was drummed into Thai children from birth that their primary duty was to support their parents, and if that duty involved selling their bodies, few had the courage to refuse.

'Thanks, but no thanks,' said Harper. He unzipped his hip-pack and pulled out a couple of hundred-euro notes. He slipped them to her. 'A tip,' he said.

'Are you sure?'

Harper laughed. 'I won it on the horses,' he said. 'Don't worry about it. Now tell me about Katrin.'

Elsa tucked the money into the top of her stockings. 'She's from Lithuania.'

'You too?'

She shook her head. 'I'm from Estonia, but we're friends. Her tits aren't real, but mine are.' She jiggled her impressive breasts to prove her point and Harper couldn't help but laugh.

The girl returned with Harper's beer and he sipped it, then chatted to her and Elsa until Sylvia came back with Katrin. Katrin's breasts were as fake as Sylvia's but she had a pretty face, long black hair and, though the dark patches under her eyes suggested she hadn't had much sleep, she didn't have the same haunted look as Elsa. She was wearing a white silk robe and, from the way it clung to her curves, nothing underneath it.

'You like?' asked Sylvia.

Harper stood up. 'I like a lot.'

Katrin shook her long, curly black hair and held out her hand. Harper took it and allowed her to lead him upstairs, along a corridor to a bedroom. There was a king-sized bed with red satin sheets but no duvet, and a mirrored ceiling. The windows were open and a soft breeze ruffled the lace curtains. There was a fridge by the bathroom door and Katrin opened it. 'Do you want a drink?'

Harper held up his beer. 'I'm good.'

'Do you mind if I have something?' she asked, pulling out a bottle of champagne.

Harper knew that if he said yes the cost would be added to his bill but he just smiled. 'Sure, why not?'

She popped the cork, filled the glass and sat on the bed. Her skin was tanned and, from what he could see, there were no tan lines. 'Sylvia tells me I partied with your friends.'

Harper nodded. 'Polish guys, a couple of days ago.'

'Tomasz?' she said. 'He was crazy. I got the feeling he hadn't had sex for a long time.' She threw back her head as she laughed, showing perfect white teeth.

Harper figured she was in her mid-twenties at most. 'That sounds about right. How long did he stay?'

'He didn't. He paid for us to go out. Me and Anna. And four other girls. Anna was for his friend. What was his name? Gabriel, like the angel?'

'Gabriel, yes,' said Harper. 'Good old Gabriel. So they gave you a good time?'

'They spent money like it was nothing and they were tipping like crazy. I told them our fee for the night and he gave me double that.'

'Did he give you his phone number?'

She shook her head. 'I gave him mine and he said he'd call me but he hasn't. He said he and Gabriel would come back last night and I waited but . . .' She shrugged. 'I suppose there are many places like the Pussycat.'

'Where was his villa?'

Her eyes narrowed. 'You said he was your friend.'

'He is, but he's on holiday and I'm not staying with him.'

She was still eyeing him suspiciously. 'Do you want to have fun or just talk?' She sipped her champagne.

Harper unzipped his hip-pack and took out a handful of hundred-euro notes. 'What's your normal fee?' he asked.

'During the day, two hundred euros for an hour.'

Harper placed two notes on the bed next to her. Then two more. Then another two. By the time he'd finished there was a thousand euros on the sheet. 'I don't do anal,' she said.

Harper grinned as he put the rest of his money back into his hip-pack. 'That's just for chatting to me,' he said.

'You don't want sex?'

'Not right now. I'm more of a night-time person.'

She scooped up the money and slid it into a drawer in the bedside table as if she was scared he would change his mind, then returned to sit next to him. She clinked her glass against his beer bottle. 'Thank you,' she said, and kissed him gently on the cheek.

'There is one thing you can do for me,' he said.

The suspicion was back in her eyes. 'What?'

'Just let me have Tomasz's address. I don't have his phone number and I want to say hi.'

'I don't have the address.'

'Ah. That's a pity.'

Her eyes narrowed. 'You're sure he's a friend?'

'Cross my heart and hope to die.' He crossed his chest solemnly.

She laughed. 'I don't have the address but I put the location on my phone. Sylvia makes us do that, just in case there's a problem when we do outcall.' As she leaned over and picked up her phone, her robe fell open and her breasts swung free. He couldn't help but admire them and she smiled when she caught his look. 'Are you sure you don't want to fool around? You've paid enough. I can ask Elsa to join us.'

'Just the address and I'll be a happy bunny,' said Harper.

She tapped on her iPhone and held it out, showing him the location of the villa. 'I can send it you, if you want?'

Harper took out his phone. 'I'll take a picture. That'll be fine,' he said. He photographed her screen, then stood up. 'Thanks. I'll tell Sylvia I came quickly but it was my own fault.'

She smiled up at him and let her robe fall open again. 'Are you sure I can't tempt you?'

Harper grinned, and looked at his watch. He really wanted to take a look at the villa, but Katrin had one hell of a body. 'You know what? You've talked me into it,' he said. He took off his shirt. 'Just be gentle with me.'

29

Fedkin found Stepan Kuznetsov sitting at a table outside a café in a side street not far from Notre Dame. There was a small steel-topped bar, where half a dozen men in overalls were drinking pastis, and a few tables where a crusty old woman begrudgingly served baguettes, Croque Monsieur and steak-*frites*. Tourists usually took one look inside and hurried away. Kuznetsov didn't smile or stand up to greet Fedkin – he had never been one for the social niceties. 'You're putting on weight,' he growled. 'And you look soft.'

'Let's do three rounds in the ring and we'll see who's fucking soft,' said Fedkin, pulling up a chair and sitting down.

Kuznetsov was always like a bear with a sore head – it was just his way. His name meant 'blacksmith', as common as 'Smith' was in the West, and he had the look of a man who worked with hot metal: big shoulders, massive forearms and scarred hands. He had been a relative high-flyer with the KGB when the Soviet Union had imploded and, like many, had moved on to work in the private sector, with as many files as he could take with him. He had married a Frenchwoman, he for the passport and she for the money

he offered, but the business relationship had surprisingly
evolved into a romantic one. They now had three children
and lived in a large duplex apartment overlooking the Seine.
Kuznetsov oversaw an investigations agency, which ran due
diligence checks for French companies on their Russian
counterparts. Russians were pouring money into France,
as they were into the rest of Europe, but it wasn't always
obvious what the source of the funds was, and while most
French companies would happily deal with an oligarch who
had a shady past, few would be prepared to go into business with a known Russian Mafia hoodlum. Kuznetsov,
with his KGB background, was often able to fill in the
blanks. He had a sideline, too, in running a black intelligence service, happy to help out any government who would
pay his fee, as well as individuals like Fedkin.

Kuznetsov had an espresso and a large brandy-filled
balloon glass in front of him. A cadaverous grey-haired
waiter came out and wished Fedkin good day in a tone
that suggested he couldn't have cared less what sort of day
he was having. Fedkin ordered a *café américain* and a brandy
to match Kuznetsov's. Kuznetsov had asked for the meeting
so Fedkin sat back in his chair, intertwined his fingers over
his stomach, and waited for him to speak.

'Your man is in Marbella,' said Kuznetsov. He held out
a gloved hand, palm upwards. Fedkin reached into his coat,
pulled out an envelope full of euros, and gave it to him.
Kuznetsov slid it inside his jacket without checking the
contents. 'He originally flew into Paris from Bangkok and
checked into a suite at Le Meurice for one night. He was
using an Irish passport in the name of Sean O'Donnell.
Then he vanished. He didn't fly out of the country and

there's no record of a Sean O'Donnell booking into another hotel. He could have taken the train or the ferry to the UK, of course.'

Fedkin nodded. He knew that Harper had been in England, but he had no intention of doing Kuznetsov's work for him. Lukin's Thai contacts were able to keep an eye on Harper's Thai mobile and he had used it in London. Fedkin didn't have a location yet but he had somebody working on it.

'Anyway, he came back to Paris because today he re-appeared at the airport as Sean O'Donnell and flew to Marbella on Vueling.'

'Vueling?'

'A low-cost Spanish airline.'

'And he's still there?'

'He hasn't flown back. But my Spanish contacts are patchy at best so I don't know what he's doing there.'

'No matter. I have people in Spain I can talk to. So, Marbella. What's in Marbella?'

'Sun, sea and sex,' laughed Kuznetsov.

'He lives in Thailand,' said Fedkin. 'He has all the sun, sea and sex he needs.'

'British gangsters,' said Kuznetsov. 'The English call that part of Spain the Costa del Crime.'

'That's what I was thinking,' said Fedkin. 'He's gone there to see someone. And the route he took suggests he wants to stay below the radar. He could have flown from London to Marbella but he chose to travel through Paris. And no record of him flying in, right?'

'Right.'

'Which means train or ferry. Which probably means he'll

travel back by the same route. You can keep a watch on the flight manifests into Paris?'

'Of course. It costs, but then everything does.'

Fedkin waved away the mention of money. 'You just let me know when he comes back. What about monitoring his phones in Spain?'

'I can ask around, but it's not something I've done before.'

Fedkin shrugged. 'I doubt he'll use his phones much anyway. And if he does he'll probably use a throwaway or a landline. He hasn't used his phone in France yet so I'm not holding my breath. The flight back is the best bet for catching him.'

Kuznetsov sipped his brandy. 'What did he do, this Englishman?'

'You know Yuri Lukin?'

'I know of him, of course. He's your client?'

'Harper shoved a bottle up the arse of Lukin's son.'

Kuznetsov tried to suppress a smirk but failed. 'A bottle?'

'A beer bottle.' He pointed a stubby finger at the man's face. 'But keep that to yourself, hear?'

30

The villa was a short drive from the coast in the area called Sierra Blanca, up a hill that gave it spectacular views of the Mediterranean, Gibraltar and Africa to the south, with the Marbella mountain range to the north behind it. It was a large plot – several acres at least – and it reminded Harper of Valentin Rostov's villa in Pattaya, a high wall topped with security wire around it and a barred gate covered by CCTV cameras. He didn't have a ladder or wire-cutters with him, and as the Poles wouldn't know him from Adam, he figured he might as well try ringing the bell and playing the lost tourist – though he made sure to park the Rolls-Royce where it couldn't be seen.

There was a brass bell push set into the concrete pillar to the left of the gate, and a grille. He pressed the bell several times but there was no response. He peered through the bars of the gate. A red Porsche was parked in front of the double garage and a black SUV closer to the house.

'Hello!' he shouted.

There was no reply. He shaded his eyes against the sun and stared at the villa for a while, then bent down and reached through the barred gate to grab a handful of gravel. He tossed a chipping towards the villa but it fell short. He tried again, harder this time, and the pebble clattered against the window. He waited a few seconds, then threw another. It, too, hit the glass. Still no reaction. Harper drew back his hand and threw the rest of the handful at the house and several tiny stones struck the window. No one came out to see what was going on. He looked around but the next villa was a hundred yards away and there was no sound of traffic on the hillside road. He grabbed the bars and climbed over the gate. He wiped his hands on his trousers and headed up the driveway to the front of the house, knowing he'd blown his chance of anyone believing he was a lost tourist.

He went through the motions of knocking a couple of times, but he already had a bad feeling about what he was going to find so he wasn't surprised when no one came to open the door. He reached out and turned the handle. The door was unlocked. It was a huge piece of carved wood but it opened easily. Harper wasn't sure what he became aware of first – the buzzing of flies or the stench of rotting flesh. Either way it told him all he needed to know about why no one had answered the door.

He found the first body sprawled across the bottom of a marble staircase. The man had been shot in the face, which was a mass of black flies. More flies buzzed around Harper as he stared down at the corpse. There were two more bullet holes in the chest, where flies were also feeding and laying their eggs, and a single spray of blood across the wall, which he thought had come from the first shot. That meant the gunman had gone for the head first and the shots to the body were overkill.

The 60-inch LED TV was showing a European football

match with an East European commentary. A dozen opened cans of lager stood on a glass coffee-table with a large ashtray overflowing with cigarette butts.

The second body was in the kitchen, face down in front of a massive stainless-steel refrigerator. There was blood spatter by the kitchen door and streaks on the tiled floor. Harper figured the man had been chased, shot in the back and the legs, and fallen down. The bullet to the back of the head had been the clincher. Harper was pretty sure two shooters had been involved. Maybe more.

They had made no effort to clean up after themselves and had left the bodies in plain sight, which probably meant they weren't local and in all likelihood had already left the country.

Harper padded upstairs. Two of the five bedrooms had been used. He found a Polish passport lying on a dressing table next to a wallet, which was full of credit cards, and two mobile phones. The passport and cards were all in the name of Gabriel Wawrzyniak. He left the wallet but put the phones and passport into his hip-pack. There was no cash in the wallet but Harper didn't think for one minute that robbery had been the motive. He opened a wardrobe and went through the man's clothing, all designer labels and brand new. He took a pair of socks from a drawer and slipped them over his hands, then wiped down the wallet and anything else he had touched.

There was no passport in the second bedroom but he found a boarding pass with the name Tomasz Twardsowski, matching the tag on a hard-shell suitcase that had been pushed under the bed. The suitcase was locked but a couple of hard stamps broke it open. Inside a padded envelope contained a thick wad of five-hundred-euro notes and an iPhone. He took off the socks and flicked through the notes. There were a hundred or so, which meant he was holding at least fifty thousand euros. 'Waste not, want not,' he muttered to himself, and slid the notes into his hip-pack, along with the iPhone. He took the envelope to the toilet, ripped it up and flushed away the pieces.

He put the socks back on and checked the rest of the room, then went downstairs and searched the ground floor quickly and efficiently. He found the CCTV monitors in a room off the kitchen. They were working but someone had taken a hammer to the computer and removed the hard drive. It was clearly a professional job.

31

Harper used a computer terminal at Marbella airport before flying back to Paris. He logged on to the Yahoo account and opened the draft folder. There was a single message from Charlotte Button, much longer than usual. He twisted the screen to the side to make sure it couldn't be overlooked and read through it slowly.

Lex, I need you to do something for me. I think I'm being followed and I need to check that the insurance policy I spoke about is still current. I can't go near it myself so I need you to visit the safe-deposit box and check that all's well. There is only the one copy left and I need you to make another and get it to me. Let me have a name that you have valid ID for and I'll have it put on the list of registered users. It's in Birmingham. You'll need a key so let me have an address where I can courier it to. Please be careful. I'm not sure who is following me but they are professionals. Let me know when you have the copy. I trust the other matter is proceeding apace. Keep me informed.

Harper read it a second time, then deleted it and typed: *Will do. Sean O'Donnell.* He added the address of a mailbox centre not far away from the ops room and continued:

Good news bad news. I found two of the guys behind the Manchester heist in Marbella but someone had beaten me to it. Gabriel Wawrzyniak and Tomasz Twardsowki. Both shot execution-style which suggests to me that someone is making sure they don't appear on the front page of the Sun. *If this is your pal Jeremy's doing then he's upped the ante. Be careful. I will send you their phones. Might be useful. Let me have an address.*

He waited for a couple of minutes. A message appeared in the folder, with a mailbox address in Fulham. Then another message:

You need to be careful. I'm not sure how long the tail has been in place. We might have been compromised in Paris. Sorry.

Harper cursed under his breath. If there had been a tail on Button he wouldn't have spotted it because he wasn't looking. But the meeting had taken place in a hotel suite that he was sure was clean, so no one would have seen them together. But the fact that Button was worried enough to mention it meant he was worried, too. He deleted it and replied, *No problem.* He added a smiley face, logged off and went to catch his flight.

32

Fedkin had booked himself into the Sheraton Hotel in Terminal Two of Charles de Gaulle airport. His gut feeling was that Harper would fly back through the airport, but if he appeared in Paris it was only half an hour away. He lay on his bed, flicking through the channels on his television, but all seemed to be French and he barely spoke the language. He found a Russian news channel but it was only propaganda and, like most Russians, he preferred to take his news from overseas sources such as the BBC and CNN. His phone rang and he picked it up. It was Kuznetsov. 'Your man is in the air as we speak, flying back to Paris.'

'Same airline?'

'Yes.'

'What terminal do they use?' asked Fedkin, sitting up.

'Three.'

Fedkin swore. 'I'd been hoping for more notice, Stepan.'

'Yeah, well, as the French say, "When there's a lack of thrushes, one eats blackbirds."'

'What the fuck does that even mean?'

'The English say, "Beggars can't be choosers."'

'You have been here too long, my friend,' said Fedkin.

'Look, I need something else from you. Manpower. Can you get two heavies for me at the airport?'

'To do what?'

'Wet work. I might have to take him out before he leaves Charles de Gaulle. I'll be playing it by ear and that'll be a lot easier if I've got backup.'

'I'll see what I can do,' said Kuznetsov.

Fedkin ended the call, grabbed his coat and rushed out of the hotel.

33

Harper checked his phones as soon he was in the arrivals area at Charles de Gaulle. There was a text message from Hansfree – TALLY HO! – which he took as a good sign. And a short voicemail from Mickey Moore, which was less optimistic, just a gruff 'Call me, you bastard'.

Harper phoned Hansfree first. 'We've had two contacts,' said Hansfree. 'I think he's getting ready to move.'

'I'm all ears,' said Harper. 'Bring me up to speed.'

Hansfree ran through what had got him excited. The previous morning, with the team in position as usual, they had seen McGovan emerge from the club much earlier than he had done on any previous day. For the first time, he seemed to be walking purposefully, as if he had a definite destination in mind. He seemed to be carrying out anti-surveillance measures, checking in mid-stride and looking back at the people walking behind him, or stepping into a shop doorway to eyeball everyone walking past. However, the team were skilled and alert enough not to arouse his suspicions, and after a few more minutes of anti-surveillance drills, evidently reassured that he was not being followed, he had set off again, this time heading towards Hyde Park. There was a packet of cigarettes in his hand. As he'd walked through the park he'd bumped into a Muslim man wearing traditional dress. The cigarette packet McGovan was holding was jolted from his hand and it fell to the ground, but he kept walking, apparently not having noticed that he had dropped it. However, a moment later the Muslim man picked it up and slipped it into a pocket of his robe.

'We're calling him Yankee One,' said Hansfree. 'He's medium build, about five foot nine, black hair, straggly beard, wearing a fawn *dishdasha* and one of those little round hats Muslims wear.'

'A *kufi*?' Harper said.

'Erm, I guess so.'

'What happened then?'

'The aim now was to "house" the newcomer and, with luck, ID him and check his background,' said Hansfree.

The team had spent the next few hours following the Yankee across London. According to Hansfree, it was an easy follow at first because the man had little tradecraft and made few attempts to check if he was being tracked, to double back or alter his route. However, to their intense frustration, they lost their quarry in Brick Lane, east London, where the indigenous population and the hordes of tourists were so dense that it was next to impossible to follow anybody.

'Wait. You lost him?' said Harper.

'We've got pictures, we'll pick him up again,' said Hansfree. 'The thing is we now know for sure Tango One is up to something. And there's more.'

'Get on with it, mate. I've got a train to catch.'

The second incident had happened yesterday afternoon.

McGovan again left the military club, walking purposefully, but this time, he'd gone along Oxford Street and entered a branch of McDonald's. After ordering his food, he glanced around as if unsure where to sit, then sat at a table next to a Middle Eastern-looking man wearing a well-worn dark suit. Although he had apparently chosen the seat at random, Tango One then spent several minutes talking animatedly to the other man. The team had been unable to get close enough to eavesdrop without the risk of compromise, but from their body language and the way they spoke to each other, heads close together and glancing around frequently to make sure they were not overheard, it was clear that whatever they were discussing, it was not the quality of their burgers.

As with the first Yankee, when McGovan stood up and left a few minutes later, the surveillance team abandoned their pursuit of him and instead focused on Yankee Two. This time they didn't lose him. They followed him as he travelled by bus to north London, and eventually housed him in a smart semi-detached property in a street mostly populated by families of similar Middle Eastern origins.

'Thank God for that,' said Harper. 'Losing one is bad luck, but if you'd lost two . . .'

'Not only did we not lose him, we've got an ID for him as well,' said Hansfree. 'He has a criminal record as an Islamic agitator and has been convicted several times for public order offences.'

'Finally some good news,' said Harper.

'Here's the thing, though, Lex, that's puzzling me,' said Hansfree. 'We've been monitoring any calls in or out of Tango One's room, but there hasn't been a single one, not even a wrong number. Nor has he posted any letters and he's not been emailing or texting anyone either. So the question is: how did those two Yankees know when and where to meet him?'

'My guess would be that he's probably been using the communal telephone in the club. Any chance we can plant a bug on that?'

'It would be pretty difficult to do. It's in a prominent place near the desk, and even if we could bug it, that phone must be used by scores of people every day, and since we don't have any audio of Tango One speaking, we'd have no way of knowing on any particular call if we were hearing him arranging a meet with a terrorist suspect or just some squaddie who was home on leave and fixing a meeting with his mates for a few pints. But I've got my thinking cap on.'

Harper ended the call and used his Thai mobile to phone Mickey Moore in Pattaya. 'The shit thickens, mate,' said Moore.

'What's happened?'

'Word around town is that Lukin has put a million-dollar contract on your head. Or a million euros. Depends who you talk to.'

'Bollocks,' said Harper.

'You put his son in hospital. Worse than that, you shoved a bottle up his arse.'

'To be fair, it was only a Singha bottle, not a fucking magnum of Cristal.'

Moore laughed. 'You're a fucking madman, Lex. Seriously, the Russians have been saying there's a hitman from Moscow on your case. I don't have a name, just that he's a fucking nasty bastard who does a lot of wet work for the oligarchs.'

'How much do they know?'

'They know your name, which means they'll have your picture and passports you've used to enter the country. Plus any information you were stupid enough to write on any of your landing cards.'

'I'm usually pretty creative on that front, Mickey.'

'We all are. But seriously, Lex, watch your back. These Russian heavies are former KGB, a lot of them, and they've got access to all sorts of black intelligence networks.'

'I'll be fine, Mickey.' He ended the call, wishing he felt half as optimistic as he'd sounded.

34

Fedkin watched Harper put away his phone. He was standing next to the two men that Kuznetsov had sent him. They were both Algerians, olive-skinned and swarthy, one tall and lean, the other an inch or two shorter with slightly bowed legs. Both were wearing leather bomber jackets and cargo pants. The taller one was named Habib and the shorter one was Aziz, but Fedkin was fairly sure they weren't their real names.

He had met them in the arrivals area just fifteen minutes before Harper's plane landed, which meant that Fedkin was stuck with them. They weren't carrying guns but both men had flick-knives with them and professed to be experts. Fedkin had shown them a photograph of Harper, but had yet to decide what to do.

Lukin wanted the man dead, but carrying out a contract killing in a crowded French airport would be difficult at best. And Lukin had seemed serious about the manner in which he wanted the Englishman killed. Fedkin could always lie about the bottle, but he was a professional and would prefer to carry out the client's wishes to the letter, if at all possible.

The two Algerians kept glancing at Harper, and Fedkin

hissed. 'Eyes on me. We split up. When he moves, we move. Do you have passports?'

The two men nodded.

'French?'

More nods. That was something. At least they could follow him onto the Eurostar, if necessary. Fedkin was carrying two passports, his Russian one but he also had a Dutch passport. It was fake but it was a good one and it would pass muster on the Eurostar.

'He will probably go from here to the Eurostar terminal, then to London. The best place to get him will probably be at Gare du Nord, but if he travels on the Métro there will be an opportunity there. Until we know where he's going for sure, stick close.'

The two men grunted and walked away.

35

Harper spotted the three men while he was on the phone to Mickey Moore. Three was an unusual number at an airport. People travelled alone, in couples or families. Three men standing together was a red flag. There could be perfectly reasonable explanations, of course. Three company representatives travelling together. Three drivers having a chat while they waited for their clients. Three guys off on a stag do. But the three men on the far side of the terminal didn't look like they worked in an office, had nothing with them to suggest they were there for an airport pick-up, and lacked the happy faces of men who were heading off for a few days of debauchery. They were big men with hard faces, two Arab-looking and the other was either former special forces or ex-cop – 'former' because the gold watch on his wrist and the cashmere overcoat hinted at a pay packet way above what a government employee received. One of the Arab men was clearly an amateur because he kept openly staring at Harper.

Harper played it cool. He doubted they would try anything in the terminal – at least, not in the areas covered by CCTV. And plenty of armed cops from the Gendarmerie Nationale were strolling around with guns on their hips, and black-uniformed soldiers with automatic weapons and impenetrable sunglasses standing in pairs.

He wandered over to a bookshop, bought himself a map of Paris, then wandered over to a screen showing the latest arrivals. He wasn't in the least bit interested in knowing the geography of Paris or what flights were due in, but the behaviour of the three men convinced him that they were indeed on his tail. Losing them wouldn't be difficult – he could catch a taxi into Paris, then run anti-surveillance on the Métro before heading for the Eurostar terminal at Gare du Nord. The problem was the three men knew which terminal he had flown into, which suggested they had access to airline or government databases. It was possible that someone had tipped them off in Marbella, but doubtful. He hadn't put himself about and it had been a flying visit. It was more likely they had been accessing flight manifests, and if they were capable of that, there was every chance they'd be able to pick him up in London.

There wasn't much he could do in the main arrivals area, but there was no CCTV in the toilets. He headed for the men's room, looking at his watch as if he was on a deadline. He pushed through the door and glanced around. To the left, four stalls, all unoccupied. To the right, a line of urinals. Also on the right, two sinks and a hot-air hand dryer. The door opened so that anyone looking in would see the cubicles. Only when the door had closed behind them would they be able to see the sinks.

Harper took his holdall and pushed it underneath one of the sinks, then pressed his back against the wall and waited. After a couple of minutes the door opened and he tensed, but he heard the rattle of a wheeled case being pulled across the tiles and started to wash his hands. A middle-aged Asian came in and headed straight to the urinals as Harper continued to wash his hands. As the Asian finished, Harper moved to the dryer. The Asian zipped up and left, and Harper took his place by the wall again.

After a few minutes the door opened. This time it was two French businessmen in dark overcoats who went together to the urinals, talking animatedly. Harper went into a stall and shut the door, reappearing after they had left.

Assuming the men were following him – and he was ninety-nine per cent sure they were – then at some point one would have to come in and check on him. The more professional they were the longer they would wait, but eventually they would have no choice because there was an outside chance that there might be another way out, a window or an emergency exit. If the roles were reversed and Harper's team was doing the following, he would send someone in if the target hadn't reappeared within half an hour.

The men following him were less patient. Twelve minutes after Harper had entered the toilet, the door opened. One of the Algerians appeared and took a step inside, his eyes on the cubicles. There was a click as the blade of his flick-knife sprang into place, and Harper knew immediately that this was more than a check to see where he was. He moved quickly, stepping behind the man as the door began to swing shut, his fingers clasping the Algerian's right hand, his left hand pushing down on the man's neck. Harper grunted as he pulled the knife into the man's chest at the same time pressing his head down. The man sank down onto the knife and gasped, then struggled as Harper pushed the knife in deeper. The man sagged and Harper let go of his neck, put both arms around him, grasped the knife and shoved it up towards the heart. The man struggled and went still. Harper dragged him into the far cubicle, sat him on the toilet and locked the door. He worked quickly, snapping the blade back into its handle, slipping it into his pocket, then patting the man down for his ID. All he had was his wallet and Harper took that. The man was breathing, barely, and while there was little blood on his clothing, Harper knew there had been catastrophic internal damage and that death was only seconds away.

He shoved his left foot between the dying man's legs and levered himself over the top of the cubicle and onto the toilet next door, then quickly took his place behind the door.

It was several minutes before the main door opened again. A backpacker with a large rucksack and a Canadian maple leaf patch on the side came in. Harper went through the motions of washing and drying his hands while the Canadian used the urinal and left.

The next person in used the near cubicle and Harper went to the urinal and pretended to use it until the man had finished.

Three more men came and went and Harper was about to call it quits when the door opened slowly. 'Habib?' whispered a man. The door opened further. 'Habib?'

The man stepped inside, looking at the cubicles. The door began to close and he looked to his right but Harper was already moving. His right hand slashed against the man's throat, splintering the cartilage. He punched him in the solar plexus with his left, doubling the man over. He pulled the knife from his pocket, flicked out the blade and stabbed the man in the heart, twisting the knife between the ribs to do the maximum amount of damage. The man went down but Harper caught him by the scruff of the neck and dragged him into the cubicle next to the first Algerian's. From the man opening the door to Harper positioning him on the toilet had taken less than ten seconds.

Harper stood over the man, breathing heavily. Again, there was little blood. The man sighed and went still. Harper pulled his victim's wallet from his jacket pocket, and took a pearl-handled flick-knife from another. He pulled the first knife from the man's chest, wiped the handle and slid it to the back of the neighbouring cubicle. Then he took the man's own knife, flicked out the blade and stuck the handle into the dead man's right hand, letting it lie on his lap. The pair were almost certainly known to the police and, with any luck, they wouldn't put too much effort into investigating their deaths.

He climbed out of the cubicle, then checked himself in the mirror above the sinks to make sure there were no stray drops of blood on his clothing, bent down, picked up his holdall and headed out of the door. He took out his phone and pretended to study the screen but in reality his eyes scanned the arrivals area. The man in the expensive coat was standing by a pillar, his arms folded.

Harper smiled coldly and walked towards him. The man unfolded his arms as he realised Harper wasn't going to turn away, but he stayed where he was, staring at Harper, his jaw clenched. Harper kept walking, his eyes never leaving the other man's face. He raised his phone smoothly and took several photographs of him as he walked. He stopped when he was just three feet away, close enough to reach him with a kick or a punch but knowing that nothing was going to happen, not then. Harper smiled and winked. 'They're dead, mate. Lovers' tiff. You never can tell with Arabs, can you?'

The man said nothing but continued to stare at Harper. His eyes were brown but they were lifeless and he didn't blink.

'Cat got your tongue, has it?' said Harper, matching the man's stare. The man wasn't a cop, he was sure of that. Wasn't a cop now and never had been. Ex-military, certainly. And probably ex-special forces. Cops, especially those who had been in the job for a few years, tended to have eyes that suggested disappointment tinged with sadness. They were used to seeing the worst side of people, and more often than not the people they dealt with would lie to them. All a cop could do was follow the rules and get on with his job, for little thanks and not much money. After a while they came to realise that, no matter how hard they worked, the world would never become a better place and bad people would always lie.

Soldiers, past and present, were used to solving their problems physically, and that showed in their eyes too. There would always be a hint of aggression in their stare, a look that said, while they were happy to resolve an issue by talking, at the end of the day they weren't scared of fighting and would be happy enough to throw a punch or fire a gun. The eyes of the man Harper was staring at weren't disappointed or aggressive. They were cold and calculating. His posture had changed as Harper had walked up. Not aggressive, not defensive, just ready. Prepared. One foot had shifted back, just a fraction. The left shoulder was slightly ahead of the right now, giving him just a bit more weight to throw behind a right-handed punch. His chin was down, just enough to protect his throat.

'See, your silence tells me a lot,' said Harper. 'It tells me that if you did speak, I'd learn something about you, something you don't want me to know. That means you're not French because if you were you wouldn't give a fuck. Not English, either, or American. But foreign for sure, and you know that if I know where you're from I'll know who sent you. You're obviously not an Arab, like your pals in the toilet, so I'm going to stick my neck out and say that you're Russian.' He smiled as the man's eyes tightened fractionally and his lips pressed together. 'And your micro-expressions show me I'm right. You're Russian. And it's not personal because there's no hatred in your eyes. You're stone cold, which means you're a pro, which means someone is paying you. And the only Russian I've pissed off recently is Yuri Lukin.' The man's jaw tightened and Harper nodded. 'And what you did right there confirms it.' He held up his phone but the man didn't look at it. He kept staring at Harper impassively. 'I've got your picture and in no time at all I'll know as much about you as you know about me. But here's the difference between us. You're an employee. You're doing this because someone is paying you. But I'll tell you now, no matter what Lukin is paying you, be it a million dollars or a million euros, it's not enough. Because for me, it's not about money. I'll kill you to protect myself and, trust me, personal protection trumps money every time. And I will kill you, don't doubt that for one second. I'm going to kill Lukin, too. I have to. He's given me no choice. And once he's dead there'll be no one to pay your bill, will there?'

He smiled and gestured at the exit with his phone. 'I'm going to walk away now. You're good so you've probably already worked out that I'm going to London. And that at some point I'll be going back to Thailand.' Harper stepped towards the man so that their faces were only inches apart, but the Russian didn't flinch. 'So here's the thing. If I see you in London, I'll kill you. In fact, if I ever see you again, no matter where, I won't say anything, I won't ask you what you're doing, I'll just kill you. And if I ever find out you're in Thailand, and I will find out, trust me, then I'll kill you.' He stared at the man for several seconds, then smiled brightly. 'Right, I'm off. You have a great day. Be lucky.' He turned and walked away, knowing full well that the Russian was staring at his back but not caring. He had meant every word he had said.

36

Passport checks were little more than cursory on Eurostar and Harper's Sean O'Donnell Irish passport was merely glanced at. He had a business-class ticket so had a free meal on the train and even managed a catnap before arriving at the St Pancras terminal. From there he caught a taxi to Paddington and reached the mailbox centre in Praed Street at three o'clock in the afternoon. He showed his Sean O'Donnell passport to the shop assistant, a tall Eastern European brunette with pale blue eyes. She handed over the padded envelope that had arrived by courier from Charlotte Button. Harper paid her and left.

He waited until he was back in his hotel before opening the package. There was a small key and the business card of a Birmingham safe-deposit company with a nine-digit identification number on the back. He put the key and the card into his hip-pack, then spent half an hour wandering around Bayswater making sure he wasn't being followed before catching a black cab to the ops room.

Hansfree was ecstatic. McGovan had apparently moved up a gear and over the past three hours had met with two more Yankees. Hansfree had housed them both – they were low-level jihadi agitators with criminal records who were already known to the authorities.

'How's he doing the recruiting?' asked Harper. 'That's what I don't understand.'

'Maybe someone else is pointing them at him,' said Hansfree. 'They go to him and not vice versa. ISIS sleepers, maybe. Sent here over the past few years and waiting to be activated. By McGovan. Or maybe for McGovan.'

Harper agreed. 'Maybe he doesn't do the initiating. They're told to contact him and he gives them their instructions. Makes sense.'

'I'm worried by how poor he is at anti-surveillance,' said Hansfree. 'He should be better than this, a lot better.'

'Why worry?' Harper said. 'It just makes him easier to follow.'

'Exactly, but if he's that careless, it suggests that either he's not as good as we thought he was, or he isn't close to going operational. If he was, he'd be taking a lot more care. But however unprofessional and careless he appears to be, we still can't afford to relax for an instant. If he suddenly switches on and we're not on our game, the whole operation could be blown. We've already worked much too hard and invested too much time to let that happen.'

Hansfree was right. 'I get the feeling you have a suggestion,' Harper said.

Hansfree grinned. 'More people,' he said. 'More feet on the ground.'

'I'm reluctant to increase the size of the team.'

'Lex, we don't have any choice. We're way too stretched as it is.'

Harper sighed. Again, Hansfree was right. And to make matters worse, he was going to have to go to Birmingham the following day on Button's errand. 'I'm guessing you have a suggestion, name-wise.'

'I've got a few people I can call, Lex. All first rate, all reliable, all prepared to work on a daily rate of a grand a shift.'

'They'd have to be reliable. This is heavy shit we're getting into. Plus, you know what the end-game is going to be. The fewer people who know, the better.'

'To be honest, without more hands to the pump the end-game could blow up in our faces,' said Hansfree. 'We've got too many balls in the air and not enough jugglers.'

'Okay, bring in what you need,' said Harper. 'I'll make sure you get the cash.' He chuckled. 'I'm assuming they'll want cash. And on the subject of being overstretched, I've got to go up north tomorrow.'

'Not a great time, Lex. Seriously.'

'Nothing I can do,' said Harper. 'Favour for a friend.' He took a Sim card from his pocket and placed it on the table in front of Hansfree. 'There's a couple of photographs of a guy who was following me at Charles de Gaulle. I think he's Russian. See what you can find out, will you?'

'I'm on it,' said Hansfree.

37

Fedkin downed his brandy and waved at the waiter to bring him another. He was sitting at a café overlooking the Eiffel Tower, his collar turned up against the wind that was blowing from the Seine to his left. There was a coffee untouched in front of him, and a cigarette that he'd started but not finished.

The confrontation with Harper had hurt his professional pride, but he had to acknowledge that he had made mistakes. He shouldn't have used the men Kuznetsov had provided. As soon as he had seen them he should have sent them on their way. They had been amateurs, clearly, and it was Fedkin's own fault for sticking with them.

Kuznetsov wasn't happy about what had happened to them, but Fedkin got the impression that it was an inconvenience rather than a personal loss. He had called him to break the news and Kuznetsov had ranted about what a difficult position he was now in, but he had sounded to Fedkin as if he was acting and that behind the bluster the man was aware that he had sent boys to do a man's job.

The waiter returned with the fresh brandy, the fourth Fedkin had ordered since sitting at the table. He had a decision to make and it was one that was going to require a lot of thought. He lit a cigarette and blew smoke towards the iconic tower. Fedkin wasn't in the least bit scared by his confrontation with the Englishman. The man was a professional, clearly. The way he had dealt with the Algerians. The way he had stared Fedkin in the eyes as he'd spoken. The body language, the words he'd used, all had indicated that the man had meant exactly what he'd said. If he ever saw Fedkin again, he'd kill him. It hadn't been a threat, more a statement of intent. And Harper had been absolutely correct when he'd said that personal protection always outweighed financial considerations. When you killed for money you planned everything down to the last detail. You wanted the target neutralised but you needed to make sure you had an escape route and a fallback position. When you killed to protect yourself, you did what you had to do. The consequences were important, yes, but at the end of the day it was self-preservation that mattered.

The contract was worth a million euros. That was big money. The only targets that paid more were heads of state and government officials. Fedkin understood the lust for revenge and had been happy enough to take Lukin's money, half up front and half on completion of the contract. But Lukin had underestimated the man he wanted dead. Harper wasn't a simple tourist. He wasn't a simple anything. And Lukin had given Fedkin the impression that Harper was on the run, which clearly wasn't the case. Harper was on a mission that involved him travelling to Marbella, Paris and London. Lukin should have known who and what Harper was. And if he did know and hadn't told Fedkin, that was a serious omission, which could have proved fatal.

The big question was what Fedkin should do next. Harper

hadn't been able to do anything but talk at the airport, not with all the CCTV cameras and armed French cops around. If the confrontation had taken place in a dark alley, things might have been different. Or maybe not.

Harper had recognised Fedkin as a fellow professional and had treated him as such. Fedkin had options. There were almost always options in life, choices that had to be made. Fedkin could ignore everything Harper had said and continue to try to fulfil the contract. He knew where Harper was – London – and his contacts in the UK were as good as they were in France. It wouldn't take much time or money to track Harper down and try to kill him. Or he could wait until Harper was back in Thailand. But the Englishman would be ready for him and wouldn't be a soft target. And if Fedkin failed, his own life would almost certainly be forfeit.

He could choose to back out of the contract. He could tell Lukin the truth that he had failed once and didn't want to try again. Or he could lie and say that he had simply failed to track the man down, that Harper was an expert at covering his tracks and that Lukin would be better to wait until the Englishman returned to Thailand. In either case Lukin would probably insist on having his money back but that would be no great loss as Fedkin had spent only a few thousand euros so far. The greater loss would be to Fedkin's reputation: he doubted that Lukin would keep the story to himself. Word would get around that Fedkin had failed and his professional reputation was paramount. Work would soon dry up if clients lost faith in his ability to follow through.

Harper had clearly meant what he had said about killing

Fedkin if he ever went near him. And he had been equally convincing when he said that he was going to kill Lukin. There had been no bravado, no bluster. It had been a straightforward statement of fact, no different from telling Fedkin what he planned to have for breakfast the next day. Lukin was well protected and he was no one's fool, but Fedkin didn't doubt for one moment that Harper would kill him, and soon. That being the case there would be no more money forthcoming from Lukin: the contract Fedkin had would end with Lukin's death. If – or, rather, when – Harper killed Lukin, Fedkin's current predicament would end because no one would know that he had failed, and no one would ask for the return of the five hundred thousand euros. His reputation, too, would be intact.

Fedkin nodded thoughtfully. That was the answer, then. All he had to do was nothing. Just wait. Harper would solve everything. The Englishman would kill Lukin, Fedkin's reputation would be unsullied, and he would get to keep the money. Fedkin finished his brandy and waved at the waiter for another. He smiled to himself, then took a long drag on his cigarette. Life was always so much easier when you dealt with professionals.

38

Charlotte Button was sitting at a coffee shop in JFK's Terminal Four. She looked at her watch and frowned. Her flight was closing in less than an hour and she still had to pass through security and Immigration, and even with her Virgin Upper Class ticket it was going to take her the best part of thirty minutes. She picked up her phone but there were no messages and no missed calls.

'Charlotte, so sorry,' said a voice to her left. It was Richard Yokely, smartly dressed as always but with a harried expression that was out of character. 'I was tied up in a meeting and then the traffic was a nightmare.'

'I'll have to go fairly soon,' she said.

'Nonsense. I'll walk you through Immigration. You can have the VIP treatment.'

'You can do that?'

He laughed. 'Of course I can. And what's the point of having friends in high places if they don't make your life easier from time to time?' He sat down at her table and gestured at her boarding pass. 'Good choice,' he said. 'Unlikely that jihadists would ever try to take down a Virgin plane.'

Button smiled. 'The joke in England was why would

anyone want to fly on a plane that won't go the whole way. Anyway, thanks for coming to see me off.' She looked around. 'Am I . . .?'

Yokely shook his head. 'No, you're good.'

'Your people are here now?'

'There are two within fifty feet of you, Charlotte. And don't even bother looking because they're the best in the business. It looks to me as if they leave you alone in the States. They just pick you up when you fly back.'

'So they're accessing airline manifests?'

'It isn't difficult, as you know. Government do it all the time and if you know the right palms to grease . . .' He shrugged. 'There will always be people who think they're not paid enough and that they deserve to earn a little on the side.'

'And have you been able to put names to the faces?'

Yokely smiled. 'Of course. I thought you'd never ask, my dear.' He took a thumbdrive from his pocket and gave it to her. 'Password protected. Your month of birth in capital letters plus today's date.'

Button put the thumbdrive in her pocket. 'You know it always causes trouble when Americans use dates,' she said. 'You mean American style, right? Month, day and year?'

'Of course.'

'You realise that America is the only country in the world to do dates like that? Everywhere else goes day, month, year.'

'Then everywhere else is doing it wrong.' He gestured at her pocket. 'Be sure you don't make a mistake, three strikes and you're out. The whole disk is wiped.'

'I'll be careful,' she said. 'And rather than keep me in suspense, can you tell me now who is on my case?'

'It's not government, which could be good news or bad,' said the American. 'We managed to identify four. Two are Israelis, both former Mossad but now in the private sector. The other two are Brits and work for a private security firm in south London. The Brits are just regular private detectives who do divorce and corporate investigations. The Israelis are more of a worry. But at this point they seem only to be interested in surveillance. There's no sense that they mean you any harm.'

'That's good to know.'

'Though, of course, that may well change if they think you don't have your insurance policies.'

'That's in hand, Richard.'

'Good to know,' he said. 'Now, how's the other matter progressing?'

She smiled thinly. 'Is that the real reason you were so keen to wave me off? Your congressman is getting impatient?'

'He's all for sending Delta Force over.'

Button laughed. 'Well, good luck with that.'

'I've explained to him that we can't use American special forces to kill British citizens on British soil. If it was out in the desert, it'd be a whole different ball game.'

'It's in hand, Richard. McGovan is under surveillance, and as soon as the opportunity presents itself, it will be done.'

'The sooner the better.'

'I hear you,' she said.

'And what about you?'

'I'm increasing my insurance. And then I'm going to talk to an old friend. See if she'll tell me what's going on.'

'If you need my help, just whistle.' He grinned. 'You know how to whistle, don't you?'

Button laughed. 'That was a great movie. I've never seen myself as Lauren Bacall but there's definitely something of the Humphrey Bogart in you.'

Yokely beamed, clearly taking it as a compliment. 'Here's looking at you, kid,' he said, and faked a salute. 'Now, come on, let's go get you patted down and on your way.'

39

Harper drove up to Birmingham early the next morning, taking a circuitous route that saw him in Reading, then Swindon and Gloucester. He took his time and avoided the motorways, doubling back and taking turns sometimes at random. Within an hour he was sure there was no one on his tail, but he still kept off the motorway. He stopped for breakfast at a small café outside Cheltenham, then cut across to Stratford-upon-Avon and spent half an hour driving around the tourist spots before heading up to Birmingham. He finally parked his car in a multi-storey in the city centre, took a small leather briefcase out of the boot, then walked around the major shopping areas, including the Bull Ring, Corporation Street and the Piccadilly and Burlington arcades. During his walk around the shops he paid cash for a MacBook laptop and a nylon carrying case. Eventually he was satisfied that he was tail-free and walked to the building that housed the safe-deposit company. He showed the O'Donnell passport and the business card with the ID number on it, then signed two forms and followed a young man in a pinstripe suit down a flight of stairs to the basement area. There was a large steel door covered by two CCTV cameras and the young man tapped in a four-digit code, then pulled the door open. It was several inches thick but Harper knew that was only for show: if anyone was going to force their way into the vault they'd simply drill through the concrete around the door.

'Ever been broken into?' asked Harper, as he followed the man into the vault.

'Never,' he said. 'State-of-the-art security in here. Infrared and motion detectors, and a laser couldn't get through that door.'

Harper smiled at the mention of lasers. There was no need for anything as hi-tech as a laser: an industrial drill would do the job. The one that had broken into the Hatton Garden Safe Deposit Company had cost just three and a half grand and had done the job in under two hours.

The assistant had a clipboard with a key attached and he used it to open one of the two locks in the flap of a box at about waist height. Harper used his own key to release the second, then the assistant lifted the flap and slid out the long metal box. He carried it out of the vault, closed the door, then took Harper along a corridor to another room, which contained just a metal table. He put the box on the table and pointed at a button to the right of the door. 'When you're ready just press that and I'll come and take the box back.'

'Brilliant, thanks,' said Harper. As the man left, Harper looked around the room. There was no sign of CCTV, which made sense because the whole point of safe-deposit boxes was that the owners wanted the contents kept away from prying eyes. He opened the box and looked inside. There was a stack of fifty-pound notes, a couple of inches thick, a small velvet bag tied with a piece of golden rope that he knew without touching contained sovereigns, half a dozen envelopes, a battered Filofax and a grey thumbdrive. Harper didn't even think about opening the letters or the Filofax. He took the thumbdrive out of the box and placed it on the metal table. He opened his laptop case and took out the MacBook. It booted up within seconds and he quickly configured it before he plugged in the thumbdrive and copied the file onto the computer's hard disk. He switched off the computer, put it back into his briefcase and the thumbdrive into the safe-deposit box, then pressed the button to summon the assistant. Half an hour later he was on the motorway, heading south to London.

He left the computer locked in the boot of his car while he went to the internet café and opened the draft message folder. He typed a new message: *All sorted*. He went to the counter and bought himself a coffee. By the time he had got back to the terminal the message he had written had gone and there was one from Button in its place: *You're an angel*.

He sat down, sipped his coffee, and typed a new message: *What do you want me to do with my copy?*

She replied a few minutes later: *Just keep it safe. You're my safety net.*

Are you OK?

I've been better.

Anything you need, just ask. Harper sat back and sipped his coffee again.

You're sweet. Stay in touch.

As Harper watched, one by one the messages were deleted.

40

Hansfree was alone in the ops room late that night when Harper turned up with a couple of coffees. 'Did you get the extra manpower?' he asked, as he flopped down on a folding camping chair.

'Half a dozen. Three are working with Maggie and three with Barry Whisper. I've got two more coming in later.'

Harper took an envelope from his jacket pocket and tossed it onto the table where Hansfree was working. 'There's thirty thousand euros to be going on with,' he said. It was part of the money he'd found in the villa in Marbella. 'I'll get more as and when you need it.' He sensed that Hansfree was unhappy about something. Just a feeling, but they'd known each other for so long that he could read the signs. 'Something happen while I was away?' he asked.

'I'm not sure. Maybe nothing.'

'And maybe something. Come on, spill the beans.'

'It was about midday. Maggie's team were following Tango One along a street just off the Edgware Road. One of the new guys, Reggie, was in the A position closest to the subject, with a woman called Nancy behind him. Maggie was working as C on the opposite side of the street, while Barry Big was mobile in a vehicle not far away, cruising, ready to take up the follow if the subject hailed a taxi or got into a car. There had been nothing to indicate anything out of the ordinary, with Tango One strolling along, apparently without a care in the world. There were enough other people in the street for the team to remain inconspicuous as they followed him. Anyway, everyone is as happy as Larry when Reggie calls it off. Break, break, break.'

'What had happened?'

'Well, Reggie says he'd seen a guy, a dark-haired man in a blue suit, olive skin scarred with pockmarks, old smallpox scars maybe. He says the man's expression didn't change as he approached, but he says that when the guy got closer to Tango One he winked.'

'Winked? He called it off because of a fucking wink?'

'Reggie's a pro, Lex. He's not a kid. He's in his seventies and spent thirty years as a follower with Five. He does a bit now and again to keep his eye in but, trust me, he's not the sort to panic.'

'He's sure it was a wink? Not just a dodgy eye or an insect or something?'

'Reggie says he saw a wink so he was doing the right thing by breaking it off. They came back here for a debrief. No one else spotted anything but Reggie was closest. He did the right thing.'

'So what's your assessment?'

'If Reggie was right, and I've no reason to doubt him, then maybe Tango One was laying a trail. The big question is how many watchers he had stationed along his route and whether any of them had been observing us long enough to be able to identify that we were following him.'

'That's guesswork,' said Harper. 'And if Reggie's as good

as you say he is, surely he'd have spotted any other watchers beforehand.'

'I think you're right,' said Hansfree.

'So, well done, Reggie, and full steam ahead,' said Harper. 'Everyone needs to be on full alert, obviously. I don't have to stress how vital it is that we all bring our A-game to work tomorrow. But the good news is that if he was laying a trail to see if there was any surveillance on him, it suggests that he may be making last-minute checks before going operational.' He raised his coffee cup in salute. 'We're entering the end-game, mate, and that's always my favourite part.'

41

Patsy Ellis unlocked the front door, placed her briefcase next to the hall table and went through to the kitchen. Her husband, Roger, was bending down to peer through the glass panel in the oven door. 'Dinner'll be ready in half an hour,' he said, without looking around.

'Where are the boys?'

He stood up and gave her a peck on the cheek. 'In with Charlie. Why didn't you tell me she was coming? I mean, there's enough to go round but some notice might have been nice.'

Ellis had to fight not to show surprise. She smiled as her mind raced. 'I'm sorry, honey, it completely slipped my mind,' she said. 'Where are they?'

'Sitting room. She volunteered to help them with their homework.'

Ellis went along the corridor to the sitting room. Charlotte Button was sitting on the sofa with the two boys, nine-year-old Jamie and eleven-year-old Harry. They both had exercise books on their laps. Button was wearing a blue Chanel suit and what looked like Chanel heels, very similar to how Ellis was dressed. 'Charlie, what a lovely surprise,' she said.

Button looked up and smiled. She brushed a stray lock of hair behind her ear. 'I'm not as good at algebra as I thought,' she said.

Harry sighed theatrically. 'I keep telling you, Auntie Charlie, it's calculus, not algebra.'

'Potato, tomato,' said Button, ruffling his hair. 'I can't believe how they've grown.' There was a bottle of wine in an ice bucket on the side table next to her and a flush to her cheeks that suggested she'd already drunk a fair bit of it.

'Well, it's been a while since you've seen them,' said Ellis. 'Boys, can you take your books upstairs while I talk to Auntie Charlie? Supper will be ready soon.'

The boys grabbed their books and clattered out of the room. Ellis narrowed her eyes. 'Seriously, Charlie. My home?'

'I'm under a bit of pressure at the moment,' said Button, quietly. 'I needed somewhere safe.'

'And you figured nothing bad could happen with my husband and sons under the roof?'

'Is that so bad? Can't an old friend pop around for a surprise visit?'

'I'd rather you'd called first.'

Button smiled brightly. 'But then it wouldn't have been a surprise, would it?' She took the bottle out of the ice bucket and held it up. 'I brought a gift. Roger said I should open it.'

Ellis smiled at the bottle. It was a Chardonnay, and a good one. It was her favourite brand, and she was sure that was no coincidence. It was also half empty.

Button poured some into a glass and held it out to Ellis. 'Cheers, then.'

Ellis took the glass and they toasted each other. 'What am I going to do with you, Charlie?' She sighed.

'Sit down, drink some wine and relive old times,' said Button. 'That's what friends do.' She sat down on the sofa and crossed her legs.

Ellis sank into an armchair and sipped her wine. 'How can I help you, darling?' she asked. 'I'm assuming you do want my help.' Ellis worked for the Joint Intelligence Organisation, the agency responsible for intelligence assessment and forward planning. It offered advice and support to the Joint Intelligence Committee, which oversaw the work of MI5, MI6 and GCHQ. No one knew more about the workings of the British intelligence agencies than Patsy Ellis. Prior to joining the JIO she had worked for MI5 and had been something of a mentor to Button.

Button took a long drink of wine. 'When we talked last, you suggested I loaded a file onto a website, which could be revealed in the event of my death.'

'Your insurance policy? I was talking hypothetically.'

'And I agreed. But to be honest, Patsy, that thought hadn't occurred to me. I put my faith in good old-fashioned hardware. Thumbdrives, three of them.'

'As I said at the time, it's the obvious thing to do.'

'Right. And two of those thumbdrives have been stolen.'

Ellis raised her eyebrows. 'Ah, that's unfortunate.'

'Please tell me it's nothing to do with you, Patsy.'

'Of course it's not. Perish the thought. Where were they? Not under the mattress, obviously.'

Button smiled. 'Safe-deposit boxes. Hatton Garden and Manchester. Both broken into by professionals.'

'Professionals who were arrested fairly promptly in the

case of Hatton Garden. Charlie, I can assure you, this is none of my doing.'

'You can see why I'd be worried, though. Two of my three insurance policies have now gone. And I really shouldn't be telling you that.'

'I don't know what else I can say to convince you that I'm not your enemy, Charlie. What happened happened. You got caught, you resigned and that's the end of it. I was just brought in so that you'd be dealing with a friendly face.'

'What about Willoughby-Brown?'

'Jeremy got what he wanted. Your job. I doubt he'd be still pursuing you.'

'Well, someone is. And they're good. Both the Hatton Garden robbery and the Manchester one were planned like military operations. And when they thought I was heading for the third, I was followed. By pros.'

'That's . . . interesting.'

'Isn't it? Whoever is on my tail they're good. Government standard. And they're able to go airside.'

'I won't ask you how you know that.'

'How sweet. I need you to check with Five and Six that they're not behind this.'

'I'm sure they aren't, but I'll check.'

Button leaned towards Ellis. 'And I need more. I need to know who it is, Patsy. Otherwise I might start to think that attack is the best form of defence. I have now put another copy out there and it's not in a box. If I continue to feel under pressure I might reach the conclusion that the best option for my safety is to go and have a chat with the editor of the *Guardian.*'

'Oh, I do hope not, Charlie. And, please, if ever you do

decide to talk to a journalist, please make it the *Telegraph*. The *Guardian*'s an awful rag, these days.' She held up her hand. 'I'm joking. I don't want you to go to any newspaper. And I know you don't either. We have the same views on journalists. Most of them, anyway.'

'There are still some serious journalists around who care about something other than how fat the latest pop star is getting,' said Button. 'The point I'm making is that, once the information is in the public domain, there's no point in anyone trying to keep me quiet.'

'That's certainly true. But once the cat is out of the bag, heads would have to roll. And you'd be first in line. You killed people, Charlie.'

'Terrorists.'

'For personal reasons. That's good old-fashioned murder, whichever way you look at it.'

'I'd happily take my chances with a jury of my peers,' said Button. She sipped her wine. 'A grieving widow pushed over the edge when she witnessed her husband killed in front of her? With the right jury I'd get probation, but even with the wrong jury I'd get ten years, out in five. You think I'm scared of five years in a British prison? I'd appreciate the rest, frankly. And it'd give me a chance to catch up on my reading.'

'Well, yes. You could see it that way. But you're forgetting that you'd be up against the whole weight of the Establishment, looking for a scapegoat to hang out to dry, if you'll forgive the mixed metaphors. With the right judge, the right prosecuting counsel, and a carefully vetted jury you might well find yourself facing a life sentence. And is there anything involving the Americans in that file, Charlie? That's the question you need to be asking yourself. Because if the Americans take an interest and they press for extradition, well, you could be spending eternity in a metal box under the ground in some Midwestern state where same-sex marriage is illegal but wedding your cousin is okay.'

Button shrugged. 'So the best thing all round is for the file to stay out of the public domain. And for that to happen, you have to make sure I stay safe and well.'

'I've already told you, darling, this is nothing to do with Five. Or Six.'

'Not officially, no. But there could be someone within the organisation who is pursuing their own agenda.' She smiled at the look that flashed across Ellis's face. 'Please, no snappy comment about pots and kettles.'

'You do see the irony, though?'

'Yes, I do.' She reached for her bag, opened it and took out a padded envelope. She passed it to Ellis, who peered inside.

'Why, thank you, Charlie, but really I have all the phones I need.'

Button smiled thinly. 'Two of the men involved in the Manchester safe-deposit heist were killed in Marbella. Executed. Gabriel Wawrzyniak and Tomasz Twardsowski. These are their phones.'

Ellis frowned. 'That's news to me.'

'Their bodies haven't been found yet. Not officially, anyway.'

'And they were involved in the robbery?'

'They have form for similar break-ins in Poland and Germany. It's the first time they've worked in the UK.' She smiled. 'And the last, obviously.'

'And the Spanish police aren't aware of this because?'

'Because they're the Spanish police,' said Button. 'They generally have trouble finding their backsides with both hands.'

'And who executed them, do you know?'

'Presumably whoever hired them. I'm guessing it's the same person who hired the guys who did the Hatton Garden job. He didn't want the Poles being picked up so . . . You can see why I'm a little nervous.'

Ellis patted the padded envelope. 'So you want me to find out who they spoke to, where they went?'

'All the information will be on their phones and Sim cards. I could probably get it done myself but it'll be quicker and easier through you. Plus you'll get to see for yourself.'

'And then what?'

'Well, I suppose that depends on who's behind this. You can either deal with it, or you can bounce it back to me. Either way it'll be taken care of.'

There were half a dozen surveillance photographs in the envelope. Ellis slid them out and looked at them. There was writing on the back: the names of the subjects and details of where the photographs had been taken. 'Those are four of the watchers who have been on my case in the UK,' said Button. 'They pick me up at the airport and stick to me like glue.' She saw the unease that flashed across Ellis's face. 'Don't worry, they didn't follow me here. They're good but they're not perfect. Two work for a British security company, two are former Mossad.'

'Are they now? That's interesting.'

'I don't think it's the Israeli government. I think whoever wants me tailed hired an Israeli company, that's all. I'm guessing they then took on extra manpower in the UK. I think whoever is having me followed also ordered the robberies and the murder of the Polish crew.'

Ellis nodded thoughtfully. 'Okay, let me see what I can do. Are you okay, darling?'

Button flashed her a tight smile. 'I've been better.'

'Stay for dinner. Roger's cooking.'

'Are you sure?'

'That Roger's cooking? Absolutely. He's doing his *hachis parmentier*. Just don't call it shepherd's pie – he'll never forgive you.'

Button chuckled. 'About me staying, I mean. Are you sure you want me here?'

Ellis raised her glass. 'Charlie, we're friends. No matter what's happened, that's never going to change.'

42

Harper was standing in his usual spot close to the military club when he heard Hansfree's voice in his earpiece. 'Lex, I've just heard Tango One on his mobile, via the in-room camera,' he said. 'He was contacting a vehicle retail site in Staffordshire and asking about the availability of second-hand Land Rovers. I've just done a quick internet search and found out that the company specialises in the sale of ex-military vehicles.'

'So it sounds like they're going for a military target, then.'

'Could be,' Hansfree said. 'Though, of course, there are plenty of civilian targets that would be easier to access using military vehicles.'

Harper thought for a few moments, then took a calculated gamble. 'Give us the details of the site, Hansfree,' he said, into the mic at his shoulder. 'Barry Big, take one of the leased vehicles to the site, I'll follow you on the bike. Maggie and Barry Whisper, remain in position, keep staking out Tango One and track him if and when he leaves. We could be on the move, everyone on full alert.'

'Roger that,' said Maggie, in his ear. 'About bloody time.'

Later that afternoon McGovan came out of the club wearing a long coat and a woollen beanie hat. Maggie May and Barry Whisper trailed him along Euston Road to Euston station, where they saw him meet the man they had named Yankee Four. He was mixed race, clean shaven, other than a small, neat moustache, and, like McGovan, was wearing a long coat. The two men went into the station and bought tickets. Maggie was behind them and overheard their destination: Lichfield in Staffordshire. She bought tickets for herself and Barry Whisper and they boarded the same train, managing to get seats at the far end of the same carriage. Throughout the two-hour journey they remained in radio contact with Harper and by the time the train arrived at Lichfield, he and Barry Big were already in position outside the station, Harper on his bike and Barry Big in one of their rental cars.

The two targets left the train and jumped into a cab, Harper on his bike in close pursuit, and the rest of the team three-up in Barry Big's car.

The taxi drove out of town for a few miles and eventually pulled up at a long-disused and abandoned airfield, now an expanse of cracked, weed-strewn concrete, dotted with heaps of fly-tipped rubble and other rubbish. A large area, surrounded by a much newer-looking steel-mesh and barbed-wire fence, enclosed the disused control tower and crew room, and the assorted old hangars, administrative buildings and bunkers, which were now housing the offices, repair shops and stores of a company specialising in the sale of ex-military vehicles. Hundreds of ex-army Land Rovers and Bedford trucks, still in their original military camouflage, were parked in rows on the concrete hard-standing around the buildings.

The two men were soon deep in conversation with a

salesman, who was showing them two ex-army Snatch Land Rovers. Harper, meanwhile, was wandering around the site, pretending to be interested in buying a vehicle, but often close enough to the group to catch snatches of their conversation and overhear what was being discussed. Eventually the two men came to an agreement with the salesman and they retired to the office to fill in the paperwork.

Harper went over to the car. The passenger side window wound down. 'Have you got any trackers with you?' he asked Barry Big.

'I never leave home without them.' He nodded at the glove compartment. Barry Whisper opened it and took out two compact devices.

'Hansfree's finest,' said Barry Big. 'They'll stick to anything metallic and once they're in place they kick off automatically. He can pick them up on any iPad.'

Harper nodded at Barry Whisper. 'Do the honours, mate, and fix those to the Land Rovers they were looking at. I've got a feeling they're going to be buying them.'

'Roger that,' said Barry Whisper. He climbed out and headed over to the vehicles. Harper went to a Bedford truck parked outside and climbed into the cab so that he could look into the office. He glimpsed McGovan handing a wad of cash to the salesman. 'Have we missed a brush contact somewhere along the way today?' he murmured, into his shoulder mic. 'Or has Tango One been packing a fortune in cash ever since we started surveillance on him? Where did that cash come from?'

Shortly afterwards the two men set off, each driving one of the ex-army Snatch Land Rovers.

Harper's team followed them back to London, Harper

taking the lead on his bike and the rest following in the car. It was after dark before the long drive back to London ended with the targets circling the capital on the eastbound M25, then turning off just south of the river. To the south-east of the junction the unearthly glare of light from the Bluewater shopping centre lit the night sky, but the two vehicles turned in the other direction, driving upstream from the Dartford River Crossing for a few miles, parallel to the south bank of the Thames, then turning off again into a light industrial estate, stopping outside one of thirty or forty units on the site, most of which looked to have seen better days.

The sprawling estate was dominated by a crumbling concrete structure, like a tower, part of a factory that must once have stood there and which the developers had not yet got round to demolishing. The units were occupied by the usual post-industrial mixture of service companies, printers, plumbing supplies, waste-product recyclers and direct-sales companies, leavened with a mixture of vacant and derelict sites, festooned with optimistic 'To Let' and 'Development Opportunity' signs. At first glance, the unit the targets had rented was no different from the others, but it stood out from its neighbours in one way: it was surrounded by a pristine new high-security fence.

Harper parked his motorbike, clambered part of the way up the concrete tower and, using a small pair of high-powered binoculars, he watched as McGovan unlocked the gates of the compound and the two men parked the Land Rovers in two lean-to garages, which formed part of the unit. The main building was a single-storey warehouse with a main entrance at the front but no windows that Harper could see. Before leaving the compound, McGovan tested the doors of the buildings, then walked around the site, checking the fence. Two twenty-foot shipping containers – one blue, the other blood red – had been parked at the far end and he examined them carefully, testing the padlocks on the doors. He waited until Yankee Four was safely outside the fence, before releasing a ferocious rough-coated German Shepherd, which had been locked up in a small shed at the side of the main building. 'Where the fuck did the dog come from?' said Maggie.

The two men left the site, locking the gate. They walked up the road together to the far end of the estate, then parted company, McGovan turning left towards Erith, while Yankee Four walked in the opposite direction, heading east.

Harper stood down the team, though Hansfree remained at his post in the ops room, monitoring the electronic equipment and the feed from McGovan's room at the military club. Before climbing down from the tower, Harper fixed a small surveillance camera to the rough concrete surface, using strips of gaffer tape to hold it in place, and adjusting it so that it was pointing at the jihadists' compound. When Hansfree's voice in his earpiece confirmed that he was receiving and monitoring the signal back in the ops room. Harper climbed down and walked towards the compound.

At that time in the evening, the other units on the site were quiet, locked up for the night, and, after making sure that the targets really had left the area and were not doubling back on their tracks, Harper walked around the perimeter of their unit, peering in through the chain-link fence. All the time he was doing so, he was being tracked by the dog, which kept pace with him all the way round. The Alsatian made no noise but its eyes never left Harper, and once or twice when it decided that he was too close, it flung itself at the fence, regardless of its own safety, baring its teeth. Even with a chain-link fence between them, Harper took an involuntary step back, startled by the savagery of the animal.

Using his binoculars, he looked closely into every part of the unit. Finally, when he was satisfied that he had seen everything there was to see on the site, he walked back to where he had left his bike and rode back into London at high speed.

43

Harper hurried up the stairs to the ops room, where Hansfree was sitting in darkness, staring at his computer screen, his face lit only by the cold metallic glow from the display. 'Give that a rest a moment,' he said. 'I need your help to access the site where the targets have stashed their vehicles and equipment.' Hansfree had his equipment cases stacked at the far end of the room, and after a few minutes' rummaging through them, he had what he needed: a battery-driven electric drill, a set of drill bits, and a fibre-optic endoscope, a super-thin, flexible extending device that enabled the user to penetrate sealed or inaccessible spaces. With the device came a couple of attachments that fitted onto the end of the optic cable: a small camera and an even smaller light.

The pair travelled in Hansfree's van, out through the hinterland of new builds, drab suburbs and fading industries that lined the south bank of the Thames.

On the way, Hansfree briefed Harper on what he'd discovered about the man he'd photographed in Paris. 'Dmitry Fedkin, assassin for hire,' said Hansfree. 'He operates mainly in Russia. Former Spetsnaz, as all the best Russian assassins are. As you know, Spetsnaz has become a catch-all for any sort of special-operations group, from the cops to bog-standard military. But Fedkin is the real thing, Alpha Group. It was created by KGB boss Yuri Andropov after the 1972 Munich Olympics massacre. The Germans fucked up big-time and the Russians wanted to make sure the same thing couldn't happen to them. They're on a par with the SAS or Delta Force. They were used as storm troopers, cracking the whip right across the former Soviet Union. After it fell apart, Alpha Group was downgraded and moved from pillar to post before being swallowed up by the Federal Security Service. Fedkin joined in 1996 and left five years ago to go private. Works for a company based in Moscow. Most of the clients are Russian Mafia or oligarchs, though these days those terms are pretty much interchangeable.' Hansfree looked across at Harper, frowning. 'Was he just following you, Lex? This guy isn't about surveillance, as a rule.'

'He didn't try anything, but he had a couple of henchmen who had a go.'

Hansfree nodded. 'Well, if this guy's on your case, you've got problems.'

'I spoke to him professional to professional,' said Harper. 'I think I'm good.'

It took them just over two hours to reach the industrial area where the targets had stored their vehicles and equipment. Hansfree parked well away from the unit and the two men studied the live pictures from the surveillance camera being relayed to his laptop before they got out of the van. All appeared quiet at the site, but they still made a covert approach, slipping between the patches of shadow in the lee of the other buildings on the site and pausing frequently for minutes at a time to look and listen before moving forward again. As they reached the compound, the German Shepherd spotted them and stood stock still as it stared at them, ears pricked.

'I can see what you mean about the dog,' Hansfree said. 'It's got a head like a bleeding alligator. Have you seen the state of those teeth? That's the most evil-looking guard dog I've ever seen.'

'It's not a guard dog,' Harper said. 'It's an attack dog. If they'd wanted a dog to work as a guard, they would have used one that barked whenever anyone walked within yards of the compound. This one is much too quiet for that, which makes it even more dangerous. Given the chance, it'll attack and kill if it can. The question is, where the hell did it come from? Muslims won't have anything to do with dogs – they reckon they're unclean. McGovan obviously has others helping him put this together.'

Harper walked parallel to the fence for a few yards, then turned back, all the time watching the dog intently. It kept its gaze just as firmly fixed on him and when he moved towards the fence and placed a hand against it, his fingers projecting through the steel mesh as if about to scale it, the dog launched itself at him in a heartbeat, its jaws closing with a snap on the point where Harper's fingers had been, its body crashing into the mesh with an impact that set the fence rattling for several yards in both directions. Harper had only just been in time as he snatched his hand away. The fact that it had attacked in total silence, without emitting so much as a growl, had been even more frightening.

Hansfree's face had gone even whiter than its usual pallor. 'Bloody hell,' he said. 'That's not a dog, it's a Terminator.'

'It's good, all right,' Harper said. 'I've got a mate who

makes a decent living training attack dogs. Normally the first stage in training a dog is to boss it. In effect you become the pack leader, and once you've dominated it, you can make it do what you want it to do. But with attack dogs it's just the opposite. You have to brutalise it, but if you want a dog to be a killer, of humans as well as other dogs, you have to defer to it constantly and retreat before it whenever it moves towards you. That tells the dog it's the leader of the pack, even when humans are around, which makes it much more aggressive and fearless.'

'That's all very interesting,' Hansfree said, 'but it doesn't tell me how you propose to deal with it.'

'I'm not quite sure myself yet,' Harper said. 'But it's going to have to die, there's no question of that. I can't see there's any way of us getting inside with the bastard thing alive. But we're going to have to make it look like natural causes or an accident, because if there are any unexplained wounds on it McGovan will know we're on to him. But I've got a plan. We'll just need a few bits and pieces before we start.' He led Hansfree back to where they'd left his van.

'Where to?' Hansfree said, as he started the engine.

'A corner shop will do.' Harper glanced at his watch. 'If you can find one that's still open, that is.'

They drove for a couple of miles before Hansfree spotted an open corner shop and pulled up outside. Harper went in and bought a can of some luridly coloured soft drink that only kids would have contemplated drinking and a packet of Haribo sweets. When he came back outside, he poured the drink into the gutter, crumpled the empty can and slipped it into his pocket. He ripped open the sweets and tipped them into the rubbish bin outside the shop, but once again he kept the crumpled packet and put it into his pocket with the can.

'What was that all about?' Hansfree said, but Harper merely winked and tapped the side of his nose with his finger.

'Now we need to find a charity shop or maybe some recycling bins would do.'

'There won't be any charity shops open, Lex – it's the middle of the night.'

'I know. It shouldn't make that much difference with what I'm looking for.'

Hansfree shot him another quizzical look, but Harper said nothing. They drove along a run-down high street where even the few shops that had not been boarded up or left empty had long since closed for the night. They passed several closed charity shops in a succession of rust-belt north Kent towns before they found what Harper was looking for. In the doorway of an Oxfam shop there was a stack of cardboard boxes and three or four carrier bags but, having rummaged through them, Harper returned to the van, shaking his head. 'No good,' he said. 'We'll have to try again.'

'If I knew what we were looking for, it might help,' Hansfree said.

'Children's shoes.'

Hansfree thought for a moment, then broke into a grin. 'Now I get it,' he said.

Having exhausted the local supply of charity shops, they drove to a large supermarket on the outskirts of a town. There was a row of recycling bins at the side of the access

road, including two for clothes and shoes. Both were full
to overflowing and several carrier bags had been left on
the ground around them. This time Harper's search was
rewarded and he returned to the van holding a carrier bag
containing two pairs of children's trainers. 'We've hit the
jackpot,' he said, with a smile.

They drove back to the industrial site, and as they walked
towards the compound, Harper paused long enough to snap
a thin branch from a spindly tree planted in a feeble attempt
at landscaping the site. He carried it with him as they moved
on towards the compound. The area was still silent and
deserted but the dog was no less alert and watchful.

Harper ignored it and, keeping his feet clear of the muddy
puddles in front of the compound's gates, he took the
trainers out of the carrier bag and placed them on the
ground, positioning them in as natural a way as he could,
then putting his own foot on top of each one in turn. He
pressed them down into the mud so that when he lifted
them up again a pair of child-size footprints had been
imprinted in the mud. He repeated the process a couple
of dozen times altogether, until it appeared that a small
group of children had paused by the gates, then moved
towards the fence and stood there for some time. To reinforce that impression, he took the crushed can from his
pocket and tossed it onto the ground, then crumpled the
empty Haribo bag into a ball and placed it at the foot of
the fence next to the gate, hooking it onto a loose strand
of wire so it couldn't blow away. He poked the thin branch
through the bars of the gate. The dog pounced on it at
once, biting it savagely and, as Harper tried to pull it back,
it broke off the end with a vicious jerk of its head.

Harper withdrew what was left of the branch and examined it carefully. The broken end was now scored with the dog's tooth marks. He nodded to himself and dropped the stick on the ground next to the gate. 'Right,' he said. 'Job done. Let's get to work.' He left Hansfree taunting the dog by rattling the fence while he quietly moved to the opposite side of the compound. The dog was puzzled and didn't know which target to pursue first, repeatedly switching its gaze from one man to the other, but Hansfree kept goading it and forced it to focus on him by repeatedly moving towards the fence and rattling it. Every time he touched the fence, the dog hurled itself at the other side of it with such force that it left a few tufts of its fur caught on the wire. It became even more confused when Hansfree put his prosthetic hands through the gate and tried to entice the dog to bite them. It needed no encouragement but found its jaws closing on steel fingers rather than flesh-and-blood ones. While the dog's full attention was focused on Hansfree, Harper seized the moment to climb up and jump over the fence at the back of the compound.

As he hit the ground, he immediately crouched in a boxer's stance, bracing himself for the onslaught from the dog. It had heard the thud as his feet hit the ground and immediately stopped biting at Hansfree's prosthetic hands. It spun around and raced across the yard towards Harper. A few feet from him, it launched itself into the air, its hackles raised, yellow teeth bared and jaws gaping, ready to tear out Harper's throat.

As the dog approached, Harper forced himself to suppress any fear and kept a cold, savage focus on the animal that was hurtling towards him. At the last possible moment before it struck him, so close that he could feel the dog's foul breath on his face, Harper grabbed both of its front legs in his hands. Just as the dog's jaws filled his vision, he put all his strength into one vicious jerk, first forcing the dog's legs inwards and then yanking them apart. He heard a distinct crack as the animal's sternum and ribcage collapsed and the jagged ends of the bones were driven deep into its heart. It was already dead as its momentum sent it crashing into Harper. He fell onto his back, with the dog pressing down on his chest.

Harper exhaled in a long, juddering breath, then pushed the beast to one side and got to his feet. It took several seconds of deep, controlled breathing before he had recovered enough to carry on. He stared down at the animal, examining the fur on its chest for any external sign of what had killed it. It looked far less fearsome in death and seemed diminished in size, more like a discarded and dilapidated fur coat than the savage and powerful creature it had been just moments before. Harper hoisted it onto his shoulders and walked over to the fence, close to where he had left the footprints. He hefted the dog up and poked its front two legs through the fence, making it look as if it had hurled itself there and become entangled.

'I get it,' said Hansfree. 'Kids tease the dog, dog goes crazy, dog dies. Think they'll buy that?'

'I don't see why not,' said Harper.

'I didn't think you were going to kill it with your bare hands,' said Hansfree. 'Where did you learn that trick?'

'In the Paras,' said Harper. 'But that's the first time I've done it for real. They're vulnerable once they leap. They lose all traction and they can't see what's underneath them.

Then it's just a matter of timing. Now let's get a move on. It's already almost two o'clock and we've still got a lot of work to do.'

Hansfree went to the gate and passed the drill and the fibre-optic endoscope through to Harper, who took them back to the unit while Hansfree kept watch. He walked around to the back of the first of the two sea-containers, and drilled a narrow-diameter hole through the steel wall near the top so that it was well above anyone's eyeline. He fed the endoscope with the light attachment through the hole and put his eye to the scope. The container was partly filled with uniforms – British Army by the look of them – in plastic bags. Next to them was a stack of wooden boxes. Harper moved the endoscope to get a better look. He caught his breath as he saw that the boxes were marked PE-4A. PE-4 was the British equivalent of the widely available plastic explosive C-4, a mixture of explosive with a plastic binder and a plasticiser to make it as malleable as Plasticine, so that it could be formed into any shape desired. An explosion could only be initiated by the combination of intense heat and a shock wave produced by a detonator. All manufacturers of C-4 and its variants, including PE-4A, routinely added to the mix a chemical tag or marker, a constituent unique to that particular batch of explosive, so that forensic teams could trace the batch's origins if it was later used in a terrorist attack or any other unauthorised way.

Harper knew that plastic explosives were not hard to find on the international black market in arms, providing you had the necessary funds, but they were almost always from corrupt sources in Russia and the former Soviet republics. However, the PE-4A labelling showed that this batch was of British origin, which was a worry.

There were other items inside the shipping container, but even with the endoscope it wasn't possible for Harper to identify all of them. Harper withdrew it, removed the light from the end and swapped it for a miniaturised camera. He then fed the endoscope back through the hole in the container wall and took a number of photographs for later analysis.

The contents of the second container were equally alarming. It held a variety of weapons, including a number of British SA-80 rifles and a tripod-mounted AT-4 Spigot anti-tank missile, a piece of ex-Soviet equipment that, despite its age, still packed a very formidable punch. The SA-80s were the L85 IW version, with IW standing for 'individual weapon'. It was the standard issue rifle for the British armed forces.

'With what they've got in the other container,' Hansfree said, 'that is some very heavy-duty kit.'

'Right,' Harper said. 'And you don't need to put something like this together just to carry out some penny-ante operation. They must be planning something big and we need to discover what it is pronto – before we find out the hard way when the bombs go off.'

Hansfree recorded everything they had seen and made a note of the serial numbers stencilled on the outside of the containers, so that their origins and the route by which they had come to the site could be traced and their onward movement tracked, if the jihadists later transferred them to a different site.

While Hansfree was doing that, Harper did a quick walk-around of the main warehouse unit. There was only one way in, which was locked and shuttered. He spent several more minutes carefully erasing every trace of his presence, including scooping up a little mud from a puddle and rubbing it over the drill holes he had made in the container walls, obscuring the thin line of bright metal that had been just visible around the edge of each hole. He slipped off his jacket and dragged it along the ground, using it like a brush to erase his footprints and the marks where the dog had dug its paws into the ground as it launched itself towards him, then took a final, careful look around, searching for any other incriminating traces he might have missed. He climbed back over the fence and walked away, with Hansfree, at a steady pace, without any visible sign of haste but putting distance between himself and the compound as quickly as he could.

44

As soon as he got back to central London, Hansfree dropped Harper close to an all-night internet café in a side street on the fringes of Soho, a few blocks north of Leicester Square. As usual, Harper seated himself at the furthest terminal from the cash desk, then left a message for Charlotte Button using the usual drafts folder technique. He kept it short and sweet: *We need to talk. Are you in London?*

He ordered a coffee and sipped it as he waited for a response. After half an hour he gave up and went back to his room in Bayswater. In the early hours of the morning his phone beeped and he rolled over to look at the screen. It was a text message: *You've got mail*. He cursed, got out of bed, dressed, and headed out. He managed to find a black cab and had the driver drop him in Soho. The area was still busy, with more than its fair share of gay couples walking home arm in arm, and Harper received a number of admiring glances, which he managed to ignore, on the way to the internet café.

Button's message was in the draft folder: *I'm in London but am pretty sure I'm being followed most of the time. I can lose them if necessary but if I slip up and they see you then we will have all sorts of problems. Call me on this number on the hour from six a.m. onwards.* He scribbled it down on a piece of paper, rearranging the last four digits, then deleted the file.

He put a new message in the drafts folder, *Six it is,* and signed off. He looked at his watch. It was four o'clock, which meant he had two hours to kill. He bought another coffee and passed the time on the internet, reading up on the weapons and explosives he'd seen in the containers and studying Google Maps of the area.

At five he caught a black cab to Bayswater, which, like Soho, was one of the areas of the city that never seemed to sleep. He spent forty-five minutes running all the anti-surveillance techniques he knew, made easier by the fact that the streets were much quieter now than they were during the daytime, then walked to Paddington station. At precisely six o'clock he called the number from a public phone on the station concourse and Button answered on the third ring. 'I'm so sorry about the cloak-and-dagger,' she said.

'Who's after you?' he asked.

'Israelis, I think. An Israeli company anyway. Though it looks as if they've subcontracted it to a UK security firm.'

'So not the government?'

'I don't know. They could be doing it at arm's length. Same as they did with the Pool. And whoever it is has access to airline manifests. I'm working on it but I can't risk putting you and your team in the firing line, so I'm going to have to steer clear of you until it's resolved.'

'I appreciate that,' said Harper. 'But there's a lot you need to know.'

'I'm listening.'

'Your man is getting ready to move. No question. He has a team in place, some Asian, some white, and he has two shipping containers filled with gear, including British Army uniforms, SA-80 rifles, anti-tank missiles and a hell of a lot of plastic explosives.'

'Explosives?'

'PE-4A, which can only have been sourced – I'm assuming stolen – from within the UK.'

'And where is this equipment?'

'An industrial estate near Gravesend, not far from the Dartford River Crossing. This is big. Huge. He's got arms and explosives and jihadists ready to go, and with the best will in the world all I have is a team of surveillance people. If you're serious about wanting to stop your man, then all you need to do is make one phone call. There's all the evidence you need to send him away for a long time.'

'It's not about sending him away,' said Button. 'The contract is for a cancellation.'

'Cancellation' was Button-speak for a killing. Someone was paying to have Caleb McGovan killed. Harper didn't know who would be paying the bill, but he could think of lots of reasons why someone would prefer a home-grown jihadist to be in the ground rather than on trial. But at the end of the day it wasn't his place to question the contract: he was just a hired hand.

'That's not a problem,' said Harper. 'I know where he is and where he usually goes, I can do it from the back of a motorcycle anytime I want. But what about the jihadists? What about his plan? Isn't that a concern?'

'Not to the person who wants the cancellation,' said Button. 'I can't go into details but it's a very personal matter and seeing McGovan behind bars really won't cut it. He wants a cancellation, end of story.'

'And that's fair enough,' said Harper. 'McGovan has clearly crossed over to the dark side, and he's exactly the sort of target you would have been sent after by HM Government in the good old days. I'm not saying he doesn't merit cancellation, just pointing out there's a lot in play here. He's got home-grown jihadists working with him, and it looks as if someone else is pulling the strings. Someone behind the scenes is putting this together because McGovan himself isn't doing enough. The industrial unit near Gravesend, for instance. He can't have arranged that. The shipping containers. The money that's paying for it all. Yes, I can cancel McGovan but all the rest will still be in place.'

Button didn't say anything and, for a moment, Harper thought that he'd lost the connection. 'Are you still there?'

'I'm here. Just considering my options.'

'Look, we know McGovan is bad. No question. Give me the go-ahead for the cancellation, then make a phone call to the authorities.'

'Except that if you cancel McGovan tomorrow, the rest will presumably scatter. You're not going to keep a street-shooting quiet, are you? The cops will be called in, he'll be identified and, yes, we'll get the containers but we'll lose the jihadists and the mastermind who's behind it.'

'Maybe. But if we continue to let them run and the shit hits the fan – what then? If you were privy to what was going to happen and didn't do anything, we'll all be accomplices before the fact. People could die. A lot of people.'

'I hear what you're saying. Let me take advice and get back to you. In the meantime, keep a close eye on things. And keep me in the loop.'

'I've got to be honest, that's bloody difficult to do with all this Secret Squirrel stuff.'

'I don't think I've got any choice,' said Button. 'If the people after me are government-sponsored they'll be able to eavesdrop on any mobile I use.'

'So you're sticking to landlines or the draft folder? That's a pain. A real pain. How about this? Get a throwaway mobile but don't use it. Send me the number. If there's an emergency I'll call you, you can ditch it immediately afterwards and get another. It'll be expensive but I guess you can afford it.'

'I'll do that now,' she promised, and ended the call.

45

Harper went straight from Paddington to the ops room to brief the team. It was just Hansfree, the two Barrys and Maggie, as Hansfree was keeping his new hires at a distance, briefing them separately by radio and phone. His man Reggie had spent the night in a van outside the club and was due to be relieved by Nancy. Harper briefed them on what he had found in the containers and Hansfree used one of his laptops to show them the video Harper had taken through the endoscope.

'That explosive is a worry,' said Barry Whisper, stating the obvious.

'It's all a worry,' said Maggie. 'Especially the uniforms. What the hell are they planning?'

'Hopefully we'll find out soon enough,' said Harper. 'We're heading out there as soon as we've got fixed up with some four-by-fours. Barry Big, can you get on that now?'

'No problem,' he said, pulling out his phone. 'Any preferences?'

'Just something that can outperform the Land Rovers the bad guys have,' said Harper. 'Hansfree, what's the story with the camera I installed?'

Hansfree tapped on his keyboard and showed them the feed from the camera that Harper had fitted to the concrete tower overlooking the target unit. It wasn't a great picture and unfortunately didn't give anything like a clear view of the containers. 'That's a pity,' said Harper. He patted Hansfree's shoulder. 'How good are the drones you were talking about?'

'As good as anything the authorities have,' said Hansfree. 'But what about piloting them? Have you got experience with drones?'

'Enough,' said Harper. 'I was on special ops with the Paras in Afghanistan and I got to fly them then. I doubt they've changed much.'

'If anything, they're easier now,' said Hansfree. 'The new models have self-stabilising sensors and GPS hover capability.'

'Then hook me up and I'll get back there,' said Harper. 'The rest of you guys can follow me down once you've got the four-by-fours sorted.'

46

Harper had no trouble launching the drone Hansfree had given him, and it took him just a few minutes to relearn the skills he had picked up in the Paras, adjusting the throttle to increase and decrease the speed, and altering the pitch, roll and yaw of the four rotors to send the drone rising, falling or moving across the sky. It was illegal to fly a drone above five hundred feet in Britain without official permission, but the legality of his actions was the least of Harper's concerns and he sent the drone soaring higher until it was no more than a speck in the sky, and the sound of its motor was lost in the traffic noise from the main road on the far side of the industrial site. He had been controlling it manually but now he set the controls to 'Loiter', causing the drone to hold to a specific GPS setting, and maintain its position stationary over the industrial unit. He called Hansfree and within five minutes Hansfree reported that he was picking up the video feed from the drone's camera.

Harper had a laptop with him and Hansfree talked him through connecting it to the video feed. Within a few minutes he was able to view the astonishingly clear pictures from above. He brought the drone down and stored it in the boot of his BMW.

The rest of the team arrived a couple of hours later, Barry Big in a Range Rover, Barry Whisper and Maggie in a Jeep Cherokee. They parked half a mile away from the industrial unit. They didn't have long to wait. At ten o'clock Harper's earpiece crackled into life. 'Tango One is in motion,' Hansfree said. 'He's heading east.'

'Vehicle?'

'He was picked up by Yankee Four in a white Honda. We're on it.'

A succession of messages let Harper and the rest of the team keep track of McGovan's progress across London and out along the south bank of the Thames. When they were ten minutes away, Harper launched the drone and called his team to full alert as their subject entered the industrial area and drove to the site.

Two other men were with McGovan: Yankee Four was driving and an unidentified Asian male was sitting in the back. Harper watched on his laptop as McGovan and the jihadists got out of the vehicle. McGovan unlocked the main gate and the two men pulled it back. As the car drove through, McGovan spotted the dead dog.

Harper watched him examine the corpse. He straightened, looked around, then peered through the fence. The quality of the video was good enough for Harper to see what McGovan was peering at – the drinks can, sweets packet and kids' footprints.

McGovan waved for Yankee Four to park the car, then jogged out of the gate and around to where the footprints were. Harper saw him pick up the stick bearing the tooth marks of the dog, then peer at the clumps of the dog's fur still clinging to the fence. McGovan squatted on his haunches to study the footprints in the mud, then went back through the gate and took another look at the dead animal. He examined the dog minutely, then began a painstaking search of the area, paying particular attention to the locks on the sea-containers. Eventually he seemed satisfied and beckoned to one of the Asians. Together they pulled the dog off the fence, carried it, now rigid with rigor mortis, and dumped it in a nearby rubbish skip.

Harper heaved a huge sigh of relief. 'He's bought into it,' he said, into his shoulder mic. 'We're in business. Stand by, stand by.'

Slowly, over the course of several more hours, more men turned up at the industrial estate. Three arrived in another white Honda, all Asian. Two white men, who didn't look long out of their teens, arrived in a van. Two of the Asians began working on the Land Rovers but the rest either went inside the containers or into the industrial unit. There was no way of monitoring their activities because even the sophisticated spy drone couldn't see through steel.

'Are you getting all these new arrivals?' Harper asked Hansfree.

'I am,' said Hansfree over the radio. 'They're all new faces. Someone is overseeing this, for sure. Tango One hasn't seen them before.'

At midday a delivery van also dropped off a number of cardboard containers at the site. By narrowing the focus of the telescopic camera on the drone and zooming it in to the maximum, Harper managed to read off the numbers, and within a few minutes, Hansfree had identified the boxes as army patrol rations.

In the afternoon the jihadists began transferring most

of the stores and equipment from the containers to the Land Rovers. The task took several hours, and when they had finished they all disappeared inside one of the containers, reappearing with armfuls of uniforms that they carried inside the warehouse. Maggie left her vehicle and came to sit in Harper's BMW to watch the feed from the drone as she snacked on a cheese sandwich and a can of Red Bull.

Some thirty minutes later, eight of the men came out. Four were Asian, three were white and one was the mixed-race man they had called Yankee Four. They were all dressed in British Army issue military camouflage gear with webbing and backpacks to match. They lined up and McGovan inspected them.

'They're getting ready to move,' Harper said into his radio. 'On your toes, everyone. Hansfree, I count eight. There are ten jihadists, right?'

'Affirmative,' said Hansfree. 'The other two must still be inside the warehouse.'

Harper brought the drone back down, flying it well away from the area before descending. He stored it in the boot of the BMW, along with the controller.

'I no longer have eyeball,' said Harper.

'I have,' said Barry Big. 'Tango One is carrying out a final inspection of the Land Rovers. Now they're getting on board. Four in each vehicle.'

'What about Tango One?' asked Harper.

'Tango One is getting into a blue VW Jetta.'

'That means they're leaving two men behind. Okay, Barry Big and Barry Whisper, you follow the convoy. Hansfree, you need to keep a team in surveillance here.'

'Understood,' said Hansfree. 'Reggie and Nancy are already in place and I have another team of four en route.'

'And the trackers are still functioning?'

'I'm looking at them as we speak.'

'Game on, then,' said Harper. He looked across at Maggie. 'You might as well stay with me,' he said.

'I could do with my bag,' she said.

Harper drove her to her SUV. She nipped out, grabbed her bag, climbed back in and they headed off in pursuit of McGovan and his convoy.

47

A few minutes later, the targets were driving counter-clockwise on the M25 and soon afterwards they turned onto the A1, heading north. It was an easy follow for Harper and his team: the men were travelling in typical military-convoy style, driving with fully lit headlamps, sticking religiously to every speed limit. After four hours they stopped at a service station to refuel the vehicles. They also filled several onboard jerry-cans. Harper could see that McGovan was very careful to ensure that only the non-Asian jihadists left the vehicles while the refuelling was taking place.

To Harper's surprise, just north of Leeds the convoy split into two, with McGovan's VW peeling off west from the A1.

Maggie told Barry Big and Barry Whisper to keep after the Land Rovers while Harper followed McGovan.

McGovan drove past Harrogate, then off the main road onto a narrow lane. On the skyline ahead of them, Harper could see the tops of the radomes of the American listening station on Menwith Hill. It was a still, chilly day, and the ground mist clinging to the moorland around the base gave the white radomes dotting the site an even more unearthly air than usual, as if they were alien craft hovering just above the ground.

Harper dropped back even further behind the VW as he saw it slow, then pull onto the grass verge. He watched as McGovan climbed out and began observing the listening station through a pair of binoculars. Menwith Hill was supposedly an RAF establishment – the sign by the gates proclaimed as much – but 90 per cent of the operatives manning the computers in the hardened concrete bunkers beneath those radomes were US personnel, and Menwith Hill could scarcely have been more American if it had been flown across the Atlantic and dropped in the middle of Kansas.

Warning notices hung from the fence every few metres and CCTV cameras on every stanchion kept watch for intruders.

'He doesn't seem worried about the CCTV,' said Maggie.

'He's standing in a blind spot,' said Harper. 'Plus the security is a hangover from the days when there was a peace camp next to the site and the guards were on perpetual full alert. But the women protesters were evicted years ago and the peace camp bulldozed so I think everyone is a bit more relaxed these days.' McGovan stayed at the site for no more than a couple of minutes, then made a U-turn and drove back the way he had come.

As soon as he saw the Jetta begin to turn, Harper drove down the lane and up a muddy farm track to a point where a copse of trees shielded him from view. He waited until the VW had passed the end of the track, then pulled out and continued to follow it as McGovan returned to the northbound A1. Driving quickly, he soon caught up with the Land Rovers that had been maintaining the same stately pace as they headed north.

As the day wore on, they continued driving still further north and crossed the county border into Northumberland. They passed to the west of Newcastle and, turning off the A1, drove deep into the Cheviots to within a few miles of the Scottish border. Harper had been in no doubt for some time about where they were heading and it was confirmed as, not long after dark, the convoy turned onto the road leading to the Otterburn Ranges, the vast training area used by the British Army.

They passed through Otterburn village, but instead of approaching the main entrance to the sprawling 60,000-acre site, with the squat guardhouse behind high steel gates topped with razor wire, they carried on along the edge of the ranges, skirting them to the east. They passed occasional conifer plantations, barely visible as belts of deeper black against the dark moorland.

They drove on even further into the wilderness, along minor roads that were now completely deserted but for the Land Rovers and the four-by-fours of the surveillance team trailing them. To avoid being detected, Harper and his team had switched off their lights and were driving using passive night goggles, which made the road show up as an eerie yellow-orange ribbon of brighter light in the surrounding moorland. The eyes of rabbits and other animals watching in the darkness shone out like torch beams.

They followed the convoy for several more miles until they turned off down a track towards the main firing range and drove into a valley, a narrow stretch of wooded, gently rising low ground between two parallel ridges. It was flanked on three sides by higher ground and visible only from directly below. The valley had a screen of fir trees close to the road, with a barrier to prevent civilian traffic entering the range's danger area, and McGovan left one of the Land Rovers there, behind the barrier but still in clear sight of any passing traffic. He also posted a sentry in full military gear, holding a rifle.

While Barry Big and Barry Whisper drove off to find an observation point on the far side of the valley, Harper found a track where he could leave the BMW out of sight. He and Maggie got out of the car and moved silently through the woods to a point where, still using their night-vision goggles, they could observe the targets. 'What the hell are they up to?' Maggie whispered, as they watched McGovan posting his sentry at the barrier. 'They're just asking to be challenged, out in the open like that.'

'They're hiding in plain sight, and the chance of anyone challenging them there is pretty remote,' said Harper. 'To any casual observer, even a passing military patrol, it'll look like another small military deployment and there are always plenty of those going on here. Once you've got yourself onto the ranges, and it's not hard because security is pretty lax, all you have to do is mount a guard, look like you know what you're doing, stay out of the red-flagged areas when the guns are firing and no one will bother you, especially here.'

'Why here in particular?' she said.

'Because it's so vast. There's a firing range down the middle so long and wide that it's the only place in Britain where the army can test fire its AS-90 self-propelled artillery pieces and the M-270 Multiple Launch Rocket Systems.

They have a maximum range of forty miles, and even with a reduced propellant charge to shorten their range, they have to be tested here because none of the other army ranges is big enough for them to be fired without the risk of wiping out a few civilian motorists or hikers enjoying a day out just beyond the ranges. There are four hundred square miles of rough moorland out there on those ranges plus some other very weird stuff. There are long-abandoned replicas of Belfast streets and Londonderry apartment blocks, where the troops used to practise before deploying to Northern Ireland, and much more recent replicas of Iraqi streets, and villages in Afghanistan as well. I kid you not, if there were some mulberry trees, a few kites flying in the sky overhead and the mountains of the Hindu Kush in the distance, you'd swear you were actually in Afghanistan.'

'You still haven't answered my question. Why are they here?'

'I'm pretty sure that the listening station on Menwith Hill is a target. That's what McGovan was looking at earlier. But I'm guessing he's here to do some training with them. It looks to me like this is the first time he's met his team and he needs to know how they'll react under pressure.'

'So we watch and wait?'

'I'm afraid so. Make yourself as comfortable as you can, though I appreciate that's not going to be easy.'

48

Once his team had settled down for the night, Harper phoned Hansfree for a private conversation. During active operations Hansfree rarely slept and Harper pictured the man sitting hunched over his computers, fuelled by Red Bull and coffee.

'Two more have arrived at the unit,' said Hansfree. 'Both white. It happened after dark so we don't have any usable pictures. And I've managed to track the serial numbers of the containers. Interesting route. In reverse we have Felixstowe, Rotterdam and Karachi. They had previously been used by the Ministry of Defence to ship stores to Camp Bastion in Afghanistan, and then, supposedly empty, they were shipped back to the UK. So the only question remaining is how the hell the weapons came to be in the hands of McGovan's mates in ISIS.'

'Who knows?' Harper said. 'The Spigot is probably old Russian Army stock left behind after the Soviet pull-out from Afghanistan in 1989. But the odds are that the SA-80s, the plastic explosives and the rest of the kit, were either stolen or captured in Afghanistan, though it's also possible that they were made in Peshawar, in north-west Pakistan. I passed through there a while ago. There are about three million people in the city and it seemed like half of them were involved in the arms trade. They claimed they could copy and make any weapon in the world. I heard one arms trader boasting that he could even make a copy of a Stinger missile. It sounded like bullshit to me but, having seen what else they can produce, I wouldn't have wanted to bet too much money on it.'

'One other thing,' Hansfree said. 'Did you see the metal stuff in the first container you looked at?'

Harper frowned. 'What metal stuff?'

'I've got some stills.' His claws tapped on the keyboard and a shot of some metal brackets filled the screen. 'They look like shelving or something?'

Harper grinned. 'Nah, they're for making shaped charges. You use them to gain explosive entry to a building by blowing out the doors or windows, or blasting holes in the walls. You pack the brackets with plastic explosive to make the charge, then set them off with electric detonators. It's a bit of an art. The SAS are masters at it but we did it in the Paras. When you use them, you have to tamp the charge with sandbags or something similar to make sure the explosion goes the way you want it to go or it can dissipate into the line of least resistance. They're the dog's bollocks when it comes to getting you into a heavily defended building. I've made one or two shaped charges in the past myself and I'm sure McGovan will have done too. The question is, what the hell is he planning to do with shaped charges?'

'What do you want me to do with the extra surveillance bodies?' asked Hansfree. 'Do you need anyone else up there?'

'Keep them on the industrial unit,' said Harper, and

ended the call. He got out of his car for some fresh air while he decided what to do about Charlie Button. He needed to tell her what was going on but standard operating procedure was for him to initiate contact through the draft email folder and he was miles away from the nearest internet café. He could access the folder through the laptop in the car, but if she was being tracked by any of the government agencies there was a chance they would follow any electronic trail to him. Using proxies wouldn't help if GCHQ was on her case, and if they traced his laptop they were perfectly capable of accessing all the files on his hard drive.

He paced up and down for a while, looking up at the blanket of stars overhead. There was little light pollution or cloud cover so he felt as if he could see to the end of the universe. The more he stared at a section of the night sky, the more stars became visible.

'Penny for them?' said a voice behind him, and Harper jumped. It was Barry Whisper, who was as quiet when he moved as when he spoke.

'Bloody hell, Barry, don't creep up on me like that,' he said. 'And why have you left your post?'

'The bad guys have bedded down for the night. Just a couple of sentries, and I guess they'll rotate them. They're here to train, right?'

'Looks like it.'

'For how long?'

'Fucked if I know, Barry. Why?'

'Because we've no water, no toilet facilities, no food. We're going to be in a pretty poor state tomorrow, and even worse the next day.'

'What are you suggesting?'

He shrugged. 'Like I said, they're bedded down for the night. I could take a run out to the main road, see if I can find an all-night place. Stock up on food and water, plastic bags to shit in, all the basics.'

Harper nodded. 'Good call.'

'You want something?'

Harper grinned. 'Anything with caffeine in it.'

'I hear you.' Barry Whisper slipped away into the darkness as quietly as he had arrived. Harper unzipped his hip-pack and took out a Samsung smartphone. He hadn't used it, or the Sim card it contained. He switched it on, launched the browser and went to the draft file. There was a message from Charlotte Button, with a list of six telephone numbers, presumably throwaway mobiles she had purchased. He took out another phone, switched it on and tapped the numbers into a memo, rearranging the final digits as a security measure.

He paced up and down, considering his options. He really didn't like calling Button mobile to mobile, even when they were both using throwaways. It wasn't just the danger of being overheard – GCHQ was able to listen out for specific voices and home in on them – it was the fact that GPS technology now meant that a phone's location could be pinpointed to within a few feet, with or without an active Sim card. It also meant a direct traceable link between Button and Harper, which wasn't good for either of them. But he had to talk to her, and soon, and the nearest internet café was probably fifty miles away, certainly not open at that time of night.

He cursed under his breath and tapped out the first of the numbers she had given him. It rang out for more than a minute before she answered. From the sound of it she was inside. Music was playing, something classical. 'It's me,' he said. Neither would be using names.

'Problem?'

'They've moved from the industrial estate,' said Harper. 'They're up near the Scottish border on the Otterburn ranges. Looks like they're going to do some training. They're planning some serious mischief, and the longer you let it run, the more the risk someone is going to get hurt.'

'How many are there?'

'There's Tango One and eight other males, some Asian, some white. There are another four back at the industrial unit in Gravesend. We've only identified three. If it was me, I'd pass this on to the SAS and get them in, slot the lot of them.'

'Unfortunately the SAS don't do that any more,' said Button. 'That's why they created the Pool.'

'I can't take on nine men armed with automatic weapons and explosives,' said Harper. 'Not when one of them is former SAS.'

'I don't need you to cancel them all,' said Button. 'Just Tango One.'

'So that's a go on Tango One, is it?'

'It is. Whenever you're ready.'

'The problem with that is he's now on an army training ground surrounded by heavily armed jihadists. It isn't a case of being able to swing by on a motorcycle and put one in the back of his head, like it was in London.'

'Can you get to him?'

'At the moment, no. At least, not without considerable risk to myself and my team. We've got one handgun between us.'

'So what are your options?'

Harper sighed. 'Watch and wait. At least while they're on the range they're only a danger to themselves. Tango One had a good look at the Menwith Hill listening station on the way up so I think he's considering that as a target. Once they're on the move we'll have a better idea of what they're up to and I might be able to get closer.'

'Do that, then.'

'My advice to you would be to get the professionals in. If this blows up and they find out that you knew about it, you could be in deep shit.'

'While I appreciate your concern, I'm in deep shit anyway at the moment. And my problem is that I don't know who I can trust and who I can't.'

'I hope you're not including me in the can't-be-trusted list.'

'You know that's not what I meant. If there is government involvement, something like this could be the last nail in my coffin.'

'Or it could be your salvation. You ride in and save the day. They might give you a medal.'

'They might. Or they might look at what happens to Tango One and start asking questions. I just want this to go away. At the moment I feel like I'm under a microscope and it's making me very nervous.'

'How is your situation?'

'It's being looked at by a couple of friends, here and in the US. Once I know who's on my case I'll know how to deal with it.'

'You're sure I can't do more to help?'

'Just take care of Tango One. And keep me in the loop. That'll be more than enough.'

'What about intel on the guys Tango One has hooked up with? Do you want that?'

'It can wait until you're back in London,' she said.

Harper ended the call and took the phone apart. He slid out the Sim card, broke it in half, pulled out the battery and threw it away, then stamped on the phone until it was beyond repair. He scraped a hole in the soil and buried it. As he straightened up he saw that Maggie had got out of the car and was watching him, clearly bemused. 'Bad news?' she said.

49

Harper and his team took it in turns to doze or catnap for a couple of hours during the night. At just after three thirty Barry Whisper returned with several carrier bags of provisions. The only place he'd been able to find open was a shop attached to an all-night filling station so he had packs of sandwiches, other snacks, bottles of water, cans of coffee and Red Bull. On the hygiene front he'd bought some toothpaste, toothbrushes, disposable razors and cans of shaving foam, plus several packs of wet wipes. He had persuaded the cashier to let him have a dozen small plastic bags, though he hadn't explained what he'd be using them for.

Well before first light the next morning, they were in position and ready to monitor the activities of the targets in the valley. Harper launched the drone and had it hover high overhead so he could watch what they were doing on his laptop.

Tutored by McGovan, five of the jihadists were taught to strip and assemble their SA-80s, and while that was going on, a further three-man team did 'dry' practice training with the Spigot anti-tank missile, assembling it, stripping it down, reassembling it, and practising range-finding, loading, reloading, and sighting – everything, short of actually firing it.

After their basic training in weapon-handling, the jihadists moved on to fire and movement drills using live ammunition, with some of the group providing covering fire while the rest were advancing towards a notional target. Known in the military as 'pepper-potting', it was the basis of all infantry manoeuvres, but the surveillance team concluded that it was as foreign to McGovan's raw jihadi recruits as Ancient Greek. However, while they were raw and untutored, they weren't lacking in bravery. Even with live fire whistling a few inches over their heads, Harper didn't see a single one flinch, or hesitate for a second in rising from cover when McGovan gave the order to move.

Screened by the terrain of the valley and the belts of forestry that surrounded it, the jihadists' training continued without any interruption from outsiders. The noise of their activities, even the rattle and crack of live firing from semi-automatics, was lost in the heavy crump of artillery and mortar rounds, and the barrages of small-arms fire from the main ranges on the other side of the hill, where various army groups and new recruits were being put through their paces.

The jihadists' training went on until just before last light, when McGovan ended the practice drills. He formed his jihadists into a circle around him and spoke to them for almost half an hour. The surveillance team could not pick up what was being said but it was obvious from the jihadists' body language – the way they sat motionless, not speaking but listening intently – that he was delivering the final briefing before their long-planned attack. When he had finished speaking, the jihadists embraced each other, then packed up all their weapons and equipment and began loading them back on to the Land Rovers. Harper concentrated on identifying which vehicle held the Spigot anti-tank missile – he was sure it would be the crucial piece of the jigsaw.

By now Harper was reasonably sure that the jihadists intended to attack the listening station on Menwith Hill, using the Spigot missile from long distance, followed by a short-range attack, probably using suicide bombers and shaped charges to gain entry, but he wouldn't know for sure until they were on the move.

50

Harper was woken just after dawn by a warning from Barry Big in his earpiece. 'Look lively, Lex, the Tangos are getting ready to leave.'

Harper was sleeping in the back of the BMW and he sat up, rubbing his face. 'What's happening?'

'They're loading up the Land Rovers. Looks like they're leaving the range.'

Maggie was awake. She had been napping in the front passenger seat and pulled it into the upright position.

'Barry Whisper, you hear this?' asked Harper.

'Roger that,' said Barry Whisper. 'I'm ready to go.'

'Okay, Barry Big take point, Barry Whisper car two. Maggie and I'll bring up the rear. Hansfree, do you still have the trackers?'

'Both are running just fine,' said Hansfree.

'Let's give them plenty of space, then,' said Harper. Maggie shifted over to the driving seat. Harper grabbed a bottle of water as he got out of the car. He rinsed his mouth, spat, then got into the front passenger seat. 'Where are they, Barry Whisper?'

'Heading for Otterburn village, probably towards the A1.'

Maggie put the car in gear and they headed off in pursuit.

Barry Big and Barry Whisper took it in turns to give updates on the progress of the three-vehicle convoy as it headed south. The Land Rovers followed the strict discipline of a military convoy, driving with headlights on and observing all the speed limits. McGovan's VW led the way but his headlights were off.

As they got closer to the intersection with the A59, Barry Big closed the gap with the convoy. He kept up a running commentary over the final mile: they would be taking the westbound route if they were heading back to Menwith Hill.

'The Land Rovers are turning off,' said Barry Big, as the convoy reached the intersection. 'But Tango One is not indicating and is not changing direction. Repeat, Tango One is leaving the convoy, continuing south along the A1.'

Harper's mind raced. It could be that McGovan was in a rush to get to the target first or that he was heading somewhere completely different. If that was the case there was a risk they would lose him because, unlike the Land Rovers, there was no tracking device on his car. 'Okay, I'll go with Tango One, you stay with the Land Rovers.' He motioned for Maggie to pick up the pace and she stamped on the accelerator.

'To do what exactly?' asked Barry Big.

'Just stick with them,' said Harper.

'Roger that, but they're armed to the teeth and all I've got is my wit and charm.'

'I'll send reinforcements. Just keep eyeballing them,' said Harper. 'Barry Whisper, you stay behind Barry Big. Hansfree, you're still tracking them?'

'Affirmative,' said Hansfree.

'Keep me posted. Maggie and I'll be with Tango One.'

As Maggie accelerated, Harper unzipped his hip-pack, took out the phone he'd used to store Button's numbers and tapped one out. It rang out for a minute and she didn't answer. He redialled and this time she picked up the call. 'The RAF station at Menwith Hill is going to be attacked,' he said.

'When?'

'The jihadists are heading there with all the gear. But Tango One is still driving south and I'm going with him.'

'What do you think's happening?'

'I'd say they're definitely getting ready to attack Menwith Hill but that might be a diversion. Get everyone's attention focused up here while they do something bigger down south.'

'What about Tango One? Are you still on schedule for the cancellation?'

'If I get him on his own, yes. That's more likely now that the main group has split off. But as I said, at the moment I've no idea where he's going. You need to take care of Menwith Hill otherwise it's going to be a bloodbath.'

'The professionals are on their way,' said Button. 'What about you?'

'I'm following Tango One. He's on his own so he's less of a threat now. But I've no idea what he's up to. You need to get Menwith Hill sorted.'

'I heard you the first time. I'll deal with it. You just concentrate on McGovan.'

She ended the call. Harper peered through the windscreen. There was still no sign of the VW Jetta and he was about to tell Maggie to put her foot down even further when she gestured with her chin. 'There he is. Just in front of that coach.' She eased back on the accelerator.

'Nice job,' he said. 'All right, everybody, we have eyes on Tango One, heading south.'

51

McGovan kept his VW at a steady 70 m.p.h. and Maggie had no trouble following him as he headed down the A1. He joined the M1 outside Leeds, and Harper had assumed that McGovan was driving back to London so he was caught by surprise when the car took the M62, heading west to Manchester.

'What's he up to?' he wondered. 'Manchester hasn't been on our radar.' He called up Hansfree and asked him for a sit rep on the Land Rovers.

'They're not moving,' said Hansfree. 'They're about a mile away from the listening station.'

'Barry Big, Barry Whisper, either of you have eyeball?'

'Roger that,' said Barry Big, in Harper's earpiece. 'They're unloading their gear. They're not going anywhere.'

'Keep well clear. The SAS are heading their way,' said Harper.

'Lex, four more Yankees have arrived at the unit,' said Hansfree. 'All Asians.'

'Four more? How many's that now?'

'That makes eight. The latest arrivals came in two cars so there are four vehicles there now.'

'Can you see what they're doing?'

'Negative on that. They're all inside the unit. To be honest, if it was me I'd be calling three nines by now. They're clearly up to something and there's enough ordinance in there to put them away for a long time.'

'Just maintain surveillance,' said Harper. 'Let's see what Tango One is up to.'

McGovan drove into the city. Maggie had to get closer to make sure they didn't lose him but McGovan didn't seem to be checking his mirrors or doing anything in the way of anti-surveillance.

Harper's mobile rang. It was Button. 'Where are you?' she asked.

'Manchester.'

'Manchester? What's happening in Manchester?'

'That's where McGovan is.'

'He's on his own?'

'Yes. And if I get the chance I'll take care of it.'

'And everybody else?'

'One of my team is with me. The rest are split between the industrial unit in Gravesend and the jihadists up at Menwith Hill.'

'That's why I'm calling,' said Button. 'The SAS are heading to Menwith Hill now. You need to make sure your people are clear by the time they get there.'

'Will do.'

'And keep me posted on McGovan.'

'Understood,' said Harper. He ended the call and switched to the radio. 'Barry Whisper, Barry Big, you need to pull out now. Back to Gravesend.'

'They're all out of the vehicles, Lex,' said Barry Big. 'I think it's going to kick off.'

'That's why you need to get the hell away,' said Harper. 'The heavy mob are moving in.' Ahead of them, McGovan's VW was slowing and indicating a left turn into a multi-storey car park. 'I've got to go,' said Harper.

McGovan stopped at a ticket machine, took a ticket, and after the barrier had gone up he drove through. Maggie followed him.

McGovan parked on the third floor. Maggie drove past and reversed into a parking space. McGovan got out of his VW and headed for the lift.

'Do I stay or come with you?' asked Maggie.

Harper had to make a split-second decision with almost no intel to go on. All he had was his gut feeling. 'Come with,' he said, grabbing his backpack. He climbed out, lifted the carpet, retrieved his gun from the hidden compartment and shoved it into his backpack. They hurried down the stairs and got to the ground floor just as McGovan stepped out of the lift. They followed him outside. McGovan was walking purposefully with no anti-surveillance techniques. Maggie slipped her arm through his. 'Cover,' she whispered.

Harper laughed. They walked faster, closing the gap. Harper realised they were heading for Manchester Piccadilly station. 'Hansfree, looks like he's catching a train,' he whispered into his radio mic.

'Where are you?'

'Manchester Piccadilly.'

'The trains run every twenty minutes to London Euston. Journey time just over two hours,' said Hansfree. 'But there are trains leaving for Liverpool, Hull, Norwich, Blackpool – he could be going anywhere.'

The pavements were relatively crowded so they were

able to stick fairly close to McGovan as he headed inside the station. He joined the queue for the ticket office. Harper let a couple of people join the line, then took his place. Maggie put a phone to her ear and faked a phone call, standing close to the ticket windows.

When it was McGovan's turn to buy a ticket they were lucky – the window was only a few feet from where Maggie was standing and she was able to overhear his destination. She nodded at Harper and went to one the automatic machines, still pretending to talk on her phone. Harper waited until McGovan had paid for his ticket before leaving the queue and joining her at the machine. 'London,' she said, feeding notes into it.

'We're London-bound, Hansfree,' Harper said into his mic. 'Get someone to meet me and Maggie, and set up surveillance there. A bike would be good.'

'No problem,' said Hansfree.

Maggie pulled the tickets from the dispenser. Harper looked around. McGovan was buying a baguette and coffee. Harper looked up at the departures board. The next train to London was due to leave in six minutes.

52

It took the twin-rotored Chinook less than an hour to travel from Hereford to Menwith Hill. The helicopter flew the last twenty miles at treetop level and came in to land some ten miles from the RAF station. The rear ramp came down and eight SAS troopers drove out on two-man silenced four-wheel all-terrain vehicles. The four passengers were facing to the rear, their carbines at the ready. They were all dressed in camouflage gear, including Kevlar helmets. The troop leader had a GPS on his handlebars and headed off cross-country. The three others followed him in an arrow formation, like geese heading home for the winter.

They got to within a mile of their target, then left their vehicles parked in a small copse that bordered a field of bright yellow rape. They hurried up a slope and lay down at the crest of a hill overlooking the Menwith Hill listening station.

Two of the troopers had high-powered binoculars and soon located the eight jihadists, who were preparing their attack. Two of the men were assembling the Spigot on its tripod, which suggested the attack was imminent.

'We need to move,' said the oldest member of the squad,

a ten-year veteran called Gary Jones, who went by the nickname Shagger, in reference to his Welsh ancestry rather than a description of his sexual prowess. He looked over at the squad's medic, a former paratrooper who had been in the Regiment for just a couple of years. 'What do you think, Dusty? Five minutes?'

'It's rough terrain,' said Dusty. 'Seven, maybe.'

'You're not in the Bird Shit now, chum. I say five.'

Bird Shit was the common nickname for the Parachute Regiment. It came from the observation that only two things fell from the sky – paratroopers and bird shit.

'I suppose the vehicles are out of the question?' said the medic.

'They'll hear us coming,' said Shagger. 'Even with the exhausts silenced.'

'We could keep to the other side of that ridge. That'll disperse most of the noise.' He pointed off to the right.

Shagger nodded. 'You'll do anything to avoid a walk, won't you?'

'Fuck it, you take the vehicles and I'll run,' said Dusty. 'But we could get a nice crossfire situation going. They wouldn't know what'd hit them.'

Shagger knew that he was right. 'Go,' he said. 'Take Jethro and Sumo with you.'

The four troopers hurried back down the slope and retrieved their vehicles. They started them up and cut across the fields.

Shagger looked through his binoculars again. The jihadists were having trouble assembling the Spigot but they were making progress and he couldn't wait too long.

'That's a Fagot, right?' asked the trooper on his left. He

was a Geordie called Beanie because of his likeness to the actor Sean Bean. 'Saw a few in Afghanistan.'

The anti-tank missile had the NATO reporting name AT-4 Spigot but the Russians called it the 9K111 Fagot, which meant 'bassoon'. It had been developed as a weapon that three men could carry and use to destroy a tank, but it would make a decent dent in the listening station. The launcher and tripod were carried by one man in a backpack, and the other two carried two launch tubes. So far as Shagger could see, the men down below had a full complement of four missiles.

'How the fuck did they get one of those?' asked Bean. 'That's a big boy's toy, that is.'

The missiles were fired with the gunner lying prone and a good team could fire one every twenty seconds. Considering the trouble they were having assembling the equipment, Shagger doubted the men he was watching would get anywhere near that.

The missiles were easily big enough to take out a tank. It left the launch tube at 80 metres a second, then a solid-fuel motor kicked in more than doubling its speed. It was a fly-by-wire weapon, which meant that the gunner had to keep aiming until the missile reached its target, up to two thousand metres away. It wasn't a weapon for amateurs.

Shagger put away his binoculars. 'Lock and load, and let's get this started,' he said. 'The enemy down there are in uniform and carrying weapons, so this is a military engagement, pure and simple. We're looking to take out the opposition, not collect prisoners.' The men nodded, all eager for the off.

They crested the ridge and headed down the slopes, their carbines at the ready.

They moved at a slow run, crouched down, spread out across the hill. It took them the best part of two minutes to reach the bottom, and then they were moving across a field. Ahead was a ditch and they went through the muddy water without breaking stride.

Ahead the Spigot team finished assembling the weapon. One of the men stood up and looked at his watch, then towards the listening station in the distance. Another was lying down, preparing to take the shot. The third was arranging the missile tubes.

Shagger increased the pace. The man who had looked at his watch shouted something and the jihadists with rifles began to move towards the listening station. It was a mile away and they weren't SAS fit, which meant it would take them at least ten minutes to cover the ground, probably longer. Shagger figured they wouldn't fire the missile until the men were closer to the installation.

'In position now,' said a voice in his earpiece. Dusty.

'Wait until we have contact,' said Shagger. The closer they got to the targets the better, though they were already within range.

The jihadists were about halfway there and the man standing by the Spigot was shading his hand against the sun as he watched his colleagues' progress. Then, slowly, he began to turn, scanning the area. Shagger knew he had two choices: to drop and hope the man wouldn't see them or to start firing. They were well within range and the closer the jihadists got to the listening station the greater the risk they would start shooting.

'Contact!' he shouted, stopped and raised his carbine to his shoulder. He fired a short controlled burst at the man standing by the Spigot and was rewarded by the sight of his chest exploding in a mass of red. The rest of his team opened fire at the Spigot gunner and his assistant. More than a dozen rounds thwacked into them and they went still.

The sound of gunfire stopped the armed jihadists in their tracks. They turned, saw the troopers and began firing but their shots went wide. The troopers dropped to lower their profiles and began to return fire. As they did, a hail of bullets ripped into the jihadists from the ridge to the side as the second SAS team opened fire.

Two days' practice on a firing range counted for nothing against highly trained SAS troopers who between them had more than a hundred years of special-forces experience including firefights in Iraq and Afghanistan. The jihadists were screaming, '*Allahu Akbar!*' as they fired, as if somehow that would help their aim. It didn't, and one by one their guns fell silent as the troopers picked them off. It was over in less than thirty seconds.

53

Harper and Maggie followed McGovan down the platform, arm in arm. They slowed as McGovan got into a carriage midway down the train. 'What do you think? Sit together or split up?' asked Maggie.

Harper knew that usually two sets of eyes were better than one and it would have made more sense to follow him separately, but the train was only going to make one stop and that was at London Euston. And a couple travelling together always looked less like a tail. 'You grab us a seat in the next carriage, I'll wait until the train pulls out.'

She climbed on while Harper took out a mobile phone. He used a new Sim card to call the third number on the list that Charlotte Button had given him. He quickly brought her up to speed. 'Can you carry out the contract?' she asked.

'I'm about to get on a train. Give me a break.'

'What about when he gets to London?'

'I'm working on it. What happened at Menwith Hill?'

'Let's just say it was a very satisfactory conclusion.'

'So we won you some Brownie points at least?'

Button chuckled. 'It would seem so, yes.'

'We might be able to add to that,' he said. He explained about the growing number of jihadists who were gathering at the industrial unit.

'What do you think's happening?'

'I'm not sure. But they have a hell of a lot of explosives there. What happened at Menwith Hill was a diversion, to get attention focused up north. I think that's why he's heading south.'

'Your people are on top of it?'

'Well, yes. In terms of surveillance. But they're not armed.'

'I've already explained that I don't want McGovan arrested. He has to be cancelled.'

'I hear that. But he's on a train. Too many witnesses.'

'Then wait until he's in London. As soon as he's cancelled, I'll send in the cavalry.'

'You're playing with fire. So long as you know.'

'It has to be done this way.'

The train was about to leave. Harper ended the call and climbed aboard, watching through the window to make sure McGovan didn't jump off at the last second. He didn't. Harper found Maggie sitting in a window seat and dropped down next to her. 'All good,' he said. 'Hansfree will have someone at Euston so we can relax. Catch some sleep if you want.' He held up his backpack. 'I'm going to pop into the bathroom and have a quick shave.'

'Maybe spray a bit of deodorant around, too.'

'Bit ripe?'

She grinned. 'Just a bit. And when you're done, pop along to the buffet car and get me some breakfast, will you?'

He saluted her. 'Yes, your ladyship.'

'Thank you so much,' she said, closing her eyes and settling back in her seat.

54

Harper and Maggie took out their earpieces while they were on the train. He used his mobile phone to keep in contact with Hansfree, making regular calls well away from the carriage where McGovan was sitting. An hour before the train was due to get in, one of the jihadists had left the industrial unit in Gravesend in a grey Volvo. Two of Hansfree's men had followed, one in a car and one on a bike. Fifteen minutes before the train arrived, Hansfree confirmed that the car had gone to Euston station.

When the train arrived, McGovan was one of the first off. Harper and Maggie followed him along the platform and onto the station concourse. Hansfree told them that a watcher called Will would be waiting for them. 'Black, bald, glasses and wearing a suit,' was the description he had given, and they spotted him at once, leaning against a shop window and studying a copy of the *Evening Standard*. Harper and Maggie closed the gap with McGovan in case their quarry headed for the Underground but there was no need to worry because he was walking slowly and looking around. An Asian man in a denim jacket and jeans nodded at him and they embraced. Laughing at nothing, Harper and Maggie walked past the two men, then waited at the exit to see what they would do.

Will had clocked McGovan and was circling, pretending to make a call on his mobile. McGovan and the man headed for another exit and Harper and Maggie followed.

'Hansfree, Tango One is heading out with an Asian in a blue denim jacket and jeans.'

'That's the driver of the grey Volvo,' said Hansfree. 'I've a bike outside watching it. We're good to go.'

'Roger that,' said Harper. 'Will, where's your car?'

'East exit,' said Will, in Harper's ear.

'Get the car ready. Hansfree, who do you have outside?'

'His name's Sammy. On a courier motorbike. He's good. He'll go ahead of the Volvo, though I think it's pretty obvious where they're headed.'

'Tell him Tango One is on the move with your man.'

'I'm on it,' said Hansfree.

Will led Harper and Maggie outside to his car. They climbed in, Harper in the front passenger seat and Maggie behind him. 'Sammy has eyeball,' said Hansfree in Harper's ear. 'They're getting into the car now. It's a grey Volvo.'

Will started the engine. He had a sat-nav on the dashboard and it booted up within seconds.

'He's on the A501, heading east,' said Hansfree.

'Probably going back to Gravesend,' said Will, pulling away from the kerb.

'Probably, but let's not go counting chickens,' said Harper.

55

McGovan did go straight to the industrial site where Hansfree had a team of five keeping the unit under surveillance and one had a drone in the air. With Hansfree's motorbike tail keeping ahead of the Volvo, Will was able to stay well back. Having a tail ahead of a target was by far the best way of running surveillance. People rarely concerned themselves with what was happening ahead of them. The biker could keep an eye on the target in his mirrors, and if the target did turn off it wouldn't take him long to double back and catch up.

Hansfree relayed through the radio that McGovan had arrived at the industrial unit. He was inside with the other seven jihadists plus the one who had driven him from the station. 'Hansfree, I'd like to have a look at the drone feed,' said Harper.

Hansfree gave him the location of the watcher who was piloting the drone and Will drove him over. The drone operator was a small man in his sixties, sitting in the front seat of a van with the name of a tropical-fish company on the side. Harper climbed in and sat next to him while Maggie squatted in the back and looked over his shoulder. A laptop open on the dashboard gave them an overhead view of the industrial unit, the two containers and the land around it.

'What's been happening?' asked Harper.

'Not much,' said the man. 'They come, they park, they go inside.'

'What about the gear in the containers?'

'They carried most of the stuff inside this morning.'

Harper sat back and spoke to Hansfree on the radio. 'Do we have registration numbers on the vehicles?'

'All of them,' said Hansfree. 'They were all sold to private buyers within the last two weeks. All taxed and insured and seem legit, but I have my suspicions.'

'Because?'

'Because they're all showing owners in Birmingham with names like Khan and Patel.'

'Do me a favour and text me each car's details. Just the registration number, model and colour. Don't bother about the owners.'

'Will do,' said Hansfree.

'I've a question for you,' Harper said, to the man operating the drone. 'If we had to, could you follow a car with one of those?'

'I'd like to say yes but, hand on heart, they're not fast enough plus you'd be playing catch-up trying to keep it in range. They're great for static surveillance or getting into difficult-to-reach places, but you need the military stuff to follow a moving vehicle.'

'That's what I thought,' said Harper. He climbed out of the van and called up the next number on Button's list of throwaway mobiles. 'Tango One is back in Gravesend,' he said. 'He's got eight jihadists with him and we haven't managed to identify most of them. He hasn't met them before, that's for sure, or we would have seen them.'

'What's he up to?' asked Button.

'Fucked if I know. They're all inside. But they're up to something, obviously. They're not here for a prayer meeting.'

'How close are you to cancelling Tango One?'

'A lot depends on his next move. If they pile into two cars and head out mob-handed, I won't be able to get near him. But if they move out separately, maybe. The problem is, what do we do then? They've got explosives, remember.'

'You're thinking suicide bombers?'

'I don't know. Like I said, they're inside. But we're not that far from central London.'

The man in the van wound down his window and shouted across at Harper, 'They're on the move.'

'I'll call you back,' said Harper, and jogged to the van. As he climbed into the passenger seat, his phone beeped to let him know he had received a text message. He looked at the laptop. One of the cars was driving away from the industrial unit. A blue Mondeo. 'Hansfree, do we have a tail for the vehicle?' Harper said into his mic.

'Affirmative,' said Hansfree.

'How many on board the Mondeo?'

'Two,' said Hansfree.

'Is it Tango One?'

'Negative.'

'Let me know if anyone else moves out. And keep me updated on that vehicle.'

'I'm on it.'

Harper looked at the drone operator. 'What did you see?'

'Two men came out. Asians. They got into the car and left.'

'Anything unusual? Were they carrying anything?'

The man shook his head. 'One thing. The passenger was wearing a coat and he wasn't wearing one before.'

Harper cursed.

'Is that significant?' asked the man, frowning.

'It is when they've got all that explosive,' said Harper. 'It could be they've spent the day building suicide vests and Tango One is now sending them on their way.'

He got out of the van and checked the text Hansfree had sent him before forwarding it to Button's mobile. He gave her two minutes to review the message, then phoned her. 'Did you get that?'

'I got it.'

'The two that have left are in the blue Mondeo. We have a tail and I can update you with texts. But you need to take care of it. The tail isn't armed. The passenger is wearing a coat that he wasn't wearing before so the suicide-bomber option is looking more likely. I think he's setting them up as suicide-bombers. Menwith Hill was a distraction to get everyone's attention focused up north. Meanwhile the real attack will be on London.'

'But are you sure?'

'Let's see what happens next. As things stand there's a car driving into London with two Asians on board, one wearing a long coat he didn't have on before. There are eight of them and four vehicles. Do the maths.'

'What do you suggest?'

'I've got a surveillance guy tailing the Mondeo but you need to get them picked up. Armed cops, SAS, whoever's available. I'm guessing they won't be primed but I wouldn't put money on it. If I were you, I'd get the Mondeo pulled over and you'll have a better idea of what's going on. But if it was really up to me I'd just shoot them in the head, to be on the safe side.'

'And there's just the one vehicle so far?'

'Just the blue Mondeo. If that changes, I'll let you know.'

Button ended the call and Harper went back to the van. He climbed in and stared at the laptop.

'Anything wrong?' asked Maggie, from the back of the van.

'We'll know in the next few minutes,' said Harper.

56

'Are you okay, brother?' the driver asked his companion. The driver's name was Omar but he didn't know the passenger's. The first time they had met was when they had arrived at the industrial unit and McGovan had insisted they did not identify themselves. Omar was the driver, and the man in the passenger seat was the *shahid*. The martyr. Under his coat he wore a canvas vest and in the vest were several pounds of explosives. He sat with his hands in his lap, staring straight ahead with unseeing eyes.

Now he nodded. 'I'm okay,' he said.

'It's a great thing you are doing,' said Omar.

'We are not to talk. We were told not to talk.'

'I know, brother. But I just wanted you to know. Respect.'

Omar looked at the sat-nav. They were north of the river, between Dagenham and Barking, just over twelve miles from their destination. Downing Street, home of the prime minister. They wouldn't be able to get close to the man, or to the house: McGovan had made that clear. The road was one of the most secure in the country, as secure as the area around the American Embassy, which would be the second target. The *shahid* was to get as close to the target as possible. There were always tourists standing at the black steel gates that blocked off the road, along with armed police from the Diplomatic Protection Group. It didn't matter who died, what mattered was that ISIS was seen to be able to strike at the heart of government.

Omar looked back at the road. He frowned. There was a black SUV ahead, just a few car lengths, that he hadn't noticed before. He braked, and as he did so he looked in his rear-view mirror. There was a second black SUV behind him.

'Watch out!' shouted the *shahid*.

Omar looked ahead again. The SUV in front was slowing sharply. Omar stamped on the brake and swore.

The *shahid* wasn't wearing his seat belt because he didn't want any pressure on the vest, and as the car braked he was slammed against the window. He fell back into his seat as the vehicle stopped. 'What the fuck, man?' he shouted. He put a hand to his head and felt blood.

Men in black overalls were piling out of the SUV. Men with guns. 'It's the fucking cops!' screamed Omar. His eyes flashed to the rear-view mirror. More armed police. 'Fuck, fuck, fuck!'

'What do we do?' asked the *shahid*.

The cops were screaming now. 'Armed police! Raise your hands! Armed police!'

'I don't know,' said Omar.

'Do I go now? Do I do it now?'

'ARMED POLICE! PUT YOUR HANDS IN THE AIR!'

'I don't know,' said Omar, again.

'I think I should. If they get closer, they'll kill us anyway, and if they kill us they win.'

Two armed cops were standing at the front of the car, their carbines at their shoulders. Both were screaming, 'Put your hands up! Put your fucking hands up now!'

'I don't know, brother. I just don't know.'

The *shahid* fumbled for the trigger. His fingers caught hold of it and he held it up. '*Allahu Akbar!*' he shouted.

He looked across at Omar and their eyes met. Omar took the *shahid*'s left hand and smiled. Together they shouted, '*Allahu Akbar!*'

The *shahid* closed his eyes and pressed the trigger.

Nothing happened.

'The switch!' screamed Omar. 'The fucking on-off switch!'

The windshield exploded and Omar saw the *shahid*'s head fold in on itself and blood sprayed across the back seat. Then he felt a punch in the face and everything went black.

57

'One of them isn't Asian,' said Harper, as he looked at the laptop screen. Two men were walking from the industrial unit towards a white Honda.

The man operating the drone nodded. 'Yeah, he went in a few hours ago. That's his car.'

The Asian was wearing a long coat. He got into the front passenger seat while the other man sat behind the steering wheel.

Harper's phone rang. It was Button. 'You were right,' she said. 'Suicide-bombers. We got them on the A13.'

'Anyone hurt?'

'No collateral damage, as they say, just the two in the car. They were shot before they could detonate.'

'There's another vehicle leaving now,' said Harper. 'The white Honda. You've got the details.'

'I'll get it targeted. How many left?'

'There are three cars still parked there. Four jihadists inside, plus McGovan. If they keep operating in pairs, we have two more. But that's supposition. They could just as easily leave alone.'

'Call me as and when they leave.'

'You could take them all out here. There'd be less risk of civilians getting hurt.'

'Just do as you're told. It's going to work out just fine.' Button ended the call.

The white Honda drove through the gates and headed towards London. 'Hansfree, make sure you have a tail on the white Honda,' Harper said into the radio.

Hansfree chuckled. 'No need to teach this grandmother to suck eggs,' he said.

58

McGovan examined the suicide vest and nodded his approval. 'You're good to go,' he said. The vest was a standard design that required next to no skill to assemble. Anyone could do it, even a child, and the design had remained the same since the concept had been developed by the Tamil Tigers in the 1980s. There were four plates of PE-4A plastic explosive sitting in four pockets evenly spaced around the vest, with a detonator in each plate, all wired to the control unit in a pocket at the back of the vest. Two wires ran from the control unit to a metal trigger. An on-off switch on the front of the belt ensured that the vest could not be detonated prematurely.

McGovan patted the shoulder of the man wearing the vest. His name was Zayn. Born in Bradford, he was a Pakistani Muslim who had spent three months fighting with ISIS in Syria before returning home, flying from Turkey to Canada and from there to the UK. 'You'll make us proud,' said McGovan. Zayn nodded but his eyes were dull and lifeless as if his spirit had already left his body.

Another of the jihadists helped fit the fragmentation jacket over the explosive vest. The explosives created the shock wave but it was the shrapnel from the jacket that would do the damage, dozens of pockets filled with nuts, bolts, nails and ball bearings. When the PE-4A was detonated, the lethal shrapnel would radiate outwards, killing or maiming anyone within fifty feet.

The jihadist muttered an Islamic prayer as he fitted the jacket, then stood back to admire his handiwork. '*Allahu Akbar*,' he said.

'*Allahu Akbar*,' muttered Zayn.

McGovan and the jihadist helped Zayn put on a raincoat. It was several sizes too big so that it would go over the vest and jacket. The jihadist buttoned up the coat, muttering another prayer, as McGovan fed the wires of the trigger down the sleeve. 'Don't forget. Only make the vest live when you're within sight of the target.'

Zayn nodded again, but didn't say anything.

'Repeat that back to me,' said McGovan, putting his hands on the man's shoulders and looking into his blank eyes.

'Only make the vest live when I'm within sight of the target.'

'Good man,' said McGovan. He beckoned Zayn's driver. He was one of the non-Asians in the group, a twenty-five-year-old Glaswegian, who had converted to Islam in Scotland, then spent a year in Syria as a foreign fighter. An ISIS talent-spotter had realised the man's potential and persuaded him that he could best serve Islam back in the UK. His name was Bruce, but McGovan didn't know if that was his family name or his first name. He didn't know and he didn't care. Names didn't matter. All that mattered was that the men did their jobs. Bruce was to drive Zayn as close to Waterloo station as he could get. Zayn was to walk into the middle of the station to detonate. 'Off you go, lads,' said McGovan. '*Allahu Akbar.*'

The two men smiled thinly. '*Allahu Akbar,*' they chorused, then headed outside.

59

Harper watched on the drone feed as the two men walked from the industrial unit towards a blue Hyundai. One was Asian, wearing a long coat. The other was white, in his twenties, in jeans and a leather jacket.

'I have a tail up and running and a bike on the way back from the A13,' said Hansfree in Harper's ear.

The two men got into the Hyundai. A few seconds later it drove away and was soon out of range of the drone's camera.

Barry Whisper drove up and parked behind the van. Harper climbed out, waved at him, then took out his mobile and called Button. 'The third team has just set out. A blue Hyundai. We have a tail on it. I'll call in the location once we know where they're headed.'

Harper ended the call and got into Barry Whisper's car. 'How's it going?' Barry Whisper asked.

'Two-man suicide-bombers. We're dealing with them as they leave. The third has just headed out and so we think there's one team left. I've a job for you, Barry, if you're up for it.'

'I'm up for it,' he said immediately.

'At least let me tell you what it is.'

Barry Whisper shrugged. 'We go back a long way, Lex. If you want something doing, I'll do it.'

Harper grasped the man's shoulder and squeezed. 'You're a star, but this is different from the normal jobs. I've got to slot this guy McGovan and I've got to do it myself. I think the best way is from the back of a bike and even I'm not good enough to drive and shoot at the same time.'

'No problem,' said Barry Whisper. 'I'll drive. What about the bike?'

'We can get it off Hansfree's guy. In fact, talk to Hansfree now, then head over with the car and come back on the bike.'

60

'There it is, dead ahead, white Honda,' said Glenn Marsden. He was at the wheel of the black BMW X5, favourite vehicle of the Metropolitan Police's armed-response unit. Sitting next to him in the front passenger seat, Jon Cooper was the most experienced of the three-man unit.

Cooper checked the registration number on the screen in front of him. 'That's it,' he said. 'Guns out, Paul.' He picked up his radio mic. 'Trojan Six Three Four, we have the target vehicle in sight.'

Paul Evans, the youngest member of the team, was sitting behind Cooper. He pulled down the seat next to him revealing the three SIG Sauer 516 assault rifles. The SIG 516s the unit used came with a telescoping stock and a thirty-round magazine. Evans slid the guns out and handed one to Cooper.

'Right, just so you know, if this is the same situation as the other Trojans had, the passenger has a suicide vest on and the driver is clear,' said Cooper. 'There's an on-off switch that has to be in the on position before the trigger is pressed so, providing we act quickly enough, we can stop the detonation.' Marsden and Evans grunted.

'Trojan Six Two One, we're right behind you. How do you want to play this?' It was Stan Mitchell, senior officer in the second armed-response vehicle that had been assigned to the situation.

Evans twisted around in his seat. A second black BMW X5 was three cars behind. 'I see them,' he said.

'We'll pull ahead and stop the Honda,' said Cooper. 'It has to be fast but we need to issue clear warnings. Any attempt to detonate and Operation Kratos applies.'

'Understood,' said Mitchell.

The Met had laid down the Operation Kratos tactics in 2002 specifically to deal with suicide-bombers, and although the term had been officially dropped in 2008, the tactics still applied: if a suicide-bomber was in danger of detonating, he or she was to be shot in the head until the threat was neutralised.

Cooper nodded at Marsden. 'Let's do it, Glenn.'

Marsden accelerated, pulling smoothly in front of the white Honda. He braked, slowly at first, but then increasing the pressure on the pedal. The driver of the white Honda pounded his horn but Marsden continued to slow. Cooper and Evans flicked the safeties off as the car stopped and piled out of the offside.

They ran to the Honda, shouting, 'Armed police!' Cooper to the passenger side, Evans covering the driver. Trojan Six Two One had pulled up behind the Honda. Traffic continued to drive past but slowly as motorists craned their necks to see what was going on.

'Armed police, hands up!' shouted Marsden. The driver kept his hands on the wheel, his mouth wide open.

'Put your hands in the air, now!' screamed Cooper.

Marsden was climbing out of the X5, his gun in his right hand. The men in the second X5 were getting out too, guns at the ready.

The passenger opened his mouth to shout and his right arm moved. Cooper fired twice. The windshield shattered and the man's head exploded.

Evans kept his weapon aimed at the driver. 'Stay exactly where you are!' he shouted.

The driver blinked, frowned, then looked at the body next to him. He glanced back at Evans, then lunged towards the body. Evans pulled the trigger. The shot took off the top of the driver's head. He fired again, twice, a professional double-tap with both shots hitting the face, dead centre.

Traffic had slowed to a crawl now and in almost every car a mobile phone was pointing at the Honda and the two dead bodies inside.

'Let's move these vehicles on and set up a roadblock,' Cooper shouted to Mitchell. 'This is now a crime scene.' He waved at Marsden. 'Glenn, move these vultures on. Anyone not out of here in double-quick time is to be charged with using their phone while driving.'

61

Harper watched as the final two jihadists walked out of the industrial unit and got into a white van with the name of a courier company on the side. 'They're taking the van,' said Harper into his mic. 'You've got a tail ready?'

'Barry Big's in place,' said Hansfree, over the radio.

'Roger that,' said Barry Big. 'Raring to go.'

'I've a bike ready, too,' said Hansfree.

'Just keep updating me. Once we know which route they're on, the cops can take over.'

'How do we stand so far?' asked Hansfree.

'Two neutralised, one on the way,' said Harper.

'Any collateral damage?'

'So far so good,' said Harper. 'Looks to me as if Tango One is now alone in the unit. So I need you to pull off all surveillance. Only those following the vehicles are to stay in play, everyone else is now off the clock.'

'You're sure?' asked Hansfree.

'I'm sure,' said Harper. 'I'll take care of Tango One. Barry Whisper will help. Everyone else can stand down, job well done.'

'Roger that,' said Hansfree. 'You just be careful. I'd hate

anything to happen to you before my money goes into the bank.'

'Good to know you have my best interests at heart,' said Harper. He patted the drone operator on the shoulder. 'We're done, mate, thanks. Pack up and head on home.'

Harper climbed out of the van and went over to the BMW. Maggie was in the driving seat, drinking from a bottle of water. He leaned down and winked at her. 'All done, the authorities will take care of it now.'

'What about Tango One?'

'I'll deal with him.'

'I'll give you a hand.'

'Nah, I'm good,' he said. 'You can stand down.' He nodded at the BMW. 'You can keep the car, sell it for whatever you can get or give it away. It's untraceable.'

'I'm happy to stay, Lex, you know that.'

'I know. But it's not necessary. I'll call you.'

She blew him a kiss. 'Make sure you do.'

As Maggie drove off, the drone came in for a perfect landing close to the van. The operator climbed out, put it into the back, waved to Harper and disappeared down the road after Maggie.

Harper went over to Barry Whisper. He took out his gun, checked it, then put it back in his underarm holster. Barry Whisper was already wearing a black full-face helmet and he handed a white one to Harper. 'Let's get this done,' said Harper, climbing onto the pillion.

62

The police took down the occupants of the blue Hyundai about three miles from central London, south of the river. There were two occupants: a Caucasian was driving, an Asian sitting in the front passenger seat. Three armed-response vehicles were involved, working together to slow down the Hyundai at a quiet section of road.

As soon as it had stopped, six armed officers surrounded the car, their SIG Sauer 516 assault rifles aimed at the occupants. They knew now that there was no doubt about the threat. Two cars had already been dealt with and both had contained suicide-bombers.

'Armed police, raise your hands!' shouted a sergeant, who had his carbine trained at the passenger's face. All the intel suggested that only the passenger was carrying explosives but both men were a threat because either could operate the trigger.

The two passengers looked at each other, their mouths open and their eyes wide. It wasn't unusual for suspects to freeze when they were confronted by armed police. It was a natural human reaction, and a result of brain chemistry rather than conscious thought. The amygdala – a small region of the brain near the top of the spine – kicks out a neurotransmitter called glutamate in response to any sign of danger. It activates the freeze response first because evolution has taught that freezing is the best way to avoid a predator. But within less than a second that same neuro-transmitter reaches the hypothalamus where it triggers the flight or fight response. That is when the heart rate jumps and adrenalin courses through the body. At that point a conscious decision has to be made – fight or run. But until that decision is taken the body stays in freeze mode. That was where the two men were as they stared out at the armed police. They couldn't run because they were in a car surrounded by policemen with guns. They couldn't fight because they had no weapons. So they froze.

'ARMED POLICE, HANDS IN THE AIR NOW!'

The passenger moved his right hand. Just his right hand, not the left. The sergeant took that to mean he was about to reach for the trigger and fired. The side window shat-tered into a thousand cubes and the sergeant fired again. The second bullet slammed into the side of the man's head and exited the other side before blowing off the top of the driver's skull. The driver slumped forward and, as he did so, two of the other officers opened fire. The windshield shattered and both men's heads blew apart. Blood, brain matter and pieces of skull sprayed across the interior. More than a dozen shots were fired, then everything went quiet.

The sergeant's eyes were stinging from the cordite in the air. He knew that, strictly speaking, neither man had made a threatening gesture, but he didn't care. If the vest had gone off everyone would have died. So far as he was concerned, two dead terrorists and no collateral damage was a perfect result.

63

Harper had his gun in his hand as Barry Whisper revved the engine. They were at the entrance to the industrial unit. The gate was open but, with no windows in the unit and the door closed, there was no way of telling what McGovan was doing inside. Time was ticking away and he didn't want to wait for ever. He tapped Barry Whisper's shoulder. 'Drive in, drive around the unit and let me off at the side. Then head back to the entrance and attract his attention. But be careful, mate – he's got some serious weaponry in there.'

Barry Whisper revved the engine again, and drove through the entrance. He accelerated hard, then turned to the left to drive by the lean-to garages. He slammed on the brakes and Harper was off the bike before it had stopped. Barry Whisper accelerated and disappeared around the back of the unit.

Harper kept close to the building as he went around to the front. He reached the corner as the bike appeared at the other side, heading for the exit.

Harper heard the door open and ducked back. McGovan was holding an L85 with a thirty-round magazine in place, and as Barry Whisper reached the exit, McGovan swung the rifle up to his shoulder. Harper knew he had to react quickly – the Heckler & Koch assault weapon had an effective range of close to 400 metres and, as ex-SAS, McGovan would be a marksman more than capable of killing Barry Whisper, even on a motorbike.

McGovan was totally focused on Barry Whisper so didn't see Harper step out and raise the Smith & Wesson until the last second, just as he was pulling the trigger. McGovan had started to turn as Harper fired and the slug slammed into his left shoulder. The impact spun him around and the rifle clattered to the ground. McGovan bent down to pick it up but Harper fired again and McGovan's right hand practically exploded. He staggered back and disappeared inside the unit.

Harper ran after him and pushed through the door. There was a small office to the left but the rest of the building was open plan, empty except for a few trestle tables piled with weapons and provisions. There was a tailor's dummy with a canvas vest on it, but no explosives. McGovan was staggering as he ran, blood dripping from his wounded shoulder and hand.

He was running towards a table on which there was another rifle. Harper shot him in the leg and McGovan pitched sideways and fell to the floor. He rolled over, then slowly pushed himself up so that he was sitting against the wall. He watched impassively as Harper walked over to stand in front of him.

'They got them all,' said Harper. 'They killed the guys you left at Menwith Hill. They didn't get anywhere near the listening station. And those suicide-bombers? All dead, mate. Not one of them even got to press their trigger. All shot in the head. Bang, bang, bang, bang. It was all for nothing. Everything you did. A total waste of fucking time.'

McGovan's shirt was now soaked with blood from the shoulder wound. His right hand was shattered and useless. What was left of it was lying in his lap. Two fingers were missing. There was blood all over his trousers.

'Get me a field dressing, will you?' asked McGovan. 'There's one on the table over there.'

'Fuck you,' said Harper. He pushed up the visor of the full-face helmet.

McGovan tilted his head on one side as he looked at Harper. 'You were in the Regiment, right? Or are you still in?'

'Never was, never will be,' said Harper. 'I was a Para, and happy with that. I couldn't be doing with all the crap you have to go through to get in.'

'But you were a soldier.' McGovan winced, and gritted his teeth. He took a long, slow breath before speaking. 'You've won. I accept that. But now I'm a casualty. I'm bleeding to death here.'

Harper shrugged. 'I'm not a medic. That's not what I do.'

'Just take me in. Let me have my day in court,' said McGovan. 'I'll tell the world why I did what I did. They need to understand.'

Harper shook his head. 'That's not going to happen. No one gives a fuck why you did what you did. You did it for a fictitious god that you believe doesn't want you to eat bacon or drink beer, a god that says women should cover their faces and not drive cars. You're fucking deluded, mate.' He tapped the side of his helmet with the barrel of the gun. 'You're a few rounds short of a magazine, not right in the head, get it? I dunno what made you become a Muslim nutter, but that's what you are. That's all anyone will remember.' He levelled the gun at McGovan's face. 'No one gives a shit who you are or why you did what you did.'

'At least I kill for something I believe in,' said McGovan, his eyes blazing with hatred. 'You kill so that your masters can continue to persecute Muslim innocents all around the world for no other reason than they want their oil.'

Harper smiled. 'You've got it all wrong, mate. I don't kill for politics or religion or because I'm ordered to. Someone's paying me to kill you, pure and simple. You killed a Yank in the sandpit. A Yank with a very important father. He wants you dead and I'm the guy who's going to make that happen. I don't care what you've done or why you're doing it. All I care is that the money goes into the bank. You're a job, mate. That's all you are. Now *Allahu Akbar* and fuck off.' He pulled the trigger and McGovan's face imploded. Blood began to pool around what was left of the man's head as Harper pumped two more slugs into his chest.

He turned and walked outside. Barry Whisper had driven back to the unit and was waiting beside the door on the bike, the engine running. Harper climbed onto the pillion and patted him on the shoulder. 'Home, James, and don't spare the horses,' he said. As the motorbike sped towards London, Harper took a phone from his hip-pack and sent Button a final text.

64

The driver of the white van checked in his wing mirror, indicated and pulled out to overtake the truck ahead of him.

'You don't have to drive so fast, bruv, there's no rush,' said the passenger.

'He's crawling along,' said the driver. 'We haven't got all day.'

'There's no rush,' repeated the passenger.

The driver eased back on the accelerator. 'Okay, whatever.'

The passenger looked across at the driver. 'What's your name, bruv?'

The driver shook his head. 'He said we weren't to know each other's names. Security.'

'Fuck that. I'll be in Heaven in less than an hour, who gives a fuck? I'm a *shahid*, mate. A martyr. Don't see why I shouldn't know the name of the brother who's driving me to Paradise.'

The driver smiled. 'Mohammed Tariq. But everyone calls me Mo.'

'*As-salamu alaykum*, Mo. I'm Ali. You went to Syria?'

'Fuck, yeah. It was something.'

'You kill anyone?'

Mo grinned. 'Fuck, yeah. They had us shoot some prisoners the first day we were there. A test, like. I wasn't sure I could do it but, fuck, yeah.' He beat a rapid tattoo on the steering wheel with his hands. 'And you?'

Ali shook his head. 'I was on patrols, mainly. Then they started giving me extra tuition. About the Koran and stuff. Said there were better ways of serving Allah than firing an AK-47. That everyone has to play to their strengths.'

'And you're okay about what you're doing?'

'Sure,' said Ali. He held up the trigger. 'This will achieve more than any bullet,' he said.

'The Houses of Parliament,' said Mo. 'You'll be like Guy fucking Fawkes.'

Ali smiled. 'He failed. I won't.'

Mo was to drop Ali on the Embankment and Ali was to walk the rest of the way. No one expected him to get inside the building, but he'd be close and the area was always packed with tourists. His aim was to approach one of the security checkpoints and take out as many police officers as possible. There would be plenty of tourists using video cameras so what happened would be seen around the world.

A black SUV moved in front of the van and Ali groaned. 'What's he playing at?'

'Relax, bruv,' said Mo. 'Enjoy the drive. Enjoy the moment. What we're doing today will resonate for eternity. Like the warriors who carried out Nine/Eleven.'

The SUV slowed sharply and Mo had to stamp on the brake to avoid a collision.

To Ali, it was as if everything was happening in slow motion. He saw armed police officers dressed in black pile out of the car in front of them. He heard shouts behind him. He heard Mo cursing. Ali smiled. He felt as if he had all the time in the world as he raised his right hand and started to squeeze the trigger.

'*Allahu Akbar*,' he whispered. He was disappointed that he wouldn't be taking out his designated target, but this way was fine. His fingers tightened on the trigger but then the windscreen shattered, something thudded into his face and everything went black.

65

Patsy Ellis removed her headset. She looked up at the massive monitor that took up almost the whole of the far wall in the operations room they had commandeered at Thames House. There were only four people in it – Ellis, Charlotte Button and two young men in shirtsleeves, who had spent the whole two hours staring at the screens in front of them without making a sound other than to acknowledge Ellis's instructions. The only interruption had been when a young man in a suit had delivered a round of teas and coffees and plastic-wrapped sandwiches, none of which had been opened.

Four locations showed on the map: the places where the suicide-bombing teams had been intercepted by the armed-response vehicles. 'All done,' said Ellis. 'No casualties. Not on our side, anyway.'

'That's a relief,' said Button. Her phone beeped to let her know she had received a message. It was Harper: JOB DONE. And a smiley face.

The two men took off their headsets, picked up their jackets from the backs of their chairs, and Ellis thanked them by name as they left.

'It would have been less stressful if you'd brought us in earlier,' said Ellis.

'But, still, all's well that ends well.'

'Charlie, if we'd missed one, it could have ended very differently.'

'But it didn't. You and the police saved the day. MI5 and the Metropolitan Police working hand in hand took out four suicide-bombers with no collateral damage. Applause all round.'

'And the man who planned it? Can you let me into that little secret? I'm sure that's what that message was, right?'

Button took the back out of the phone, removed the Sim card, and broke it in half.

Ellis smiled. 'It would have been so much funnier if you'd swallowed it,' she said.

'The mastermind was a former SAS man, Caleb McGovan. He converted to Islam at some point and offered his services to ISIS. He appears to have sold them on the idea of a joint operation – the attack on Menwith Hill and the multiple suicide-bombers.'

'And where is this Caleb McGovan now, pray tell?'

'An industrial unit outside Gravesend.'

'Dead or alive?'

'He didn't make it, I'm afraid.'

'Why do I get the feeling you're not telling me everything, Charlie?'

'It was a very complicated situation. I had a lot of ducks to line up.'

'You could have told me what was happening much

earlier. This has all been very much on the fly, and that's never the best way of working, as you know.'

'Hand on heart, Patsy, I didn't get the full picture until very recently.'

Ellis sipped her tea. 'And who killed Caleb McGovan?'

'Probably best we put it down to friendly fire and leave it at that. There'll be surveillance footage of McGovan setting up the suicide-bombers so I don't think anyone will be shedding any tears for him. If the SAS or the police want to take the credit for it, I don't think anyone will be complaining.'

'And who was all this for, Charlie? Who were you working for?'

'Does it matter? We took out an ISIS cell, thwarting what would have been a series of very damaging attacks. The security services and the police come out of it smelling like roses.'

'When you put it like that, of course I sound like I'm looking a gift horse in the mouth. It would just be nice to know who's been pulling your strings.'

Button flashed Ellis a tight smile. 'Client confidentiality, I'm afraid.'

'Of course. And as you said, Charlie, all's well that ends well.'

'And the quid pro quo? Can you tell me now who's been making my life a misery?'

Ellis grinned. 'Actually, I can,' she said. 'And after what's happened today, the chance that you'll ever have any problems with Five or Six in the future is slim to none.'

66

Harper's team split up and went their separate ways. There was no group hug, no drinks down at the pub, they just left. Their fees would be paid into their offshore bank accounts and they wouldn't speak again until the next time they were needed. The only member of the team left in the ops room when Harper arrived was Hansfree, who was sipping a coffee, his feet on the table. He looked exhausted, which was hardly surprising since he'd functioned with almost no sleep over the past four days. 'All's well that ends well,' said Hansfree.

'It was a close-run thing,' said Harper. 'The guys you brought in did a bang-up job. Tell them I'll put them through for a bonus. You, too. After what we did today, we should all get fucking knighthoods.'

'I won't be holding my breath on that score,' said Hansfree. 'The money'll do just fine.' He swung his legs off the table and reached for a black thumbdrive with his right claw. He held it out to Harper. 'Everything you need is on there,' he said. 'IDs on the jihadists we identified, surveillance pictures of them all.'

Harper took it and slipped it into his hip-pack. He planned to put the documents in the drafts folder for Button to use as she wanted. 'There's something else I need you to do for me before you pack up,' he said. He unfolded a piece of paper and gave it to Hansfree. 'Can you rig up something like that for me?'

It took Hansfree only seconds to work out what it was. 'A detonating circuit?'

'Yeah, using a Sim card. It needs to be totally fail-safe.'

Hansfree grinned. 'My stuff always is, Lex. You know that.'

'How much do I owe you?'

Hansfree held up the sheet of paper. 'For this? On the house. Just make sure the rest of my fee goes into my bank account.'

'It's already there.' Harper jerked a thumb at the stack of boxes and cases. 'Do you need a hand with your gear?'

'Reggie and a few of my guys are coming over, so I'm all sorted. How soon do you want this circuit?'

'As soon as,' said Harper. 'I need to get back to Thailand.'

'Couple of hours should do it,' said Hansfree, reaching for a circuit board and a soldering iron.

'Perfect,' said Harper. 'I've got something else to pick up, so I'll catch you later.'

He went downstairs, getting a friendly wave from Mr Singh as he headed out. He caught a black cab to Chinatown and wandered around the restaurants, appearing to look at roast ducks hanging from their necks in the windows but actually checking reflections for tails.

The shop he was looking for was above a dim-sum restaurant. It had its own door on which there was a small brass sign with a dozen or so Chinese characters and below it, in English, DR LI, CHINESE MEDICINE AND

ACUPUNCTURE. Harper pushed open the door and went up a narrow flight of stairs that turned to the right and led to a beaded curtain that he pushed through.

Dr Li's shop was lined with wooden cabinets containing glass-fronted drawers of dried herbs, plants and leaves. On one of the walls posters of the human body showed what looked like acupuncture or pressure points marked in Chinese characters, and four framed degree certificates, which Harper had never examined too closely. He didn't care what, if any, professional qualifications Dr Li had. All he cared about was that he produced results. The man himself came out of a side room where he had an examination table, polishing his spectacles. He was short and plump with a totally bald head and pixie-like ears. He peered at Harper with screwed-up eyes, put his glasses on and smiled. 'Mr Lex, long time no see. What can I do for you?'

Dr Li had lived in London for the best part of forty years but he still spoke like an extra in a kung fu movie.

'Something a little special, Dr Li.'

'Anything for you, Mr Lex, always a pleasure.'

By the time Harper got back to the ops room, Hansfree had finished the circuit. It wasn't much bigger than a mobile phone, with a slot for a Sim card and a socket for a nine-volt battery. There didn't seem to be an on-off switch but there were two wires that could be connected when necessary to make the circuit live.

'You didn't say anything about a timer, right?' said Hansfree.

'Yeah, phone only, and it'll be line of sight because I don't want there to be any mistakes.'

'That'll fit the bill, then,' said Hansfree. 'You'll need to put in a Sim card and a battery, then run the red wires to the detonator. The circuit is inert until you connect the black wires together. At that point a call to the Sim card activates the circuit and Bob's your uncle.'

Harper wanted to shake hands but he always felt awkward touching Hansfree's prosthetic claw so he punched him gently on the shoulder. 'You're a star,' he said.

'A five-year-old could put that together,' said Hansfree. 'Next time give me something difficult.' He saluted with his right claw. 'It's been a pleasure, Lex. As always. Keep me in mind for your next job.'

'You're always top of my list, you know that,' said Harper. He headed downstairs, dropped off a wad of banknotes with Mr Singh by way of thanks, and caught a black cab to Bayswater. When he got back to his room, he transferred the contents of the bottle Dr Li had sold him to a small white plastic bottle that had once contained eye-drops, easily small enough to pass through airport security. The circuit board Hansfree had built went into a side pocket of his holdall, along with three of his mobile phones. He doubted that the circuit would show up as suspicious on any scan but even if they did examine it there was no battery in it and it didn't contravene any airport security regulations. He was good to go.

67

Harper was lying on his bed, staring up at the ceiling, when there was a soft knock on his door. He reached for the gun under his pillow, then smiled to himself as he realised that, generally, killers didn't knock. He swung his feet off the bed, opened the door and relaxed when he saw Charlotte Button. 'I wanted to catch you before you went,' she said. She was wearing a dark blue suit and carrying a Chanel bag with a gilt chain. She had tied her hair back and had on almost no makeup. She looked tired and Harper had a sudden urge to hug her, which he resisted because, at the end of the day, she was his boss and he was the hired hand.

'I'm flying back this evening,' he said, 'but I'm glad you dropped by.' He picked up the thumbdrive Hansfree had given him. 'There are surveillance pictures of the bad guys. Might be helpful.'

She took it from him and thanked him.

'So are you back in HM Government's good books?' he asked. 'You saved a lot of people today.'

'You mean you did. You did a great job.'

'It was a close-run thing,' said Harper, sitting down on the bed and waving her to the one chair in the room, next to the plywood dressing table. She looked at its dusty seat and grimaced, but sat down anyway. 'But all's good, yeah? Your client got what he wanted, and the authorities took out a jihadist cell. But I guess that's not why you're here, right?'

She nodded and forced a smile. 'I know who's been giving me grief,' she said. 'His name's Malik Sharif but he uses Malcolm. Malcolm Sharif. One of the richest Pakistanis living in the UK. He's been on the *Sunday Times* Rich List since 2012. And, ironically, we helped him get there.'

'We as in the government?'

'The Pool, specifically. Sharif is very close to a member of the cabinet. That member of the cabinet pushed through Sharif's citizenship papers. And it turns out that, as part of a quid pro quo, Sharif passed them some very damaging intel on another Pakistani businessman based in Birmingham. The intel showed that the businessman was a direct threat to our national security and it was decided to use the Pool to eliminate the threat without an embarrassing trial.'

'Embarrassing why?'

'Because the same minister who got Sharif his papers also fast-tracked the businessman's citizenship application. If that had become public knowledge, it could have brought the government down. Can you imagine what a field day the press would have had – "British Minister Gets Citizenship For Al-Qaeda Mastermind"? The Americans wouldn't have been best pleased, either. So, as I said, the job was given to the Pool. All well and good, except it now turns out that the businessman was totally innocent. Sharif faked the intel. He wanted the businessman out of the picture so that he could take over his companies, and that was what happened. Shame on me for not checking more closely, but the order came from the top and I was told it had to be done.'

'I hope it wasn't one of my contracts.'

Button shook her head. 'It wasn't.' She looked around the room. 'I don't suppose there's a minibar, is there?'

'With a nice cold Pinot Grigio in it?' He laughed. 'Charlie, this place is sixty quid a night, cash, no questions asked. I don't think they even change the sheets. So Sharif arranged for the safe-deposit boxes to be raided?'

'I'm assuming so. That's conjecture. But what isn't conjecture is that he's having me followed. He's been doing it through an Israeli security company. Former Mossad. It's all been one step removed but there's no doubt it's him. Somehow he'd got to hear about my insurance policies and was worried that if anything happened to me his dirty little secret would get out. He has a lot of enemies back in Pakistan so if he was stripped of his citizenship and sent packing, he'd lose everything. Including his life, probably. He obviously figured that he'd be safer if I wasn't around. He paid the Israelis to track down my insurance policies, remove them and presumably me, too.'

Harper nodded. 'Now what? I'm assuming a stern talking-to isn't going to get this sorted.'

Button tried to smile but Harper could see how worried she was. 'Can you do it for me, Alex? Can you cancel Malik Sharif before you go back to Thailand? For your usual rate, of course.'

Harper grinned. 'Charlie, honey, this one's on me. It'll be a pleasure.'

68

Malik Sharif lived in a mansion in St John's Wood, not far from the one owned by the former Beatle, Paul McCartney. Sharif's mansion was twice the size of McCartney's, standing alone in a large garden with a double garage at the side. Harper was parked outside the house when Sharif arrived home at just after six in the back of a chauffeur-driven Rolls-Royce. He let himself into the house and there didn't appear to be anyone around to greet him. Harper was able to get to the rear garden and watched the house as darkness fell. A woman was in the kitchen, too portly and plain to be Mrs Sharif. He watched her cook a meal, then disappear into the house. Security was non-existent, pretty much, with no CCTV, no bodyguards and an alarm system that seemed unused.

Harper was wearing dark clothing – black jeans, and a bomber jacket over a black pullover – and had a small backpack with him. He had brought a sandwich and a bottle of water, and consumed them as he watched the rear of the house. A light went on in a room on the top floor, then ten minutes later it went off. A flickering through the curtains suggested that a television had been switched on, but at just before one o'clock it stopped.

An upstairs sash window had been left partly open, a bathroom by the look of it, and there was a drainpipe that could be climbed, but the sunroom, with sliding windows, was a better bet. Harper couldn't see any motion-sensitive floodlights on the house, but he kept close to the hedge as he made his way towards the sunroom. It was locked but he had a screwdriver in his backpack, which was all he needed to pop the lock. He slid open the door and stepped inside, then moved through into the kitchen. The absence of feed bowls meant he was unlikely to bump into a dog. It looked as if Sharif felt so safe in his adopted country that he didn't need security. Harper smiled to himself. Big mistake. He took his gun out of the backpack, tiptoed into the hallway and up a large, winding staircase.

Sharif was fast asleep in the master bedroom, spread-eagled on his king-size bed like a stranded starfish. He was in his sixties, overweight, with a neatly trimmed beard and receding hair. His spectacles were on the bedside table, with a glass of water and a gold watch. He was snoring loudly, his belly rising and falling in time with his breathing.

Harper doffed his backpack and took out padded cuffs attached to lengths of rope. He put the gun on the bed and carefully lashed Sharif's wrists to the ornate brass headboard and his ankles to the legs at the bottom of the bed. Sharif grunted in his sleep but didn't wake up. It was only when Harper took a strip of cloth from his backpack and tied it around the man's mouth that his eyes fluttered open. He groaned and tried to rub his face but realised his hands were tied and began to struggle. Then he saw Harper standing over him. He tried to speak but the gag muffled everything except a frightened grunt. 'Don't struggle, mate, it'll soon be over,' said Harper. He reached into his pocket and took out a syringe containing some of the liquid he had purchased from Dr Li in London's Chinatown. He had more than he needed, certainly more than enough to take care of Sharif. It was a chemical isolated from *Gelsemium elegans*, a highly toxic yellow-flowered shrub found only in a remote region of China. It was the perfect assassin's weapon – just a few drops would trigger a heart attack. For years the pretty flowers had been harvested and the chemical used by the Chinese Ministry of State Security to kill those it wanted out of the way without the necessity of a trial. In recent years the Russians had discovered the compound and had also used it with great success. Death always came quickly and a cursory examination would show that it had been a heart attack.

Sharif's eyes widened in terror and he began to struggle but the bonds held firm. Harper held the syringe in front of the man's face and grinned at him. 'You tried to hurt a friend of mine, mate, and there's a price to be paid for that. Charlotte Button. You put the fear of God into her, do you know that? Getting those places robbed, getting those Poles killed, and for what? To protect a secret that was never in any danger of getting out? You should have let sleeping dogs lie, because this is one dog that's come back to bite you in the arse.'

Harper walked to the bottom of the bed. He held Sharif's left foot tightly, and pushed the needle into a vein between the big toe and the one next to it. Sharif tried to kick free but Harper had a grip like a vice and he slowly pushed down the plunger. When the syringe was empty, he stood back. The gelsemium began to work in seconds. At first

Sharif went still, a look of pure panic in his eyes. Then his body went into spasm: his back arched and his eyes bulged. He held that position for a good ten seconds, as taut as a bow, then collapsed back onto the bed. His chest heaved and his breath came in short gasps, making the gag pop back and forth. Suddenly he went still. Harper waited a full minute before checking for a pulse in the man's neck. Finding none, he removed the cuffs and placed them, with the empty syringe, in his backpack.

He rearranged the duvet over the body, took a minute to check that he hadn't left anything incriminating behind, then slipped out of the room, went downstairs and out through the sunroom. Five minutes later he was in a black cab, heading back to Bayswater.

69

Harper was fairly sure that the Russians would be watching the Thai airports, or at the very least keeping track of arrival cards. It was easy enough to do. Every foreigner who arrived at any of the country's airports had to fill in a landing card and have his photograph taken. A bribe of a few hundred dollars would get you a copy of the card and the photograph. If he was going to get back into Thailand without the Russians knowing, he'd have to enter by land. That was easy, too, as the country was bordered by Malaysia, Myanmar, Laos and Cambodia.

He decided on Malaysia because he could take the train from Kuala Lumpur. He flew from London to Belfast, showing a driving licence as ID, then caught a taxi south to Dublin Airport. From there he flew to Amsterdam on an Irish passport and caught the midday KLM flight that arrived in Kuala Lumpur at just after six in the morning. He booked into a hotel at the airport, ate steak and chips, then slept for most of the day. He checked out at five o'clock in the evening and caught a cab to the main railway station where he bought a ticket to Bangkok. The train left at nine fifteen p.m. and, even though he had a sleeping cabin, he stayed awake for most of the night. Eleven hours later he arrived at Padang Besar, a Malaysian town that bordered Songkhai province in Thailand. The town on the other side of the border was also called Padang Besar though the locals referred to it as Pekan Siam. It was a popular destination for Thai and Malaysian tourists who could take advantage of the duty-free shopping complex between the border checkpoints.

Harper's Irish passport was scrutinised but he wasn't photographed. He checked into a cheap hotel to eat and rest, then caught the early evening train to Bangkok. Again he had a sleeping cabin and managed to grab a few hours' sleep before arriving in Bangkok shortly after midnight. He caught a taxi to Pattaya and phoned Mickey Moore on the way.

70

The Russian stretched out his legs and grunted. The chair he was sitting on was comfortable enough but he had been there for six hours and his buttocks were starting to complain. More than two dozen people had entered or left the condominium building but none had matched the photograph he had concealed in the magazine on his lap. He was looking for an Englishman in his thirties, tall but not too tall, fit but not too fit, average-looking. In fact there was nothing memorable about Alex Harper, which was why the Russian was constantly having to look at the photograph. His colleague sitting on the other side of the reception area seemed to be equally uncomfortable. Both men were former Russian special forces. They had served in Ukraine and the north Caucasus and were happier with guns in their hands and bullets whizzing overhead than sitting in chairs.

The Russian bent down and picked up his cup of Starbucks coffee. It was the third since he had arrived at the building, and he would be needing the bathroom soon. That was why there were two of them. Mirov had been clear on that: someone had to be there all the time. He sipped his coffee and nodded at his colleague, who nodded back.

A motorcycle taxi driver walked in, with a tattoo of a cobweb across his neck and a steel chain around his neck from which hung five Buddha symbols. Two women in matching lime green suits were standing behind the counter and the guy spoke to them in Thai, then looked around the reception area. He took out an iPhone, made a call, then walked around talking loudly, the phone pressed to his ear. The Russian was impressed that a motorcycle taxi driver owned an expensive iPhone, unless it was a Chinese knock-off. He had realised soon after he'd arrived in the country that nothing in Thailand was as it seemed at first glance. Watches were often fake, as were designer labels, and more often than not the famous Thai smile was a mask for something more sinister. The Russian wasn't a big fan of Thailand but Mirov was paying big bucks and the boss, Yuri Lukin, had a huge operation in Moscow that promised even richer pickings in future, providing the Russian made a good impression.

The motorcycle guy was talking animatedly, waving his hand up and down as he stalked around the reception area, passing within a few feet of the Russian, then heading off to the far side, clearly annoyed at something. Then he took the phone away from his ear, shouted something at the two girls, and left. The Russian smiled at his colleague. At least something had happened to break the monotony.

He looked at the glass doors to his left. They were the only way to get to the lift lobby, and beyond the lifts were the stairs. Anyone going in or out of the apartments had to pass through the doors, which were operated from inside and outside by a keycard system. If Alex Harper returned to his apartment they would spot him, no question.

The motorcycle taxi driver went outside. His bike was standing by the main entrance but he ignored it and walked to a black Humvee that was parked on the road. The tinted window rolled down as he approached the vehicle and Mickey Moore grinned at him. 'How did it go, Adisorn?'

'There are two in there, Khun Mickey,' said the man. 'They look like Russians.' He passed the phone through the window and grinned as Mickey handed him a thousand-baht note in return. 'Anytime, Khun Mickey,' he said, putting his palms together and bowing, the traditional Thai *wai*.

'You take care, Adisorn,' said Mickey. As Adisorn headed back to his bike, Mickey went through the photographs on the phone. The Thai had been right: they looked like Russians. Big, hard men who clearly weren't waiting in Harper's condominium building to give him a welcome-back vodka. He grimaced, tossed the phone onto the passenger seat and drove off.

71

Harper had the taxi drop him on Second Road and went down Soi 15 to Walking Street. It was two o'clock in the morning so most of the Chinese and Korean tour groups had gone home, leaving the strip to the drunks, bar girls and sex tourists. A young contortionist was doing her thing for a group of onlookers under the watchful eye of a man whom Harper hoped was her father. She was standing on her hands with her legs over her head, using her feet to put on a pair of sunglasses. She couldn't have been much more than twelve years old. A group of uniformed cops were sitting at a table nearby in front of a police van, handing out tourist information and clearly unconcerned about any possible breach of the child labour laws.

Groups of young Thai men in black uniforms and scantily dressed dancers were in the street, trying to entice customers into their bars, without much luck. Most of the men, and women, who walked past Harper had the blank-eyed faces and slack jaws caused by too much alcohol, too much ear-shattering music and, in all likelihood, a fair amount of illegal drug-taking. Harper had a Singha beer baseball cap pulled down over his face as he threaded his way through the drunks to the Ice Bar. There were two sections: a trendy cocktail bar and the Ice Bar itself, a refrigerated unit with an industrial door and plate-glass windows overlooking the street. The cocktail bar was comfortably air-conditioned while the Ice Bar was maintained at twenty degrees below zero.

Mickey and his brother Mark were in the cocktail bar, chatting with the owner. Mickey saw Harper first and grinned broadly. 'You look like shit, mate.' He was a big-chested man in his early fifties, with hair that had receded almost halfway back and a dark tan that emphasised the blue of his eyes. He had a thick gold chain around his neck from which hung a gold Buddha image in a gold case. There was another thick gold chain on his right wrist and a chunky gold Patek Philippe watch on the other. He was wearing a white silk shirt with the sleeves rolled up and Versace jeans.

Harper grinned. In comparison to Mickey, he looked like a tramp. 'I came overland, from Malaysia.'

Mickey walked over and gave him a hug and a slap on the back. 'Drove?'

'Train.'

'How was it?'

'Like you said, I look like shit. But at least I came in under the radar.'

Mickey released his grip on Harper and stepped to the side to let his brother grab him in an equally painful hug. Mark was younger than Mickey by about eight years but was a couple of inches taller, with an even bigger chest. Like Mickey, he wore a gold chain around his neck but on his wrists he had a large Cartier watch with multiple dials and a metal Khmer bracelet that he claimed made him invulnerable to bullets. That was what the Khmer magic man who had sold it to him had said, but Mark had never put it to the test. He was also wearing designer labels – a pair of Armani jeans and a Ralph Lauren shirt, the real thing, not the knock-off copies that were sold all over Pattaya. The Moore brothers spent a lot of money on their appearance. That wasn't how Harper liked to operate. His watch was a cheap Casio and he never wore fashion brands. Labels were easy to identify and remember, and expensive watches stuck in people's memories. He preferred to be as forgettable as possible.

Mark punched Harper on the shoulder. 'Yeah, and then you walk straight into the lion's den. You must have balls of bloody steel, mate. Red Oktober is less than a hundred yards away.'

'This is the last place they'll be looking for me,' said Harper.

'Hide in plain sight?' said Mark 'It's still a risk, mate. You're coming home with us tonight.'

'Nah, I'll be fine.'

'Fuck that, do as Mark says,' said Mickey. 'We checked out your condo. There's a couple of Russian goons camped out in Reception.' He pulled an iPhone from his back pocket and showed him the photographs the motorcycle taxi driver had taken earlier that day.

Harper scowled at the picture. They were big men and certainly looked Russian. 'Fuck.'

'So we're booking you into Casa del Moore,' said Mark. 'No arguments.'

Harper nodded. 'Okay.' He indicated the large refrigerator door. 'But we need to talk now.'

Mickey waved a hand at the owner. 'Okay if we have a conference?'

The owner flashed him a thumbs-up and Mark pulled open the door. Most of the patrons borrowed one of the bar's fur-lined parka jackets as they knocked back a selection of freezing-cold flavoured vodkas and tequilas, but Mickey, Mark and Harper went in as they were.

There was a small bar made of clear plastic that looked like ice in the corner where a waitress in a padded coat with the hood up was looking glumly through a plate-glass window at the passers-by in Walking Street. Her smile flashed on as soon as they came in and she gestured at the bottles in front of her. 'What can I get you?' she asked. Her only company was a Thai man in a polar bear suit.

'Three chocolate vodkas,' said Mickey. 'And one for you. And one for the fucking bear.' He patted the polar bear's shoulder. 'I don't know how you put up with it, mate, standing with your balls freezing for ten hours a day.'

The bear shrugged.

'He's got a job, hasn't he?' said Mark. 'Plus he gets all his booze free.' Mark shivered and rubbed his forearms. 'Plus he's got a nice comfy suit to keep him warm.'

The girl poured five chocolate vodkas. Mickey raised his. 'To our mate Lex. Life's never fucking boring with you around.'

The three men raised their shot glasses. So did the girl. The bear pulled back his head to reveal a Thai man in his forties with a gap-toothed grin. He picked up a glass with his paw and raised it in a salute. All five downed their drinks in one and slammed their glasses onto the bar. Mickey took out his wallet and gave the girl and the bear a thousand baht each. 'Give us five minutes alone,' he said. They hurried out and slammed the door behind them. The Moore brothers often used the Ice Bar to discuss business. It was totally soundproofed and there was a huge rattling air-conditioning unit on full to keep the temperature down so there was zero chance of anyone inside being overheard.

'Right. I need a silenced gun,' said Harper. The three men were leaning over the bar, their heads close together and their backs to the window. 'Mine is in my apartment and I can't get to it. Ideally I'd like something Russian. A 9mm PB silenced pistol would be favourite.'

'That shouldn't be a problem,' said Mickey.

'And I'll need explosives.'

'What sort?' asked Mark.

'The sort that go bang.'

Mickey laughed. 'Yeah, but there are big bangs and small bangs. And bloody huge bangs. Spectaculars, the IRA used to call them.'

'Nothing fancy,' said Harper. 'Just enough to blow up a car. In fact, not a whole car just the back bit.'

'Are you going to war, Lex?' asked Mickey.

'Just taking care of business,' said Harper. 'They started it.'

'Well, to be fair, you did stick bottles up the arses of two leading lights of the Russian Mafia,' said Mark.

'After they'd beaten up a friend of mine. And they sent someone to kill me in Paris. So if I don't make a bold statement now, this is going to drag on and on.'

'Why not just shoot the fuckers?' asked Mark.

'Because a bomb will muddy the waters,' said Harper. 'It'll leave some doubt. I was thinking you could ask your

Cambodian Army mates. I'm sure they've got some spare.'

'I'm sure they have,' agreed Mickey. 'They should be able to get the PB for you, too.'

'So are we good? Explosives and a detonator. Two to be on the safe side.'

'What about a timing circuit?'

'I'm sorted on that front. How soon can you get it for me?'

'How soon do you need it?' asked Mickey.

'As soon as.'

'Then I'll fly over today. Providing we pay in cash we should have the stuff in Bangkok within twenty-four hours.'

'How much do I owe you?' asked Harper.

'Buy me a chocolate vodka and we'll call it quits.' Mickey slapped him on the back. 'Least I can do for a mate who's willing to go to war with the Russian Mafia.'

'It's not a war, mate,' said Harper. 'It's not even a fucking skirmish.'

72

A rmed police were standing at the two entrances to the compound where the Moore brothers lived. There was a tradition in Thailand of police officers hiring themselves out as security guards, usually in banks and jewellery shops, but Mickey's police contacts were as good as Harper's and there were always at least four on duty outside the compound. The two at the main entrance saluted his black Humvee as they drove by, which Harper thought was a nice touch. They were wearing white T-shirts, brown police uniform trousers, with shiny black boots, and had Glock pistols in nylon holsters on their hips.

There were six Thai-style villas around a central building, set in twelve acres of landscaped gardens with towering palms and spreading fruit trees. The main building had a large landscaped pool and a terrace protected by a pagoda-type roof where the brothers had regular barbecues. To the front of the main building a car parking area had spaces for more than two dozen vehicles. There were two black Range Rovers, a red Porsche, another black Humvee, a Bentley convertible, an old MGB sports car, and several Toyota saloons that belonged to the staff. Mickey parked the Humvee next to its twin, then jogged up the stairs and through the carved doors at the top. There was a double-height hallway with a vaulted teak ceiling and a seven-foot tall golden standing Buddha statue, wreathed in garlands of purple and white flowers. The hallway led to a huge room filled with overstuffed sofas and teak planters' chairs, a large LCD television on one wall and a library of paperback books. It was the compound's chill-out area. Leading off it was a dining room with a table long enough to seat twenty, and another room, which served as a private cinema with a dozen reclining seats and sofas.

Harper and Mark followed Mickey down a hallway to the double-height bar area, which had vaulted teak ceilings with large wooden-bladed fans turning slowly above their heads. It looked like a five-star hotel bar, with leather sofas and armchairs, and a mahogany counter complete with beer taps and a full range of spirits. Glass-fronted fridges held wine and soft drinks, and there was even a popcorn machine. The luxury-hotel feel was spoiled somewhat by the three pinball machines, a Wurlitzer jukebox and a massive fruit machine behind the pool table.

Two men were playing pool. Like Mickey, they were in their early fifties, well-muscled and tanned by the fierce Thai sun. Harper knew them both – Davie Black and Barry 'Baz' Wilson. Like the Moore brothers they were skilled armed robbers, though unlike the Moores they had done time. As a teenager, Davie had been caught robbing a post office with a chair leg in a supermarket carrier bag, and Baz had tried to run a Securicor van off the road in Liverpool and ended up in hospital, then prison after slamming his car into a lamp-post. Both had learned about the Moore brothers while behind bars and met up with them after their release. They had been part of the crew for the past fifteen years.

The Moores and their team had been responsible for some of the most spectacular heists and robberies in Europe over the past couple of decades. They rarely struck more than once a year, their haul was never less than a million pounds, and everything they did was planned to the last detail, usually by an expert hired for the job, although as their fame had grown it was more usual for someone to approach them with a plan. It was a faultless business model that had made them all multi-millionaires. But they spent what they earned, pretty much. Harper had tried to convince them to join him in his various drug-trafficking enterprises, in particular shipping cannabis from North Africa into the European Union, but they were old-school villains, and while they were happy to use drugs recreationally, they had always refused to get into the business. 'Better the devil you know, mate,' Mickey always said.

Davie and Baz stopped playing and came over to them.

'Bloody hell! Lex Harper! How's it going, stranger?' Harper turned and grinned at the good-looking guy in a wheelchair, who had propelled himself in from next door. His name was Terry Norris, the youngest of the crew. Ex-army, a weapons expert, who was as good as anyone Harper had ever met, Norris had severed his spine in a motorcycle accident and was unlikely ever to walk again. Ramps and lifts all around the compound ensured that he could go wherever he wanted.

'All good,' said Harper, shaking the man's hand.

'I heard you've been winning friends and influencing people,' said Terry.

'That's why he's here,' laughed Mickey. 'We're taking him under our wing.' He pulled open a double-doored fridge and took out a bottle of Heineken. 'Anyone else want one?' he asked.

'What do you think?' asked Mark.

Mickey tossed him a beer. 'Davie? Baz?'

'We're sorted,' said Baz, nodding at a bottle of brandy on a shelf by the pool table. It was half empty.

'Lex?'

'I'm good,' said Harper. He had spotted two Thai girls lying on one of the sofas, entwined in each other's arms. Mickey saw what he was looking at and waved his beer bottle at them. 'Who are they?'

'They're with me,' said Baz. 'Ning and Nong, I think. Ning for sure, Nong I could be wrong about. They're lesbians. You can take them for a spin if you want when they wake up.'

'Why would I want to fool around with lesbians?' asked Mickey. 'Doesn't that sort of defeat the purpose?'

'They're happy enough for you to join in,' said Baz.

'Mate, I've told you before, I don't want your sloppy seconds. Look, Lex is going to be staying in the empty villa.' He grinned at Harper. 'You're welcome to Ding and Dong if you like.'

'Ning and Nong,' said Baz.

'I'm good,' said Harper.

'Whatever,' said Mickey. He looked at his watch. 'Guys, I'm off to Cambodia first thing so I'm going to have to hit the sack if I'm going to get any sleep at all. Take care of Lex. Lex, mate, the chef's on duty twenty-four/seven so order what you want.'

'You still play pool, Lex?' asked Baz.

'Been known to,' said Harper.

'Let's play doubles. You and Terry against me and Davie. Thousand bucks a game.'

Terry looked up at Harper and winked. 'You up for this?' asked Harper.

'Money in the bank, Lex. And they can break.'

73

Mickey Moore caught an early morning Bangkok Airways flight to Phnom Penh. The journey took just over an hour and an army Land Rover was waiting for him as the plane taxied up to the terminal. As the rest of the passengers hurried towards Immigration and Customs, two soldiers carrying AK-47s escorted him to their vehicle and whisked him out of the airport.

They turned off the main road on the outskirts of Phnom Penh, then rattled along a dusty single-track road through the Cambodian countryside for the best part of an hour, eventually arriving at the army firing range, which Moore and his crew visited several times a year. It was intended for Cambodian troops to hone their skills but the army was happy for tourists to have a go – at a price. Pretty much any weapon owned by the military was available, from simple handguns through AK-47s to bazookas. Hand grenades could be thrown for fifty dollars a go, and RPGs for five hundred. The army could also be creative in the targets it supplied. Barrels full of water were the target of choice for the machine-guns, but chickens could be supplied at five dollars a time. And larger weaponry, even hand grenades, could be hurled at cows and water buffaloes, as long as enough cash was handed over. Moore had heard that, providing enough money was paid, human targets could be provided from the local prison, but he figured – or hoped – that was just a rumour.

There were several firing ranges and a number of buildings that could be used as practice areas. The Moore brothers would come over with their crew to rehearse robberies on the range before flying to the UK to carry out the real thing. Their attention to detail at the planning stage was one of the reasons they had never been caught.

The colonel was sitting under a large canopy made of palm fronds in a La-Z-Boy chair overlooking one of the target ranges. At his side a stainless-steel ice bucket contained a bottle of Johnnie Walker Black Label while another held ice and several bottles of soda water. There was also a plate of sliced pineapple, a Smith & Wesson .44 Magnum and his peaked cap.

He grinned when he saw Mickey climb out of the Land Rover and pulled the handle on the side of his chair to lower his feet. He stood up and hugged Mickey. 'Always a pleasure to see you in my country, Mickey.'

'Sam, good to see you, too,' said Mickey, patting him on the back.

The colonel's full name was Samang, which was Khmer for 'lucky', but most Westerners ended up shortening it to Sam.

Sam hugged Mickey again, then waved him to a chair that was the twin of his own. A very pretty girl with waist-length hair, wearing a traditional Khmer purple silk sarong, came over and poured Mickey a whisky and soda, then refilled the colonel's glass. The two men toasted each other,

drank, and sat down. The girl picked up the plate of pineapple and offered it to Mickey. He took a piece, dabbed it
in a ceramic pot filled with chilli, sugar and salt, and popped
it into his mouth.

'So, what can I do for you, my friend?' asked the colonel.

Mickey waited until the girl had walked away, then said,
'Explosives. What do you have?'

Sam held up his palms to the heavens. 'I have whatever
you want,' he said. 'C1, C2, C3, C4, CA, CB.' His grin
widened. 'A veritable alphabet.'

'What would be best for taking out a vehicle? A car?'

'You can't go wrong with C4,' said Sam.

'How much would you need?'

'To destroy the vehicle? Or just kill the occupants?'

'The occupants.'

The colonel nodded thoughtfully. 'Half a kilo would
suffice.'

'Can you deliver it to me in Pattaya tomorrow?'

'It's urgent?'

'I'm afraid so,' Mickey confirmed.

'Then of course tomorrow can be arranged. It will be
expensive.'

'No problem. It's a ten-hour drive, right?'

'Not necessary, my friend. I will have it delivered from
Siem Reap. Five and a half hours, maybe six. I can have
it in Pattaya by midnight.'

'Perfect. How much. I'll need a couple of detonators,
too.'

'Of course.'

'And something a little special if you have it. A silenced
pistol. A Russian one, if possible.'

Sam laughed. 'You're not planning to assassinate someone are you, Mickey?' He drained his glass, then waved for the waitress to refill it, and Mickey's.

Again, Mickey waited until she had left before answering the colonel's question, though he knew Sam was joking. 'It's for a friend,' he said.

'Of course it is,' said the colonel. 'But it's none of my business who does what with what. We have several Makarovs and PB pistols in the armoury and I'm sure there's a least one with a working suppressor.'

'Excellent. And the cost? For everything?'

'Including delivery, three thousand dollars, my friend.'

Mickey reached inside his jacket, took out an envelope and counted thirty hundred-dollar bills. There was no need to do anything but pay up front because the colonel had never let him down.

'Always a pleasure doing business with you, Mickey.' The colonel slipped the notes into the pocket of his tunic.

'And you, Sam.'

The colonel raised his glass. 'You should stay for lunch. A rich American is going to fire a machine-gun at a cow and we'll barbecue what's left. We'll have you at the airport in plenty of time for the early evening flight.'

Mickey raised his glass in salute. 'Sounds like a plan.'

74

Police Colonel Somchai Wattanakolwit kept his eyes on the ball, swung back the club and tried to clear his mind of everything accept the shot he was about to make. He started his swing, relaxed into it, and was rewarded with a satisfying crack as the ball soared into the air.

'Nice shot,' said a voice behind him, and Somchai turned to find himself looking into the amused eyes of Lex Harper.

'You shouldn't go creeping up on someone like that,' said Somchai. 'Not when I have my gun in my golf bag.' He handed his club to the nineteen-year-old girl caddy. She was wearing a tight-fitting white T-shirt, a short white skirt and dark blue panties, as were the twenty-year-old driver of his golf cart and the girl who was responsible for supplying him with cold beers and even colder towels. Somchai was wearing a pink polo shirt and blue and green checked trousers with a snakeskin belt. His three fellow players – all off-duty policemen – were equally brightly dressed, each with a golf cart and three caddies to attend to his needs.

Harper wasn't dressed for golf – he had on blue jeans and a cheap grey hoodie and didn't appear to have shaved that day. 'Now, this is a pleasant surprise,' said Somchai.

'I had no idea you were back in Thailand.' He stepped forward, put his arm around Harper's shoulders and led him away from his golfing buddies.

'Hopefully very few people do,' said Harper.

'You should bring your clubs next time,' he said.

'I don't own golf clubs,' said Harper. 'I don't have the patience.'

'That's the whole point,' said Somchai. 'It teaches you patience. There is something very Zen-like about golf. I think that's why we Asians enjoy it so much.'

One of his caddies came over and gave them both iced towels. Harper slapped his on the back of his neck. It was a hot day, well into the high thirties. Expats always claimed that Thailand had two seasons. Hot, and very hot.

Somchai turned to watch the next golfer teeing up his shot. 'You know that Yuri Lukin has hired some very heavy hitters?' he said.

'I sort of thought that might happen,' said Harper, keeping his voice low so that it wouldn't carry.

'And security has been increased at Valentin's compound for when he and Grigory Lukin are released from hospital.' Somchai rubbed his cold towel around his neck. 'Though I gather it will be a few days yet before the doctors allow them to leave. You did a lot of damage, it seems.'

'Allegedly,' said Harper.

'It's good to see you have retained your sense of humour, my friend,' said Somchai.

The golfer hit the ball with a resounding thwack that sent it soaring into the air and Somchai nodded appreciatively. He smiled at Harper. 'I'm not sure that you coming back to Pattaya was a good idea.'

'I need to get this sorted, Somchai. I can't spend the rest of my life looking over my shoulder.'

Somchai seemed uncomfortable. 'My friend, as much as I'd like to, I can't protect you. Yuri Lukin is paying off the boss of my boss and even higher, and I can't go against them.'

Harper shook his head. 'It's not your protection I need, Somchai,' he said. 'It's your permission.'

Somchai frowned. 'My permission? For what, may I ask?'

Harper's smile broadened. 'Your permission to protect myself.'

Somchai chuckled. 'Oh, by all means, my friend. You do what you have to do.' He patted Harper on the back. 'And I wish you all the luck in the world.'

75

Mark prodded the massive T-bone steaks that were sizzling on the grill while Baz and Lex looked on, drinking bottles of Heineken. 'Japanese beef,' said Mark. 'Can't beat it. The cows get a bottle of beer every day, a massage and probably a happy ending for all I know. Best beef in the world. And the most expensive.'

Aerosmith was blaring from the stereo system and braziers had been lit around the pool, casting flickering shadows over the water. Half a dozen Thai girls were playing in the water and more were sprawled around the cabanas. It was party night, but pretty much every night was party night at the compound.

'See anything you like, Lex?' asked Mark, waving a pair of stainless-steel tongs. Harper wasn't sure if he was referring to the girls or the steaks. The barbecue was huge and the table next to Mark was piled high with steaks, chicken and fish, and another laden with salads, sauces and vegetables. The Moore brothers had three chefs between them working round the clock, all hired from top hotels on much-improved salaries. The girls were also paid, and Harper recognised several top dancers from the city's best go-go bars. Baz had left the compound at just before eight in one of the Humvees and had returned with six of the girls, all obviously pleased at being asked to spend an evening partying rather than dancing around a chrome pole. Mickey had arrived at the compound at just after six and had phoned in the rest of the girls, most apparently regular visitors to the compound. Two were dancing topless at the side of the pool while two more had appointed themselves bartenders and were walking around refilling glasses and offering fresh beers.

'Lex, how do you want your steak?' asked Mark, waving his tongs in the air.

'Just cut the hoofs off and throw it over.' Harper laughed. 'The rarer the better.'

Mark stuck his fork into a steak and slapped it onto a plate. Harper took it, helped himself to potato salad and a roasted ear of corn, then went to sit down at a long table where Terry was already tucking in. 'I keep forgetting how large you guys live,' said Harper, as he cut into his steak. Blood oozed out over his plate, which was just how he liked it.

'Dunno how long it'll last,' said Terry. 'The Russians are going to spoil it for everyone.'

'How so?'

'You know how so,' said Terry. 'You've been here long enough. We have a string of genuine businesses, property, restaurants, a couple of diving companies. We all have work permits and pay tax.' He waved his knife at the ground around them. 'We can't own this place because only Thais can own land, but it's in a company we control so all good. The Thais let us live here and we respect that by not shitting on our doorstep. But you know as well as I do that the Russians are a whole different ball game. They run prostitution here, all sorts of scams, ATM fraud, protection rackets, and they've started trading Thai girls into Russia. You've seen what they've done to Walking Street. Wall-to-wall Russian hookers, these days. There'll be a backlash before long, and when it comes all foreigners will be hit, not just the Russians.'

Davie Black sat down with a plate of steak and chicken. Harper grinned. 'No veg?'

'Like my South African mates say, chicken is a fucking vegetable,' said Davie. 'You guys talking about the Russians?'

'I was just telling Lex, the shit is gonna hit the fan sooner rather than later.'

Davie started hacking at his steak. 'What about you, Lex? Have you got a plan B?'

'I've always got a plan B,' said Harper. 'But I'm happy enough here.'

'Cambodia, that's where we'll be going,' said Davie. 'If there is a clampdown, we've already got a spot picked out. Fifteen acres, our own lake. We've had a place designed and it could be up and running in six months if we need it.' He waved a chunk of steak in front of Harper's face. 'Tell you what, we'll fix you up with a villa. What do you think, Tel? Lex is one of the guys, right?'

'Hell, yeah,' said Terry.

'I appreciate the offer, seriously. But I don't live well with others.'

'Lone fucking wolf, is Lex,' said Davie.

Harper grinned. 'Yeah, that's my Red Indian name. But, seriously, thanks for the offer. If ever I turn gay I'll take you up on it.'

The two men laughed, and despite the banter, Harper was genuinely touched. The crew was the closest thing he had to family and he knew they felt the same.

One of the compound's estate managers, a middle-aged Thai who had worked for the Moores for more than a decade, hurried over to the cabana where Mickey was lounging with two dark-skinned Thai girls in matching stars-and-stripes bikinis. The man had a whispered conversation with him, then hurried away. Mickey got to his feet, kissed one of the girls, then went over to Harper's table.

'The gear's arrived,' said Mickey. 'We need to give it the once-over so that the guy can get on his way.'

Harper stood up and followed him to the main building, then out to the car park. There was a minivan with the name of a Thai tourist company on the side, along with the logo of a smiling elephant wearing a floppy hat and holding a cocktail glass with an umbrella in it. There were no passengers in the van, just a driver, who was wearing sunglasses even though it was ten o'clock at night, and a woman who might have been his wife. Mickey opened the side door, pushed back the middle row of seats, then pulled up the grey carpet. There was a metal door set into the floor and four holes with hexagonal screw heads. The woman twisted in her seat and handed him an Allen key, which he used it to remove the screws before he pulled up the panel. Underneath a compartment contained three cloth-wrapped packages. Mickey took out the largest and unwrapped it. It was a block of C4 explosive, sealed in plastic. On top of it were two detonators, each with twin wires. Mickey laughed. 'You'd have thought they'd wrap them separately,' he said.

'No need,' said Harper. 'Without a power source it's as safe as Plasticine.'

Mickey rewrapped the package and handed it to Harper. The second contained a gun, and the last a silencer, with two eight-cartridge magazines.

Harper nodded his approval and Mickey rewrapped them, handed them to him, then screwed the panel into place and put the carpet back. He gave the Allen key to the woman, along with a couple of thousand baht, which earned him a respectful *wai* from her and her husband. Mickey slammed the door and the minivan drove off to the main entrance, where the gate was already rattling open. Two police officers clicked their heels and saluted as it drove onto the road.

'Drop the gear in your villa and we'll get stuck into our steaks,' said Mickey. 'Mark and I will give you a hand tomorrow.'

'You don't have to, really. This is my fight.'

Mickey put his arm around Harper's shoulders. 'It's our fight, mate. You're one of us. They fuck with you, they fuck with the whole crew.'

76

The limousine spent all morning parked inside the Valentin compound. Mickey had arranged for a team of motorcycle taxi riders to take turns following the vehicle and to stay in touch on their mobile phones. The driver was Russian, but from his height and build, he wasn't a bodyguard. He didn't seem to be especially well trained either, and apparently wasn't aware that he was being tailed. The motorcycle riders stayed in touch with Mickey through mobile phones. The Moore brothers had more than a dozen riders on retainer. They ran errands and were often a useful source of intelligence about what was going on around the city.

At just after two o'clock in the afternoon, Mickey took a call from one of his spies that the limousine had left the compound. He went out to the pool where Harper was sitting in one of the cabanas with Mark. 'The limo's on the move,' he said. 'Heading to Pattaya City. Do you want to check it out?'

Harper nodded.

'I'll come with you,' said Mark, grabbing a shirt.

'I can do it myself,' said Harper.

'Fuck that,' said Mark. 'All for one and one for all.'

Harper headed back to his villa. The device was in a teak cupboard in the hall. It was a simple enough build: the two detonators were embedded in the plastic explosive, which was connected to the circuit that Hansfree had built for him in London. It was sitting in a grey plastic Tupperware box to which Harper had superglued several powerful magnets. The whole thing was about nine inches long, six inches wide and three inches deep. He placed it in a black nylon kitbag and carried it over to the main building, where Mickey and Mark were waiting for him. They walked together to the parking area. 'We'll take one of the pick-ups,' said Mickey, grabbing a set of keys from a line of hooks by the front door. 'The Hummers and the Range Rovers attract attention.'

'Yeah, funny that,' said Harper.

They went out of the main building and over to a white four-door Toyota pick-up truck with tinted windows. Mickey and Mark sat in the front and Harper climbed into the back.

Mickey took another call while they were driving down the road towards the coast. 'He's in the Central Festival Department Store,' said Mickey, as he shoved the phone back into his pocket. 'This should work.'

'That thing isn't going to go off accidentally, is it?' asked Mark, twisting around in his seat and pointing at the holdall.

'It's phone-activated,' said Harper. 'All sorts of fail-safes built into the circuit. It was done by an expert.'

'Yeah, and experts said the *Titanic* was unsinkable,' said Mark. 'What happens if someone calls a wrong number?'

'You don't just make a call. You enter a three-digit number and then it goes bang. No code, no explosion. And C4 is pretty much inert without a detonator. You can set fire to it and use it to boil water if you want to.'

'Fuck me, mate, that's what electric kettles are for,' said Mickey.

'Yeah, well, sometimes when you're in the desert in Afghanistan and feel like a brew, there isn't an electric kettle to hand, and that's when a little block of C4 comes in handy.'

'Did they ever give you a medal for what you did in Afghanistan?' asked Mark.

Harper shook his head. 'Sand up my arse. That's all I took home with me.'

It took twenty minutes to drive to the Central Festival Department Store. It was midway down Beach Road, a seven-storey shopping complex that advertised itself as the largest in Asia. Above it towered the Hilton Hotel.

One of Mickey's motorbike spies was waiting at the entrance to the car park and slid into the back of the pick-up next to Harper. Mickey drove into the multi-storey car park under the complex and the motorbike guy gave him directions for finding the limousine. Because of its length the limo had been parked across two spaces at the far corner of the car park, next to the wall.

'Driver shopping in Big C,' said the motorbike guy.

'We've got a few minutes at least,' said Mickey. 'How do you want to handle it, Lex?'

Harper looked around. Two security guards were standing by the entrance to the complex, and another was sitting at a table next to a VIP parking section. The structure was busy with shoppers heading to and from their vehicles. 'A diversion would be nice,' he said.

Mickey grinned. 'No problem,' he said. 'Just give me the nod when you're ready.'

Harper climbed out of the pick-up. So did the motorcycle taxi driver, who hurried off. Harper walked casually over to the limo, then past it. He turned and nodded at the pick-up, though the heavily tinted windows meant he couldn't see Mickey or Mark. Almost immediately Mickey revved the engine, put the truck in gear and drove into a parked Honda. There was a sickening crunch, followed by the Honda's alarm going off. Immediately all of the security guards ran towards the pick-up. All heads turned to see what was going on and Harper stepped between the limo and the wall, then dropped down. He unzipped the holdall and took out the Tupperware container, lay on his back and slid under the vehicle. He placed the container midway between the rear seats, choosing a spot that wasn't too close to the exhaust. He pushed it against the metal and heard a reassuring click as the magnets bit. He gave it a tug and it wouldn't budge. Even if it hit a pothole or two, the powerful magnets would hold it in place. He shuffled out from under the vehicle, zipped up the holdall and stood up.

Several dozen shoppers were now staring at the pick-up and the Honda's alarm was still blaring. Mickey was out of the truck, apologising loudly and profusely. A middle-aged Thai lady had appeared, pushing a shopping-laden trolley, and from the way she started shouting it appeared that it was her Honda Mickey had rammed. He went to her, still apologising.

Harper walked away and waited at the car-park exit. Five minutes later the pick-up appeared, a small dent and a slight scrape on the bumper the only physical signs of the collision. Harper climbed into the back. 'You owe me twenty-five thousand baht,' said Mickey.

'No problem,' said Harper. 'Was she okay?'

'Mate, I barely touched her car. A bit of panel-beating, a touch of paint, and she's good to go. It was a five-year-old Honda, for fuck's sake. She's quids in and she knows it. She went away as happy as Larry. I gave all the security guards five hundred baht and they saluted me as I drove off. I love this country.' He headed away from the beach, making for the compound. 'And you? Your gizmo's all hooked up.'

'Good to go,' said Harper.

'Now what?'

'The trap's set. I just need the bait. I'll do that tonight.'

'I'll tell you something, Lex,' said Mark, 'I sure hope you never get pissed off at me.' He turned in his seat to punch Harper's shoulder. 'Underneath that happy-go-lucky exterior, you're one mean son of a bitch.'

Harper grinned and settled back. 'They started it, mate. But I'll sure as hell finish it.'

77

Lex Harper had never been a fan of hospitals and tried to avoid them as much as possible. He didn't like the smells, or the sounds, or that so many people died in them. He had on a white coat with 'DOCTOR' above the chest pocket, a stethoscope hanging around his neck, horn-rimmed spectacles and a medical mask over his mouth and nose. He kept his face away from any CCTV cameras as he walked through the hospital, but was confident he wouldn't be recognised if anyone looked through the footage later.

It was just before midnight, and while the emergency centre was as busy as ever, dealing with road-traffic accidents, drug overdoses and the aftermath of drunken brawls, much of the rest of the hospital was quiet. He was wearing black trainers that made barely any noise as he walked along the tiled corridor and along to the emergency stairs.

He took the stairs up to the ICU floor. Two nurses were sitting in the station at the other end of the corridor but they were deep in conversation. One glanced up, saw the white coat, smiled, and went back to her chat. There was a long window in the side corridor that looked onto four intensive-care suites, each with a patient lying in a bed surrounded by a battery of monitoring equipment. To the left of each doorway, the name of the patient was written on white card. One of the names was Thai, one was Japanese and the other two were in English: HELEN FIELDS and GRIGORY LUKIN. There were two nurses in the ICU to the far left, the one occupied by the Japanese patient. They were leaning over him and had their backs to the window. There were no medical staff in the other three units.

Another window to the right overlooked four more units. Two were Arabic names, one was Thai and another Japanese. Harper figured that Valentin Rostov must have recovered enough to be moved to a general ward. Not that it mattered: it was Lukin he had come for.

Harper went back to the first window and along to the glass door that led to the units. He pushed it open and immediately heard the electronic beeping of the various monitoring devices used to track the vital signs of the patients. He tiptoed to Lukin's unit, taking a syringe from his pocket and sliding the protective plastic cover from the needle. The syringe contained the rest of the gelsemium he had bought from Dr Li. Only if a forensic expert went looking for gelsemium would the true cause of the Russian's death be identified, and Harper was pretty sure that the Thais wouldn't be doing that.

Lukin's eyes were closed and his mouth was open, revealing broken and cracked teeth. The Russian's right arm was in plaster, hanging in a sling, as were both his legs. Harper smiled to himself. At least the Russian's last few days would have been painful. He'd earned it, after what he'd done to Pear.

Harper padded over to the intravenous drip and held

the tube with his left hand, about six inches from where it went into Lukin's arm. He pushed the needle into the tube and slowly pressed down the plunger. In a matter of seconds the contents of the syringe had been injected into the tube. Harper replaced the cap on the needle, put the syringe into his pocket and went to the door. As he left the room he heard Lukin's bed begin to shake as the Russian went into spasm, but he didn't look back. He kept his head down as he walked along the corridor to the emergency stairs. When he reached the ground floor and walked across the hospital car park, Grigory Lukin was already dead.

78

Less than twenty-four hours after Grigory Lukin was declared dead of a heart attack, his father's Gulfstream jet landed at Bangkok's Don Mueang airport. Yuri Lukin insisted that the door be opened before the immigration officers arrived and paced up and down as he waited for them. His passport was examined, the cash bribe was pocketed, and he got into the back of the stretch limousine. Two white four-by-fours bracketed the vehicle, each with three men inside. Lukin recognised Volkov and Myshkin but it was the first time he'd seen the others. Mirov picked up on Lukin's unease. 'They're good men.'

'They'd better be,' snarled Lukin. 'I'm fed up with you hiring fuckwits. Why was no one guarding Grigory in the hospital?'

'He was in the ICU and they wouldn't let us post guards. And there were always people about.'

'And what the fuck happened?' growled Lukin. He grabbed a bottle of vodka and poured himself a shot, which he downed in one.

'A heart attack, the doctors say. Grigory was overweight, he used drugs, and that plus the attack—'

'Grigory was as strong as a fucking horse,' said Lukin,

pouring himself another shot. 'What about that fucker Valentin?'

'Valentin's still in the hospital.'

'Did he have protection? Were his fucking guards protecting him?'

Mirov shook his head. 'Boss, I keep telling you, we weren't allowed guards in the hospital. They said they'd call the cops.'

'We own the fucking cops,' said Lukin. 'You should have had fucking cops in there sitting by his bed. That shit Harper attacked my son, and now he's fucking well killed him.'

'Boss, I'm not convinced it was anything other than a heart attack.'

Lukin's eyes hardened. 'Harper killed my son. And you, you fucker, you let it happen.'

'Boss, really, he had a heart attack.'

Lukin smashed the vodka glass against the side of Mirov's head. It shattered and Mirov yelped and fell backwards, blood streaming from his cheek. Lukin had cut himself and he held his bleeding hand out in front of Mirov's nose. 'Now look what you made me do,' he said. He shoved Mirov in the face, pushing him against the window, smearing blood across his nose. 'Look what you made me fucking do!'

'Sorry,' mumbled Mirov.

Lukin growled, shoved him in the face again, then grabbed a napkin from a stack on the bar and held it to his bleeding hand. Mirov took a handful and pressed them against the cut in his cheek. They went red immediately.

'You get blood on the leather and you'll pay to have it

cleaned.' Lukin stared out of the window as he dabbed his cut hand. Mirov took more napkins and held them tightly to his wound.

They drove in silence for half an hour while Lukin downed half of the vodka in the bottle.

'Where's the body now?' he asked eventually.

'Still in the hospital,' said Mirov. 'They were waiting to see if you wanted to take him back to Moscow or cremate him here.'

'Here? Why the fuck would we leave him here? He is a Russian and will be buried in Russia. But first, I want them to do a proper autopsy. I don't think for one moment he had a fucking heart attack. He had the heart of a lion, my son. That fucker Harper killed him and I want to know how. And I want Harper found. I want him found and brought to me so that I can kill him myself.'

'Yes, boss,' mumbled Mirov.

Lukin stared out of the window. 'Where are you fucking taking me?'

'Valentin's villa. We've upgraded the security and there is CCTV covering all the walls, cameras inside, too. We hired three more guards.'

'Yeah, well, that was locking the fucking stable door after the horses had fucking bolted, wasn't it?' He poured himself more vodka. 'It's not about the number of men, it's about the quality. You can hire all the fuckwits you want but if they sit on their arses counting crows you're throwing your money away. Fuck that, you're throwing *my* money away. My fucking money.'

'They're good men, boss. I brought them in from Moscow.'

'And what about Harper? Do we know where he is?'

'We've been watching the airports and he hasn't turned up. And we have a couple of guys staking out his apartment.' Blood was dripping down his chin and soaking into his shirt.

'Whatever it takes to track him down, you do it? Do you hear? Money's no fucking object.' Lukin swallowed a shot of vodka and refilled the glass. 'I told Grigory not to fucking waste his time here. If he wanted to fuck Asian hookers we've got all we need in Moscow. Thai restaurants, too, if it's the food he likes. He should never have come here. I told him, Moscow is where the money is.' He knocked back another shot of vodka. 'How quickly can we get the body flown back to Moscow?'

'You want the autopsy done first, right?'

'Yes, of course.' He downed another vodka. 'Actually, no, fuck it. We can do that in Moscow. I don't trust them to do it right here. They fuck everything up. Fly the body to Moscow and we'll have the tests done there.'

'I should be able to get the paperwork done this afternoon. It'll need some money to make it go smoothly. . .'

'Don't bother me with the fucking details,' snapped Lukin. 'Just get it done.'

'Yes, boss,' said Mirov. Blood was still dripping from his face and he knew the wound needed to be stitched. But he also knew that if he were to say anything to Lukin he'd likely smash a second glass into his face.

The car slowed. Ahead, a pick-up truck was loaded with cardboard boxes tied together with rope. The stack was three times as high as the vehicle and the driver was having trouble controlling it.

The SUV ahead of the limousine had already overtaken the truck.

'Look at this fucking idiot,' said Lukin. 'How is that not going to end badly? And what the fuck are our so-called bodyguards doing?' He sneered at Mirov. 'This is supposed to be a fucking convoy, right? The pricks in that car are supposed to be watching over us. So why the fuck did they overtake the truck and leave us here? Who trains these fucking morons?'

'I'll talk to them,' said Mirov. He fished in his pocket for his mobile phone as he pressed more napkins to his bleeding cheek.

Lukin leaned forward and waved the vodka bottle at the driver. 'Get by this moron, will you, before that load falls all over the fucking car?'

The driver pulled out and stamped on the accelerator, passing the pick-up truck but narrowly missing a bus that was headed their way. They caught up with the first SUV.

'These roads are fucking death traps,' said Lukin, settling back in his seat.

'We're nearly there,' said Mirov. He pressed the number for one of the bodyguards in the leading SUV.

Lukin poured himself another shot of vodka and sat back in his seat. 'If that bastard Harper's in the UK, we'll have to send people after him,' he said.

'Yes, boss.' The phone rang out, unanswered.

'But he might still be in fucking France. Bastard, bastard, bastard. I'll rip his fucking eyes out with my own hands.'

The limousine turned off the main road and headed up the hill to Valentin's villa. The SUV was about fifty yards ahead, indicating a left turn. 'Here we are,' said Mirov. He put his phone away. He glanced over his shoulder. The second SUV was where it was supposed to be, about fifty metres behind them.

'About time. We're out of fucking vodka,' growled Lukin, tossing the empty bottle into the drinks cabinet. He looked to his right, past Mirov. A man was sitting astride a motorcycle at the side of the road. It was the bike Lukin noticed first. A Triumph Bonneville. A classic British motorcycle. Lukin was a fan of big bikes: he had two Harleys in Moscow and a Honda Goldwing, but he had never been a fan of British models. The driver was wearing a leather motorcycle jacket and a full-face helmet with a tinted visor. As Lukin watched, he took off his helmet and grinned towards the car. Lukin frowned. The man's face was familiar. 'What the fuck?' he muttered to himself.

Mirov twisted in his seat, trying to see what Lukin was staring at.

'It's fucking Harper!' shouted Lukin, pointing at the man on the bike. 'That is fucking Harper!'

Harper put his helmet onto one of the bike's mirrors as the limousine drove by.

Lukin and Mirov turned to stare out of the rear window. 'That is the fucker, isn't it?' Lukin shouted.

'I . . . I don't know,' stammered Mirov.

'It is! It fucking is! Stop the fucking car!' Lukin screamed at the driver at the top of his voice. 'Stop the fucking car now or I swear I'll rip your fucking head off!'

The driver stamped on the brake and Lukin grabbed at the seat to steady himself. He looked out of the back window as he reached for the door handle. They were about a hundred yards from the motorbike now but he could see that Harper was still grinning. In his hand he was holding a mobile phone. Then the SUV behind them blocked his view. Lukin instinctively knew what was coming and he took a breath, preparing to bellow. There was a flash, a deafening noise, and his whole body felt as if it was on fire. Then there was nothing.

79

'Keep looking out of the window,' Valentin said, to the man sitting next to him. 'If you see anything, anything at all, you tell me.'

'I will,' said the man. His name was Dubov and he had flown in from Moscow two days earlier. He was a big man, barely out of his twenties, and as hard as nails. He was one of three heavies who had been recruited as extra protection and all came highly recommended.

'That bastard Harper killed Lukin and Mirov, and I'm damn sure he killed Grigory, too.'

'They can't get you in here, sir,' said Dubov.

'You say that, but he blew up a fucking limo,' said Valentin. He was lying on a trolley in the back of a private ambulance. His head was bandaged, his jaw hurt like hell and he was still damaged internally, but he knew he had to get out of the hospital. At least in the villa he could be guarded by men with guns. Getting a tame doctor out to treat him in his own home would be a matter of money, and he could buy in round-the-clock nursing care. There was another bodyguard riding up front with the driver and he was carrying a gun under his jacket, as was Dubov. There were SUVs front and back of the ambulance but that hadn't inspired Valentin with confidence as they were the same vehicles that had supposedly been guarding the limousine. He had insisted that they check underneath the ambulance, twice, before he got in.

Dubov had a transceiver and called ahead to the villa to talk to one of the four bodyguards there. 'We're five minutes away,' he said.

'The house is secure,' said the man. His name was Yerkhov and, like Dubov, had served in the Russian special forces for five years before realising there was more money to be made in the private sector. Russian businessmen and crime lords had spread across the world and disputes, business and criminal, were often settled with violence, so overseas protection had become as necessary as passports. Dubov and Yerkhov commanded six-figure dollar salaries, plus all expenses, and were never short of work.

'Check again,' shouted Valentin. 'Check everywhere. Under the beds, in the cupboards, check every fucking inch of the place.'

'The boss wants you to check again,' said Dubov. 'Then be at the gate to meet us.'

'With guns,' shouted Valentin. 'Make sure they have guns.'

'They will,' said Dubov.

'Tell them!' shouted Valentin, and grunted in pain as the ambulance went over a pothole.

'Mr Rostov says you should have your guns with you,' said Dubov, into his transceiver.

The ambulance engine was labouring as they went uphill. Valentin's heart was racing, partly through the pain he was suffering but mainly because they were now on the stretch of road where Lukin and Mirov had died. The bomb had destroyed most of the rear of the limousine but the blast had gone upwards so the driver had emerged relatively unscathed, albeit with burst eardrums. The police had managed to find Mirov's head pretty much intact but all they had found of Lukin was a foot and a hand. Valentin closed his eyes and said a silent prayer, gasping as the ambulance hit another pothole.

Dubov smiled down at him reassuringly. 'Don't worry, sir. We're arriving at the villa now.' He opened his jacket to show him the pistol that was nestled in a brown leather underarm holster. 'If there's any trouble at all we're locked, loaded and ready to go.'

80

Mickey Moore came out of the main house, holding a bottle of Heineken in one hand and a KFC bucket in the other. He walked towards where Harper was sitting by the pool, which was Olympic size, with two diving boards at the deep end, but built in the style of a tropical lagoon. There were two curved artificial beaches, complete with sand, palm trees, and rocks that were large enough to sunbathe on. At the shallow end there was a Jacuzzi big enough to hold a dozen people, which it often did on party nights. Half a dozen teak cabanas, their roofs fringed with palms, stood around the edge of the pool, and at one side there was a brick-built barbecue that was the size of a regular kitchen.

The pool tended to be the focal point of the estate during the day, though Baz, Davie and Terry were still in their villas nursing hangovers. Harper was in one of the cabanas, holding the Russian 9mm PB silenced pistol that had come from Cambodia as Mark watched and drank a beer. The gun had been specially designed for Spetsnaz units when it was introduced in 1967. Harper planned to leave it at the scene, hoping that a Russian gun would muddy the waters in any investigation by the Thais and by Valentin's associates.

The gun was still in production in what had originally been known as the Izhevsk Mechanical Plant, which had been founded in 1807, the time of Tsar Alexander I, and had gone on to become one of the largest arms manufacturers in the world, producing cannons, missiles, and the famous Kalashnikov assault rifle. PB stood for *pistolet beschumnyi*, or 'noiseless pistol'. It was based on the standard Makarov pistol and fired standard Makarov ammunition, but it had been designed so that rounds were always fired subsonically. To achieve that, the barrel had two small holes that allowed some of the propellant gas to escape into the silencer. Even without the silencer screwed in, the gun was still quieter than a standard Makarov.

'We've just had a KFC delivery,' said Mickey, as he reached the cabana.

'Clearly,' said Mark, helping himself to a chicken leg from the bucket.

'Are you sure you don't want us along for the ride?' Mickey asked Harper.

'It's my fight,' said Harper, his eyes on the gun.

'Yeah, but we're the musketeers,' said Mark, waving his chicken leg like a sword. 'All for one and one for all.'

The weapon was well oiled and appeared to have been cared for, but Harper was taking no chances. As the Moore brothers watched he stripped it down, checked the component parts, then reassembled it.

'He's showing off,' said Mark.

'He knows what he's doing,' said Mickey. 'But I still think you'd be better going in mob-handed.'

Harper shook his head. 'Then it'll be a war, and if they find out you're involved, they'll come after you.'

'I ain't scared of no steenking Russians,' said Mark, in a fake Mexican accent.

Harper laughed. 'Mate, I'll be in and out like a fucking Ninja. I'll do what has to be done, toss the gun and Robert's your father's brother.'

'They'll know it was you,' said Mickey.

'Not necessarily. And with Valentin, Grigory and Lukin dead, someone else will take over and I doubt that revenge will be high on his list of priorities. But I'll cross that chicken when I get to it.' He stood up. 'I wouldn't mind a test firing.'

'Be our guest,' said Mickey.

The three men walked away from the pool. 'I'll go and warn security,' said Mark. 'Suppressors are good, but they're not perfect.' He jogged towards the front gate.

Mickey and Harper walked to the far end of the estate where there was a clump of palm trees. 'Do you want me to stand with an apple on my head?' asked Mickey.

'Would you?'

Mickey laughed. 'Actually, I would, mate. I've seen you shoot. I know how good you are.' He picked up a loose coconut, about the size of a man's head. 'But this'll do.' He tossed the coconut about ten feet away. Harper chambered a round, aimed and pulled the trigger. There wasn't much in the way of recoil and the sound was equivalent to that of a balloon popping, not the soft hiss that silenced weapons made in movies. No suppressor was perfect, which was why the professionals called them suppressors rather than silencers. The bullet thwacked into the middle of the coconut.

'Happy?' asked Mickey, waving his bottle of Heineken.

'I will be when it's Valentin's head I'm shooting at,' said Harper.

'Go for the chest,' said Mickey. 'It's a bigger target.'

Harper opened his mouth to reply until he saw from the look on the man's face that he was joking. 'Fuck you,' he said.

'Fuck you too. Just be careful.'

81

Harper was insistent that he would take care of Valentin himself, but he allowed Mickey and Mark to drive him to the villa. They took one of the estate's nondescript pick-up trucks with a folding ladder in the back.

Harper sat in the front passenger seat with the PB in his lap as Mickey drove. He was wearing a dark sweatshirt and black jeans, with black trainers and skin-tight black gloves. He had borrowed a black nylon shoulder holster from Mickey that allowed him to carry the pistol, and silencer, under his left arm. It was a fair enough fit, though he would have to be careful not to snag the silencer when he pulled it out. Mark sat behind him with two pump-action sawn-off shotguns next to him. 'Just in case,' he'd said.

They parked a couple of hundred yards from the villa and Mickey switched off the engine and lights so their night vision would kick in. 'You've got your phone, right?' said Mickey.

'Yes, Mum.'

'Fuck off, you soft twat. If anything goes wrong, you call us and we'll be in like Finn.'

'It's Flynn, mate. In like Flynn.'

'Flynn, Finn, whoever the fuck he is, we'll be in like him if there's any sign of trouble,' said Mickey.

'It'll be fine.'

'Well, you say that, but there's CCTV covering all the walls and by all accounts a shedload of former Spetsnaz thugs inside.'

'It's late. They'll be asleep. And Valentin's gonna be dosed up on painkillers.'

'There'll be someone watching the CCTV monitors,' said Mark.

'You say that, but you know most of the time that's not true. No one sits and watches a screen all night.'

'You need a diversion,' said Mickey. 'That's what you need.'

'Oh, fuck! You're not going to wear the clown suit again?' sneered Mark.

'That was twenty years ago,' said Mickey. 'And it worked, didn't it? We got clean away with the takings.'

'No thanks to those fucking clown shoes you had on.'

'He's taking the piss,' Mickey said to Harper. 'I was wearing trainers. Seriously, you need some sort of distraction at the gate. Get security focused on that and you can slip in unnoticed.'

'Like what?'

'A couple of drunken motorcycle taxis at the gate. I can fix that up, no bother. Let me give a mate a call.'

Harper nodded. 'Okay. It can't hurt.'

Mickey spent a couple of minutes on the phone, then grinned as he put it away. 'Ten minutes, Lex. It'll give you time to get set up.' He patted Harper's shoulder. 'And I'm serious. You get in trouble, call.'

Harper climbed out of the truck. He picked up the light-weight ladder and two old rice sacks and jogged towards the rear wall. The security wire had been replaced and there was now a weatherproof CCTV camera trained along the top of the wall. It hadn't been done by experts as it could clearly be approached from behind. There was another camera at the far corner but that seemed to be pointing at the ground. Harper figured there was a blind spot of twenty feet or so, but he couldn't be sure. He pulled on a ski mask and crouched near the base of the wall.

After about ten minutes he heard several motorcycles coming up the hill. Three, maybe four. Then the engines cut out and he heard laughing and Thai shouting. Then smashing glass. Soon afterwards he heard angry Russian voices. Then 'Fuck off, you drunken bastards!' shouted in accented English.

There were Thai yells, and Harper recognised several choice Thai swearwords. He placed the ladder against the wall, climbed up, snipped out a section of the security wire and threw the sacks over the broken glass. He slipped over, pulled the ladder after him and used it to climb down into the compound. The shouts were louder now and it sounded as if the motorcycle taxi drivers were up for more than shouting.

Harper crept over the grass to the main building. The lights were on downstairs, and in the two smaller buildings closer to the entrance. From where he was crouched, he could see the silhouettes of three big men looking towards the gate. Another had approached it and was shouting through the bars. He made out four Thais in green tunics and faded jeans stalking back and forth, shouting and waving their arms. One threw a bottle, which smashed against the gate. The three silhouettes moved closer to it, all shouting now.

He worked his way along the wall to the back entrance and inside. The house was in darkness. He pulled the silenced gun from its holster under his arm and crept towards the main sitting area. He heard a Russian voice, and the crackle of a transceiver. Two men were looking out over the swimming pool and the bay beyond. From where they were standing they could hear the shouts at the front gate but not see what was going on. One had a transceiver to his ear and was barking into it in Russian. Harper recognised one word: *khuyesos*. 'Cocksucker'.

He wasn't thrilled at the idea of shooting two men from behind but he knew that, given the chance, they'd have no qualms about doing that to him. He waited until the man on the transceiver had paused for breath, then shot him in the back of the head. Blood and brain matter sprayed over the window and the body began to fall, seemingly in slow motion, to the floor.

The other man began to turn but Harper had already taken aim and the second shot was also to the head, sending a virtually identical spray across the window. He followed the first to the floor, the only sound being the thud as he hit it.

Harper stood for a while, listening. Both shots had seemed louder than they had in Mickey Moore's compound, probably because the sound echoed off the walls of the villa, but he doubted that anyone outside would have heard anything. He turned and went back into the hallway and along to a closed door. He was pretty sure it led to the bedrooms. He reached out for the handle and said a silent prayer that Valentin was alone. If there was a doctor or a nurse with him, things could get complicated. While Harper was perfectly happy to shoot armed Russian bodyguards, unarmed civilians were a different matter.

He twisted the handle and the door opened into a corridor. He realised he had been holding his breath and exhaled, then took a long, slow breath, and exhaled again. To his right there was a door with a slatted panel at the bottom, which he guessed led to a laundry room. The shouting at the gate faded as he padded along the marble floor. He was in a corridor with Thai silk panels hanging from polished teak rods. He passed a teak and glass cabinet full of opium paraphernalia, including dried poppy heads, scrapers and cutters for extracting the drug, and pipes of various shapes and sizes. At the end of the corridor there was another set of double doors, ornately carved with matching dragons. There were two handles and he pulled them towards him, slowly at first, then with more force when he found they weren't locked.

He saw movement to his left and went down into a crouch as he brought the gun up. A man in a tracksuit was pushing himself up out of a winged chair and reaching for a gun on a side table. Getting up had been a big mistake, Harper thought. Putting the gun on a side table had also been a mistake. Combining the two meant that the confrontation could end in only one way. Harper fired and hit the man square in the chest. His eyes opened wide in surprise and he slumped back in his chair. There was a sucking sound from the wound, which frothed with red bubbles. More blood trickled from between the victim's lips. He wasn't dead, not yet, but he was no longer a threat.

The sound of the shot woke Valentin. He was lying in a king-size bed, propped up on two pillows. An intravenous drip was connected to his left arm. He began to grunt and thrash like a stranded fish, his eyes wide and panicking. Harper walked towards him, the gun aimed at the centre of his chest. There was no need to say anything. Valentin knew what was happening and why. And so did Harper. Snappy one-liners were only for the movies. He pulled the trigger and shot Valentin in the face, then turned away. The bodyguard in the chair was dead now: his eyes were closed and his chest had stopped moving. Harper put the silenced PB into the man's right hand and picked up the bodyguard's gun, a Glock, shoving it into his underarm holster. If nothing else, the silenced weapon in the bodyguard's hand would make muddy waters even muddier.

He slipped out through the kitchen and ran across the compound, bent double. There were angry Russian shouts from the main entrance but the Thais clearly weren't backing down and were giving as good as they got.

He put the ladder against the wall, climbed over and dropped to the ground. The Thais stopped shouting and shortly afterwards he heard the motorcycle engines start up.

He reached the pick-up truck as the motorbikes were driving down the hill. 'How did it go?' asked Mickey, as Harper climbed in and pulled off his ski mask.

'All good,' he said.

'Where's my fucking ladder?'

'I left it there,' said Harper.

'Well, go back and fucking get it,' snarled Mickey. His face broke into a grin. 'Only messing with you,' he said.

He switched on the engine but kept the lights off as he drove away from the villa. 'All's well that ends well, huh?'

'I hope so,' said Harper.

'It's over, mate. These Russian gangsters, they don't give a shit about each other. There's no honour among Russian thieves. They'll pick over what's left of Lukin's business and move on. They won't care about you.'

'Good to know,' said Harper. 'And thanks. For everything.'

'No need,' said Mickey. 'We're mates and mates take care of each other.'

'All for one and one for all,' said Mark, punching the air. 'Can we go and get drunk now? I need a beer.'

'Amen to that,' said Harper. 'And I'm paying.' The phone in his hip-pack buzzed and he pulled it out. It was a text message. Just three words: *You've got mail.*

Finding
Gobi

Finding Gobi

The true story of a little dog and an incredible journey

DION LEONARD

HarperCollins*Publishers*

HarperCollins*Publishers*
1 London Bridge Street
London SE1 9GF

www.harpercollins.co.uk

First published in the US by W Publishing Group, an imprint of Thomas Nelson, 2017
First published in the UK by HarperCollins*Publishers* 2017
This paperback edition 2018

4

© Dion Leonard 2017

Dion Leonard asserts the moral right to be
identified as the author of this work

All photographs used with permission. Photographs from
the 2013 and 2014 Kalahari Augrabies Extreme Marathon are
courtesy of KAEM; photographer Hermien Webb.

A catalogue record of this book is
available from the British Library

ISBN 978-0-00-822796-8

Printed and bound by CPI Group (UK) Ltd, Croydon CR0 4YY

MIX
Paper from
responsible sources
FSC www.fsc.org **FSC™ C007454**

For my wife, Lucja.
Without your endless support, dedication, and
love, this never would have been possible.

PROLOGUE

THE CAMERA CREW FINISHED UP LAST NIGHT.
Someone from the publisher arrives tomorrow. I can still feel the jet lag and other side effects of forty-one hours of travel in my body. So Lucja and I have already decided to make this, our first run of the year, an easy one. Besides, it's not just the two of us we need to think about. There's Gobi to consider.

We take it easy as we pass the pub, drop down beside Holyrood Palace, and see the clear blue sky give way to the grassy mountain that dominates Edinburgh's skyline. Arthur's Seat. I've run up there more times than I can remember, and I know it can be brutal. The wind can be so strong in your face that it pushes you back. The hail can bite into your skin like knives. On days like those, I crave the 120-degree heat of the desert.

But today there's no wind or hail. There's nothing brutal about the air as we climb, as if the mountain wants to show itself off in all its cloudless glory.

As soon as we hit the grass, Gobi is transformed. This dog that's small enough for me to carry under one arm is turned into a raging lion as she pulls forward up the slope.

"Wow!" says Lucja. "Look at her energy!"

Before I can say anything, Gobi turns around, tongue lolling out, eyes bright, ears forward, chest puffed. It's as if she understands exactly what Lucja's said.

"You haven't seen anything yet," I say, pushing the pace up a bit in an attempt to loosen the strain on the leash. "She was just like this back in the mountains."

We push farther up, closer to the summit. I'm thinking how, even though I named her after a desert, I first saw Gobi on the cold, rugged slopes of the Tian Shan. She's a true climber, and with every step we take, she comes more and more alive. Soon her tail is wagging so fast it blurs, her whole body bouncing and pulsing with pure joy. When she looks back again, I swear she's grinning. *Come on!* she says. *Let's go!*

At the top, I soak in all the familiar sights. The whole of Edinburgh is spread out beneath us, and beyond it is the Forth Bridge, the hills of Lomond, and the West Highland Way, every one of whose ninety-six miles I have run. I can see North Berwick, too, a full marathon distance away. I love the run along the beach, even on the tough days when the wind is trying to batter me down and every mile feels like a battle all its own.

It's been more than four months since I've been here. While it's all familiar, there's something different about it as well.

Gobi.

She decides it's time to descend and drags me down the hill. Not down the path, but straight down. I leap over tufts of grass and rocks the size of suitcases, Lucja keeping pace beside me. Gobi navigates them all with skill. Lucja and I look at each other and laugh, enjoying the moment we have longed for, to be a family and finally able to run together.

Running isn't usually this fun. In fact, for me, running is never fun. Rewarding and satisfying, maybe, but not laugh-out-loud fun. Not like it is now.

Gobi wants to keep running, so we let her lead. She takes us wherever she wants to go, sometimes back up the mountain, sometimes down. There's no training plan and no pre-mapped route. There are no worries either. No concerns. It's a carefree moment, and for that and so much more, I'm grateful.

After the last six months, I feel like I need it.

I've faced things I never thought I'd face, all because of this little blur of brown fur that's pulling my arm out of its socket. I've faced fear like I've never known before. I've felt despair as well, the sort that turns the air around you stale and lifeless. I've faced death.

But that's not the whole story. There's so much more.

The truth is that this little dog has changed me in ways I think I'm only just beginning to understand. Maybe I'll never fully understand it all.

Yet I do know this: finding Gobi was one of the hardest things I've ever done in my life.

But being found by her—that was one of the best things.

PART 1

1

I STEPPED THROUGH THE AIRPORT DOORS AND out into China. I paused and let the chaos take a good hard whack at my senses. A thousand revving engines in the car park ahead did battle with a thousand voices around me as people shouted at their phones.

The signs were written in both Chinese script and what looked to me like Arabic. I couldn't read either language, so I joined the crush of bodies that I guessed were waiting for a taxi. I stood a foot taller than most people, but as far as they were concerned, I was invisible.

I was in Urumqi, a sprawling city in Xinjiang Province, way up in the top left corner of China. No city in the world is as far from an ocean as Urumqi, and as we'd flown in from Beijing, I watched the terrain shift from razor-sharp snow-capped mountains to vast stretches of empty desert. Somewhere down there a team of race organizers had plotted a 155-mile route that took in those freezing peaks, the incessant wind, and that desolate, lifeless scrubland known as the Gobi Desert. I was going to run across it, knocking out a little less than a marathon a day for four days, then almost

two marathons on the fifth day, and an hour-long sprint for the final six-mile stage that would bring the race to a close.

These races are called "multi-stage ultras", and it's hard to think of a more brutal test of mental and physical toughness. People like me pay thousands of pounds for the privilege of putting ourselves through pure agony, shedding up to 10 per cent of our body weight in the process, but it's worth it. We get to run in some of the remotest and most picturesque parts of the world, and we have the safety net of a dedicated support crew and highly trained medical crew on our side. Sometimes these challenges can be excruciating, but they're also life changing, and reaching the finish line is one of life's most rewarding experiences.

Sometimes things don't go so well. Like the last time I tried to run six marathons in a week. I ended up in the middle of the pack, in agony. At the time it felt terminal, as if I'd never compete again. But I recovered just enough for one last shot. If I could run well in the Gobi race, maybe I'd yet have some more running in me. After all, in the three years since I'd taken up running seriously, I'd found out how good it felt to be on the podium. The thought of never competing again made me feel queasy inside.

If things went wrong, as they had for another competitor in the same race a few years back, I could end up dead.

According to the Internet, the drive from the airport to the hotel was supposed to take twenty or thirty minutes. But the closer we got to the hour mark, the more agitated the driver became. He had started out grouchy when he realized I was an English-speaking tourist and quoted me a price three times as much as I was expecting. It had got only worse from there.

By the time we pulled up outside a redbrick building, he was waving his arms and trying to shove me out of the cab. I looked out the window, then back at the low-resolution image I'd shown him before we started the journey. It was kind of similar if you squinted a bit, but it was obvious that he hadn't brought me to a hotel.

"I think you need some glasses, mate!" I said, trying to keep it light and get him to see the funny side. It didn't work.

Begrudgingly, he picked up his phone and yelled at someone on the other end. When we finally made it to my destination twenty minutes later, he was livid, shaking his fists and burning rubber as he sped away.

Not that I'd been bothered. As much as ultra-running batters your body, it also assaults your mind. You learn pretty quickly how to block out distractions and mildly annoying things like lost toenails or bleeding nipples. The stress coming from an enraged taxi driver was nothing I couldn't ignore.

The next day was a different story.

I had to travel a few hundred miles out of the city by bullet train to get to the race headquarters in a large town called Hami. Right from the moment I arrived at the station in Urumqi, I knew I was in for a journey that would test my patience.

I'd never seen such security at a train station. There were military vehicles everywhere, temporary metal roadblocks funnelling pedestrians and traffic past armed guards. I'd been told to allow myself two hours to get on the train, but as I stared at the great tide of people ahead of me, I wondered whether it was going to be enough. If the previous day's taxi ride had taught me anything, it's that if I missed my train, I wasn't sure I could overcome the

language barrier and re-book another ticket. And if I didn't get to the race meeting point that day, who knew if I would even make the start?

Panic wasn't going to help me get anywhere. I took control of my breathing, told myself to get a grip, and shuffled my way through the first security check. By the time I cleared it and worked out where I needed to go to collect my ticket, I discovered I was in the wrong qucuc. I joined the right one, and by then I was way down on my time. *If this was a race*, I thought, *I'd be at the back*. I never ran at the back.

Once I had my ticket, I had less than forty minutes to clear another security check, have my passport stared at in forensic detail by an over-eager policeman, force my way to the front of a line of fifty people waiting to check in, and stand, open-mouthed, panting and staring frantically at signs and display boards I couldn't read, wondering where the heck I had to go to find the right platform.

Thankfully, I wasn't entirely invisible, and a Chinese guy who'd studied in England tapped me on the shoulder.

"You need some help?" he said.

I could have hugged him.

I just had time to sit down at the departure point when everyone around me turned and watched as the train crew swept past us. It was like a scene out of a 1950s airport, the drivers with their immaculate uniforms, white gloves, and air of complete control, the stewardesses looking poised and perfect.

I followed them onto the train and sank, exhausted, into my seat. Almost thirty-six hours had slipped by since I left home in Edinburgh, and I tried to empty my mind and body of the tension

that had built up so far. I looked out the window for something to interest me, but for hours on end the train just sliced through a bland-looking landscape that wasn't cultivated enough to be farmland and wasn't vacant enough to be desert. It was just land, and it went on for hundreds and hundreds of miles.

Exhausted and stressed. This was *not* how I wanted to feel this close to the biggest race I'd faced so far in my short running career.

I'd taken part in more prestigious events, such as the world-famous Marathon des Sables in Morocco, universally agreed to be the toughest footrace on earth. Twice I'd lined up alongside the thirteen hundred other runners and raced across the Sahara Desert as the temperature topped 125 degrees in the day and sank to 40 at night. I'd even finished a respectable thirty-second the second time I ran it. But fifteen months had passed since then, and a lot had changed.

I had started taking note of the changes during another 155-mile race across the Kalahari Desert in South Africa. I'd pushed myself hard—too hard—to finish second overall, my "first-ever podium finish" in a multi-stage. I'd not kept myself hydrated enough, and, as a result, my urine was the color of Coke. Back home my doctor said I'd caused my kidneys to shrink due to the lack of liquid, and all that running had left them bruised and resulted in blood in my urine.

A few months later I'd started having heart palpitations during another race. I could feel my heart beating wildly, and I got hit by a double blow of queasiness and dizziness.

Both those problems flared up again almost as soon as I started the Marathon des Sables. Of course, I ignored the pain and forced myself through it, all the way to a top-fifty finish. Trouble was, I'd pushed myself so hard that as soon as I got home, my left

hamstring went into violent and agonizing spasms every time I tried to walk, let alone run.

For the first few months I rested; then for the next few I was in and out of physiotherapists' consultation rooms, all the time hearing the same-old same-old: I just needed to try whatever new combination of strength and conditioning exercises they were suggesting. I tried them all. Nothing helped me to run again.

It took the best part of a year to find a physiotherapist and a coach who both had running expertise and knew what was going on to discover the truth: part of my problem was that I wasn't running correctly. I'm tall—well over six feet—and while my long, steady, loping stride felt easy and natural, I wasn't firing up all the muscles I should have been using, so I had sharp, painful spasms in my legs every time I ran.

The race in China was my first chance in a tough competition to try out my new, faster, shorter stride. In many ways I was feeling great. I had been able to run for hours on end at home without pain, and I'd followed my usual pre-race diet better than I ever had before. For the previous three months, I'd avoided all alcohol and junk food, eating not much more than chicken and vegetables. I'd even cut out coffee, hoping that would put an end to the heart palpitations.

If it all paid off, and I ran as well as I thought I could do in China, I'd tackle the prestigious race that the organizers were putting on later in the year—across the Atacama salt plains in Chile. If I won there, I'd be in the perfect shape to get back to the Marathon des Sables the following year and make a real name for myself.

I was the first passenger off when we pulled into Hami and at the head of the pack as we surged towards the exit. *This is more like it*, I thought.

The guard manning the security checkpoint put a quick end to my joy.

"What you do here?"

I could see a long line of taxis outside the door, all waiting beside a vacant pavement for my fellow passengers to lay claim to them. I tried to explain about the race and say that I wanted to go and get a cab, but I knew it was no use. He looked quizzically back and forth between me and my passport, then motioned me to follow him into a trailer that doubled as an office.

It took half an hour to explain what all the packets of energy gels and dried foods were for, and even then I wasn't convinced he believed me. Mostly I think he let me go because he was bored.

By the time I got out and approached the pavement, the crowds had all gone. And so had the taxis.

Great.

I stood alone and waited. I was fatigued and wanting this ridiculous journey to be over.

Thirty minutes later a taxi pulled up. I'd made sure to print off the address of my hotel in Chinese script before I'd left Urumqi, and as I showed it to the driver, I was pleased to see that she seemed to recognize it. I climbed in the back, squashed my knees up against the metal grille, and closed my eyes as we pulled out.

We'd only got a few hundred feet when the car stopped. My driver was taking on another passenger. *Just go with the flow, Dion.* I didn't see any point in complaining. At least, I didn't until she turned to me, pointed to the door, and made it perfectly clear that the other passenger was a far better customer, and I was no longer welcome in the cab.

I walked back, spent another twenty minutes getting through

the inevitable security checks, and lined up once more, alone, at the deserted taxi stand.

Another taxi came, eventually. The driver was happy and polite and knew exactly where to go. In fact, he was so confident that when he pulled up in front of a large, grey building ten minutes later, I didn't think to check that I was at the right hotel. I just handed over my money, pulled my bag out after me, and listened to him drive away.

It was only when I walked into the entrance that I realized I was in the wrong place entirely. It was not a hotel but an office block. An office block in which nobody spoke any English.

For forty minutes I tried to communicate with the office workers, they tried to communicate with me, and the phone calls to I-didn't-know-who failed to get us any closer. It was only when I saw a taxi drive slowly past the front of the building that I grabbed my bag, ran out, and begged the driver to take me where I needed to go.

Thirty minutes later, as I stood and stared at the empty bed in the budget hotel the race organizers had booked, I said out loud my solemn vow.

"I am never, ever coming back to China."

It wasn't the frustration of not being able to communicate properly or even the muscle aches and serious fatigue that were bothering me. All day I'd fought hard against the urge to worry, but as one thing went wrong after another, I ended up getting nervous. It wasn't logical, and it didn't make sense. I'd reminded myself again and again that I had allowed plenty of time to get from Beijing to the race start, and I figured that even if I'd missed my train, I could have found a way to put things right. And I knew, deep down, that

any aches I'd picked up from the previous couple of days would soon shake themselves out once I started running.

Even so, by the time I arrived at the hotel near the race head-quarters, I was more anxious than I'd ever been before any race I'd ever run. The source of my nerves wasn't the journey, and it wasn't the knowledge of the physical challenges that lay ahead of me. It was something far, far deeper than that.

It was the worry that this might be my last race ever and the fear that maybe I was never going to win a race—winning had been the only thing that motivated me to run competitively in the first place.

Tuesday, 3 January, 1984. The day after my ninth birthday. That was when I first understood how quickly life can change. The day had been a great one, soaked in beautiful Australian summer sunshine. In the morning I'd ridden my bike over some jumps I'd put together while Mum and Dad read the papers and my three-year-old sister played out in the yard near Nan's downstairs flat at the far end of the house. I'd finally managed to perfect my somersault on the trampoline, and after lunch Dad and I went out with our cricket bats and a few old balls. He was just recovering from a chest infection, and it was the first time in ages that he'd joined me for a bit of sport outside. He taught me how to hold the bat in just the right way to hit a ball so hard and high that it sailed way out over the scrubby grass and beyond the far boundary of our property.

When I finally came inside in the late afternoon, I found the house to be full of the smells of Mum's cooking. She steamed her chocolate pudding for hours and made Bolognese so rich that I

would hold my head over the pot and inhale the aroma for as long as I could before the heat got to be too much.

It was a perfect day.

Like any nine-year-old, I denied I was tired when it came time to go to bed, but soon enough I was drifting off to sleep, vaguely aware of Mum leaving for her Tuesday night aerobics class while Dad watched cricket on TV with the sound turned down low.

"Dion!"

I didn't want to wake up. It was dark and my head was still half-stuck in its curious dream world.

"Dion!" I heard Dad's voice again. There was no other noise in the house, no TV, and no sound of Mum anywhere.

I didn't know why he'd be calling me like this, and I let myself drift back to sleep.

I couldn't tell you how much longer Dad went on calling my name, but at some point I knew I had to get up and go and see what he wanted.

He was lying on his bed, under a sheet. He didn't look at me when I came in, and I didn't want to go too far into the room. His breathing sounded all wrong, as if he was having to use all the strength he possessed to drag even the smallest lungful of air in. Something told me he was really sick.

"Go and get your grandmother straightaway, Dion."

I ran downstairs and knocked on Nan's front door.

"Nan, you've got to come," I said. "Dad needs you. Something's wrong."

She came right out, and I followed her back upstairs. I remember thinking that because she used to be a nurse, Dad would be okay. Whenever my little sister, Christie, or I was hurt, Nan would always make us laugh as she tended to our wounds, telling us stories

from when she worked in a war repatriation hospital as a head nurse in charge of the others. She was a tough woman, a fighter who I believed held within her hands the power to make any illness or pain disappear.

As soon as she saw Dad, she left to call an ambulance. I stayed with him while she made the call, but as soon as she came back, she told me to leave the room.

Christie was asleep in the next room. I stood and watched her, listening to my dad's breathing grow worse and Nan talk in a voice I'd never heard her use. "Garry," she said, a little louder than normal. "The ambulance is coming. You're having an asthma attack. Keep calm, Garry. Stay with me."

Christie woke up from the noise and started crying. "Dad doesn't feel well, Christie," I said, trying to sound strong like Nan. "But people are coming to help."

I raced across the hallway to open the door as soon as I heard the ambulance pull up outside. I watched as the paramedics carried a stretcher and breathing apparatus up the set of stairs. And I looked on in silence as Mum rushed into the house a few minutes later. I listened to the sound of Mum's sobbing coming from the bedroom, not understanding what it meant. When they wheeled Dad out a while later, I didn't want to look at him. He was still struggling to breathe, and his head was shaking. I could hear the noise of one of the wheels under the stretcher as it squeaked along.

I followed everyone outside, where the streetlights and headlights and blinking hazard lights all made the night look out of time. As the medics were loading Dad into the back of the ambulance, he told Mum he loved her. I stood by Nan's side, the grass cold against my bare feet. "Things will be okay," said Nan. I didn't know who she was speaking to.

Christie, Nan, and I stayed back while Mum went off with Dad in the ambulance. I don't know how long we were alone, or even what we did. But I remember that it was around midnight when the front door finally opened. Mum came in with a doctor beside her. Neither of them had to say anything at all. Nan and I both knew what had happened. Soon Mum, Nan, and I were crying. Not long after, the phone started ringing. Nan answered, her voice low, the calls never lasting more than a few minutes. When the doorbell rang and the first neighbours arrived and hugged Mum tight, I disappeared to my room.

On the day of the funeral, I watched as Dad's coffin was wheeled toward the hearse. I broke free from Mum's hand on my shoulder and ran out to stop it. I draped as much of myself as I could around the timber box, but it was no use. My arms couldn't reach all the way around. When my sobbing got so hard that it hurt my chest, someone peeled me away.

2

SOON AFTER DAD'S DEATH, MUM MOVED DOWN-
stairs, where Nan took care of her and Christie and me. It was as
if Mum became a child again, and in doing so she couldn't be a
mum to us anymore.

I may have been just a nine-year-old kid, but any fool could have
spotted the signs. The day I walked in on her in her bedroom, tears
barely dry on her cheeks, confirmed the fact that she wasn't coping.

That was a few weeks after Dad's death. It took a few months
for me to find out that her troubles were not just caused by grief.
She and I were in the kitchen one evening. She was cleaning—a
new obsession that had started recently—and I was sitting at the
table reading.

"Dion," she said, "Garry wasn't your dad."

I don't remember crying or running off to hide. I don't remember shouting or screaming or asking my mum to explain further. I
have no memory of what I said next. I have no recall of how I felt.
A blank void exists where so many memories should be. I can only
imagine how painful that news must have been for me to wipe all
trace of it from my mind.

15

But what I know for sure is that the wound that had been inflicted on me by my dad's—Garry's—death became so deep that it changed everything about me.

Even today my mum will cry when she and I talk about Garry's death. She'll say it took only a twenty-minute ambulance ride for everything in our lives to change. She's right, but she's also wrong: it might have taken minutes for life to be thrown into chaos, but it took only four words for my grieving heart to be ripped completely apart.

I held tight to my secret. Within a year or two of finding out the truth about myself, I was ashamed of my past: not only was I the kid without a dad at home, but I was the only one I knew who also had a single parent. The regular stream of visitors that poured in after the funeral had long since stopped, and our dwindling finances forced Mum to go out and find work. Whenever she was at home, she spent hours repeatedly cleaning the house and listening to Lionel Richie songs played loudly on the stereo in the pristine dining room.

In my mind, it seemed like all my friends came from perfect families, and because they all went to church, I'd take myself on Sundays as well. I wanted to feel as though I belonged, and I also liked the fact that I could help myself to a handful of small cakes after the service. I didn't mind the sermons so much—sometimes they even made me feel better about myself. But the way people responded to me, as I hovered near the tea table at the end of the service, made it clear to me that they saw me differently from everyone else. I could hear them whispering behind my back. As soon as I turned around, the awkward silence and fake smiles would come out.

Mum started getting phone calls as well. I'd try to creep out into the hallway and watch as she stood, her face turned to the wall, shoulders hunched. Her words were clipped and the calls short, and sometimes when they were over, she'd turn around and see me watching and tell me about the latest gossip people were spreading about us in the town.

Soon enough I encountered the ostracism myself. When I went to a friend's house to visit one Saturday afternoon, I could see his bike on the grass out front, so I knew he was in. His mum, however, said he couldn't come out to play.

"You can't see Dan," she said, pulling the screen door closed between us.

"Why not, Mrs. Carruthers?"

"You're a bad influence, Dion. We don't want you coming around."

I walked away devastated. I didn't drink, swear, act up at school, or get into trouble with the police. Okay, so I was a little greedy with the small cakes at church, but other than that I was always polite and tried to be kind.

She could only have been referring to one thing.

I didn't have a name for it at the time, but I quickly developed a strong dislike for being made to feel I was being excluded. By the time I was fourteen, I was well aware of precisely where I belonged in life: on the outside.

I sat, as I always did, alone and away from everyone else as the race staff welcomed the runners and started the safety briefing. The race was organized by a group I'd not run with before, but I'd been in enough of these meetings to know what was coming.

The biggest danger for anyone running a multi-stage ultra in desert heat is when heat exhaustion—your standard case of dehydration, cramps, dizziness, and a racing pulse—tips over into heatstroke. That's when more drastic symptoms arrive, including confusion, disorientation, and seizures. You won't know it's happening; you won't pick up the signs yourself. That's when you end up curling up in a ditch or making wrong decisions at precisely the time when you need to be getting out of the heat, replacing salts and liquid, and drastically reducing your core temperature. If you don't, you can slip into a coma and end up dead.

The race organizers said that anyone they suspected of being on the edge of heat exhaustion would be pulled from the race immediately. What they didn't say was that six years previously, one of their competitors in the same race had died from heatstroke.

The microphone was passed to an American woman. I recognized her as the founder of the race. "This year we've got some great runners competing," she said, "including the one and only Tommy Chen." There was a round of applause from the hundred runners in the room, who all shifted focus to a young Taiwanese guy who had his own personal film crew standing beside him, capturing the moment. We then listened to a whole load of stuff about how Tommy was going for the win, how he already had some great results behind him.

When I was back home, I had researched the runners I thought were the main contenders, so I knew Tommy was one of the best around. I knew he was a genuine multi-stage superstar and would be tough to beat.

Before I'd left Scotland, I'd read an e-mail from the organizers listing the top-ten runners they expected to do well. I wasn't mentioned at all, despite having beaten a few of them in the past.

A bit of me was still annoyed about it but not because my ego was bruised. There was no reason why they would have expected me to do well. Having not raced since a 132-miler in Cambodia eight months before, I felt I had become a forgotten nobody, and I didn't blame them for passing me over.

I was annoyed with myself. I'd started running only three years earlier but already had enjoyed a few podium results. Coming to the sport so late, I knew I had only a tiny window in which to prove myself, and taking eight months off to recover had felt like a waste of precious time.

Before the briefing we had a kit check to make sure we each had the mandatory equipment required for the race. Even though we carry all the food, bedding, and clothes we will need for the entire six-stage, seven-day race, the aim is to keep our bag weights to a minimum. For me, that means no change of clothes, no sleeping mat, and no books or smartphone to keep me entertained at the end of the race. All I bring is a sleeping bag, a single set of clothes, and the absolute minimum amount of food I can get away with. I bank on 2,000 calories a day, even though I know I'll burn closer to 5,000. I return home looking like death, but the lighter bag is worth it.

Later that day we were boarded onto buses and taken to the site where the race would begin, a couple of hours outside of Hami. I made small talk with a guy next to me, but mainly I kept quiet and tried to block out the noise of the three guys who had come from Macau behind me who were laughing and talking loudly the whole way. I turned around and half-smiled at them a few times, hoping that they'd pick up on my subtle hint for them to shut up. They

just grinned back and carried on with their party. By the time we stopped, I was pretty fed up and hoping to get off and find some peace and quiet to start mentally preparing for the race ahead.

The locals put on a beautiful exhibition of regional dancing and horse riding, including a game that looked like polo but was being played with a dead sheep. I snuck off to find the tent I'd be staying in to claim my spot. On most multi-stage ultras, runners get assigned tent mates to camp with throughout the race. You never know who you're going to get, but you can at least make sure you don't get stuck with a terrible sleeping spot.

I stood in the old army surplus tent and wondered where to put myself. I never liked being near the door because of the draft, and the back of the tent often got a little cold too. I decided to chance it and take a spot in the middle, hoping that my fellow campers wouldn't keep me awake by snoring or making a fuss.

I gave my kit a final check as the first three tent mates arrived. They looked sound enough and didn't cause a ruckus as they chose their spots.

My heart sank when I heard the sound of laughter, looked up, and saw the three guys from Macau walking in.

Even though it was summer, the temperature was noticeably colder when the sun started to set. The local mayor gave a speech that I couldn't understand, but the display of Mongolian dancing and high-speed horse riding was enough to keep me occupied for a while. Some of the runners were sitting around, eating their evening meals, but I wandered around. I got sidetracked looking at Tommy Chen's film crew, but soon enough I was thinking about getting back to the tent. When people started asking one another what type

of shoes they were running in, how much their bags weighed, or whether they'd brought any extra supplies, it was definitely my cue to leave. Getting involved in those kinds of conversations on the day before a race starts is never a good idea. The minute you encounter someone who is doing something different, you'll end up doubting yourself.

I checked my watch—six thirty. Time to eat. Even though waiting can be hard when I'm nervous and it's dark already, I always make sure I eat at the right time the night before each day's race. You don't want to eat too early and have your body consuming the calories before you're actually running.

I got my food, climbed into my sleeping bag, and ate in silence in the tent.

I made sure I was asleep before anyone else came back.

3

PEOPLE ALWAYS GET UP WAY TOO EARLY ON the first day of these races. Their nerves get the best of them, and two or three hours before the start, the camp is buzzing with people packing and repacking their bags, eating their food, talking, and worrying about whether they've packed their bags right and eaten the right amount of breakfast at just the right time.

I get it. I've been there myself. But that's not how I operate anymore. I have a routine that's tried and tested.

Start minus ninety minutes—wake up, get dressed, visit toilets.

Start minus sixty minutes—keep warm in tent, eat high-calorie breakfast.

Start minus fifteen minutes—pack up sleeping bag and inflatable mattress, leave tent, and join start line.

To anyone watching, however, the last hour of my routine looks a little weird. I stay in my sleeping bag right up until it's time to leave, even when I'm eating my can of All Day Breakfast. While everyone else is hopping up and down outside, having eaten their dehydrated meals, I'm curled up in my bag, beanie hat pulled tight

23

over my head, tucking into a cold can of beans, sausage, bacon, and mushrooms. I get a few looks because no multi-stage runner in their right mind would ever carry canned food; it's just not worth the weight. But I take just one can that I eat before the race starts, and the 450 calories are more than worth the bemused stares as people wonder what kind of amateur I am.

It tastes especially good knowing that for the next six days I'm going to be eating nothing but cold, rehydrated meals that taste like salmon or Bolognese-flavoured pasta, the occasional strip of biltong—dried and cured meat from South Africa—a few nuts, and dozens of energy gels. I'll be sick of this food before the end of the week, but it's lightweight nutrition that keeps my bag weight down.

I savoured every cold mouthful. I couldn't see the three Macau boys anywhere, but I could tell that the rest of my tent mates—two Brits and one American—were staring at me like I was a fool who was way out of his depth. Nobody said anything, and once I'd eaten, I lay back down and curled up as tight as I possibly could in my bag. I guessed they were probably still staring.

With a quarter hour left, I climbed out of the sleeping bag, packed my things away in my rucksack, and headed for the line. People stared as I knew they would. They always do when they see me coming on the first day. My skin-tight running top is bright yellow and covered in my sponsor's logo. And because I'm tall and skinny, I look like a banana. While confident in my pre-race preparation and training, I always start to question myself, seeing the start line. As much as I try to avoid it, I end up thinking the other runners look better than I do. They all seem to be fitter, stronger, and look more like endurance athletes while I suddenly feel like

an amateur again. The only way through it is to clench my jaw, hide behind my sunglasses, and tell myself it's time to get down to business.

For a lot of runners, the act of lacing up their shoes, heading out the door, and letting their lungs and their legs find their perfect rhythm as they run through nature is a beautiful thing. It's about freedom, peace, and the moment when all time seems to stop and the stresses of daily life fade.

I'm not one of those runners. My wife is. Lucja runs because she loves running. She races because she loves the camaraderie and the sense of community. Not me. I don't love running. I don't really like it either. But I do love racing. I love competing.

It took me thirty-seven years to realize that racing was for me. For most of my teens and twenties, I played competitive cricket and hockey. Right from the start I loved the action of a well-bowled ball, a perfectly struck cover drive, and a rocket of a shot that sails into the top right corner of the goal. To me, both of those sports have the potential to fill me with the kind of peace and happiness that Lucja describes when she runs. But even though I could master the technical aspects of hitting and bowling, I never could deal with the dynamics of playing as part of a team. I've watched myself fly off into a rage at my underperforming teammates so many times during matches that I know I'm more of a solo sport kind of guy.

I played golf for a while and got pretty good too—good enough to hustle the weekend players on courses throughout the western suburbs of Sydney and come back home with enough

money so Lucja and I could eat for the rest of the week. But there was something about the pressure and the need to fit in with all those etiquette rules that riled me. After I threw one too many tantrums and broke one too many putters, I finally decided that golf was not for me either.

When it came to running, I discovered, quite by accident, that my competitive side returned. We had moved out of London and were living in Manchester at the time. It was New Year's Eve, and I was listening to a friend from cricket go on and on about how he was going to take part in a half marathon in the spring. Dan was talking about bringing down his personal best of 1 hour 45 minutes. Thanks to Lucja, I knew enough about running to know that was an okay time, not amazing but better than a lot of people could run. Dan was quite fit as well, so I reckoned he was probably right in feeling confident about becoming a bit faster.

But he was just so cocky about it all. So I put down my beer and spoke up.

"I reckon I could beat you."

Dan laughed. The music was loud, and he had to lean in to make sure he'd heard correctly. "You what?"

"I could take you. Easy."

"You're not a runner, Dion. No way."

"Dan, I'm so confident I'll even give you five minutes."

The conversation got a bit wild after that. People were laughing and shouting, and pretty soon the deal was done. If I didn't beat Dan by five minutes, I'd take him, his wife, and Lucja out for dinner. If I won, he'd be the one paying.

Lucja gave me the kind of look that said, *Here we go again.* I

just smiled back and held up my hands. As far as I was concerned, I'd just won a free sumptuous meal for the two of us.

The race was at the end of March, and I knew I had a double mountain to climb. I'd been running for a year or two, but never farther than two or three miles at a time; any more than that and I'd just get bored and fed up. I've always hated running when it's cold or wet—and Manchester in January and February serves up nothing but cold and wet. So a few weeks went by, and my training had barely begun.

Dan is one of those runners who can't resist coming back from a run and posting his times on Twitter. It wasn't long before his overconfidence began to show, and when I started to read how far he was running and how fast he was getting there, I had all the motivation I needed to get off the sofa and hit the streets. I knew that as long as I pushed myself to run farther and faster than the times Dan was posting, I'd be able to beat him.

I lined up alongside Dan and Lucja at the start line. Dan was looking fit and up for it. Lucja was loving the pre-race-hype and crowd-warm-up routine from the announcer whose job it was to get everyone pumped for the race start. I was feeling out of place among the thousands of other runners who all had what looked like better sports equipment than I had.

"You know I have very expensive taste in wine, Dion," Dan said. "You're going to need a second mortgage to pay for the meal tonight."

I didn't say anything. Just smiled.

"Seriously, mate," he said, looking genuinely concerned. "Are

you all right for this? It feels hot already. Don't push yourself harder than you should."

I was feeling nervous. My mouth was dry, and it was all I could do to suck as much air as I possibly could into my lungs.

The gun was fired, and we were off. Dan was at my side, and we were going at a fair pace already. Lucja dropped back, and the two of us carried on together. He seemed strong and in control. I felt fine about keeping pace with him, happy that we were finally under way.

When we passed the first mile marker, it hit me that I had only twelve more in which to gain five minutes on Dan. So I did the only thing I could think of. I decided to give it everything I had, running as hard and as fast as I could. Pretty soon my lungs were in agony, and I felt as if there wasn't enough air in the sky to keep me going. I wanted to slow down just a little and recover, but I forced myself to keep up the pace. Those five minutes were going to come my way only if I kept pulling away from Dan.

Never once did I look back. Somehow I knew it wouldn't help. If I saw him close, I'd probably panic, and if he was too far back already, I might end up slowing down. I knew that the race was going to be won or lost in my head. If I kept focus and pushed on, I'd avoid distraction.

Dan was right about it being a hot day. I'd never experienced heat like it at that time of year in Manchester before, and all through the morning the noise of the crowd was broken up by the sound of ambulance sirens as they raced to help exhausted runners.

For me, though, the heat wasn't a threat. It was like a welcome friend. It reminded me of my childhood in Australia. I'd spend hours on summer days playing cricket or riding my bike in temperatures pushing up to 110 and 120 degrees. It wasn't anywhere near

that hot during the race, but all the same I found myself getting stronger as the heat increased and the miles passed by.

At least I did until mile eleven. That's when I started to feel myself slowing down. My legs were numb and weak, as if someone had stripped half the muscles from them. But I kept running, pushing hard and reminding myself what was at stake: my pride.

I crossed the line in 1:34, a respectable time for a first-ever half marathon, and nine minutes faster than Dan's previous personal best. Was it going to be enough? He'd set off pretty fast, and his training had put him in line to beat it. All I could do was crouch at the finish, feel my lungs begin to recover, and watch the clock tick by and hope not to see him.

It was Lucja who crossed a little more than five minutes after me. We high-fived each other and smiled as we waited the best part of another ten minutes for Dan to finally come home.

"What happened?" he said once he had recovered a little. "You just sped off. You must have done more training than you let on."

I smiled and gave him a pat on the back. "You need to get off Twitter, mate."

The start line at the race was much like any other start line at any other race around the world; everyone doing their own thing to cope with the nerves. I was at the side, second or third row back from the front, trying to distract myself by looking at the others around me. Tommy Chen was there, looking focused and pretty damn good. He had his camera crew to the side and plenty of fans among the pack. "Good luck, Tommy," someone called out. "Hope you smash it!"

"Yeah, thanks," he said, shifting his feet back and forth. I

watched as the smile fell quickly from his face. He was just as nervous as the rest of us. Maybe more so. I knew he was one of the up-and-coming stars of multi-stage ultras, but he'd come in second in the first of the five races the organizers hosted that year. The pressure was on him to deliver.

To keep myself busy for another minute or so, I did one more final check of my kit, making sure the straps were tight enough across my chest, the food I needed during the stage was in the correct pockets, and my bright yellow gaiters were covering my shoes properly. I knew we'd be running up a sand dune pretty soon in the day, and the last thing I wanted was to spend the four or five hours that followed with pieces of grit irritating my feet, which could possibly lead to blisters and other foot issues.

The start horn sounded, and what little noise there was from the small crowd disappeared from my world. The race began on a wide stretch of grass, and as we got under way, the usual crush of people was surging down the middle. You get all sorts wanting to take the lead on that first day, and I don't mind so much. That's the beauty of these races—even though world-class athletes are lining up alongside happy amateurs, there is no sense of hierarchy or rank. If you want to run at the front and can keep up the pace, then be my guest.

I had guessed that the start would be a little bit tricky, with the runners bunching up as they usually did, so I'd put myself far out wide of everyone else. I didn't want to be tripped off the line, and if I went off fast enough, I could get ahead of the slower runners before the course narrowed and dropped down into a rocky canyon.

My plan worked as I soon fell in closely behind Tommy after the first 100 meters. It hadn't been raining in the night, but the

rocks were slippery from the morning dew. I struggled to keep my footing and felt a bit uneasy and took it steady, just like Tommy. I guess we both knew that if we put a foot down wrong and twisted an ankle, we'd have no choice but to put up with a whole lot of pain for another 150 miles or, worse yet, a Did Not Finish.

I heard someone move up behind me and watched as a Romanian guy flew right past me. He was skipping over the rocks as if they were mini trampolines. Once Tommy knew he was behind him, both of them pulled away from me a little. *Keep it steady*, I told myself. *No need to worry.* I had put together a detailed stage-by-stage race plan with my coach before I'd left Scotland. We'd looked back at my other races and noticed that I'd been making the same mistake a lot of the time.

I tended to start slowly and then make up ground as the week went on, particularly on the long day, which had become one of my strengths, when the stage typically covered fifty miles or more. The truth is I'm just not a morning person, and the first morning always seems to hit me hard. I've often found myself twenty minutes down on the race leaders at the end of day one, which makes it close to impossible to make back up.

Even in training runs I struggle to get going, and for the first mile or two, I always question whether I want to keep going. I spend those first few minutes feeling like I'd rather be doing anything other than running. But if I push through it, I'm usually fine, and during the last half of a run, I'll be flying.

I trusted that as long as I kept Tommy and this Romanian guy in my sights, I'd be all right. If I was close at the end of stage one, keeping pace but not overcooking, I'd be putting myself in the best possible position for the rest of the week.

Halfway through the day, when the Romanian started to tire

and fell back so far behind us that I could no longer hear him, I looked up and saw a sand dune towering up ahead. It was steep and wide, easily three hundred feet high. I'd seen dunes like it in Morocco, but this one seemed different somehow. The sand on the side looked harder and more compact, but the path I had to run up was soft and offered almost no resistance at all.

There's a key to running up a sand dune, and I learned it the hard way back when I first competed in the Marathon des Sables. I didn't know that you have to keep your stride as short as you possibly can, ensuring a quick cadence to avoid the sand breaking underneath your feet and slowing you down. I didn't know that sometimes the longer path is easier than the shorter one. As a result, I tanked and came in so late at the end of the first day that I was seriously considering dropping out altogether.

Tommy attacked the dune ahead of me, but after just a couple of strides it was obvious that sand in the Gobi Desert was not like the Saharan stuff. It must have rained in the area overnight, and the sand was darker, clumpier. It gave way with the slightest pressure, falling away like weak clay, and at times I had to use my hands to gain a little extra grip. We weren't running up it; we were scrambling.

Once we were finally at the top, I could see the dune more clearly. The only option was to run along the narrow peak that stretched ahead for almost a mile. On both sides, the dune fell away, and if anyone put a foot wrong, he'd end up falling all the way down to the bottom. It would take ages to clamber back up, wasting precious time and precious energy.

Tommy was loving it. "Look at this view!" he shouted. "Isn't it magnificent?"

I said nothing back. I'm scared of heights and was terrified that I'd fall. I moved ahead as cautiously as I could. More than once my

foot slipped, and I threw my arms out in a desperate attempt to regain my balance. At that point I didn't particularly care how much ground Tommy made on me. All I could do was stare at where my feet were heading and hope that the sand held.

As much as I hated being on top of the dune, when it came time to run down it, I was in heaven. I put a bit of power into my legs and sprinted down as fast as I could. By the time I hit bottom, I overtook Tommy. I felt his surprise and heard him keeping close behind me.

We ran side by side for a while until the Romanian caught up with us, and then the three of us traded the lead from time to time. The course took us through muddy fields and over bridges, alongside a giant reservoir. The vast sands and cruel heat of the Gobi Desert were a couple of days away, and we ran through remote villages that belonged in another century. Tumbledown buildings squatted on the land like an abandoned movie set. Occasionally we'd see locals, standing and staring impassively at us. They never said anything, but they didn't seem bothered by us either. It wouldn't have made any difference to me either way. I was flying by this time, full of hope that the race in the Gobi Desert might not be my last race after all.

4

I WAS BORN IN SYDNEY, NEW SOUTH WALES, but grew up in an Australian outback town in Queensland called Warwick. It's a place that barely anyone I meet has visited but one that contains the kind of people everyone can recognize. It's farming country, with traditional values and a strong emphasis on family. These days it's changed a lot and become a small, vibrant city, but when I was a teenager, Warwick was the kind of place that would fill up on a Friday night. The pubs would be crammed with hardworking men looking for a good night out involving a few too many beers, a couple of fights, and a trip to the petrol station— which any self-respecting Australian calls the 'servo'—for a meat pie that had been kept in a warmer all day and was hard as a rock.

They were good people, but it was a cliquish town at the time, and everyone knew everyone else's business. I knew I didn't belong among them.

It wasn't just the scandal of my abnormal childhood and family situation that prompted people to react badly. It was the way I behaved. It was who I had become. I went from being a polite, pleasant little kid to an awkward, pain-in-the-ass loudmouth. By the

time I was fourteen, I was the class joker, riling the teachers with my crowd-pleasing comments, getting thrown out of class, and swaggering my way out of the school gates as I walked to the servo for an early afternoon pie while the other fools were still stuck in class.

And when my school year ended and the headmaster greeted each of us with a handshake and a friendly word about our futures at the final assembly, all he could say to me was, "I'll be seeing you in prison."

Of course, there was a reason for all this, and it wasn't just the pain of losing my dad—not just once but twice over.

I was falling apart because everything at home seemed to me to be falling apart.

It seemed the loss of her husband hit my mum hard. Really hard. Her own father had returned from the Second World War traumatized, and like so many men, he turned to alcohol to numb the pain. Mum's childhood taught her that when parents are struggling, home isn't always the best place to be.

So when Mum became a widow in her early thirties with two young children, she coped the only way she knew how. She retreated. I remember days would go by and she'd be locked in the bedroom. I cooked meals of eggs on toast or spaghetti out of a can, or else we went to Nan's, some other neighbour's house, or, if it was Sunday, church.

From what I could see, Mum would go through phases where she became fixated with keeping the house immaculate. She cleaned relentlessly, and on the odd occasion that she did cook for herself, she'd clean the kitchen frantically for two hours. Neither I nor my

little sister, Christie, could do anything right. Kids being kids, if we'd leave crumbs around the place, smear our finger marks on windows, or take showers that lasted longer than three minutes, it might upset her.

Ours was a half-acre, filled with trees and flower beds. While Mum and Dad used to love working in it together, after Dad's death it was up to me to get out and keep it tidy. If I didn't do my chores, I felt life wasn't worth living.

When Mum would start nagging at me, pretty soon she'd be yelling at me and screaming. "You're useless," she'd say. I'd scream and yell back, and soon we both would be swearing at each other. Mum never apologized. Nor did I. But we both had said things we'd later regret.

We argued endlessly, every day and every night. I'd come home from school and feel like I had to walk on eggshells around the house. If I made any noise or disturbed her in any way, the whole fighting thing would start up again.

By the time I was fourteen, she'd had enough. "You're out," she said one day as, following yet another storm of mutually hurled insults, she pulled out cleaning supplies from the cupboard. "There's too much arguing, and nothing you do is right. You're moving downstairs."

The house was a two-storey home, but everything that mattered was upstairs. Downstairs was the part of the house where nobody ever went. It was where Christie and I played when we were little, but since then the playroom had become a dumping ground. There was a toilet down there, but barely any natural light, and a big area that was still full of building supplies. Most important for my mum, there was a door at the base of the stairway that

could be locked. Once I was down there, I felt trapped, stopped from being part of the family life above.

I didn't argue with her. Part of me wanted to get away from her.

So I moved my mattress and my clothes and settled into my new life—a new life in which Mum would open the door when it was time for me to come up and get food or when I needed to go to school. Apart from that, if I was at home, I was confined to the basement.

The thing I hated most about it was not the fact that I felt like some kind of a prisoner. What I hated about it was the dark.

Soon after Garry's death, I started sleepwalking. It got worse when I moved down, and I would wake up in the area where all the broken tiles were dumped. It'd be pitch black; I'd be terrified and unable to figure out which way to turn to switch on the lights. Everything became frightening, and my dreams would fill with nightmare images of Freddy Krueger waiting for me outside my room.

Most nights, as I listened to the lock turn, I'd fall on my bed and sob into the stuffed Cookie Monster toy I'd had since I was a kid.

Normally I don't take a mattress with me on a race, but I was worried my leg injury might flare up at some point crossing the Gobi Desert, so I'd packed one specially. I blew it up at the end of the first day and tried to rest up. I had a little iPod with me, but I didn't bother putting it on. I was fine with just lying back and thinking about the day's race. I was happy with third place, especially as there was only a minute or two between me, Tommy, and the Romanian, whose name I later found out was Julian.

Instead of an army surplus tent, we were in a yurt that night, and I was looking forward to it being good and warm as the temperature dropped. Meanwhile, though, I guessed I'd have to wait a while before any of my tent mates returned. I ate a little biltong and curled up in my sleeping bag.

It took an hour or so before the first two guys arrived back. I was dozing when I first became aware of them talking, and I heard one of my tent mates, an American named Richard, say, "Whoa! Dion's back already!" I looked up, smiled, and said hi and congratulated them on finishing the first stage.

Richard went on to say he was planning on speaking with the three Macau guys as soon as they got in. I'd slept all through the first night, but according to Richard, they'd been up late messing with their bags and up early talking incessantly.

I wasn't worried too much, and thinking about Lucja and how she'd got me into running in the first place, I drifted back to sleep.

I first tried running when we were living in New Zealand. Lucja was managing an eco-hotel, and I was working for a wine exporter. Life was good, and the days of having to hustle the golf courses for food money were behind us. Even better, both our jobs came with plenty of perks, such as free crates of wine and great meals out. Every night we'd put away a couple of bottles of wine, and on weekends we'd eat out. We'd take Curtly, our Saint Bernard (named after legendary West Indian cricketer Curtly Ambrose), out for a walk in the morning, stopping off at a café for sweet potato corn fritters or a full fry-up of eggs, bacon, sausage, beans, mushrooms, tomato, and toast. We might get a pastry on the way home, crack open a bottle of something at lunch, then head out in

the evening for a three-course meal with more wine. Later we'd walk Curtly one more time and get an ice cream.

People would tell me I was a big lad, and they were right. I weighed 240 pounds and was heavier than I had ever been in my life. I didn't do any exercise, was an off-again on-again smoker, and had created a dent in the sofa where I lay and watched sports on TV. I was twenty-six and eating myself to death.

The change came when Lucja made some new friends who loved running and fitness. She got onto her own health kick and started slimming down. She explained that she wanted to look good in a bikini, and I—like a typical guy from my part of the world—told her she was being ridiculous.

But I didn't believe what I said. I knew she was made of strong stuff, that she was determined and was going to see this through.

Lucja quickly got into running and found that she was completing her three-mile loop faster and faster.

"You're so unfit and unhealthy, Bubba," she said, calling me by the name I was now beginning to dislike. "I could beat you."

I was lying on the sofa at the time, watching cricket. "Don't be stupid. I could beat you easily. You've only been at it for six weeks."

In my mind, I was still a sportsman. I was the same kid who could spend all day playing cricket or running about with his friends. Besides, I had something that Lucja lacked—a killer competitive instinct. I'd competed so much as a teenager and won so many matches that I was convinced I could still beat her at any challenge she threw at me.

I found some shorts and tennis shoes, stepped over Curtly, who was sleeping on the front step, and joined Lucja on the street outside.

"You sure you're ready for this, Bubba?"

I snorted in disbelief. "Are you kidding? There's no way you're winning."

"All right then. Let's go."

We kept pace—for the first fifty feet. After that, Lucja started pulling away from me. My brain was demanding that I keep up, but it was impossible. I had nothing to give. I was like an old steamroller whose fire had gone out, gradually getting slower and slower.

By the time I'd covered another hundred feet, I stopped moving altogether. Up ahead, the road made a slight turn and went up a hill. The defeat felt heavy within me.

I stood bent over, hands on knees, retching, coughing, and gasping for breath. I looked up to see Lucja way ahead of me. She looked back at me for a second, then carried on running up the hill.

I was enraged. How could I get beaten? I turned around and walked back home. With each step, the anger was joined by something else. Panic.

The healthier she became and the more weight she lost, the greater my risk of losing her. On the day of the run, I knew she wouldn't stop, that this wasn't just a phase or a passing fad. She was determined, and I knew she'd keep going until she was happy. And when she reached that point, why would she stay with a fat bloke like me?

I woke up again but this time to the sound of the Macau boys coming back into the tent. They were all pumped up at having completed the first stage and were spreading out their kits, looking for their evening meals. That was when Richard pulled off his headphones and started talking to them in what sounded to me like perfect Mandarin.

Judging by their reaction, they understood every word he said, and they were taking it seriously. They looked like schoolboys being told off, not knowing where to look. As Richard was finishing, he pointed at me. They all stared in silence, grabbed their food from their bags, and slipped out of the tent.

"What did you say?" asked Allen, one of the British guys in the tent.

"I told them that tonight they had to be quiet and more organized. They've got to get their stuff organized before dinner, come back, and rest. That guy's here to win."

They all turned and looked at me.

"Is he right?" asked Allen. "Are you here to win?"

"Well, yes," I said. "I'm not here for fun, if that's what you mean."

Richard laughed. "We got that impression. You're not exactly sociable, are you?"

I laughed too. I liked this guy.

"Yeah, some of that's because I'm cold, and some of it's just how I get through these races." I paused. "But thanks for saying that to them."

It was six thirty in the evening when I shuffled out of my sleeping bag and wandered outside the yurt carrying a bag of dehydrated whatever-it-was I was going to eat that night. While we have to carry all our own food, bedding, and clothes on a multi-stage ultra, at least our water is provided. I found the fire where water was being boiled and made up a chilli con carne–flavoured meal. It tasted pretty bland, just like it always did, but I reminded myself I wasn't there for fun. It had the bare minimum calories I required to keep going, and I needed to eat every last bit of it.

Everyone was sitting around the fire and chatting. I liked the idea of resting in its glow and soaking up the heat for a while, but all the seats were taken, so I crouched down on an uncomfortable rock and ate. After scooping the very last traces of food from the corners of the bag, I headed back to the yurt. It had been a good day—a really good one, in fact—but I'd need a solid night's sleep and an equally good day tomorrow to keep my number three slot. I'd started the day as an unknown. I guessed that from now on people would be a bit more aware of me in the race. And that could make things difficult.

It was when I got up that I saw a dog. It was maybe a foot tall and sandy coloured with great dark eyes and a funny-looking mustache and beard. It was walking around between the chairs, getting up on its hind legs and charming people into giving it bits of food. Getting runners to part with any of their food this early in the race was no mean feat.

Clever dog, I thought. *There's no way I'd feed it.*

PART 2

5

THE YURT HAD BEEN SO HOT I'D BARELY BEEN able to sleep all night, but as I walked out the next morning, the air was cold enough to make me shiver. The ground was wet, and the Tian Shan up ahead appeared to be covered in low dark clouds that were surely going to dump more rain on us.

With a few minutes to go before the eight o'clock start, I took my place on the start line at the front of the pack. After coming in third yesterday, I felt as though I belonged there.

People were a lot less nervous than before. I could even hear some of them laughing, though I tried my best to block out all distractions and focus on the challenge ahead. I knew we'd face mile after mile of ascent as we headed up into the mountains, followed by some dangerous descents. We were already at an altitude of seven thousand feet, and I guessed that some runners would already be struggling with the lack of oxygen. Today was going to make things harder by taking us up to more than nine thousand feet.

My concentration was broken by the sound of more laughter and a little cheering behind me.

"It's the dog!"

"How cute!"

I looked down and saw the same dog from last night. It was standing by my feet, staring at the bright yellow gaiters covering my shoes. It was transfixed for a while, its tail wagging constantly. Then it did the strangest thing. It looked up, its dark black eyes taking in my legs first, then my yellow-shirted torso, and finally my face. It looked right into my eyes, and I couldn't look away.

"You're cute," I said under my breath, "but you'd better be fast if you're not planning to get trodden by one hundred runners chasing after you."

I looked about to see if anyone was going to come and claim the dog and get it out of the way before the runners took off. A few other runners caught my eye, smiled, and nodded at the dog, but none of the locals or the race staff seemed to notice.

"Does anyone know whose dog this is?" I asked, but nobody did. They were all too focused on the ten-second countdown to the race start.

"Nine . . . eight . . . seven . . ."

I looked down. The dog was still at my feet, only now it had stopped staring at me and was sniffing my gaiters.

"You'd better get away little doggie, or else you're going to get squashed."

"Five . . . four . . ."

"Go on," I said, trying to get it to move. It was no use. It took a playful bite of the gaiter, then jumped back and crouched on the ground before diving in for another sniff and a chew.

The race began, and as I set off, the dog came with me. The gaiters game was even more fun now that the gaiters moved, and the dog danced around my feet as if it was the best fun ever.

It seemed to me that the cute moment could become annoying if it carried on for too long. The last thing I wanted was to trip over the little pooch and cause injury to it or myself. Then again, I knew there was a long stretch of single track coming up in which it would be hard to overtake a lot of the slower runners, so I wanted to keep up the pace and not lose my position with the front runner.

I was thankful when, after a quarter mile, I looked back down and saw that the dog wasn't there. *Probably gone back to its owner at the camp*, I thought.

The track narrowed, and we entered a flat forest section that lasted a few miles. I was in second, a few feet behind a Chinese guy I'd not seen before. Every once in a while he'd miss a marker—a pink paper square about the size of a CD case attached to a thin metal spike in the ground. They were hard to miss, and in the forest sections there was one of them every ten or twenty feet.

"Hey!" I'd shout on the couple of occasions that he took a wrong turn and headed off into the forest. I'd wait for him to track back, then fall in again behind him. I guess I could have let him keep going or shouted my warning and then carried on running, but multi-stage runners have a certain way of doing things. If we're going to beat someone, we want it to be because we're faster and stronger, not because we've tricked them or refused to help when we could. After all, pushing our bodies as hard as we do, everyone makes mistakes from time to time. You never know when you're going to need someone to help you out.

The forest fell away as the path started its climb into the mountains. I kept up the six-minute-mile pace, concentrating on keeping my stride short and my feet quick. My body remembered the hours I'd spent with my coach standing beside the treadmill, beating out the rapid cadence to which he wanted me to run. His shouts of

"one-two-three-one-two-three" were like torture at first, but after a few sessions of spending a whole hour running like that, three minutes on then one minute off, my legs finally got the message. If I wanted to run fast and not feel the crippling pain anymore, I had no choice but to learn how to run this way.

I saw something move out of the corner of my eye and forced myself to look down for a fraction of a second. It was the dog again. It wasn't interested in my gaiters this time but, instead, seemed happy just to trot along beside me.

Weird, I thought. *What's it doing here?*

I pressed on and attacked the incline. Zeng, the Chinese guy who was leading, is an accomplished ultra-runner and had pulled away from me a little. I couldn't hear anyone behind me. It was just me and the dog, side by side, tearing into the switchbacks. The path was interrupted by a man-made culvert. It was only three feet wide, and I didn't think anything of it, leaping over the fast-flowing water without breaking stride.

I could tell the dog had stayed behind. It started barking, then making a strange whimpering sound. I didn't turn back to look. I never do. Instead, I kept my head in the race and pushed on. As far as I knew, the dog belonged to someone back near the camp. The little thing had had a pretty good workout for the day, conned some runners out of some high-calorie food, and now it was time to head home.

I was fifteen when I told my mum I was leaving the dingy basement and moving in with a friend. She barely said anything. It seemed to me she didn't care. I guess since I'd already been staying with friends whenever I could—and the fact that when I was

around, Mum and I fought endlessly, trading insults like boxers at a weigh-in—it couldn't have come as much of a surprise. In fact, it was probably a relief.

I moved in with a guy named Deon. "Dion and Deon?" said the woman who ran the hostel when Deon introduced me. "You're kidding, right?"

"No," said Deon. "Straight up."

She snorted and turned away mumbling. "I've heard it all now."

Deon was a year older than me, had left school already, and was an apprentice bricklayer. He'd had his own troubles at home.

Even though we were both finally free from the struggles at home, neither of us was too excited about life in the hostel. The walls were paper-thin, and everyone else living there was older and freaked us out. The hostel was filled with homeless people, travellers, and drunks. Food was always going missing from the communal areas, and barely a night went by without the whole hostel waking up to the sound of a fight breaking out.

While I was still at school, I also took a part-time job pumping petrol at the servo. It brought a little bit of money in but not enough, and I had to rely on Deon to help with the shortfall each week.

I only just managed to keep up with my schoolwork, but none of my teachers showed any sign of caring about where I was living or how I was coping with life away from home. In fact, I don't think any of them knew about my new living arrangements, and I wanted to keep it that way. I was embarrassed to go back to the hostel and tried to hide the truth from my classmates with their perfect, loving family homes.

Deon was the kind of guy who could charm the birds from the trees. We'd sneak into the pub on a Friday or Saturday night, have a few beers, and try to chat up some girls. I'd let Deon do

the talking, much like I'd let him do the dancing. Aussie blokes from towns like mine didn't dance in those days, and it was almost inevitable that when he finally came off the dance floor, Deon would take a mouthful of abuse and a few thrown punches. He'd just laugh them off.

One Sunday afternoon as we lay on our bunks wasting time, we heard shouting in the corridor outside. Someone was calling Deon's name, saying he was going to kill him for sleeping with his girlfriend.

The two of us froze. I stared at Deon, who looked for the first time ever genuinely scared for his life. We both tried to act tough when we were in the hostel, but we were just kids—who at that moment were terrified we were about to get our heads kicked in. Luckily the blokes didn't know which room we were in, and they kept moving up and down the corridor until they eventually left. That was enough of a shock to get us to move out of the hostel as soon as possible.

The Grand Hotel was a step up from the hostel, but it wasn't much of a hotel. It was just a pub with a few rented rooms at the top. Instead of addicts, drunks, and homeless blokes, the Grand was home to guys who worked on the railroad or in the local meat-packing plant. One was an ex-pro pool player who had once beaten the national champion but had drunk all his talent away. Another was a traveller who had run out of money and simply decided to make Warwick his home. I liked listening to him talk. "Any place can be all right," he'd say, "as long as you accept what's wrong with it."

I felt much happier at the Grand than I did at the hostel. I liked being in the company of the kind of people who had chosen their lot and were happy with it, even if it meant not having the perfect

wife, the perfect house, and the perfect family. I felt free living among them, and for the first time in years, it seemed to me that all the things my mum had said that made me feel worthless and unwanted, an unlovable screw-up and a disappointment, might not necessarily be true. Maybe I could learn to get by after all.

The barking and whimpering continued until I was twenty feet past the culvert. Then there was silence. I had a moment of hoping the dog hadn't fallen into the water, but before I could think about it much more, there was a familiar flash of brown beside me. The dog was back by my side again.

You're a determined little thing, aren't you?

Soon the track became even steeper as the temperature dropped lower. The cold air had numbed my face and fingers, but I was sweating. The increase in altitude made my breathing tight and my head a little dizzy. If I was going to run without stopping all the way up the mountain, I knew I'd have to dig in even more than usual.

I hate mountain running. Even though I live in Edinburgh and am surrounded by the beauty of the Scottish Highlands, I avoid running outside and up hills whenever possible. Especially when it's wet, cold, and windy. But give me a desert baked in 110-degree heat, and I'll be as happy as any runner out there.

People often ask me why I like running in the heat so much. The answer is simple: I've always felt the most freedom when I'm running beneath a blazing sun.

It started when I was a kid. After Garry died, I turned to sport in the hope of finding refuge from the troubles at home. I'd spend hours outside playing cricket or hockey. Time would stop when I was outside, and the more I ran and pushed myself, the heavier my

breathing became, and the louder my heart beat, the quieter the sadness and sorrow grew within me.

Maybe you could say that running in the heat was a form of escape. What I do know for sure is that as I ran in the Gobi Desert, I was no longer running to get away from my past. I was running towards my future. I was running with hope, not sorrow.

My pace slowed as every step became its own battle. There was snow all around, and at one point the track ran alongside a glacier. At other times the mountain would drop away at the side. I guessed there were some pretty dramatic views this high up, but I was thankful the cloud was so low that it was impossible to see anything more than a thick wall of grey mist. The experience was surreal, and I couldn't wait for it to be over.

The checkpoint finally came into view, and I heard people call out the usual encouragement. Once they saw the dog, they shouted a little louder.

"There's that dog again!"

I'd almost forgotten the little dog at my side. All the time that I'd been struggling up the hill, the dog had kept pace with me, skipping along as if running 2,500 feet up into the sky was the most natural thing in the world.

Once I was at the checkpoint, I faced the usual range of questions about how I was feeling and whether I had been drinking my water. Checkpoints are there to give runners an opportunity to refill their water bottles, but they're also a chance for the race team to check us over and make sure we are fit to carry on.

This time, however, it was the dog who got far more attention than me. A couple of volunteers took some photos as the dog sniffed

about the checkpoint tent. As soon as my bottles were full and I was ready to go, I moved out, half expecting this might be the point when the dog decided to leave me in favour of a better meal ticket.

But when I and my yellow gaiters started running out, the dog joined me straightaway.

If the climb to the top of the mountain had been tough, then the descent was its own unique sort of pain. For more than five miles the route took me straight down a path covered in rocks and loose stones. It was brutal on the joints, but like any runner, I knew that if I ran at anything less than 100 per cent, I'd get caught by who-ever was behind me.

And that's exactly what happened. I was feeling sluggish and struggled to hit anything close to my maximum pace on the descent, and soon enough Tommy glided past me, quickly followed by Julian.

I was annoyed with myself for giving too much on the ascent. I'd made a basic error, the kind I knew better not to make.

I checked myself. Getting annoyed could lead me to make another basic error. At times in the past, I'd let myself obsess about a mistake I'd made. Over the course of a few miles, the frustration would build and build until I'd lose all interest in the race and bail out.

I tried to distract myself by concentrating on the view. Coming down from the mountain at one point, I thought I saw a giant lake ahead of us, stretched out wide and dark beneath the grey skies. The closer I got, the more it became clear that it wasn't a lake but a huge expanse of dark sand and gravel.

As the path flattened, I settled into a steady six-and-a-half-minute-per-mile pace, bursting through the final checkpoint, not

bothering to stop for water. I saw Tommy, Zeng, and Julian up ahead and found they hadn't opened up the gap as much as I had feared. They were racing one another hard, and with less than a mile to go, there was no way for me to catch them. But I didn't mind so much. I felt good to be finishing strong without any hint of pain in my leg. I could hear the drums that played every time a runner crossed the finish line, and I knew that finishing a close fourth for the day would hopefully be enough to keep me in third overall.

Just as at each of the day's checkpoints, the dog was the focus of attention at the finish. People were taking pictures and filming, cheering for the little brown mutt as it crossed the line. The dog seemed to like the attention, and I could swear it was playing to the crowd by wagging its tail even faster.

Tommy had got in a minute or two before me, and he joined in the applause. "That dog, man! It's been following you all day!"

"Has it had any water?" asked one of the volunteers.

"I have no idea," I said. "Maybe it drank at some of the streams on the way." I felt a little bad about it. I didn't like the idea of it being thirsty or hungry.

Someone found a small bucket and gave the dog some water. It lapped it up, obviously thirsty.

I stepped back, wanting to leave the dog to it and get away from the crowds a little. Again I thought it might wander off and go find someone else to follow, but it didn't. As soon as it finished drinking, it looked up, locked eyes on my yellow gaiters, and trotted over to my side, following me wherever I went.

It was hot in the camp, and I was glad we'd left all that horrible alpine cold up in the mountains. From now on the race was going to be about coping with the heat, not struggling through the cold. From tomorrow onward we'd be in the Gobi Desert. I couldn't wait.

As soon as I sat down in the tent, the dog curled up next to me—and I started thinking about germs and diseases. It's crucial during a weeklong race to keep as clean as possible because without any access to showers or wash basins, it's easy to get sick from anything you touch. The dog was looking right into my eyes, just as it had earlier that morning. I had a few hours before my six-thirty meal, so I pulled out one of the packs of nuts and biltong. The dog's stare was unbreakable.

With a piece of meat midway to my mouth, it struck me that I hadn't seen the dog eat a thing all day. It had run the best part of a marathon, and still it wasn't trying to beg or steal any of the food I had in front of me.

"Here you go," I said, tossing half the meat down onto the tarpaulin in front of it, instinct telling me that feeding by hand wasn't a risk I wanted to take. The dog chewed, swallowed, spun around a few times, and lay down. Within seconds it was snoring, then twitching, then whimpering as it drifted deeper and deeper into sleep.

I woke up to the sound of grown men cooing like school kids.

"Ah, how cute is that?"

"Isn't that the dog from last night? Did you hear she followed him all day?"

She. The dog had run with me all day, and I'd never thought to check what sex it was.

I opened my eyes. The dog was staring right at me, looking deeper into my eyes than I would have thought possible. I checked. They were right. It wasn't an it. It was a she.

"Yeah," I said to Richard and the rest of the guys. "She stuck with me all day. She's got a good little motor on her."

Some of the guys fed her, and again she took whatever she was given, but gently. It was almost as though she knew she was getting a good deal here and she needed to be on her best behaviour.

I told the guys I'd been wondering where she came from and that I'd guessed she'd belonged to whoever owned the yurts we'd stayed in the previous night.

"I don't think so," said Richard. "I heard some of the other runners say she joined them out on the dune yesterday."

That meant she had put in almost fifty miles in two days. I was staggered.

It also meant she didn't belong to the people back at the previous camp or to one of the race organizers.

"You know what you've got to do now, don't you?" said Richard.

"What?"

"You've got to give her a name."

6

I STOPPED RUNNING LESS THAN A MILE IN AND
cursed my stupidity.

The last twenty-four hours had brought all kinds of weather our way, from the snow and rain of the mountains to the dry heat that greeted us as we came down to camp. All night high winds had been tearing at the sides of the tent, and when I got up, the temperature was the coldest for any start yet.

The cold bothered me. I'd been looking forward to the day, knowing it was going to be flatter and hotter, but, instead, I'd found myself shivering on the start line. While the other runners went through their pre-race routines, I'd thrown off my backpack, rummaged around inside, and pulled out my light jacket, completely upsetting my usual precise and carefully prepared race start.

And now I was taking it off again. After a few minutes the sun had come out, and the temperature had started to rise. I should have been happy about it, but I could feel myself start to overheat in my wet weather gear. With five hours of hard running ahead of me, I had no choice but to stop.

As I pulled at zippers and plastic clips and shoved the jacket away, I noticed Tommy, Julian, and two others run past and reclaim the lead.

Then one more runner approached, and I smiled.

"Hey, Gobi," I said, using the name I'd given her the night before. "You changed your mind, did you?"

She'd spent the night curled up at my side, but once I got to the start line that morning, she'd disappeared among the crowd of other runners. I'd been too focused on the weather to worry about her. Besides, if the previous twenty-four hours had taught me anything, it was that she was a determined little thing. If she had other plans for her day, who was I to stop her?

But there was Gobi, looking up at me as I fastened my bag, then down at my gaiters. She was ready to go. So was I.

I pushed hard to catch up with the leaders and was soon tucked in behind them. I knew a long stretch of the race went through a section of large boulders, and I remembered how light on his feet Julian had been when we hit similar terrain the first day. I didn't like the thought of watching him skip away from me again, so I pushed my way up past the third and fourth runners, then overtook Julian and Tommy.

Being out in front again felt good. My legs felt strong, and my head was up. I could hear the gap between me and the other runners grow bigger with every minute that passed. I was able to run hard, and whenever I started to tire, all I needed to do was glance quickly down at Gobi. She didn't know anything about running technique or race strategy. She didn't even know how far I was planning on running throughout the day. She was running free, running because that was what she was made to do.

I followed the pink course markers all the way to the boulder section. The flat path I'd been on veered to the right, but the markers carried on straight ahead, through the rocks that looked big, unstable, and like they were going to make it almost impossible

to keep up any kind of pace. But there was no avoiding them, and I scrambled up, feeling the smaller rocks shift and move beneath me as I went. I hoped I wasn't going to twist an ankle, and envied Gobi's ability to bound effortlessly over them.

I knew Julian was going to be quicker than me in this section, and as we approached the peak, I could hear him closing in behind me. But as I finally reached the top, instead of pushing ahead and trying to hold him off as long as I could, I froze.

I could see everything from up there. The checkpoint sat off in the distance, with a small village we would run through before it. I could see the way the boulder section sloped off ahead of us for another thousand feet, the pink race markers plotting the course as it returned to the flat path that led to the village, the checkpoint, and beyond.

None of that was what I was looking at.

My gaze, just like that of Julian and the other two runners who had pulled up alongside him, was firmly fixed on the solitary figure running off to the right.

It was Tommy.

"Whoa," said Julian. "Not right."

Tommy had somehow skipped the entire boulder section and gained a bit of time. By my calculations he'd made ten minutes on us.

All three of us were furious, but Tommy was too far ahead to hear us if we shouted. So we set off as a pack with renewed fire in our bellies, determined to catch him.

We could see Tommy at the checkpoint ahead as we ran through the village, but by the time we reached it ourselves, he had disappeared over a ridge a few hundred feet away.

I decided to pause long enough to raise the alarm and make

sure someone had a record of what happened. The member of the organizing team looked at me as if I was an idiot when I first tried to explain it.

"Say that again, please?" she said.

"Tommy Chen missed that whole rocky section back there. I don't know if he did it deliberately or not, but it's not fair."

"We'll look into it later," she said, giving me the brush-off.

"Tommy cut corner," said Zeng, who'd been with us and seen it all. "Not right."

Again, she didn't seem to care all that much. Soon we were back out of the checkpoint, trying to catch up with Tommy. He had almost a mile of tough terrain on us, but I had rage on my side. I pushed the pace up to a six-and-a-half-minute mile and worked hard to start reeling him in. Julian and the others stayed back a little, but I didn't mind. I was on a mission.

The path was undulating, and there were only a few times when I could see Tommy clearly. At one point there was only a half mile between us when he turned around, saw me running hard towards him, turned back, and sprinted off as fast as he possibly could.

I couldn't believe it.

There's an etiquette to these races. If you realize you've gained an unfair advantage over other runners, you hang back, let them catch up, and allow the proper order to be restored. I've made this kind of error myself in another race. It's easy to do in the battle for the lead, but it's better to settle while on the race course rather than after the run is completed.

I pressed on after him, but after working so hard to try to narrow the gap, and having let myself get so angry, I soon felt tired. I heard footsteps behind me, and Julian overtook me. The heat started to rise, and the race moved onto a long, flat road that

extended off for miles into the distance. I started to feel bored, then frustrated with myself.

Previous experience had taught me that feeling this way was toxic. But it had also taught me how to deal with it.

In my first-ever ultra-race—a full marathon with a six-mile loop added onto the end—I'd started to feel tired at around the twenty-mile mark. By the time I approached it, I was done. I wasn't enjoying the running, and I was fed up with getting overtaken by men and women who were much older than me. I'd done it only to keep Lucja company, and even though I was about to complete the 26.2 miles in a respectable 3:30, I gave up inside. I stepped off the course, headed back to the car, and waited for Lucja to join me.

It took hours.

As I sat in the car and watched the rest of the field put in the hard work that I wasn't prepared to put in myself, I started to feel like I'd let myself down.

The field had thinned, and the only people still running were the kind of people who looked as if this event was a once-in-a-lifetime achievement. Lucja was fitter, faster, and stronger than all of them, and I was beginning to wonder what had happened. Eventually I got out of the car and walked back along the last mile of the course, looking for her. I found her soon enough, running slowly alongside a guy who obviously had a pretty serious leg injury. Lucja had struggled with fatigue toward the end of the race, but she had toughed it out.

I watched her cross the finish line and felt myself start to choke up. The mental strength and compassion Lucja showed that day has stayed with me ever since. I try to emulate her often when I'm

racing, and at my best I can dig deep and tough out all kinds of pain and discomfort. But there are days when the voices calling me to quit shout louder than the voices calling me to keep on going. Those are the toughest days of all.

As I watched Julian disappear into the distance and tried not to think about how far ahead Tommy had gotten, I knew I was missing Lucja. But a quick glance down at Gobi was enough to bring back my focus and take my mind off the thing with Tommy. She was still beside me, still skipping along. Just by being there, Gobi made me want to keep going.

The long, flat section ended and gave way to scrubland. I'd noticed during the start of the stage that if Gobi saw a stream or puddle, she would occasionally run off to the side of the course and take a drink. Since the boulder section we'd not seen any water at all, and I wondered whether I might need to give her some of my own water. I didn't want to stop, but I was also starting to feel responsible for the dog's welfare. She wasn't a big dog, and her legs weren't much longer than my hands. All that running must have been hard on her.

So, initially at least, I was relieved when I saw the streams up ahead. Gobi trotted off and had a drink out of one of them, but if she'd been able to see what I could see, she wouldn't have been nearly so happy.

Beyond the stream I could see Julian, on the far side of a river that must have been at least 150 feet wide. I remembered that the organizers had spoken about it while I was shivering on the start line a few hours earlier. It was going to come up to my knees, but it was possible to walk across.

The sight of Julian spurred me on, and I didn't hesitate to wade in, checking that my bag was strapped on tight and high on my back. It was colder than I imagined, but I welcomed the chance to cool down a bit.

It was soon clear that the water was definitely going to reach my knees, and possibly even higher. The current was fast as well, and combined with the slippery rocks underfoot, I felt unsteady. I could handle continuing the race with wet shoes, for they'd dry out soon enough. But if I slipped, fell, and got my bag wet, not only would it become heavy and uncomfortable, but most of my food for the rest of the week would be ruined. One wrong foot, one tiny fall, and my race could be all over.

I was so focused on getting myself across that I didn't stop to think about Gobi. I guess I assumed that she'd find her own way across the river, just as she had with the culvert the day before.

This time, however, her barking and whining didn't stop. With every step I took, it became more desperate.

I was a quarter way across the river when I finally did what I had never done before in a race. I turned around.

She was on the bank, running up and down, looking right at me. I knew Julian was ahead by a few minutes, but I wondered how long it would be before someone came up behind me. If I went back, would I lose a place as well as valuable minutes?

I ran back as best I could, tucked her under my left arm, and waded back out into the cold water. I'd not picked her up before, and she was so much lighter than I imagined she would be. Even so, it was so much harder crossing with her. Using only my right arm for balance, I edged forward.

I slipped more than once, one time going down hard on my left side, getting Gobi and—I guessed—the bottom edge of my

bag wet. But Gobi didn't complain, nor did she wriggle or try to escape. She stayed calm, letting me do my job and keep her safe.

I put her down when we reached a small island in the middle, and she trotted around as though the whole thing was a great adventure. Once I'd checked that my bag wasn't seriously wet and made sure it was as high up my back as I could get it, I called for Gobi, who immediately ran back to me. I scooped her up and continued on as before.

She scrambled up the bank on the other side a lot quicker than I did, and by the time I was clear of the mud and the undergrowth, Gobi had shaken herself off and was staring at me, obviously ready to get back to the race.

The dirt road ahead soon led us to another man-made culvert, though this one was altogether bigger than the previous one Gobi had jumped across. I didn't stop at all this time, just picked her up and lifted her over.

There was a moment when I had her in front of me, her face level with mine, that I swore she gave me a look of genuine love and gratitude.

"You're ready, aren't you, girl?" I said, unable to stop smiling as I put her back down and watched her start to jump about. "Let's go, then."

It was only when I looked up that I saw an old guy on a donkey. He was watching us both, his face completely expressionless.

What must I look like? I wondered.

7

RACE ORGANIZERS LIKE TO TEASE RUNNERS,
and the final stretch of the day went on for miles. My GPS watch
told me that we were close to finishing, but I couldn't catch a glimpse
of the camp anywhere. All I could see was the path disappearing off
into the distance, rising and falling over a series of ridges.

I was a couple of miles out, and by my calculations, I'd lost
so much time when my pace had dropped earlier and then when I
helped Gobi across the river, that Tommy and possibly even Julian
would have finished. So I was surprised when I crested one of the
ridges and saw both of them a mile up ahead. Neither of them
appeared to be going at a decent pace. Instead, it looked to me like
they were walking. I wondered whether, maybe, Tommy was holding back deliberately to allow others to catch up and make amends
for what had happened earlier. Or maybe he was just struggling in
the heat and was unable to go any faster.

Either way, I thought I might just have a shot at narrowing the
gap between us, but I wanted to do it without letting them know.
I didn't want them to realize I was chasing them down and pick
up their own pace. I had only so much more energy to give for the

day. As the road went down into another dip, hiding me from view, I sprinted as fast as I possibly could. When I reached the top and could be seen again, I slowed right down. Gobi thought it was all great fun and pushed me hard on the sprints.

I didn't see Tommy or Julian for the first couple of ridges, but when I crested the third, the gap between us had been halved. They were definitely walking, and I ran the next two dips even faster.

I knew I was getting closer with each sprint, and when I came up for the fifth time, my lungs burning, I was barely two hundred feet behind them. They were just about to disappear from view for the final dip down, and I could see that the finish line was just ahead.

I had time for one last sprint before I switched tactics and started to run with a bit of stealth. The last thing I wanted to do was alert them to the fact that I was chasing them, so I went from running as fast as I could to running as quietly as possible.

By keeping up on my toes, and taking care to avoid any loose stones, two hundred feet soon turned into one hundred. Then eighty. Then sixty. I was amazed that neither of them heard me or looked back.

When the gap between us was thirty feet, and the line was another hundred feet beyond them, I decided I was close enough and kicked into the fastest sprint I could manage. I got a few paces closer before Julian turned and saw me, but even though Tommy started running, I had gained too much ground for either of them to make up.

I crossed the line first, with Gobi close on my heels in second. The sound of the finishing drum couldn't drown out the shouts and cheers from the small crowd of organizers and volunteers.

I knew that the few seconds I'd put on Tommy would make no difference at all when it came to the end of the seven-day race,

but it felt like a good way to respond to what had happened. I wanted him to know that even though I respected him and all he'd achieved as a runner, I wasn't going to sit back and let him have everything his own way. If he was going to win, he'd have to do battle with me out on the course fair and square.

"That was amazing," said one of the race organizers. "You're having a super race."

"Oh, thanks," I said. But I didn't want to have my ego stroked. I wanted to see how she was going to deal with the Tommy situation. "Can I come and have a chat with you later today about Tommy Chen cutting the course before checkpoint one? I'm not in the right frame of mind now, but you need to know what happened earlier."

A lot of the anger had gone, but I knew I still had to be careful about what I said. After all, Tommy was the star of the show.

I ended up giving my version of events and waiting in the tent with Gobi curled up at my side while the investigation continued. The woman asking the questions also spoke with the other runners, the checkpoint staff, and Tommy. I'd said that I thought a fifteen-minute adjustment was fair, but in the end Tommy had just five minutes added onto his day's time.

I was a bit disappointed and maybe a bit worried about how Tommy would take it. I went in search of him and found him in his tent. He was in tears.

"Do you have a minute to talk, Tommy?"

"I didn't see the markers," he said as soon as we got outside. I thought that was unlikely. Those little pink squares were hard to miss, and any seasoned runner who spends time at the front of the pack quickly learns how important it is to continually scan the

route ahead and keep on course. Besides, he was behind me at the time, and my bright yellow shirt was hard to miss.

"Okay," I said. "I don't want any hard feelings about today. It's all done with now. Let's not hold any grudges, shall we?"

He looked at me, his face set firm and his tears long gone. "I didn't mean to do it. I didn't spot the markers."

I left it at that. There was nothing else to say.

Back in my tent I got a bit of encouragement from Richard and Mike for finishing first, but it was the incident with Tommy that they wanted to talk about. I wasn't so interested in discussing it and wanted to put the whole thing behind me.

"I take my hat off to you, Dion," said Richard. "You did something nice there."

"How come?"

"Us runners farther back really appreciate your taking a stand on this. We've all got to stick to the same rules. Plus, you've done the right thing talking to Tommy and burying the hatchet."

"Yeah, well, we'll see what Tommy's capable of tomorrow," I said. "Maybe I've just stirred up a whole hornets' nest of trouble for myself."

I didn't get much sleep again that night. It was hot in the tent, and I had too much white noise playing out in my head. At one point Richard left to go to the bathroom, and when he came back, Gobi growled at him. I liked the feeling that she was looking out for me.

The next day was a desert session over rocky, hard-packed ground under a cruel sun. We'd already agreed the night before that it would be too much for Gobi, so she'd travel to the next camp in a volunteer's car. I was up early, out of my tent way before my usual fifteen-minute mark, trying to find out who was going to

take her and making sure that person was going to keep her cool and hydrated throughout the day.

When it came time to say goodbye, I felt a tiny shiver of worry about her. She'd attached herself so clearly to me, but would she be okay with a bunch of strangers for the day? Would I see her again, or would she set off on another adventure?

The day's race was a hard run right from the start, partly because of the change in terrain. Where the previous day had served up a mix of undulating paths, rivers, and boulders to keep runners alert, the fourth day was a series of endless flats between checkpoints that hid beneath the horizon, miles and miles apart.

Underfoot there were the same old rocks that had snagged plenty of runners' feet already, but instead of scrubland or dusty trails, we were now running across the compressed shingle that made up the black portion of the Gobi Desert.

I spent the whole day running into a headwind, watching out for rocks, and trying not to get frustrated by the constant sound of eating and drinking that was coming from over my shoulder.

It was Tommy.

Almost from the start of the day, he had positioned himself behind me. Not ten feet behind me or a few feet to the side. Right behind me, his feet falling in perfect sync with mine. With his body tucked in where the wind resistance was at its weakest, he was slipstreaming, just like a road cyclist or a migratory bird. Only, with Tommy, it was obvious he had no intention of ever giving me a break and taking the lead for a while.

As he ran behind me, leaving me to navigate the route and suck up the vicious headwind, he got himself fuelled.

Nuts. Gels. Water.

He spent the whole day eating and drinking and saying absolutely

nothing to me. Even when Zeng overtook us both, Tommy didn't move. He was my shadow, and there was nothing I could do about it.

I started to wonder about Tommy's motives. What was he up to? Did he plan on stalling me? Was he planning to break away and leave me in his dust? I knew he would want to erase yesterday's loss and be all about winning the stage, so why was he staying behind me? Then I started to think about Gobi. I missed her biting at my gaiters to get me to speed up.

For most of the day, though, I coped well enough and refused to let Tommy's presence get me down. In fact, it gave me the extra incentive I needed to ignore the headwind, put up with the boredom, and grind out a steady, solid pace.

At least, that's how I felt until we approached the final checkpoint. I knew it was just over four miles from the finish, but with the sun now at its highest in the sky and the temperature feeling like it was in the low hundreds, I started to feel dizzy.

When I was finally in the shade of the checkpoint, I took a moment to enjoy the lack of heat and steady myself. Tommy, on the other hand, didn't even pause. He nodded and exchanged a couple of words with one of the team and carried straight on. I don't think he even broke stride.

I decided to take my time, filling up both my water bottles so that I had the full fifty ounces. When I finally moved out, Tommy was six hundred feet ahead of me. He looked strong and in perfect control. It was clear he was on a mission, and I soon realized there was no way I was going to catch him.

Julian and Zeng caught me soon after and didn't waste any time behind me. They went off in a pair, hunting Tommy down, while I felt as though my wheels had just come off.

I couldn't get going. No matter how hard I tried, no matter how

much I told myself not to slow down, I could feel my legs turn to concrete.

This wasn't like the day before, when the boredom and fatigue had been equal factors. This was purely physical. I'd spent three hours running in full heat into a scorching headwind. I simply didn't have much strength left.

I'd been here before.

It was back in 2013. Even though I'd got my weight down from 240 pounds to the mid-170s, I still had the taste for good food and good wine. So when it came to choosing my first-ever marathon to complete, I picked one that took place in France, in the heart of wine country. Each mile marker had a refreshment station that offered either local wine or local delicacies. And because it was all about the good vibes and not about the time, all the runners had to dress up as animals.

I went as a pig.

Some people skipped a few of the stations, but not me. By the time I reached the halfway point, I'd put away vast quantities of meat, cheese, and oysters as well as a half-dozen glasses of wine. I had a little bit of pain from where my skin was chafing at about the three-quarter mark, then developed some leg and lower back pain just after the twenty-mile point.

The sun was getting fierce, and even though Lucja was dancing about like a prizefighter at the end of a first-round knockout, I slowed down. I felt nauseated; I was finding it hard to concentrate or see straight, and the sharp, stabbing pain in my back had me seriously worried.

Lucja got me to the end that day, though I barely remember

the final mile. She helped me back to the hotel, got me drinking plenty of water, and told me that it would all be okay as I shivered beneath the blankets on the bed.

We were only a few months away from our first 155-mile multi-stage ultra—an event that would see us cross parts of the inhospitable, unforgiving Kalahari Desert in South Africa. Lucja's training had been going well, and we both knew she'd be fine. But me? Who was I kidding?

"I can't do it, Lucja. I'm just not like you."

"Just sleep on it, Dion. We'll worry about it tomorrow."

Tommy was too far ahead for me to see him, and Julian and Zeng were almost out of sight too. I was finished. There was nothing left. My legs were like strangers to me, and my head was drifting into thoughts I couldn't control.

Maybe this was going to be my last race after all.

Maybe I was all washed up.

Maybe coming here had been one big mistake.

I heard the drum long before I saw the finish line. I'd been overtaken by a fourth runner in the final mile, but I was past caring. All I wanted was for the day to be over. For everything to be over. I could imagine Lucja telling me to sleep on it, that I'd feel better after some rest and food, but another voice within was telling me to pack it all in completely.

When I turned the final bend and saw the finish line, Gobi was there. She was sitting in the shade, on a rock, scanning the horizon.

For a moment she stayed motionless, and I wondered whether she'd recognize me.

Then she was a blur of brown fur in motion. Leaping from the

rock, she tore over the ground towards me, tail up, little tongue flapping.

For the first time that day, I was smiling.

It had been the hottest day yet, and the sun was dangerously intense. The camp was near an old sheep station, and I tried to rest up in one of the barns, but the metal sides had turned it into a furnace. I settled for the tent, where the air was stale and the temperature was above 110 degrees. With Gobi curled up at my side, I drifted in and out of sleep. Part of me was looking forward to the chance to lie back and recover, but these times in the tent were the moments when I missed Lucja most of all.

Even before I came to China, I knew racing was going to be hard without her there. Work commitments meant she couldn't join me, but this was only the second race we hadn't entered together. And even though we hadn't run side by side since that first marathon in France, where I'd dressed as a pig—with her as a bumblebee—I relied on her in so many ways, especially at the end of each day. She'd be the one who would get out of the tent and be sociable with the other runners, and whenever I became frustrated or was bothered by something, she'd always help take the sting out of it. In more than one race, she'd talked me out of quitting entirely. I needed her, especially when unexpected problems came up as they did with Tommy.

But today had taught me something else. I missed Gobi. She was a great distraction from the boredom of hour after hour of running across an unchanging landscape. The way she ran—determined, consistent, committed—inspired me too. She was a fighter who refused to give up. She didn't let hunger or thirst or fatigue slow her down. She just kept going.

It was a bittersweet moment, for I knew what was coming tomorrow.

Day five was the long stage. Almost fifty miles in even hotter temperatures. I'd already made arrangements for Gobi to be looked after by the organizers again, and I knew they'd take good care of her.

Long days have always been my speciality, even more so when the heat is cranked up. But after only two days of running with Gobi at my side, something had changed. I was beginning to enjoy running with her, watching her little legs power through the day. I knew I'd miss her again.

I didn't get much sleep that night. The air was too hot and still to get comfortable, and after four days of running without having a shower or even changing my clothes, my skin was coated in a thick layer of dried sweat and dirt. Gobi couldn't settle either. She got up a few times, trotting out of the tent to go and bark at the sheep. I didn't mind, and nobody else in the tent complained. I guess we were all too busy trying to get our heads ready for what was coming next.

8

I MIGHT HAVE GROWN UP IN AUSTRALIA, BUT I still have to train for the heat. Living in Edinburgh means going months without the temperature rising above 60 degrees, and if I didn't take matters into my own hands, I'd not be able to cope out in the desert.

The solution was to turn the spare bedroom at home into a mini heat chamber. I bought two industrial heaters—the kind you'd expect to see drying out a house that's been flooded—as well as two small portables. I bought a heavy blind for the window and discovered that if it's just me in there, the thermometer will top out at 100 degrees. If I can persuade Lucja to join me, it'll rise a little higher.

The sessions are brutal. I wear winter running tights, a hat, and gloves, and set the incline on the treadmill as high as it will go. The humidity is intense, and even when I don't wear a backpack loaded with six or seven kilos (thirteen to fifteen pounds) of sugar or rice, I still struggle as I get into the second and third hour.

I'd put in more of these sessions in my training for the Gobi Desert event than I had for any other race. And when I wanted to change things up and run in some scorching dry heat, I'd pay

a hundred pounds for an hour-long session in the heat chamber at the local university. Lucja said she'd never seen me so determined and focused, and I knew I had no other option. I'd run the Marathon des Sables twice already, where the heat even topped 130 degrees from time to time, but I'd never felt much pressure to perform back then. At Gobi, I knew it would be different. The guys on the podium would be the ones who coped with the heat.

Day five started an hour earlier, at seven o'clock, and as I stood on the start line, I went through my race plan for the hundredth time. Go quick through the road section at the start, take the desert section steady but strong, and then—depending on the heat—drop the hammer and race it home. I was still third overall, but there were just twenty minutes separating number one from number four. I needed a good day. I simply could not afford to mess up anything.

From the beginning of the day, I ran the way I wanted. I was out front, leading the pack at times and then dropping back to let someone else carry the burden for a while. I was concentrating hard on my stride and missed the markers at one point. I led the pack the wrong way for a minute until someone called us back. We tracked back, still in formation, to where the runner was waiting for us to resume the lead. There was no need for anyone to try and get an unfair advantage. The course and the heat were enough of a challenge by themselves.

The terrain was less helpful. The first six miles were through thick tufts of camel grass occasionally interrupted by brief sections of uneven asphalt. After that, we moved onto the "Black Gobi" sand. It was still early, but already it felt like the temperature was more than a hundred. It was obvious that the heat was going to be cruel, and I let

myself ease up a little on the pace. A couple of people overtook me, but I didn't mind. I had a plan to stick to and guessed that in a few hours, as the sun really started to attack, I'd be overtaking anyone who had pushed himself too hard in this middle section.

I let my mind drift to Gobi, wondering what she was doing while I was running. I also made a point of noticing the scenery around us, knowing that I was unlikely to see it ever again, and hoping to keep my mind from slipping into boredom. As soon as we had hit the black sand, all signs of human life fell away. On previous days we had run through remote villages where curious locals stood and watched in the shade of their single-storey houses. At other times the route had taken us along dried-up riverbeds as wide as a football field where people stopped and stared, and across wide-open plains where the ground was the colour of fire. But as we pushed deeper into the Gobi Desert, there were no signs of human life. Nobody could make a life for himself in terrain so brutal.

As I entered the fourth checkpoint, I went through my usual routine of filling my bottles, taking a salt tablet, and asking about the temperature.

"It's 115 degrees now," the medic said. "But it's going to hit 120 soon enough. You want one of these?" He handed me a hot Pepsi. It was the only time the organizers had given us anything other than water to drink. Even though I could almost feel it burn my throat, I gulped it straight down.

"Thanks," I said. "You got any rehydrate solution?" I'd been popping salt tablets throughout the day, but with half the race still to come, I wanted to make sure I had enough to last. He took one of my bottles and made up a salt and sugar drink.

"You sure you're okay?" he said, taking a closer look at me as he handed it back.

"I'm fine. I'm just taking precautions."

Before I left, I checked the timings of the runners ahead of me. Tommy, Zeng, and Julian were among them, and they were only a quarter of an hour up the road. I was surprised they weren't further ahead and decided to step up the pace a bit. After all, I was hydrated, I'd just taken on an extra 150 calories from the Pepsi, and it was getting hot. I was ready to attack and knew that if I stayed strong, I'd probably catch them within the next one or two checkpoints.

I caught Julian at the next one, checkpoint five. He didn't look great, but he didn't look finished either. What interested me was the fact that Tommy and Zeng had left only minutes before I'd arrived. I quickly dug in my bag and pulled out the secret weapon I'd been holding in reserve this whole race. My tiny iPod.

I clipped it on, poked the earbuds in, and hit play as I headed back out into the heat. I knew the thing only had a few hours of battery life, which is why I'd never turned it on during any of the long afternoons I'd spent in the tent or at any other point in the race. I'd wanted to keep it for a moment when I needed a boost, and this was the perfect opportunity.

I listened to the playlist I had carefully put together over the previous months. The list included some big songs, a few surging anthems that I knew would get my feet going. But the real rocket fuel was Johnny Cash. When that baritone filled my ears with lyrics about outsiders and the kind of men everyone always writes off, I felt my spirit lift. He was singing just to me, calling me to push harder, run faster, and prove the doubters wrong.

When I finally saw Tommy at checkpoint seven, he looked awful. He was slumped on a chair, and two or three volunteers were

desperately trying to cool him down, spraying him with water and fanning him with their clipboards. He looked at me, and I could tell right then that I had him.

I turned away to give him some privacy, filled my bottles, and popped another salt tablet. Zeng had just left the checkpoint, and in front of him was a guy we all called Brett, a Kiwi runner who was having an excellent day, and an American female runner named Jax. I knew I could still win the stage, but I also knew I didn't need to. I wasn't concerned about Brett and Jax finishing ahead of me because both their overall times were hours behind mine.

All that mattered was that I passed Zeng, who was probably now five minutes ahead of me for the stage; as long as I did that, the twenty-minute overall lead I held on him before the day started would remain. With only six miles to race in the last day stage, there was no way I could lose the overall time, and the winner's medal would be mine. There were two checkpoints left to run, and a total of ten or twelve miles. If I kept going like I had been, I'd do it.

As I was putting some water on my head, I listened to what the doctor was saying to Tommy.

"You're very hot, Tommy, and we'd rather you go out with Dion than on your own. Will you do that?"

I fiddled with my earbuds and pretended not to hear. I didn't want to leave the guy stranded, but I was racing to win. If he couldn't keep up, I wasn't going to carry him.

As I checked my bag straps and prepared to move off, Tommy pushed himself off the seat and stood next to me.

"Are you sure you're okay, Tommy?"

"Yeah," he said, his voice hoarse and faint. "I'm just struggling. It's too hot."

We moved out. In the few minutes that I'd been in the shade

of the checkpoint, someone had turned up the heat a few more degrees. It was like running in a forced-air oven, and the sun cut like needles into the flesh on my arms. I was loving it. Even though I wondered whether I should have reapplied the sunscreen I'd put on in the morning, nothing could wipe the smile from my face.

There was no breeze and no shade. Everything was hot—the air, the rocks, even the plastic trim and metal zippers on my backpack. All that existed out there was heat.

But I knew I wanted to catch Zeng. I didn't know how strong he was or whether he was struggling, but I knew I felt about as good as I possibly could, given the conditions. This was my chance. I had to take it.

We were only a few hundred feet out from the checkpoint, and already Tommy was struggling to keep up. But he was a tough runner, and he wasn't going to give up on the race anytime soon.

We were in a straight gravel section, one where the pink markers were placed every fifty feet. "Come on, Tommy," I said, trying to get him to pick up his pace. "Let's run the flags."

We ran to the first marker, then walked to the next one before running again. We carried on like that for a half mile, and soon the track became sandy and opened out into an even wider area. All around us were sand canyons, twenty-foot-high walls of compressed dust and dirt as far as the eye could see. It looked like the surface of Mars, and if it was possible, I could have sworn that there was even less air and more heat in there.

Tommy was no longer at my side. I knew he'd drop back eventually. *This is it*, I thought. *Time to move.*

I ran through four or five flags, feeling my breathing hold steady and my pace remain solid. It felt good to be running free again, good to know that with every step I was reeling in the guy ahead.

And yet there was something nagging me. I couldn't stop thinking about Tommy. Was he okay? Was he still with me? Was he going to make it out here on his own?

I slowed down.

I stopped.

And then I looked back.

Tommy was swaying like a drunkard. His arms were flailing, his balance destroyed. He looked as though he was in an earthquake, and each step forward was a battle against invisible forces. I watched him, willing him to shake it off and start running toward me.

Come on, Tommy. Don't bail on me now.

It was a futile wish, and within a few seconds I was running the three hundred feet back to where he was swaying and staggering on the spot.

"Tommy, tell me what's going on."

"Too hot." His words were slurred, and I had to grab him to stop him from falling over. It was a little after one in the afternoon, and the sun was directly above us. I knew it was only going to get hotter, and I looked about for some shade, but there was none at all, just a series of windblown rocks off to the side.

I checked my watch. We were just over a mile into the section with another three to go until the next checkpoint. I thought about telling him to turn back, but he was in no state to go anywhere by himself. It was all up to me.

Do I go back, or do I go on? I wondered.

Tommy fumbled for his water bottles. One was completely empty, and he drained the other in a couple of gulps. I guessed that we'd left the checkpoint twenty or thirty minutes before, and that when we did, Tommy must have left with full bottles. That meant he'd drunk seventy ounces in no time at all.

"I need to pee," he said, pulling down his pants. His urine was like molasses.

He slumped down in the sand, right in the full glare of the sun. "Need to sit," he said. "I need to sit. Can you wait?"

"There's no sitting here, Tommy. You've got to get into some shade." I looked back to see if I'd missed anything, but there was nothing that could shield him from the sun. I hoped I'd see some other runners too, but there was nobody.

I scanned ahead. I thought I could see a path of shade to the side of a rock formation about a mile in the distance. It looked as though it might be big enough to offer Tommy some protection from the sun, and it struck me as our best hope.

It took another twenty minutes to reach it. I had to drag Tommy with one arm through the sand while carrying his backpack and giving him as much of my water as he wanted. I tried to keep him talking, but I couldn't think of much more to say than "Keep coming, mate. We're nearly there." He barely said a single word in return.

I knew how serious Tommy's condition was. He was dizzy, disoriented, and soaked in sweat. It was a clear case of heat exhaustion, and I knew that if I didn't cool him down soon, it could slip into heatstroke. From that point he'd be at risk of falling into a coma in as few as thirty minutes. After that he would need special medical equipment to keep him alive.

I finally managed to drag him to the sand rock and put him in the small rectangle of shade that fell beside it. I unzipped his shirt, hoping to let out any heat that I could. I was shocked by how pale his skin was. He looked half-dead already.

Tommy half fell onto his side and peed some more. His urine was even darker this time.

What am I going to do? I could feel the urge to panic but fought

as hard as I could to keep my emotions in check. I guessed that we were probably halfway through the stage. I ran up a slight hill to see if there were any signs of life, but there was nothing and no one around.

"Listen, Tommy," I said as I crouched back at his side. "You need help. I'm going to keep going to the next checkpoint and get them to drive back to you, okay?"

"I don't want to run anymore," he said.

"I know, mate. You don't have to. Just stay here and wait for them to come. Don't move."

I gave him the last of my water, made sure his feet were tucked up in the shade, and ran.

My head was full of numbers. I calculated I had just lost forty-five minutes. I had given away the last forty ounces of my water, and I had just under three miles left to run before I could get any more. It was 120 degrees and likely to get even hotter over the next hour. If I hadn't looked back when I did, Tommy might already have spent thirty minutes in heatstroke. If I hadn't looked back, he might have already slipped into a coma.

As I ran, I scanned ahead for the markers but also looked far into the distance in the hope of seeing a vehicle or someone else who could help. Still nothing.

After the numbers came the questions. Why had I looked back in the first place? Had I sensed something? Was something or someone guiding me to help Tommy? And had I made the right decision to run ahead? Would Tommy have got help quicker if I'd gone back?

To save time, I tried to cut the course. I lost the markers for a while and started to panic. I was in a gully, feeling trapped. My

heart was racing, and I feared, for the first time, that I might have made a terrible mistake.

I cleared a ridge and saw that I was back on track. In the distance, a mile off, I could see the checkpoint. It shimmered like a mirage, and no matter how fast I tried to run, it didn't appear to get any closer.

Half a mile out, a race vehicle approached. I waved it down and told them about Tommy and where to find him.

"You've got to get there quickly," I said. "He's in real trouble. And I'm out of water myself. You haven't got any water, have you?"

The little they had was enough to get me to the checkpoint, and as soon as I made it there, I sat down and ran through the Tommy story again. I took on as much water as I could and ran through my symptoms. But having run with too little water in me and too much pressure to raise the alarm, I'd already pushed myself too hard. I was feeling queasy and weak. At least I was aware of my symptoms. That meant I was thinking straight. I didn't have heat exhaustion, yet.

I asked about Zeng and was surprised to hear that he was only twenty minutes ahead. Twenty minutes? That meant the overall result was in the balance. Zeng had cancelled out the lead I'd had on him at the start of the day, but I still had a chance.

I found it hard not to think about death as I ran. I wondered if we were near the place where the other runner had died of heat-stroke back in 2010. And I thought about Tommy too. I felt sad to think that he might be in a coma even now. I hoped he wasn't. I hoped I'd done enough. Suddenly, having been so angry about him gaining five minutes on us at the boulder section seemed silly.

Half a mile after leaving the checkpoint, my chest started to feel strange. It was as if it wasn't pumping correctly, as though I had

a band wrapped tight around my lungs. Whenever I took a drink of water, it felt like it was boiling. Gradually I slowed down. I was feeling ill. Soon I was shuffling along, my feet scuffing and stumbling like I was half-asleep.

I was terrified of just one physical symptom: heart palpitations. I'd had them two or three times before. My chest would feel like I was going to explode, the sweat would pour out of me, and I'd feel sick and faint. The doctors had linked it to me drinking too much coffee, and ever since then I'd cut out caffeine in the build-up to a race. But the memory of it still bothered me, and out there in the heat of the Gobi Desert, I could feel the symptoms all lining up. And if my heart did start to freak out again, I knew I couldn't blame it on coffee this time. If I started having palpitations out here, it could only mean that something serious was happening.

I spotted a race vehicle parked up ahead of me. I knew it was there to offer emergency assistance, and I must have looked like a viable candidate as I staggered up. When I was close enough to hear the engine running, the volunteers jumped out.

"Are you okay? Do you want some water?"

"I need to sit in the car," I said. "I don't feel well."

I didn't know if it was in the rules or not, but I didn't care. I needed to cool down immediately.

I yanked on the rear door and threw myself and my bag down onto the backseat. The AC was on full blast, and it was like stepping into a refrigerator. It was beautiful. I closed my eyes and let the cool air get to work.

When I opened them again, I had to blink and rub my eyes to check that I had read the dash properly. "Does that really say 132 degrees?" I said.

"Yeah," said the guy behind the wheel. He and the other

volunteer didn't say anything else, but I could see him watching me closely in the rear-view mirror.

"Can I have the water?" I asked, pointing at a bottle that had a frozen cylinder of ice inside. I was convinced that it was the best drink I'd ever had in my entire life.

I pulled a gel from the pouch around my front. It was hard to get my hands to work properly, and some of the sticky substance ended up on my chin, chest, and the car seats. I figured I'd wait the ten minutes it usually takes for a gel to kick in, then be off. But as the time passed, I felt steadily worse.

My head was drifting, and I was finding it almost impossible to keep my eyes fixed on any one thing for more than a few seconds. The band around my chest wound tighter with each breath, and I could feel my lungs grow heavy within me.

"Come on," I said to myself, long after the gel should have worked. I was trying to summon the energy to pick up my bag and move, trying to command myself to get out and keep going, but nothing happened.

The cold air wasn't working as I hoped it would, but the thought of opening the door and stepping back out into that heat once more made me scared. Even if I could get my body to obey me and haul myself out of the car, could I even make it to the next checkpoint, let alone the finish?

It was at that point when my chest exploded. My heart started racing, and I was panting, desperate to pull in any air I could.

I glanced up and caught the driver looking back at me in the mirror. In his eyes I saw fear. Fear and panic.

It set off a second explosion within me. Only this time it wasn't my heart that started racing; it was my mind. For the first time ever in my life, I was genuinely scared for my safety. For the first time ever, I wondered if I was about to die.

9

COME ON! NOW, DION, NOW!

It was no use. No matter how tightly I closed my eyes or gritted my teeth, I couldn't make myself move from the back of the car. All I could do was breathe in the cold air and hope that something would change.

Minutes slipped by. I tried another gel. I tried stretching to relieve the pressure in my chest. I tried to remember my race plan. Nothing worked.

I wondered what had happened to Tommy. I hoped the car had reached him in time and the volunteers had been able to get him the help he needed. My best guess was that his race was over.

I had been looking out of the car for a few minutes when it hit me that I'd not seen any other runners for a long, long time. I thought about the gap I needed to make up.

"How did Zeng look when he came past?"

"Not great. He was struggling a lot and just walking."

That was all I needed to hear. I'd wasted fifteen minutes in the car, so I now needed to make up thirty-five. If he was still having a hard time, there was a chance I could do it. And if I did, I'd be in the overall lead.

I got out of the car with some trepidation but anxious to make up for the time I'd lost. I could feel the heat, and it took me a while to catch my breath and steady my feet. But eventually I was running again. Not fast, but steady.

That pace didn't last very long. I had enough energy to run only a few hundred feet, but after that I was walking again. At least my heart had stopped its wild beating, and I was able to think more clearly. I managed to run the flags for the remaining miles, stumbling ahead, looking at nothing but the pink markers before me, and thinking about nothing other than placing one foot in front of the other.

Eventually I was confronted by a series of tall, wind-formed cliffs. I crested a sand dune that ran through the middle and saw the finish line up ahead.

Just like the day before, Gobi was waiting for me in the shade. She ran out to join me for the last two hundred feet, but as soon as we crossed the line, she ran, panting, back to the shade, where she collapsed in a heap.

"Any news on Tommy?" I asked one of the volunteers.

He smiled and arched his eyebrows. "It's amazing," he said. "They got him cooled down, and eventually he started walking again. Filippo's with him, and they're doing okay."

I knew Filippo Rossi, a Swiss runner who was having a good day. I was delighted and relieved in equal measure to hear that he and Tommy were together.

The two other finishers—Brett and Zeng—had clearly been home for a while, and when I saw that the gap between Zeng and me was forty minutes, I knew he'd nailed it. We had the one stage left to run, and since it was only a handful of miles, I would never be able to make up that time in so short a distance.

When Tommy finally crossed the line with Filippo at his side, the whole camp was buzzing. Everyone knew what had happened by then, and Tommy's remarkable recovery and resilience were given all the praise they deserved. Nobody seemed to know anything about me helping him in the first place, but I didn't mind so much. What meant more was the hug Tommy gave me when he first saw me. He was in tears, and I was welling up. There was no need to say anything at all.

I waited in my tent as I had done every afternoon, drifting in and out of sleep with Gobi curled up at my side. I hoped none of the other runners still out on the course had come as close as Tommy had to being in serious trouble, and I wondered how Richard, Mike, Allen, and the Macau boys were. Despite the less-than-perfect start, I'd come to like the Macau boys. They genuinely cared for one another and had spent every evening giving one another massages. They were good guys, and, in a way, I was going to miss them.

It struck me that I could have won the race but only if I hadn't stopped to help Tommy. That didn't seem like a price worth paying, just to finish one place higher on the podium, even if it would have been my first overall multi-stage victory and a huge boost for my running future. Stopping to help Tommy had cost me, but I was glad with the way things worked out. Assuming that everything went okay on the final six-mile stage of the last day, my second-place podium position was secure. I wasn't ready to celebrate, but I was happy enough. I had already proved to myself that my running career still had some life left in it.

Darkness had fallen by the time Richard, Mike, and Allen got back. They'd been out in the sun all day, and they were suffering

for it. They looked like the walking dead, stumbling around the tent, their faces equal parts red with sunburn and pale with exhaustion. But it was over, and by the time the last one was back, the mood in the tent was different. Everyone relaxed more than usual, relieved to be so near the end of the race.

I woke up to the sound of the tent falling down. There was no sign of the Macau boys, and Mike was shouting at us to get up. I scooped up Gobi and crawled outside. A wind had struck up from nowhere, bringing the sand with it. It stung, but Gobi and I joined the others and lay on top of the tent to prevent it from flying off while Richard went in search of help.

The night was full of the sounds of two-way radios crackling, tents being flattened, and Chinese voices shouting back and forth. By the light of dozens of headlamps, I could see the volunteers running around the camp, desperately trying to put the tents back up.

The wind picked up and developed into a full-on sandstorm. It was impossible to see anything that was more than two or three hundred feet away, and we heard that the last runners out on the course had been held at checkpoints and were being driven back to camp.

After an hour of waiting for someone to come and help with the tent, I called Gobi to follow and went in search of a woman called Nurali. She had been introduced to us when we arrived at the first camp site. I'd been watching her shout orders and grow increasingly frustrated with her team as the winds raged.

"Can you get your guys to put up our tent, please?" I said to her.

"Yes, but we have many tents to put up first."

"I know you do," I said, "but we asked an hour ago, and still nothing's happened."

"Not my problem," she shouted.

I knew she was under a lot of pressure, and I could sympathize with her doing battle with the elements, but this seemed a little dismissive to me. "No," I said, "we've all paid thirty-seven hundred dollars to be here. It is your problem."

She muttered something I couldn't understand, turned, and walked off.

The wind picked up, and a sense of panic rose among the people running around. It was the kind of wind we get up in the highlands of Scotland, so maybe that's why I wasn't so worried. The sand didn't bother me either. All I had to do was copy what Gobi did and curl up tight with my head away from the wind, and I found I was fine.

After midnight we heard that the sandstorm was about to get worse. Nobody was getting any sleep, and after fifty miles of exhausting running, we all needed to recover, so the organizers decided to abandon the camp for the night. We joined the other runners who were huddled against one of the many large rock formations and waited for the buses to come. The level of fear in the air seemed to increase as we stood there, and before long the dust and sand were in our mouths, ears, and eyes. But I knew it was just another uncomfortable set of feelings to get through. We'd all experienced far worse in the previous twenty-four hours, but the unknown is always more intimidating than the familiar.

As dawn broke, the bus took us to a low building at the entrance to a national park twenty minutes away. It was a strange little museum with displays of million-year-old fossils and dioramas that showed a wide and random collection of natural habitats. Of course, Gobi

made herself at home, especially in the rainforest section that was full of fake trees and fake plants. I couldn't help laughing when she relieved herself under one of them.

Within minutes we had trashed the whole place, turning it into a refugee camp for 101 sweaty, smelly runners—and one not-quite-house-trained dog. The museum staff didn't mind, for the shop at the other end of the museum was selling drinks and snacks at a record rate.

The day was already scheduled as a rest day, given the gruelling nature of the previous long stage, and we spent the time sleeping, eating snacks, drinking sodas, and talking among ourselves.

I didn't retreat into my sleeping bag or take off somewhere else. Instead, I stayed and talked with Richard, Mike, and Allen.

"What are you going to do about that little one?" said Mike in the afternoon, pointing at Gobi.

It was a good question, and one that I'd been asking myself during the long stage. I knew that the two days I'd run without Gobi had been hard and that somehow I'd got attached to her. I didn't want to leave her to fend for herself out here.

There was more to it than that. Gobi had chosen me. I didn't know why, but I knew it was true. She had a hundred other runners to choose from, and dozens of volunteers and staff, but from the very first time I saw her and she started nibbling at my gaiters, she had hardly ever chosen to leave my side.

Gobi was a tough little trouper too. She had run more than seventy miles over three legs of the race without eating a thing during the day, and I'm sure that given the chance, she would have clocked up a whole lot more. She obviously had been scared of water but had pushed ahead and trusted me to help her. She had

given everything she had to keep up with me. How could I leave her behind when I finished the race?

For every reason I could find for wanting to help Gobi, there were equally strong arguments for walking away. I had no idea what kinds of diseases she was carrying, whether she belonged to anyone, or how I could even go about doing something to help. This was China, after all. I was pretty sure that not a lot of people would be queuing up if I asked for volunteers to help me find a home for a stray dog of unknown origin. If the stories were true, wasn't there a chance she'd end up getting killed and eaten by someone?

So I didn't do anything about finding her a forever home right there in China. I didn't ask any of the many race crew members who had taken a shine to Gobi, and I didn't even bring it up with my tent mates.

I didn't ask because it wasn't an option I wanted to consider.

I had a better plan.

"You know what, Mike? I've made up my mind. I'm going to find a way to bring her home with me."

It was the first time I'd spoken those words out loud, but as soon as I said them, I knew it was the right thing to do. I had no idea if it was even possible, but I knew I had to try.

"That's great," said Mike. "I'll chuck in a few quid to help out if you like."

"Really?"

"Me too," said Richard.

I was amazed and touched as well. As far as I could tell, all Gobi had done for my tent mates was growl when they came back in the tent at night, keep them awake by chasing sheep, and beg them for scraps of food anytime she caught them eating. But I was

wrong. In the same way Gobi had inspired me, she'd inspired them a bit too.

"Any dog that tough," said Richard, "deserves a happy ending."

By the time we lined up on the start for the final day, the sandstorm had passed. As in all multi-stage ultras, the final day is nearly always a short run of between six and ten miles. And, like in every other multi-stage I'd been in before, the thought of being an hour or two away from the final finish line brought out the best in the runners. While they'd been hobbling around like the walking dead during the recovery day in the museum, they set off at the start of the last day as if it were a Saturday morning sprint down at the park.

I had Gobi by my side, and she seemed to know something special was going on. She didn't chew my gaiters as we ran. Instead, she kept perfect pace with me, occasionally looking up at me with her big dark eyes.

The weather was cool with a slight drizzle as we ran, and I was happy that Gobi wouldn't overheat. There were no checkpoints because the last stage was so short, so I stopped every couple of miles to give her some water from my hand. She never refused, and it amazed me how much she had learned to trust me in just a few days.

I'd spent a bit of time looking at the race positions while we were in the museum. As I'd suspected, I had no chance of catching Zeng, and Tommy's near escape had cost him dearly. He'd been overtaken by Brett, the Kiwi who had stormed to victory on the long stage. I was still twenty minutes ahead of Brett, and if I kept ahead of Brett, my second-place finish would be secure.

I'd done just that all the way, but as I stopped at the halfway stage on the crest of a sandy hill to give Gobi a drink, I saw Brett approach me from behind. He stopped next to me. I must have given him a quizzical look, for he smiled and shrugged.

"I could hardly run past you as you're giving her a drink, could I?"

I smiled back. "Thanks," I said.

I put the bottle back in its holder on my bag's shoulder strap, gave Brett a nod, and carried on racing as though nothing had happened.

We stayed like that for the rest of the stage. I finished the stage fifth, Brett sixth, with Gobi between us. Medals were given out and photos taken straightaway, and soon afterward a celebration feast ensued with beer and a traditional barbecue, kebabs, and breads as big as pizzas stuffed with herbs and meat and all kinds of delicious things. I savoured mouthfuls of delicious mutton and let Gobi lick the grease from my fingers. There was a lot of laughing and hugging and the kind of smiles you get only when you know you're surrounded by good people, enjoying a moment that you're going to remember for years to come.

I had started the race as I always did, keeping to myself, focusing on the run and nothing else. I ended it as I have ended every other race, surrounded by friends.

But the race across the Gobi Desert was different. The lows had been lower, and the highs had been higher. The experience had changed my life. So it was only right that in return I should do everything I could to help change Gobi's.

PART 3

10

I WATCHED GOBI FROM OUT OF THE BUS WIN-
dow. She was busy eating up all the scraps of kebab that had been
left behind from the barbecue. Nurali was organizing the rest of
the volunteers who had just loaded the last of the runners onto the
other bus. Gobi stopped. She looked up. Was it just me, or had
she worked out that something was wrong? The bus engine kicked
into life. Gobi, startled a little, started running up and down. She
looked just like she did when I turned back at the river. She was
looking for something. For someone. For me. Her tail was down,
and her ears pinned back. I felt an almost irresistible urge to haul
my aching body out of the seat, climb down out of the bus, and go
and scoop her up into my arms again.

This is ridiculous, I thought to myself. I felt like a dad watching
his kid walk through the gates for his first day of school.

The bus began to pull away as I watched Nurali call Gobi to
her side, give her a bit of meat, and ruffle the shaggy brown mop of
fur that sat like a bird's nest on the top of her head.

I sat back and tried to think of something else. Anything.

The bus journey back to Hami could not have been more different from the drive we had made away from it a week earlier. Back

then I'd sat and only said a few words to my neighbour. I'd grown increasingly frustrated with the noise of the Macau boys behind me, and more than once I'd turned around hoping they'd get the hint and shut up.

On the drive to Hami, I would have paid good money to sit near the Macau boys and hear them laughing and chatting. I would have welcomed the distraction. Sadly, the three of them were on a different bus, and in the quiet that fell upon my fellow passengers as they gave in to the post-race, post-barbecue, post-beer drowsiness, I was left alone with my thoughts.

Why was this so hard? I had no idea I was going to feel this way. And this wasn't goodbye. I was going to see Gobi again in a couple of hours.

That plan was about as simple as any plan could be. Nurali, the woman who'd been kind of dismissive during the sandstorm, was going to drive Gobi back to Hami, where we'd have the award dinner, and I'd be able to say a proper goodbye to the dog. After that Nurali would take Gobi back home with her to Urumqi as I flew back to Edinburgh. I was then going to make all the arrangements to have Gobi flown back to begin her new life with Lucja, me, and Lara the cat back in the UK.

How long would it take? I didn't know.

How much would it cost? No idea.

Would Nurali look after her? Absolutely. That was one thing of which I was confident. Nurali might have been a little off with me when the camp was blowing apart, but I'd seen the way she ordered people around and got things done. She was a fixer, and I could tell that without her the whole Gobi race never would have happened. She was exactly the kind of person I was going to need to get things done. Besides, I'd seen her slip Gobi enough food

treats over the week to know that Nurali had a soft spot for the dog. Gobi would be fine with her. I was sure of it—just like I was sure that I was bringing Gobi home, even if it cost me a thousand pounds and took a month or two.

Gather together a bunch of runners who haven't showered, washed, or changed their clothes for a week as they've sweated their way across a desert, and they'll smell bad. Put them all on a hot bus for two hours, and the air inside will turn about as foul and putrid as you can possibly imagine.

So as soon as we arrived back in Hami, I was desperate for a shower. I cleaned myself up and rested a little, guessing that I'd catch up with Nurali and Gobi at the meal in the evening.

By the time I arrived at the restaurant, I was kind of missing Gobi already, even though it had been only a few hours. Besides, I'd only ever seen her out in the open or in a tent. How would she cope being in a town, with roads and traffic, restaurants and hotels?

I realized that there was so much I didn't know about her. Where had she been living before she joined the race? Had she ever even been inside a house before? How would she react to being shut inside from time to time? How old was she? Perhaps most important of all, did she like cats?

So much had happened the week of the race, but months, maybe even years, of Gobi's life before the race would forever be a mystery to me. I'd watched her playing when she thought I wasn't looking, and I was pretty sure that she was less than a year or two old. As for what had happened to her beforehand, I was at a total loss. If she had been mistreated, she didn't have any scars and certainly wasn't carrying any injuries that had stopped her from

running well over seventy-seven miles in total. So why had she run away? Had she got lost? Was there an owner somewhere out near the sand dune on the edge of the Gobi Desert currently fretting about his little dog who had gone missing?

Everyone I had spoken to thought this was unlikely. Gobi wasn't the only dog I'd seen on the run, and even the few hours I'd spent in Urumqi and Hami told me there must have been thousands of dogs roaming the streets in both places. Stray dogs were everywhere, and all the Chinese I had spoken to told me that Gobi must have been one of them.

At the restaurant I looked for Nurali and Gobi, but there was no sign of either of them. None of her team was there either, only the race organizers. I found one of them and asked about Nurali.

"I thought she was supposed to be coming here and bringing Gobi with her," I said.

She looked confused. "No, Nurali was never going to be coming here. She's got too much to do back at the finish line."

"Is she coming here at all before we leave tomorrow?"

"I can't think why she would."

I walked away, deflated.

It bothered me that I wasn't going to get to see Gobi to say goodbye properly. And it bothered me that the plan we'd sketched out wasn't being followed. Had something been lost in translation? Had something gone wrong already? Was Gobi still okay?

The thing that bothered me most was the fact that I could feel myself starting to stress about it. Part of me wanted to do what I normally did after a race and switch off from everything for a few weeks—from dieting, from running, from having to force myself to become so laser-focused on the one goal ahead of me. I wanted to relax and not care.

But that wasn't even an option. I did care. Feeling protective of Gobi wasn't a switch I could simply flick off.

I was distracted throughout much of the awards night, but I listened hard as Brett got up to receive his third-place medal and gave a powerful but brief speech. "What I'd like to say is that for everyone who has sacrificed their race to help other people, I take my hat off to you. It shows what great human beings are in this world."

I couldn't have put it better myself. I'd been able to do something to help Tommy, but I was far from the only one. Filippo had stopped too, and there had been so many other examples of people's putting themselves second and choosing to put someone else first. From the way the Macau boys looked out for one another to the ways people who had been total strangers at the start of the week gave constant encouragement to one another. One of the things I love most about these events is that as you push yourself to the absolute limits of physical endurance, you make some of the deepest friendships of your life.

Of course, I didn't know any of that when I signed up for my first multi-stage ultra. In fact, I wasn't even sure I'd make it to the start line, let alone finish the whole thing.

Our ultra-marathon journey began around Christmas 2012. Lucja's birthday is on 23 December, and in the months beforehand she'd been talking about wanting to move up from marathons and take on something tougher. So I'd bought her a beautiful coffee-table book called *The World's Toughest Endurance Challenges*. I'd looked through it before wrapping it, astounded by events such as the Marathon des Sables, the Yukon Arctic Ultra, and the Yak

Attack in Nepal, billed as the highest (and, I guessed, the most dangerous) bike race in the world.

This was before I'd taken part in the half marathon where I ran myself into the ground to win a free meal from my friend, so I was utterly convinced that every single one of the events in the book was beyond me. Still, I thought it might be kind of fun to dream about doing one of them one day a decade or more down the road. And in the festive atmosphere, with a bottle of champagne open beside us, I was feeling pretty good about life as I watched Lucja open the book, so I said these fateful words: "Whatever page you open to, that's the one we're going to do together."

I sat back, took a drink, and watched Lucja's eyes grow wide as she saw the cover.

"Wow," she said, looking at it front and back, "this is amazing."

She closed her eyes, opened the book to a random page, and stared.

Silence. I watched her scan the page, absorbing every detail.

"Well, Dion, it looks like we're doing the Ka-la-har-ree Extreme Marathon."

"What the hell's that?" I asked.

She didn't look up but carried on, staring at the page, calling out the brutal facts: "Northwest of South Africa, near the Namibian border . . . you run 155 miles . . . six stages over seven days . . . temperature is in the 120s . . . carry your own food . . . only get water at certain times . . . and it's in the desert."

I thought hard about my response. This was her birthday after all, and I wanted the gift to be a nice thing.

"No chance."

"What?" she said, looking up at me. "I reckon it sounds pretty good."

"Listen, Lucja, there's no way we could do that. What if something happens to one of us? And what do you mean you have to carry your own food? They don't give you anything at all? How is that even possible?"

She looked back at the book, flipped a couple of pages, and then slid it over to me and pulled out her iPad. I stared at the pages, a feeling of dread starting to grow within my guts.

"There's a whole bunch of blogs from last summer's race up here on the site," Lucja said. "And there's a Facebook page . . . and a contact form."

I stopped her. "Lucja, it says it's a couple of thousand pounds each. And that's without flights."

"So?"

"So we could just have a nice holiday in the sun somewhere. Why would we want to do something stupid like running across a desert?"

Lucja looked hard at me. It was the same look she'd given me as I lay on the couch in New Zealand and she challenged me to the run. I knew that this was one of those pivotal moments in our lives.

"You said we're doing it, Dion. So we're doing it."

I backed off, figuring that saying no was only going to make her more determined. I stopped talking about it and assumed that by the time Christmas was over, she'd have forgotten all about it.

I was wrong. After Christmas, Lucja was more determined than ever, and with the race only ten months away, she felt she had to move fast. She contacted the race rep, downloaded the application form, and told me she was ready to do it.

It was my last chance to stop her, and I threw the very best reason I could think of at her.

"How are you going to go without having a shower? What about your hair? Your nails?"

"I don't care about that. I'm not bothered. The Orange River runs through one of the stages, and I can wash my hair that day."

I tried a different line of attack: "Johannesburg's got one of the highest murder rates of any city in the world. Do you really want to fly in and out of a city like that?"

"Dion, I'm doing it. Are you going to come with me?"

I thought for a while.

"We've got to work off all our Christmas fat."

She just stared.

It was New Zealand all over again. I knew I wasn't going to be able to stop her, and I didn't want to. I'd always loved Lucja's courage and her enthusiasm, and I knew my life had been so much better since I met her. I wanted to make sure she was going to be okay out there, too, even if it meant doing something as ridiculous as running across the Kalahari Desert.

"Okay," I said. "I'm in."

I hadn't spoken to Lucja since the night I stayed in Urumqi. Some runners had paid fifty pounds to be able to send e-mails and post blogs during the race, but not me. I didn't want to be distracted, and I knew Lucja would be able to check the race organizer's website for daily updates on my times and race position. So it was in Hami, after the awards dinner, that I finally got to phone her after more than a week apart.

I was actually a little nervous. I had to find a way to tell her I wanted to bring a stray Chinese dog back to live with us. We hadn't had a dog since Curtly the Saint Bernard. Both of us had taken

his death badly; we had an unspoken agreement that neither of us really wanted to go through that kind of pain again.

As I prepared to dial, I ran through my speech one more time. "Isn't it great that I finished second? And something weird happened too. A little dog followed me, and I'm beginning to wonder about maybe bringing her home to live with us."

If Lucja was on my side, I knew it would happen. If she wasn't, bringing Gobi home would be a lot harder than I thought.

The phone rang, and I took a deep breath.

Even before I could say much more than hello, Lucja started talking.

"How's Gobi?"

I was stunned. "You know about Gobi?"

"Yeah! A lot of the other runners have mentioned her in their blogs, and she's even made it into a few official race updates. She's a pretty little thing, too, isn't she?"

"Yes, she is. I wanted to talk to you about something—"

"You're bringing her home? As soon as I heard about her, I knew you'd want to."

Having been away from cities and civilization for a week, the transfer from the Urumqi train station to the airport left my head spinning. I had forgotten how crowded the city was and how impossible it was to make myself understood. Even something as simple as checking in for my three-leg flight back home took three times as long as it should have. Everywhere I went there were crowds of people, and every official stared at me with thinly veiled suspicion.

I remembered why I'd vowed never to return to China.

Had meeting Gobi changed how I felt? Perhaps. The run had

matched my previous best—second place in the 2014 Kalahari Augrabies Extreme Marathon—and it had brought Gobi into my life. But I still found it hard to imagine myself coming back. Without knowing any of the language, it was just too hard to get things done.

I was approaching the gate for my flight back to Beijing when I saw all the race organizers waiting to board.

I knew the boss had taken an interest in Gobi, and I wanted to make sure she didn't forget once she got back from the race. I thanked her for getting Nurali to look after Gobi while I went back home to make the arrangements.

She handed me her business card. "It's been fantastic to see the story of you and Gobi take shape. If we can help make it happen, we will."

It was only when I got on the plane that I wondered why I hadn't asked the boss about why Nurali hadn't shown up at the awards dinner in Hami. I guessed I didn't want to appear pushy or like I was going to be an awkward person to deal with. But as the plane taxied and I drifted off, I wondered whether maybe there was something more to it than that. I was trusting Nurali to take good care of Gobi, but did I know her that well? Why hadn't she come to Hami? Was it really just an error of communication, or was it a sign that things might not go so smoothly after all?

Don't be paranoid, I told myself. *Sleep on it. These things always look better in the morning.*

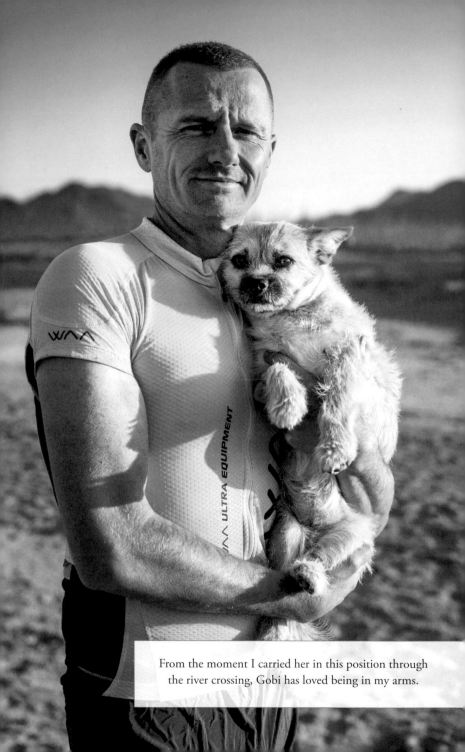

From the moment I carried her in this position through the river crossing, Gobi has loved being in my arms.

My heart has never forgotten my first
dog, Tilly. When my family moved
from Roma to Warwick, we had to
leave her behind with a farmer.

I was five in this photo; those skinny
legs would come in handy one day.

I loved bike riding, moving as
fast as I could, and I taught
Christie how to ride too.

Garry and me at eight—within a year,
it would never be the same again.

My skinny legs kept getting longer,
and I started to play cricket and hockey.

My grandmother was my last
connection to any real, loving family.

Deon Hansen was my best
mate when we were growing up.

My sister and mother were with me
on Lucja's and my wedding day in Italy.

I was sucking in all the water I could during that 2013 155-mile race in the Kalahari Desert.

I had a surprising smile on my face, thanks to Lucja's being with me after a run in the 2013 Kalahari race.

On day one of the 2014 race across the Kalahari Desert, I was gunning for the lead.

Day six was another marathon in the 2014 Kalahari race.

I nailed the long stage (nearly fifty miles) in six hours and fifty minutes in the Kalahari race in 2014.

I enjoyed a little bit of coolness with the temperature at 122 degrees in the 2014 Kalahari Desert race.

Lucja and I were proud as punch of each other in the 2014 Kalahari Desert: she finished second in the women's race, and I finished second in the men's.

I completed a non-stop sixty-two-mile race in the Gobi Desert in 2016.

Urumqi was plastered with these reward posters when Gobi was lost.

Where next? The search team and I worked out our next location to search for Gobi.

We bloody well found her—one of the best nights of my life!

I hosted a celebration dinner for the Ma family and all the volunteers who helped in the search for Gobi.

Richard and I celebrated Gobi's return.

Gobi and I met Chris for the first time in Beijing. Chris had been instrumental in directing the search party and offering advice to find Gobi.

Gobi and I did some sightseeing outside Beijing at the Great Wall.

Gobi was feeling sorry for herself after that hip operation to mend the injury she suffered in Urumqi.

The time immediately after Gobi's operation was tough for both of us.

While staying in Beijing, I often had to wear a pollution mask.

Kiki was the most amazing woman: she did everything possible to help Gobi and me in Beijing and organized our next steps to meet the requirements for departure.

Once all the requirements were met, Gobi and I were finally ready to leave China and start our journey home to the UK.

Time to fly! Gobi and I started the countdown, leaving Beijing for Paris.

Even though it took longer than imagined, I kept my promise
to get Gobi to the UK and had a great feeling upon our arrival.

Chilling together on Arthur's Seat,
Gobi and I were still in complete
amazement that we were finally home.

Lucja, Lara, Gobi, and I
celebrated our first Chinese New
Year together as a family.

Gobi and I had our first run together on UK
soil in my home city of Edinburgh, Scotland.

11

LUCJA MET ME AT THE EDINBURGH AIRPORT with some bad news. While I'd been flying, she'd looked into the process of bringing a dog into the UK.

"It's not going to be easy," she said. "You'd have thought the hardest part of the whole thing would be getting Gobi *out* of China, but from what I can tell it's getting her *into* Britain that's going to be tough. There's more red tape than you can imagine."

In between missing Gobi and looking forward to seeing Lucja again, I'd done a fair bit of imagining. I'd imagined Gobi held in quarantine, our having to pay astronomical vet bills, and the whole thing's taking months on end.

It turned out I was pretty much correct.

She'd need to spend four months in quarantine, and that wasn't going to be cheap. But the really bad news was where she would have to serve her time.

"Heathrow," said Lucja. "That's the only option."

By Chinese or American standards, the four hundred miles that separate our home in Edinburgh from London's main airport isn't all that much. But in the UK, it's an epic journey that costs

hundreds of pounds in petrol or flights, plus even more for hotels and taxis. Life in London isn't cheap, even for dogs.

The more we looked into it, the more we discovered that Lucja had been right about the costs and complexities of bringing a dog to the UK, but we'd underestimated how hard it would be to get Gobi out. In a battle for which country could wrap up the problem in the most amount of red tape, it looked like China was going to win.

Every pet-moving service we e-mailed came back with the same answer: no. Some of them didn't elaborate, but from the ones that did, we began to understand the full depth of the problem.

In order for Gobi to leave China, she would need a blood test; then she'd have to wait thirty days before being allowed to fly out of either Beijing or Shanghai. Simple enough, perhaps, but getting her on a plane out of Urumqi meant that she first had to undergo a health check by a vet, get a microchip, and have official approval from someone, somewhere, in the Chinese government. Oh, and there was one more thing: to fly from Urumqi to Beijing or Shanghai, Gobi had to be accompanied by the person who was taking her out of the country.

"Any chance of Nurali doing all that?" said Lucja.

"I couldn't get her to put up my tent in the sandstorm. There's no way she'd do all that."

"Could we get someone to drive her to Beijing?"

A few minutes on Google and the answer was clear. A thirty-five-hour, eighteen-hundred-mile drive across mountains, deserts, and who-knows-what-else wasn't much of a Plan B.

After a week of getting nothing but rejection e-mails from pet transport companies, a chink of light emerged. A woman named

Kiki e-mailed Lucja back, saying that her company, WorldCare Pet, might be able to help, but only if we could persuade Nurali to carry out some of the essential medical work. I hoped for the best and went ahead and asked.

To my surprise as well as my gratitude, Nurali e-mailed right back. Yes, she could get Gobi seen by the vet, and yes, she could make sure Gobi had all the right tests Kiki's company required. She'd even go ahead and buy a crate so that Gobi could fly in the hold.

This was the best possible outcome.

But Gobi's move wouldn't be cheap. Kiki estimated that it would cost a minimum of £5,000 for her to get Gobi back to the UK, and we'd figured out that we'd end up spending another £1,500 on quarantine and a whole lot more on travel to and from London to visit Gobi.

Bringing Gobi to our home would cost a lot of money, and we needed to think hard about whether we could do it. Part of me wanted to pay for everything ourselves, not out of pride or anything like that, but simply because bringing Gobi back was something that I—and now Lucja—wanted to do for Gobi's sake as well as our own. We weren't bringing Gobi back as an act of charity or a show of great kindness. We were bringing her back because, strange as it might sound, she was already a part of the family. And when it comes to family, you don't count the cost.

As much as all that was true, I wanted to be realistic. If anything went wrong at any point, we both knew that the total could easily exceed £10,000. When I'd told people at the end of the race that I wanted to bring Gobi home, Allen, Richard, and quite a few other runners had all said they wanted to help and would make a donation. In the days after I got home, I received more than a few

e-mails from competitors at the race, asking how they could give money to the Gobi fund. I knew that Gobi's courage and determination had touched many people, so it wasn't surprising that they'd want to hand over a few pounds to help make sure that she had a good, safe life ahead of her.

So Lucja and I sat at the computer and set up a crowdfunding page. When it came to putting in a target, we both paused.

"What do you think?" she said.

"How about this?" I said, typing in "£5,000" on the form. "We'd never get it, but it's probably the most realistic estimate of how much it's going to cost to get her here."

"And if we get only a few hundred pounds, it'll help."

Over the next twenty-four hours, my phone chirped a few times to tell me that a handful of donations had come in. I was grateful for each and every gift from my fellow runners, knowing that even a few pounds given here and there made the task ahead a little bit easier. More than the money, however, I loved reading the comments people wrote. Helping Gobi made them happy. I hadn't quite expected that.

I also didn't expect the phone call Lucja received on the second day after the crowdfunding page went live. The guy introduced himself as a journalist and said he'd seen the crowdfunding page and asked to speak to me. He explained how he'd found Lucja's number on her site that promotes her as a running coach. It felt a bit weird to know that a stranger could track us down like that, but when he explained why he was calling, I was intrigued.

He wanted to interview me and write an exclusive feature about Gobi for his newspaper, the *Daily Mirror*.

Journalists from papers such as his don't always have the best reputation. A few years earlier the *Daily Mirror*, along with several other papers, had been caught up in a phone-hacking scandal, and trust was still low. But the guy sounded genuine enough, so I decided to say yes and see what would happen. At the very least, it might be fun to post it on Facebook and get a few more people reaching for their wallets.

Before the call ended, the journalist reminded me that it was an exclusive and that he was concerned I might talk to other journalists and give them the story before he had a chance to publish.

"Mate," I said, then laughed. "You can do what you like with the story; no one else is going to care about it."

We did the interview by phone the next day. He wanted to know all about the race and how I'd met Gobi, how far she'd run with me, and how I was hoping to bring her back. I answered all the questions, and though I was a little bit nervous at first, I felt okay with how the interview went.

I didn't know whether to be anxious or excited when I went to buy a copy of the paper the following day. I skimmed through the pages, wondering what I was going to find.

What I didn't expect was a full page with great photos from the race and a really good write-up. But that's what I saw, sitting beneath the bold headline: "I Will Not Desert My Ultra-Marathon Pal." The journalist got all the facts right, and he even had a quote from the race founder, who said, "Gobi really became the race's mascot—she embodied the same fighting spirit as the competitors." I liked that.

I'd been in a paper before, when I finished sixth in my first ultra, and I'd had a few mentions on race blogs and in a few running magazines, but this was a whole other level. It was weird but

in a good way, and I quickly put messages up on the crowdfunding site, Facebook, and anywhere else I could think of. I thought it would be a pretty good encouragement for anyone who had already made a donation.

I had checked the crowdfunding page as I went to pick up the paper that morning. It was at almost £1,000, with about six or seven people having donated. An hour after I put the paper down and started making my third coffee of the morning, something amazing happened.

My phone went wild.

It started with a single notification. Someone I'd never heard of had just donated twenty-five pounds. A few minutes passed, then came another message, telling me someone else I'd never heard of had given the same amount. After a few more minutes, there was another. Then another. Then someone gave a hundred pounds.

I was astounded and even a little confused. Was this real?

A few more pings and a few more minutes passed, and I checked on the Internet to see whether the article in the paper was also on the *Daily Mirror* site. It was there all right, and in the few hours that it had been live, it had been shared and liked by hundreds of people.

I'd never imagined anything like this could happen.

The online version of the article described the story as the "Heartwarming bond between ultra-marathon man and the stray dog he refuses to leave behind".[1] Something happened in me when I read those words. I'd known all along that my heart had been

---

1 Jonathan Brown, "Heartwarming Bond Between Ultra-Marathon Man and the Stray Dog He Refuses to Leave Behind", *Mirror*, 27 July, 2016, updated 28 July, 2016, www.mirror.co.uk/news/real-life-stories/heartwarming-bond-between -ultra-marathon-8507261.

warmed by Gobi and that I refused to leave her behind, but I'd not used those words with the journalist. It was his description, and the fact that he had seen the significance of my meeting Gobi in much the same way that I did was encouraging.

Maybe that's why people are making these donations, I thought. *Maybe they see what he saw too.*

Twenty-four hours after the piece came out in the paper, the crowdfunding page showed that the £5,000 target had been met. But it didn't stop there. People kept on giving, all of them strangers to Lucja and me, all of them somehow moved by the story of this little dog who for some unknown reason chose me and wouldn't give up.

As well as constant updates about the donations, my phone started to pop with messages from other journalists. Some of them messaged me through the crowdfunding site, others through social media or LinkedIn. It was hard to keep track of them all, but I wanted to get back to every one of them.

The UK papers contacted me first—another tabloid, then a couple of the mainstream papers. I suspected that the approach the journalists took would vary from paper to paper, that perhaps they might want to know about different aspects to the story. But they were all happy to ask the same questions: Why were you running in China? How did you meet Gobi? How far did Gobi run? When did you decide to bring Gobi home? Will you run with her again?

The first time I heard that last question, it made me stop. I realized that in all the busyness and planning, I'd never thought about what life would be like when Gobi came home to Edinburgh. Would she expect twenty-five-mile walks each day? How would she

cope with city living? And if I did ever run with her again, would she stick to my side as she had before, or would she want to head off by herself into this strange new world with all its distractions?

There was so much I didn't know about Gobi's past, and there was so much I didn't know about our future together. I guess that's what makes the start of all relationships so exciting—even the ones with scruffy stray dogs.

After I'd had a few interviews with different newspapers, I got a message from someone at the BBC. Phil Williams wanted to interview me for his show on Radio 5 Live later that night, and even though I was starting to feel a bit tired from all the talking, no way was I going to turn him down.

The interview turned out to be the best thing I could do at the time. The producers combined the audio of my interview with video footage they'd managed to get from the race. The little one-minute video was more popular than I think even they imagined. Before long it had been viewed 14 million times, making it the second-most-viewed video on the BBC site.

After that, things really took off.

I did interviews with other BBC shows and stations; then the TV people started calling. I spoke with other channels in the UK, then ones in Germany, Russia, and Australia. I got on Skype and did interviews with CNN, ESPN (where Gobi's story was in the top-ten plays of the day), Fox News, ABC, the *Washington Post*, *USA Today*, the Huffington Post, Reuters, the *New York Times*, and podcasts, including the *Eric Zane Show*, which, in turn, gave the story a boost to a whole other level.

All along, the total on the crowdfunding page just kept rising. People from all over the world—Australia, India, Venezuela, Brazil, Thailand, South Africa, Ghana, Cambodia, and even

North Korea—pledged to give what they could to the cause. Their generosity was humbling as well as exciting. I'd been to some of these places, and I knew the kinds of lives a lot of the people in them lived.

Within the space of a few days, everything had changed for Lucja and me. We'd been a little unsure about whether to do the crowd-funding and felt aware of just how big a challenge it was going to be to get Gobi home. In the space of twenty-four hours, nearly all of that concern was wiped out. Having Kiki's support and getting so many pledges from people meant that we knew beyond doubt that the biggest obstacles had been taken care of: we had the expertise to get her back and the funds to make it happen. Everything seemed to be falling into place.

Almost everything.

Nurali wasn't answering any of our e-mails.

12

"I JUST DON'T SEE IT, LUCJA. I DON'T SEE HOW
it's going to happen."

We were lying in bed, waiting for the alarm, having our first conversation of the day, but the words had an eerie familiarity about them. I'd said the same thing many times in the week that had passed since the *Daily Mirror* article came out. While the crowdfunding page was up to almost £20,000, all we were getting from Nurali was silence.

Every time Lucja and I talked like this, I had tried my best to explain what I knew of Nurali and Urumqi. I had told her how the city was this crazy, busy place, and everyone there was rushing around doing their stuff. "Nurali thrives on being busy, so I can't imagine she's sitting at home with her feet up. She's probably got a hundred other projects going on, and there's no way she's going to take time off to help us. Looking after a little dog has got to be way down her list of priorities."

"So we need to remind her that this matters. We need her to remember how important this is, don't we?" said Lucja.

I remembered the night of the sandstorm. "Nurali's one of

those people who won't help if she thinks you're being a pain. If we stress her out, I reckon she'll go even slower just to piss us off."

We sat in silence for a while.

"Do you think she's seen all this stuff on Facebook?"

There was no way that would have happened. With no Facebook or Twitter making it into China, and almost no Western news channels on TV, I couldn't imagine how any of the buzz we were experiencing had made it back there.

"So what do we do?"

Silence settled on the room again. The conversation always came undone at this point. We were stuck, unable to get out. We were powerless to make anything happen. We could do nothing other than wait.

Even though Nurali was silent, the rest of the world was not. Along with Kiki's e-mails asking if we still wanted her to help, we started to see an increasing number of comments on the Facebook page asking for updates. People, rightly so, were wondering what was going on. They wanted to know how the process of getting Gobi ready to travel was going and when she was coming home. They wanted photos, video, and news.

I couldn't blame them. If I'd have given money to a cause like that, I'd feel the same way. I'd want to know the dog was being looked after and the owners were acting diligently and responsibly. I'd want evidence that everything was moving forward. I'd want to know the whole thing wasn't a scam.

Though Lucja and I were desperate to provide people with the reassurance they wanted, we couldn't do it. All we could do was post vague messages about how everything was in hand and we

were taking the first steps in what was going to be a long, long journey. We rationed our news and photos the way we rationed our food on a long desert stage.

A few more days slipped by, and still we received no response from Nurali. I could tell that Kiki was finding all this waiting a bit frustrating, but she clearly understood the unique nature of the challenge ahead of us. She offered to e-mail Nurali herself, and we gladly agreed. Hopefully the fact that Kiki was Chinese would solve any language and cultural problems.

The supporters, on the other hand, were getting more vocal, and more and more requests for information were being made. I began to worry that if we didn't come up with some concrete news soon, the huge wave of positive support might back away from us. Worse still, people might turn against us. So I decided to call one of the race organizers.

"This is a big deal now," I told her. "It's not just me who cares about bringing Gobi back; it's gone global. It feels like thousands and thousands of people are watching and wanting to know what's going on. The ones who have donated are like shareholders, and they want answers."

She listened and told me that she understood. "I'll make it happen," she said.

When the call ended, I felt a weight fall from me. If the race organizers were going to get involved, we'd be fine. They master-minded a whole series of races that took place on four different continents; surely they could get a little dog reunited with her master.

Sure enough, Kiki got an e-mail from Nurali a week later. Everything was fine, though Nurali did agree that there was a lot more to be done than she had first anticipated. She and Kiki agreed that Nurali would keep on looking after Gobi, but that Kiki

would send someone out to Urumqi to take care of everything that needed to be done before Gobi could fly back to Beijing.

This was good news. But the process was taking so much longer than either Lucja or I had hoped. What mattered most was that Gobi was safe, Nurali was still taking care of her, and Kiki would soon have someone in Urumqi putting the plan into action.

Nurali even e-mailed some pictures, and we were able to give the supporters a full progress update. It did the trick and answered most of the questions people had. The press inquiries kept on coming, and I spoke with magazine journalists for the first time as well as more radio stations.

For the first time since arriving home from China, I felt truly confident that everything was going to work out.

The next week, however, I started to get nervous. Nurali had gone silent again. It was so frustrating. Two weeks had dragged by since we launched the crowdfunding site, and we were no closer to getting Gobi the medical care and tests she needed to begin the process of flying her back home.

I e-mailed the race organizer again to see if she could help, but instead of getting a reply from her, I received one from her office. They said she was in America, as was Nurali. They wrote that Gobi was being looked after and that Nurali would be back in China in a few days and all was good. They passed on a message saying that the organizer planned on talking everything through with Nurali when they were together.

Lucja and I didn't know what to think. We were a bit annoyed that it was going to be yet another week until Kiki could get someone out to see Nurali and get things moving, but we had known there could be speed bumps along the way. And who knew, maybe Nurali would catch some of the coverage of the story when she

was in America and get a clearer picture for herself of how much attention Gobi was getting.

Nurali was as good as her word. When she was back in China a few days later, she e-mailed Kiki and promised to get things happening quickly.

Great, I thought, when Kiki told me the news. *Not long now.*

A day later I checked in with Kiki: **Any word from Nurali on when you can send your person out to Urumqi?**

Her reply was quick.

Dion, I have not heard back from Nurali. Kiki.

I waited another day.

Any news today, Kiki?

Again, Kiki got straight back.

No.

I e-mailed the race organizer again: **Why's this all taking so long? Don't tell me something's happened.**

The next day, Kiki had nothing to report, and my inbox didn't get anything from the race organizer either.

Another day passed, and from the moment I woke up, I knew something wasn't right. Sitting in bed, waiting for the alarm again, I was as wired as if I were already on my third coffee. I couldn't tell Lucja exactly what I thought was wrong. "But there's a problem," I said. "I just know there is."

I got up and checked my phone, knowing it was already late afternoon in China. Among the handful of e-mails from journalists and the great pile of notifications from the crowdfunding page, one stood out:

To: Dion Leonard
From: **** ****
Date: August 15, 2016
Subject: Gobi
Dion, I need to ring you.

When the race organizer and I spoke later that morning, there was a part of me that wasn't surprised by what I heard. She told me that while Nurali had been away in the United States, her father-in-law had been looking after Gobi. She'd run away for a day or two but come back for food. Then she had gone missing again and hadn't returned at all. Gobi had been missing for several days now.

"You've got to be kidding me," I said. I was trying to remain calm and not explode with a barrage of expletives. I was bloody furious. "What are they doing to find her?"

"Nurali's got people out there looking. They're doing their best to find her."

Doing their best? I had serious doubts about that and was upset that Gobi had been able to escape. I'd had so much time to think about Gobi, I'd run every possible scenario through my head. I was paranoid. The version of events that the organizers were relaying didn't seem quite right to me. Nurali had been quiet for so long, I was worried Gobi had gone missing a lot earlier, and they didn't tell me about it because they thought they would find her. If I was right, that meant Gobi had already been on the run for ten days or more.

All kinds of scenarios flashed across my mind. None of them were good, and I did my best to shut them out. This was no time for panic. I needed to act.

"So what can we do?" I asked, not having a clue what should happen next.

"Nurali's doing all she can."

Somehow, that didn't seem like enough.

I phoned Lucja at work and told her that Gobi had gone and that I seriously doubted whether Nurali was looking for her as had been suggested. Then I phoned Kiki and went through the story all over again.

"Let me speak with Nurali," she said. That was the first suggestion I'd heard all morning that made any sense.

When she called back, Kiki told me she had her doubts about the whole story. It just didn't add up.

"Okay," I said, putting my suspicions aside for a moment. "But what's next?"

"What we need to do is get more people involved in the search."

"How can we do that? Nurali's the only person I know in Urumqi."

"I know someone here in Beijing who has experience finding dogs. He runs an adoption shelter in Beijing. Maybe he can help."

I didn't have to wait long for Kiki to call back a second time. She had spoken to her friend Chris Barden from Beijing's Little Adoption Shop, and as I listened to the advice she relayed, I knew he was the right man for the job.

"First, we need a poster. It has to have recent photos of Gobi, a good description of her, and the location where she went missing. It needs a contact number and, most important, a reward."

"How much?" I asked.

"He says five thousand RMB to start."

I did my calculations. Five hundred pounds. I'd gladly pay ten times that if we needed to. After giving it some thought, I settled on £1,000 for the reward.

"We have to get the poster everywhere, especially digitally. Do you have WeChat?"

I'd not heard of it, but Kiki filled me in on the WhatsApp/Twitter hybrid that the Chinese authorities did not block.

"Someone needs to set up a WeChat group to start sharing the news. And then we need people on the street handing out the posters. Chris says that most dogs are found within two to three miles of the place they went missing. That's where we need to concentrate all our efforts."

The thought of putting this plan into action and expecting it to work made my head spin. I knew from experience that Gobi could easily cover two or three miles in twenty minutes, so she could be way beyond Chris's boundary. But even if I put that to one side, I couldn't imagine where Gobi might be because I had no idea where in the city Nurali lived. All I knew for sure was that Urumqi was about as densely packed as anywhere I'd been in Asia. A two- or three-mile radius could contain tens—if not hundreds—of thousands of people. Nurali was my only hope for getting the word out on the street, but I didn't know if she could do it.

Thankfully, Kiki saved the best news until last.

She told me that Chris knew someone who lived in Urumqi, a woman called Lu Xin. When her own dog had gone missing, Chris had helped with the search. He'd already asked her, and she said she'd help, even though she'd never led a dog search before.

I exhaled a great breath of gratitude.

"That's amazing, Kiki. Thank you so much." I was blown

away by the kindness of these people I'd never even met, who had jumped into action at a moment's notice. I hadn't prayed since I was a kid, but I certainly said a few words of thanks right there and then.

I went back to waiting for news. It was lunchtime in Scotland, but the end of the workday in China. I knew I wouldn't hear anything more from Kiki until the next morning.

I'd been home from China for nearly four weeks and had started back at work almost immediately, squeezing in the interviews and e-mails in the early mornings, late evenings, and weekends. I work from home some of the week, and on the other days I'm in the office, down in the south of England. On the day I found out Gobi was lost, I was in the flat, but as the afternoon dragged on, I wished I was anywhere but there. Being at home alone was hard. Harder than running across the black Gobi Desert. All I could think about was Gobi.

When the working day finished and Lucja came home, we talked about what to do. Both of us knew we had to let people know about Gobi being lost, but phrasing it the right way was hard. We knew so little, but we didn't want people filling in the blanks.

After a few false starts, late that night, I finally posted the words I hoped would alert people and help get Gobi back safely:

> Yesterday we received a phone call that Gobi has been missing in Urumqi, China, for a number of days, and she has still not been found. We are simply devastated and shocked to hear that she is now on the streets of the city, and our plans to get her to the UK are up in the

air. It has literally been the worst 24 hours, and I know that my pain and grief will be shared by you all. Please understand Gobi was well cared for and looked after in Urumqi, and this has been an unfortunate incident.

Today the below information and reward has been released on Chinese WeChat. The Urumqi animal shelter has also kindly assisted in providing a group to look for Gobi, and we are also organizing to employ locals to look for Gobi across the streets and parks of the city.

If anyone can provide any information on Gobi's whereabouts, please contact us as soon as possible. We hope and pray Gobi can be found safe soon and will keep you updated with any progress.

Just like to say we are so appreciative of all the funding and support provided to Gobi so far. I can confirm there are still 33 days to go on the crowdfunding page, and if Gobi is not found during this time, then no money will be taken from the pledges.

Dion

Within minutes I could hear my phone alert me to the responses as they came in. It was slow at first, then faster and faster, like a slow jog turning into an all-out sprint.

For a while I didn't pick up. I didn't want to read what people were writing. Not that I didn't care what they thought. I did care. I cared a lot. But I had no more news to give them, and there was nothing else I could do.

My only option was to sit and hope. Hope that Gobi was still okay. Hope that this woman Lu Xin—whom I'd never even heard of before I woke up that morning—would work miracles and build

up a big enough search team to flood the area with posters so that someone somewhere who had seen Gobi and who cared enough to act would phone in and claim the reward.

Who was I kidding? There was no hope of success.

As the last light of the summer evening slipped from the sky, my thoughts turned darker. I remembered something else that Kiki had told me during our last call of the day. She said that Chris met Lu Xin when her own dog went missing. He was the one who had advised her on the search.

Lu Xin's dog was never found.

PART 4

13

THERE'S BARELY AN AUSTRALIAN ALIVE WHO
hasn't heard of the ultra-runner Cliff Young. The man's an inspiration to all of us, not just endurance athletes. To anyone who has ever faced an insurmountable challenge that nobody believes can be overcome, Cliff's story offers hope.

On Wednesday, 27 April, 1983, Cliff Young turned up at the Westfield shopping mall in the western suburbs of Sydney, looking for the start line to a remarkable race. The route led to another Westfield shopping mall, 543.7 miles away in Melbourne.

The race was widely considered to be the toughest of its kind, and the assembled field included some of the best in the world, men in their prime who had trained for months to reach peak physical condition for the event.

Cliff stood out from the handful of runners who had gathered for the brutal race. He was sixty-one years old, wore overalls and work boots, and had removed his dentures because he didn't like the way they rattled when he ran.

While most people assumed he was either a spectator or a

maintenance guy who'd gotten slightly lost, Cliff collected his race number and joined the other runners.

"Mate," said one of the journalists when he saw Cliff on the line, "d'you think you can finish the race?"

"Yes, I can," said Cliff. "See, I grew up on a farm where we couldn't afford horses or tractors, and the whole time I was growing up, whenever the storms would roll in, I'd have to go out and round up the sheep. We had two thousand sheep on two thousand acres. Sometimes I would have to run those sheep for two or three days. It took a long time, but I'd always catch them. I believe I can run this race."

The race started, and Cliff was left behind. He didn't even run right; he had this weird-looking shuffle where he barely lifted his feet from the ground. By the end of the first day, when all the runners decided to stop and get some sleep, Cliff was miles and miles behind them.

The pros knew how to pace themselves for the run, and they all worked the same plan of running for eighteen hours a day and sleeping for six. That way the fastest among them hoped to reach the end in about seven days.

Cliff was working with a different plan. When they resumed the race the next morning, the other runners were shocked to hear that Cliff was still in the race. He'd not slept and had shuffled his way right through the night.

He did the same thing the second night as well as the third. With each morning came more news of how Cliff had jogged through the night, breaking down the lead that the runners half his age tried to stretch out in the day.

Eventually Cliff overtook them, and after five days, fifteen hours, and four minutes, he crossed the finish line. He had broken

the record by almost two full days, beating the five other runners who finished the race.

To Cliff's surprise, he was handed a winner's cheque for $10,000. He said he didn't know that there was a prize and insisted he had not entered the race for the money. He refused to take a cent for himself and instead divided it equally among the other five finishers.

Cliff became nothing short of a legend. It was hard to know what footage of him people loved most: the shots of him shuffling along highways in slacks and a casual T-shirt or the images of him chasing sheep around the pasture, wearing gum boots and a look of pure determination.

I was a kid when the Aussie news networks covered Cliff's story. He was a celebrity, a genuine one-of-a-kind who had done something amazing that made the whole nation take notice. It wasn't until I became a runner myself that I appreciated how remarkable his achievement was. And it wasn't until Gobi went missing and I found myself on a flight back to China that I returned to his story and drew inspiration from it.

The day after I posted the news that Gobi was missing, we were flooded with messages from people all over the world. Some were positive and full of sympathy, prayers, and good wishes. Other posts expressed fears that Gobi would eventually end up being eaten. It was the first time I'd ever thought about the possibility, but it didn't strike me as very likely. Even though I'd spent only ten days in China, I had a feeling that the rumour of the Chinese as dog eaters was probably off the mark. Sure, I'd seen stray dogs around the place, but I'd seen the same in Morocco, India, and even Spain. Instead of being cruel, every Chinese person who'd

taken an interest in Gobi had treated her with care and affection, nothing less.

While I appreciated people's warm wishes and could handle their panic, there was a third type of message that I just didn't know what to do with:

How the hell did that happen?! Seriously????

I knew something like this would happen . . . What a horrible place for that dog to be lost too. I'm disgusted for how this was handled.

How on earth was the dog able to escape????

These "caregivers" had one job to keep this precious small dog safe and these [supposed] guardians failed her! . . . How do you lose a dog you were supposed to be watching until she could be ADOPTED!

I felt bad. In fact, I felt terrible. So many people had given so much money—about £20,000 by the time she went missing—and now Gobi was gone. I knew that in the eyes of the public I was fully responsible for Gobi. I accepted that and knew the blame stuck with me.

If I'd handled things differently, Gobi wouldn't have gone missing. Yet what else could I have done? When I finished the race and left Gobi with Nurali, I assumed it would take only a few weeks before we'd be reunited in Britain so Gobi could begin the quarantine process. Had I known how hard it was going to be to get her across China and then out of the country, I would

have hired a driver and taken Gobi back to Beijing myself. But all I knew, at the time I finished the race, was that Nurali—who seemed to me the very best person for the job—was happy to help. At the time it seemed enough.

I was tempted to reply to each message, but they were coming in even faster than they had after the *Daily Mirror* article had hit. Every few minutes there was a new comment, and I knew that it was best just to give people the space they needed to vent their anger. There was no point in getting drawn into any arguments.

Besides, there was another type of comment that started to get my attention.

I wonder if it's a kidnap situation due to all the publicity surrounding her story.

Even though I can get annoyed with people when they mess up, I'm generally a very trusting person. I'd never thought of Gobi's escape as anything other than an accident. The more I read of these messages, however, the more I started to wonder.

I hope this wasn't intentional or that someone wasn't behind this. Forgive my suspicion, but I don't understand how this could happen! Gobi's story went global, and I just hope someone (not Dion) isn't trying to make money off taking her. Missing for days, and you were just notified?

The comments did make a good point. Thousands of people around the world were following the story, and the crowdfunding total was visible to all. Was it hard to imagine someone trying to

make some easy money by dognapping Gobi and hoping we'd pay a reward for her safe return?

I was supposed to be working, and I tried my best to get on with the reports I had to write, but it was hard going. I must have spent most of the day distracted by all these thoughts and questions. I felt like a feather in a storm: powerless and at the mercy of forces far, far stronger than me. By the time Lucja came home from work, I was exhausted.

She'd been following the feedback throughout the day, and while I had been sidetracked by the posts that looked for someone to blame, she'd been struck by the ones that tried to find a solution:

Can you fly there to look? She'll feel you and find you! Please use the funds to keep her safe until she flies home with you. This is devastating.

She is looking for you. Heartbreaking. I am praying she is found safe. I don't think anyone would think twice if you used some of that crowdfunding money to offer a reward for her safe return. Has this been put out to the media outlets to get the word out?

I'd been home for six weeks and had about the same amount of time left before going to another 155-mile race in the Atacama Desert in Chile that October. I'd not picked up any injuries in China, and I'd been able to resume my training almost as soon as I got home. I was convinced that I was going to be in the best possible condition to go out and win Atacama, especially now that

I knew some of the runners I was going to be up against, such as Tommy and Julian. And if I won Atacama, I'd go to Marathon des Sables in 2017, ready to score a top-twenty place. In the whole history of the race, no Australian had ever finished higher.

Making a sudden trip to China to search for a lost dog was not part of my training plan. Six weeks out from Atacama, I should have been clocking one hundred miles a week on the treadmill in my improvised homemade sauna. Instead, I was doing nothing. All my training had fallen away as the search for Gobi overtook my life.

Putting Atacama aside, I had other good reasons for not going back to China. I'd hardly been at my best at work in the previous weeks, and asking for even more vacation time without giving my employers any notice would be pushing their goodwill to the absolute max. If I were in their position, I knew exactly what I'd say.

And if I did go, what could I honestly hope to achieve? I couldn't speak the language, I couldn't read Chinese, or whatever version of Arabic it was that I'd seen in Urumqi, and I had even less experience searching for lost dogs than the woman who was leading the search. If I went, I'd be wasting their time as well as mine.

In the end it didn't take long for me to change my mind. It wasn't that all my doubts were suddenly answered or that I had a profound sense that if I went, I'd find Gobi. I decided to go because of a simple, compelling fact I shared with Lucja late on the second night after I'd been told Gobi was missing: "If I don't go, and we never find her, I don't think I'd ever be able to live with myself."

And so it was that I found myself sitting by a departure gate in the Edinburgh airport, ready to embark on a three-flight, thirty-plus-hour journey back to Urumqi. I snapped a photo of my flight

itinerary and posted it online. With so many people being kind and generous in the previous days, I wanted them to know I was doing all I could to help.

Only four days had passed since the phone call, but I flew with the knowledge that the people who had given so generously to help bring Gobi home wanted me to go back and find her. We had set up a second crowdfunding site, called Finding Gobi, to pay for my travel as well as the costs that the search party was already incurring—printing, gas, drivers, staff, and food. As with the Bring Gobi Home site, people's generosity had left both Lucja and me speechless. We smashed our target of £5,000 within the first couple of days.

I went with the blessing of my boss as well. When I'd started to tell him that Gobi had gone missing, he didn't wait for me to finish. "Just go," he said. "Find the dog. Sort it out. Take whatever time you need."

As for Atacama, that was the one problem to which I couldn't find a solution. I knew that going back to China would be pushing my time-off allowance at work and meant cancelling my plans to race in Chile, but I decided there was no use worrying about it. If I lost Atacama but found Gobi, all would be worthwhile.

I boarded and checked Facebook one final time. Dozens of messages had come in, all of them full of encouragement, positivity, and good faith. Many of the comments said the same thing: these people were praying for a miracle.

I agreed. That was exactly what we needed. Nothing less would do.

Somewhere in the sleepless fog of the all-night flight, the story of Cliff Young came into my mind again.

Like me, he had no idea that he was going to cause such a stir when he ambled up to the start line in 1983. I'm guessing he didn't have a clue that he was going to win it either. But he knew he could make the distance. Experience, self-belief, and a little bit of not knowing what he was up against all helped give him the confidence he needed.

Was I going to find Gobi? I didn't know. Was I going to be able to do what people suggested and get the local media to cover the story? I didn't know that either. Did I have any experience of ever having done anything like this before? None at all.

But I knew I had the heart for the fight. I knew my desire to find Gobi was as strong as any desire I'd ever had within me. Whatever it took, I knew I wasn't going to rest until there was nowhere left to search.

14

TEN MINUTES AFTER WE DROVE AWAY FROM
the airport, I finally worked out what I didn't like about Urumqi.
I'd been too distracted to notice when I came through the city as
I'd been travelling to and from the race, but as I sat in the back
of Lu Xin's car next to the translator, I listened to her explain the
reasons why every street light and bridge was covered with closed-
circuit TV cameras. I finally understood. Urumqi felt oppressive.
It felt dangerous. In an odd way, it reminded me of living in the
hostel in Warwick when I was fifteen. The threat of violence was
all around, and I felt powerless to defend myself.

According to my translator, Urumqi is a model for how the
Chinese state tackles political unrest and ethnic tensions. There's
a history of violence between the indigenous Uighur people, who
practise Sunni Islam and who see themselves as separate from
mainstream China, and the Han Chinese people, who have been
encouraged by the Chinese state to migrate into the area with the
incentive of tax breaks.

In 2009, Uighur and Han took to the streets, fighting each

other with iron pipes and meat cleavers. More than one hundred people died, and almost two thousand were wounded.

"You see that place?" asked my translator, whom I nicknamed Lil. She was a local girl who happened to be studying English at the university in Shanghai. When she heard about Gobi, she signed up, and right from the start I connected with her.

We had hit traffic and were crawling past a wide patch of open ground bordered by razor-wire fence and guarded by soldiers holding automatic weapons at the entrance. The soldiers were carefully watching people as they lined up to pass through an airport scanner. To me, it looked like a military facility.

"That's a park," Lil told me. "Have you been to one of the train stations here?"

"Oh yeah," I smiled. "That was fun trying to get through. What are there, two layers of security to go through?"

"Three," said Lil. "Two years ago Uighur separatists launched an attack. They used knives and set off bombs. They killed three and injured seventy-nine. Then, a few weeks later, they killed thirty-one and wounded ninety at a market."

In the wake of the 2009 violence, the Chinese authorities installed thousands of high-definition closed-circuit TV cameras. And when the knife attacks, bombings, and riots resumed a few years later, they installed even more, as well as putting up scanners and miles of razor wire and flooding the streets with heavily armed soldiers.

Lil pointed out a new police station that was being built on a tiny scrap of land, then another identical one under construction farther down the road. "This month we have a new Communist Party secretary. He was the top official in Tibet, so he knows how to manage ethnic tension. All these new police stations and security checks are thanks to him."

I didn't think Lil was being sarcastic, but I couldn't be sure. As she continued talking, I got the sense that she thought little of the Uighur people.

"When Communist forces arrived in the Xinjiang region sixty years ago, Chairman Mao put the clock forward permanently. He wanted every region to be on the same time as Beijing. But Uighur people resisted, and their restaurants and mosques still run two hours behind. When Han Chinese wake up and start work, most Uighur are still asleep. We're like two different families living in the same house."

It was all very interesting, but I hadn't slept on the flights. All I wanted to do was get to my hotel and hibernate for a few hours.

Lil said there wasn't time for the hotel.

"Lu Xin wants you to meet the team. They spend the afternoons looking in the streets around where Gobi went missing and handing out posters. We'll take you to the hotel later."

Ever since I'd heard about Gobi's disappearance, I'd been frustrated at what seemed to be a lack of action, so I couldn't complain now.

"All right," I said, as we pulled up at a traffic light alongside an armoured vehicle packing enough firepower to take down a bank. "Let's do it."

When we parked at the top of a residential street and I finally saw the area where Gobi had gone missing, my heart sank. Blocks of flats eight or ten storeys high lined the street. Traffic surged along the main road behind us, and in the near distance I could see an area of scrubland that looked like it led all the way off to a series of mountains in the distance. Not only was the area densely packed

with people and dangerous traffic, but if Gobi had decided to head for familiar territory and run off in the direction of the mountains, she could be miles and miles away. But if she'd stayed in the three- to five-mile radius as Chris had suggested, we'd have to knock on thousands upon thousands of doors.

I'd not talked to Lu Xin much in the car, but as I stared about, she stood beside me and smiled. She started talking, and I looked to Lil for help.

"She is telling you about when she lost her dog. She says that she felt just like you do now. She also says that Gobi is out there. She knows it, and she says that together we will find her."

I thanked her for her kindness, although I couldn't share her optimism. The city was even bigger than I remembered, and one look was enough to tell me that the area that Nurali lived in was full of places a dog could go missing. If Gobi was injured and had found somewhere safe to hide, or if she was being kept against her will, we'd never find her.

Lu Xin and Lil were deep in conversation as they led the way down the street. I followed on behind with the rest of the search team: a handful of people about my age, mainly women, all clutching post- ers and smiling eagerly at me. I nodded back and said *nee-how* a few times, but conversation was limited. I didn't mind so much. Somehow the prospect of finally being able to walk the streets and put up some posters—to actually *do something* for once—made me feel better.

We turned a corner, and I saw my first stray dog of the day. It was bigger than Gobi and looked more like a Labrador than a terrier, with teats hanging low on the ground, like a sow.

"Gobi?" queried one of the ladies next to me. She was wearing a white lab coat and clutching a stack of posters; she smiled and nodded eagerly as I stared back at her. "Gobi?" she asked again.

"What? Oh no. Not Gobi," I said. I pointed to the pictures of Gobi on the poster. "Gobi small. Not big."

The woman smiled back and nodded with even more enthusiasm.

I felt the last ounce of hope evaporate like steam.

We spent the rest of the afternoon walking, putting up posters, and trying to calm down the woman in the white coat—who Lil told me was a doctor of Chinese medicine—whenever she saw a dog of any kind.

We must have looked like a strange collection of freaks as we followed behind Lu Xin and Lil—the sensible, normal-looking ones. There was me, the only non-Chinese I'd seen since leaving the airport, standing a foot taller than anyone else, looking worried and sad. Alongside me was Mae-Lin, a particularly glamorous woman (a hairdresser, apparently) who carried herself like a 1950s movie star and was accompanied by a poodle with blue dye on its ears and a summer skirt around its waist. Then there was the woman whom I nicknamed "the doctor", with her perpetual smile and eager cries of "Gobi? Gobi?" which she shouted as she ran off down random alleys and around the back of blocks of flats. When the strays got close, the doctor would reach into her pocket and pull out some treats.

It was obvious that all of them loved dogs, and as we walked and talked with Lil, I learned why.

"Stray dogs are a problem in China," she said, translating for Lu Xin. "Some cities will round them up and kill them. That's how they get into the meat trade. But that doesn't happen here—at least, not in public. Most Uighur think dogs are unclean, and there's no way they would have them as a pet in their house, let alone eat them.

"So the dogs roam the streets. They can sometimes be danger-ous, so people kill them. That's what we're trying to change. We want to look after the strays, but we also want to show people that they don't need to be scared of dogs and they should look after them too."

I was sure that Nurali was a Uighur, and I didn't quite know how to take Lu Xin's news.

"Do you think Nurali would have looked after Gobi well?"

Lu Xin looked awkward.

"What is it?" I asked.

"We've been talking to people, and we think Gobi might have gone missing before Nurali thinks she did. We think Gobi may have escaped earlier."

"How much earlier?"

She shrugged. "Maybe one week. Maybe ten days."

I'd suspected as much all along, but it was still painful to hear. If Gobi really had been missing for so long, the distance she could have covered was vast. She could be far, far away from the city by now. And if she was, I'd never find her.

All throughout the afternoon we saw strays, but they were always alone. They avoided the main roads and trotted down the side of the quieter ones. It was like they were trying to keep themselves out of sight.

It was only after a few hours that we saw our first pack of strays. They were sniffing around a patch of bare earth a few hun-dred feet away, and because I was tired of walking and wanted to cut loose and run for a while, I told my fellow searchers that I was going to head off and quickly check them out.

It felt good to run.

When I reached the place where the pack of dogs had been, they'd already scattered. The patch of land wasn't totally empty,

and in one corner there was a half-finished cinder-block structure. Instead of turning around and going back to rejoin the others, I decided to poke around.

The weather was so much hotter in August than it had been at the end of June, and the sun was fierce that afternoon. I guess that was why there weren't any other people around and the noise of the traffic had subsided. I stood in the shade of the half-built building, enjoying the stillness.

Something caught my attention. It was a familiar sound, one that took me back to the day when Lucja and I went to retrieve Curtly, our Saint Bernard.

I went around the back of the building in search of the source. I found it soon enough.

Puppies. A litter of two, maybe four or five weeks old. I watched for a while. There was no sign of their mum, but they looked well enough. Even though Urumqi was clearly not a haven for pets, the dense housing meant that there must have been plenty of opportunities for a dog to scavenge food.

With their big eyes and clumsy paws, the puppies weren't just cute; they were adorable. But as with all mammals, that helpless, cuddly phase would pass. I wondered how long they'd have before they would be forced to fend for themselves. I wondered whether they'd both make it.

I heard the others calling my name as I approached them. They were clearly agitated, and the doctor ran out to grab my hand and hurry me back to Lil.

"Someone has seen a dog they think is Gobi. We need to go."

I didn't know what to think, but there was a buzz in the air.

Even Lu Xin was looking hopeful, and as we drove the half mile to the location, the chatter in the car became increasingly animated.

By the time we got there, I was starting to believe it too. Then again, I probably would have believed anything; I hadn't slept properly in thirty-six hours, and I couldn't remember the last time I had eaten.

An old man holding one of our posters introduced himself to Lil as we parked. The two talked for a while, the old guy pointing to the picture of Gobi on the poster and indicating that he'd seen her some way down a track that ran around the back of a block of flats.

We went where he suggested. I tried to tell people that their habit of calling out "Gobi! Gobi!" as we walked was pointless, given that Gobi had been known by that name for only a few days. She was smart but not that smart.

Nobody took my advice, and the cries of "Go-bi! Gooooo-bi!" continued. After thirty minutes of wandering, I was beginning to tire. The surge of adrenaline I'd experienced when the news of the sighting first came in had long gone, and I was ready to call it a day and get to the hotel.

The flash of brown fur a few hundred feet ahead stopped us all in our tracks. There was a moment of collective silence. Then chaos erupted.

I ran hard towards the dog, leaving the sound of the others calling out far behind me. Could it really be Gobi? The colour was right, and it looked like the same size as well. But it couldn't be her, could it? Surely it couldn't be this easy?

The dog was nowhere to be seen when I got there. I carried on searching, running down the network of alleys and dirt paths that connected the blocks of flats.

"Gobi? Gobi! Dion! Dion!"

The shouting came from behind me, somewhere back near the main path.

I raced back.

The searchers were gathered in a knot, crowding around. They parted as I approached, revealing a tan-coloured terrier. Black eyes. Bushy tail. Everything was a match. But it wasn't Gobi. I knew it from ten feet away. The legs were too long and the tail too short, and I knew from looking at the dog that it had none of Gobi's spirit. It was sniffing around people's feet as if their legs were tree trunks. Gobi would have been looking up, her eyes digging deep into whatever human happened to be close at hand.

The others took some convincing, but eventually they accepted it.

The search would have to continue.

Back in the hotel, in the minutes before my body gave in to the deep tiredness that had been growing all day, I thought back on the afternoon.

The members of the search team were wonderful people— dedicated and enthusiastic and giving up their time for no financial reward whatsoever—but they didn't have a clue about Gobi. They were searching a whole city that was full of strays for a single dog, and all they had to go on was a home-printed poster with a couple of low-quality images.

They'd never seen her in person, never even heard her bark or watched the way her tail bobbed about when she ran. What chance did they have of recognizing her in a city like this?

Finding Gobi was going to be like finding a needle in a haystack—maybe an even greater challenge than that. I was an idiot for ever thinking that I'd be able to do it.

15

YOU COULD SAY I'M AN ADDICT. THE FEELING I get when I'm in a race, when I'm right at the very front, is a powerful drug. At some races, like the Marathon des Sables, if you're the guy at the head of the pack, you'll have a car ahead of you, helicopters tracking you from the air, and a whole load of drones and film crews capturing your moment in full high-definition glory. It's fun, but the real buzz doesn't come from all that horsepower and technology. What gets me fired up is the knowledge that behind me is a herd of one thousand runners—all running a little bit slower than me.

I've spent a couple of days running like that in Morocco, and I've been fortunate enough to compete in a heap of other races too. Every time I'm one of the front runners, whether there are choppers overhead or nothing but damp-looking volunteers sheltering from the Scottish weather, the high stays with me for days afterward.

In fact, I don't even have to be in first place to get my win-junkie fix. I'm also a realist, and I know that I'm never going to win a race like the Marathon des Sables. Those top-ten slots are the preserve of the most gifted endurance runners on the planet. I'm

just a hobby runner who came to the sport late in life after a decade of life as a fat bloke stuck on the couch. Against professional athletes who have spent their lives running, the odds are never in my favour.

That means I must set my goals carefully. At an event where the best in the world are running, *winning*, for me, is a top-twenty finish. The buzz I'd get from finishing that high up the table at Marathon des Sables would be every bit as sweet as an Atacama gold spot.

I'm thankful that in the few years I've been running, I've become well acquainted with the highs of my sport. I also know the lows, and there's nothing I hate more than being unable to compete. Being injured to the point where I can't move as quickly as I think I should really kills me. Being overtaken by people I know I'm faster than hurts like a knife in my heart. Being so down on myself that I choose to stop and bail on a race entirely, as I did on my very first ultra, is about as bad as it gets.

Those experiences can leave me feeling drained and depressed. I get angry with myself and frustrated to the point of wanting to throw it all away. In those times I'm not much fun to be around.

Searching for Gobi on the hot summer streets of Urumqi, I could feel the crash coming. I could tell it was going to be a big one.

I'd been on a high since finishing second in the Gobi Desert race. Part of that was the success of the run, part was the continued success in my training, and a whole lot of it was thanks to the excitement about bringing Gobi home. As soon as she went missing, I kicked into action mode—first working out how to find her, then how to tell the supporters, then how to get myself out to Urumqi to join in the search. Life had been frantically busy right from the moment of that dreaded phone call, and I'd not had a chance to stop.

All that changed once I arrived in Urumqi. When I woke up for the first time in the hotel, the reality of the situation finally caught up with me. I was convinced all was lost.

I knew I needed to put on a brave face for the rest of the search team, so when Lu Xin came to collect me soon after breakfast, I put on my sunglasses and my biggest smile and tried to pretend that everything was fine.

We spent the morning resuming our poster campaign, working systematically along the streets and putting a poster on the windscreen of every parked car that we could see. More often than not, if we returned to the street an hour or two later, we'd find all the posters removed and piled up in a rubbish bin.

We had a couple of arguments with the guys whose job it was to keep the streets clean. The first time it happened, the old man wouldn't listen to Lu Xin's attempts at an explanation. The second time it was the doctor who stepped up. She faced off with another old guy, and this one was putting his heart and soul into the shouting. Flecks of spit were flying from his mouth as he ripped up a handful of the posters that he'd swiped from the first few cars. The doctor got up in his face, shouting just as loud. They were both speaking so fast that I didn't bother asking Lil to translate, but I could tell the doctor was refusing to back down.

Eventually she won. The old man took a good hard look at me, put up his hands, and backed away. The doctor's performance was as much of a surprise to the others as it was to me, and we all stood, staring in awe when she turned back towards us.

That was about the only good moment of the day. The rest of the time I spent trying not to let my thoughts spiral away from me.

It was almost impossible. All it would take would be a glimpse of the mountains in the distance, and I would worry that Gobi had tried to head back to the kind of terrain with which she was familiar.

Midway through the afternoon there was another flurry of activity as news of a possible sighting came in. Someone had sent a picture this time, and it was clear to me that the dog looked nothing like Gobi. I was all for giving it a miss, but the rest of the team wanted to check it out. After the previous day's letdown, I was surprised the team was still so positive.

The dog wasn't anything like Gobi, of course, and I went back and sat in the car as soon as I could. I probably looked as though I was desperate to keep going, and, in a way, I was. But all I really wanted was just a moment's rest. Wearing the fake smile was killing me.

By the time Lu Xin returned me to the hotel, it was late at night. We'd got rid of thousands of posters along miles and miles of parked cars. We'd argued with street cleaners, begged with shop-keepers, and seen countless drivers return to their cars and throw the posters to the ground without even looking at them. I had not eaten since breakfast, was still jet-lagged, and was told that the hotel restaurant had already shut down for the night.

I ordered some room service, took a drink from the minibar, and tried calling Lucja. No reply. So I waited some more and took another drink. Then another.

When Lucja called back, a great surge of sadness flowed out of me, like water down a drain after the plug is pulled after a bath. I couldn't talk for a minute or more. All I could do was cry.

When I finally caught my breath and wiped my face, Lucja had some news for me. She'd been e-mailing Kiki since I left

Edinburgh, and they'd both agreed that with me in Urumqi now, we needed to do all we could to get the local media to cover the story. She had spent a lot of the day getting in touch with outlets, and after a lot of communication difficulties, she had arranged for one of them to come and interview me the next day.

"It's just a local TV show," she said. "It's not much, but it's a start. Maybe it'll kick things off, like the *Daily Mirror* article did."

"I hope so," I said. We both knew my heart wasn't in it.

"Hey," she added. "Someone on Facebook said that you need to make sure those posters aren't just in Chinese but are also in whatever language the Uighur read. You've done that, haven't you?"

"No," I sighed, eyeing another drink. "Lucja, this whole thing's impossible. If she went farther into the city, there's traffic everywhere and great packs of stray dogs that would probably rip her to pieces. If Gobi went out to the mountains, she could be a hundred miles away by now, and even if we could somehow know what direction she went in, there are no roads to follow. All we've done is hand out posters, and now we find out that none of the locals can read them. We're finished even before we've begun."

Lucja knows me well enough to let me rant a while longer. Only when I'd run out of words did she speak again. "You know what I'm going to say, don't you?"

I did. But I wanted to hear her say it anyway.

"Sleep on it. It'll all look different in the morning."

For once Lucja was wrong. I didn't wake up feeling optimistic, and we didn't have any breakthroughs as we continued the search in the morning. We went through the usual routine of distributing posters, getting into arguments, and dealing with the depressing sight of those mountains in the distance.

There was one difference, however: the search team was now

considerably bigger. Along with Lu Xin, Lil, the hairdresser, and the doctor, many others had now joined our team. At one point, later during the search, I counted fifty people, twenty of whom chose to search all through the night while I was sleeping. They were remarkable people, and I could never thank them enough.

Doing the TV interview in the hotel later was a good idea. It reminded me of the surge of interest that we'd had back when the fund-raising kicked off. I'd not done any interviews since Gobi had gone missing, mainly by choice. With no news to share, there didn't seem to be much point.

The local TV station was different. The reporter wanted to know why a guy from Scotland would come all the way to this city to search for a dog, and he seemed to like the fact that the search was being led by locals.

Whatever the station did with the story, it worked. The next day we had two new volunteers join the search and more than a dozen requests for interviews from Chinese TV stations and newspapers. Just like the *Daily Mirror* and BBC coverage back home, that first Chinese TV interview had gone viral, unlocking interest from all over the country. One TV station even sent a crew along to follow me for a two-hour live broadcast of the search out on the streets.

Not all the attention was positive. Lu Xin took a call from a woman who claimed she had seen Gobi in a vision and that Gobi was running through snow-capped mountains. I dismissed it out of hand, but I could tell that a few of the searchers were interested.

So I said, "Tell her if she's any good at having these visions, she needs to have one that has a bit more detail in it. We need to know exactly which one of these mountains Gobi is in."

I knew nobody was going to get the joke.

The following day the new posters arrived, with the message in both Chinese and whatever version of Arabic the Uighur use. We got the same disinterested reaction from people, but at least the media interest continued to rise.

People started coming up to me on the street wanting to have their photo taken. My lack of Chinese and their lack of English meant we'd hardly ever be able to talk much, but they all seemed to have heard about Gobi and wanted to take a few posters with them. Every time that happened, I reminded myself that if this all worked out right, it was only going to take one poster to do it.

Along with the Chinese media, the international outlets started to get interested again. Lucja had worked the phone hard at home, and after a day's searching in the streets, I'd get back to the hotel and speak to journalists and producers in the UK and the US. It meant staying up late and not getting much sleep, but it was a whole lot better than sitting around feeling powerless and depressed.

Ever since I arrived in Urumqi, I'd been relying on Lu Xin and her team. We had no offers of help from the authorities or other organizations. We were on our own—that much was clear.

Over the years a lot of people have told me that—given the way my childhood turned sour—they are surprised I'm not messed up. I tell them my childhood contained some hardship, but it also gave me the tools I needed to survive. All that pain and loss gave me a certain kind of toughness, and running gave me the chance to put it to good use. Pain, doubt, fear. I discovered that I'm good at blocking them all out when I'm running. It's as though I have a switch I can flip on or off at will.

I use that blocking ability at work too. I don't give up when it looks like all is lost, and I won't take no for an answer. That mental toughness I learned as a kid has helped me in many ways. I'm grateful for it. But losing Gobi was a shock. It taught me that I'm not as tough as I think.

After everything she had done to stick with me, I couldn't just forget about her. I couldn't flip the switch and move on. I couldn't stop myself from fearing the worst, from doubting our chances, or from feeling the tremendous pain of knowing that—day by day—I was losing her.

16

DAY FOUR IN URUMQI WAS ALMOST IDENTICAL
to all the others. I was up at six o'clock, eating dumplings with the
rest of the search team in a café in a converted shipping container.
We were talking about how long Gobi had been missing: officially
it had been ten days, but none of the volunteers believed that. They
all thought she'd been missing for at least twice that.

A new girl joined us, Malan—bringing our number that morning up to ten. Malan told me that she had seen me on TV the night
before and was so moved by the story that she contacted Lu Xin
and asked if she could come along and help. She proved her worth
right from the start, suggesting we distribute the Uighur-language
version of the poster in a nearby Uighur neighbourhood.

The homes were all single storey, a patchwork of loose bricks
and rusted metal roofs. Every other street we'd been down had been
wide and clean and lined with cars parked on the side. This Uighur
neighbourhood had narrow, twisting alleys, few cars, and a lot of
goats caged up in spaces not much bigger than a hotel bathroom.

I wondered if this was the first time in the Uighur part of town
for the Han Chinese members of the search party. If it was, they

didn't show it. They just got on with the job of putting posters into as many hands as was physically possible.

The only difference in the day came in the afternoon when Lu Xin left me at the hotel to do another interview while she drove to the airport to pick up Richard, my tent mate from the Gobi race. He lived in Hong Kong, and his work took him all over China. He and I had kept in touch since the race, and he'd been a generous supporter of the Bring Gobi Home fund-raising. When he found out that he was going to be a short flight away from me in Urumqi, he offered to come and help with the search for a few days.

I was excited about having a friend come and join me, and the fact that Richard was fluent in Mandarin was another bonus. I was also looking forward to being able to run. Ever since arriving in Urumqi, I'd ambled around the streets at the same tortoise-slow pace as the rest of the search team. I'd tried getting them to pick it up a bit, but it was no use.

Richard and I went for a run in a park near the hotel as soon as he came back from the airport. I'd had my eye on the mountains all along and had seen several villages in the scrubland that separated the city from the hills. I wanted Richard to help me cover some miles and hand out a bunch of posters among the locals up there.

Richard had other plans. I didn't know it at the time, but Lucja had been in touch with him already, asking him to look after me because she knew I was stressed and not eating properly.

After the run, we met up with the team. Lu Xin looked anxious as Lil told me about a few phone calls she'd taken. That was nothing new. The more posters we'd hand out, the more calls we'd get. Mostly they were false alarms, but sometimes they were from people asking if we would increase the reward if they brought Gobi

in. They were time wasters, and after the first few, Lu Xin stopped telling me about them.

These calls were different. I could tell she was hiding something. I pressed her to tell me what was going on.

"Just someone being bad," she said. But I wasn't satisfied.

"Tell me. I want to know."

"Lu Xin took a call this afternoon. They said that Gobi is going to be killed."

At first I didn't get it, but as the news sank in, I felt sick. If this was a joke, it was despicable. If it was real, I was terrified.

I'd calmed down a bit by the time I returned to the hotel, but the interview with BBC Radio later that evening was a bit of a disaster. I was feeling particularly hopeless and depressed about the search, and even though I knew how important it was to sound upbeat and positive, to make it clear that this was not a hopeless case, I failed. I was exhausted, worried, and unable to see how we could ever hope to find Gobi. It was not my finest media hour.

Even though I'd been feeling so flat, I'd wanted to do the interview because of a piece that had appeared in the Huffington Post two days earlier. Under the headline "Missing Marathon Dog Gobi May Have Been Snatched by Dog Meat Thieves", the piece quoted someone from Humane Society International who said that it was "very worrying that Gobi has gone missing in China, where between 10 and 20 million dogs are killed each year for the dog meat trade".[1] From everything that Lu Xin had told me, the dog meat trade was not common in the region we were in, especially

---

1 Kathryn Snowdon, "Missing Marathon Dog Gobi May Have Been Snatched by Dog Meat Thieves, Humane Society International Warns", Huffington Post, 22 August, 2016, www.huffingtonpost.co.uk/entry/gobi-missing-marathon-dog-may-have-been -snatched-by-dog-meat-thieves-humane-society-international-warns_uk_57baf 263e4b0f78b2b4ae988.

given the large number of Muslim Uighur who lived there. There was no way they would ever eat a dog, which they considered to be as unfit for human consumption as a pig.

Not only was the piece inaccurate, but it was also not helpful. We had our small band of dog lovers joining in the search, but we needed the local and national Chinese media to cover the story and help convince the wider population in the city to care about a little dog. Chris and Kiki had already advised me to stay positive and never say anything critical of the state while I was being interviewed, and I knew that if the authorities felt that the story was being used by the Western media to paint the Chinese as dog-eating barbarians, I'd lose all hope of ever getting their help again.

The truth was that the local search team had been great. I wanted to tell the BBC and all the supporters back home what amazing support we'd received from the general public as well as the authorities. I wanted to make it perfectly clear that everyone I'd met had been helpful, kind, and generous. I couldn't have asked for more from the team, the Chinese media, and Kiki back in Beijing. Even if we never found Gobi, their support had been phenomenal.

That's what I wanted to tell the BBC that night. Instead, I sounded as though I was ready to end it all.

Richard rescued the situation with a few beers and a good meal. We talked about things that had nothing to do with Gobi or the search, and Richard told me he was a former US marine. He wouldn't tell me any more than that, although when the conversation did return to Gobi, he had some interesting theories on what had happened to her.

"None of this adds up," he said. "Even without those calls, it

still looks wrong to me. I don't think it's got anything to do with Nurali being in the US or her father-in-law accidentally letting her escape. I think that the moment Gobi's story went viral and the fund-raising kicked in, someone spotted a chance to make some money. That's all this is about, Dion—money. This is a shake-down. The call will come."

I wasn't so sure. Part of me didn't believe him because I couldn't imagine anyone would go to such lengths for just a few thousand pounds. Then there was a part of me that didn't believe him because I just didn't want to. I couldn't stand the thought that Richard might be right and that Gobi's survival depended on whether some idiot thought he could get enough money out of us to make it worthwhile. What if Gobi's captor changed his mind? What if he got cold feet? Would he return her carefully to Nurali, or would he treat her like any other failed business experiment and dispose of her as quickly as possible?

My phone buzzed with a message from Lu Xin.

Look at this photo. Gobi?

I wasn't convinced. The quality of the image was poor, but what I could see of the eyes didn't look right at all. Plus, there was a deep scar on the dog's head that Gobi didn't have during the race.

I sent a quick reply saying that it wasn't Gobi, but Richard wasn't so sure.

"Don't you think we should go and have a look?" he said.

I was tired and tried to brush him off. "Mate, we've had almost thirty of these, and they're always the same. It'll take an hour and a half to get up there, see the dog, have a chat, and then get back. It's getting late, and we've got to be up early tomorrow."

Richard looked at the photo again. "Looks a bit like Gobi to me."

Lu Xin sent another message thirty minutes later. This time it was a better-quality image, and someone had enlarged the eyes and pasted them next to the photo of Gobi from the reward poster. Maybe she and Richard did have a point.

Richard was convinced when I slid the phone over to him. "We've got to go," he said.

We drove into the gated community and parked in between a shiny Lexus and a couple of BMWs. A whole bunch of the cars had foot-long red ribbons tied to one of their wing mirrors—a sign that the cars hadn't long left the dealership. The neatly tended gardens and wide apartments themselves spoke of wealth. This was clearly one part of Urumqi that I'd not seen.

As we followed Lu Xin, I told Richard that we were wasting our time. And as the front door of the residence opened to reveal every single person in the search team, plus another ten or more strangers I'd never laid eyes on, I couldn't help but sigh. Any hope I had of being out of here quickly and back to bed was blown out of the water.

Because of the crowd of people, I couldn't see much, and the noise was intense too. I couldn't even tell where this Gobi look-alike was at first, but as I pushed a little deeper into the room, a knot of people at the back stepped aside and a streak of sandy brown shot across the room and jumped up at my knees.

"It's her!" I shouted, picking her up and thinking for a moment that I'd slipped into a dream. She soon started making that same excited, whimpering, yapping sound she'd made whenever I'd been reunited with her at the end of a day apart on the run. "This is Gobi! It's her!"

I sat on the couch and took a good look at Gobi. Her head didn't look like I remembered it. There was a big scar across it, a mark as wide as my finger running from near her right eye back behind her left ear. I knew she didn't know her name, but whenever we'd been on the run or in the camp, all I had to do was make a little clicking sound, and she'd come straightaway. So I put her down on the ground, took a step to the other side of the room, and clicked.

She was by my side like a shot. It was her all right. There was no doubt in my mind. No doubt at all.

The noise levels in the room exploded. People were shouting and calling out her name, but I wanted to check Gobi over and make sure that she was okay. I found a couch and looked again, running my hands up and down her back and legs to check. She winced when I touched her right hip, obviously in pain. She was okay to stand and could put some weight on it, but between the hip and her scar, I knew she was lucky to be alive. Whatever had happened to her, it had been quite the adventure.

Gobi was burrowing into my lap like a newborn puppy, and the others crowded around for photos. I understood their excitement, and I was so grateful to them for their help, but it was a moment that I really would have enjoyed being alone. Well, just Gobi and me.

The doctor got a little overexcited and wanted a selfie with Gobi. She picked her up and must have touched her hip, because Gobi let out a loud squeal of pain and jumped out of her arms and back into mine. After that, I didn't let anyone else get too close. Gobi needed some protecting, even from the people who loved her.

It took an hour for the hysteria to calm down and the full story to emerge. Richard translated while Mr Ma, the house owner, explained how he had found her.

He'd been in a restaurant with his son earlier in the evening. His son had been telling him about this girl he'd seen that afternoon—the newest member of the search team, Malan. She had been putting up posters that she'd added handwritten messages pleading with people not to throw away the posters because it was sad that the dog was missing and a man had come all the way from the UK to find her. Mr Ma's son had thought that was a kind thing for her to do.

As they walked home from their meal, they saw a dog, looking hungry and tired, curled up at the side of the road.

"That's the same dog, Dad," he said. "I'm sure of it." He made his father wait while he ran back a couple of streets to where they'd passed some of the posters.

When they called out to Gobi, she followed them the short walk home, where they then phoned the number on the poster and sent the photo to Lu Xin. When she relayed my message that I didn't think it was a match, it was Mr Ma's son who scanned the poster, took a better-quality photo, and made it clear how similar the eyes were. He was convinced even if I wasn't.

"So what do we do next? We take her back to the hotel, right?"

Richard translated. Then both he and Lu Xin shook their heads.

"They won't let you. No hotels in the city will ever allow a dog in."

"Really?" I was shocked. "But after all this? After all she's been through?"

"They're right," said Richard. "Maybe you can try and talk to the manager and see if he'll let you, but I doubt it. I stay in hotels all over, and I've never seen a dog in one."

It was past eleven o'clock, and I was too tired to argue, either with my friends or with a hotel receptionist.

"We should ask Mr Ma to keep her here tonight," said Lu Xin. "Then you can buy all the things you need for her, like a lead and collar, food, bowls, and a bed, and then collect her tomorrow."

Lu Xin had a point. I'd been thinking so long about Gobi being lost that I'd never come up with a plan for what we should do when we finally found her. I was totally ill equipped and felt bad at the thought of saying goodbye to Gobi and heading back to the hotel. But the others were right; it was the only sensible option.

I looked at Gobi, curled up beside me on the couch. She was going through that same twitch and snore routine that she had on the first night she slept beside me in the tent.

"I'm sorry, girl," I said. "I've got a lot to learn about being your dad, haven't I?"

On our way back to the hotel, I rang Lucja. "We bloody well found her!" I said the moment she picked up. Both of us didn't say much for a while. We were too busy crying.

PART 5

17

THE HOTEL MANAGER WAS A STRANGE GUY.

I had spent enough time driving around the city to know that the hotel was one of the very best in Urumqi. He'd let us use one of the meeting rooms downstairs to carry out numerous interviews, and the story was all over national TV. So I was convinced that if I asked nicely, he'd do us a favour. I thought he'd bend a couple of rules, if he had to, and let Gobi stay in the hotel. Surely the guy would understand how an opportunity like this would be good for business.

"No," he said.

His English was better than that of most people I'd met, but I tried repeating the request, a little slower this time.

"Can the dog stay in my room? She's only little. It'll be good publicity for you."

"No," he said again. He understood perfectly what I was asking. "We don't ever let dogs stay in the hotel." He paused a moment, then spoke again, his voice lowered. "But I would be willing to help."

I did some internal high fives. Even if it cost me a few hundred pounds, I knew it would be worth it to keep Gobi safe.

"Perhaps the dog could stay in one of the rooms that we use for staff training."

It didn't sound ideal, but I didn't have many other options. "Can I see it?"

"Of course," he said. "This way, please, Mr Leonard." Instead of taking me deeper into the hotel, he led me out of the revolving front door, past the security guard with the standard-issue bulletproof vest and rifle, across a busy car park, and through a set of doors that didn't appear to have any locks at all on them and swung in the breeze, like saloon doors from an old-time western.

That wasn't the worst part. The room itself was a disaster.

It wasn't so much a training facility as a dumping ground. The place was full of cleaning bottles and broken furniture. The door itself didn't appear to be closable. The manager saw me looking at it and tried to shoulder it shut as well as he could, but there was still a Gobi-sized gap at the bottom where she could easily crawl out.

"I can't keep her in here," I said. "She'd run off."

"So?" he said, turning away and walking back out into the car park.

Like I said, he was a strange guy.

Richard and I had already been out first thing and bought a selection of Gobi essentials in the sprawling market beyond the hotel car park. There wasn't much choice, but we managed to buy a lead and collar, a couple of bowls, and some food. And as we walked, we hatched a plan for what we'd do if the hotel manager turned us down. And it looked like we'd have to resort to Plan B.

Back at Mr Ma's, Gobi was just as excited to see me that morning as she had been the night before. I was relieved about that

and to see also that Mr Ma obviously had looked after her well. In all the chaos of the night before, I'd not forgotten that Richard suspected there was some foul play at work. But the more I talked to Mr Ma and saw that he was a regular guy who dressed as if he were going to head to the gym but not actually do any work, the more I trusted him. And when I found out he was a jade dealer, that did it for me. He obviously didn't need the money. There was no "shakedown" going on here.

I told Mr Ma that I wanted to give him his reward at a special dinner we were going to hold for the search team the following night. He agreed to come along but insisted he didn't want the reward money. Just as Richard, Lu Xin, Gobi, and I were about to leave, another man—wearing what looked to me like a fake smile—entered the house. I'd not met him before, but he did look familiar.

"I am Nurali's husband," he said, as he shook my hand with what felt like an iron grip. I knew he meant business.

I remembered where I'd seen him. He was one of the drivers at the race. Gobi was down on the ground, and he knelt to pick her up.

"Yes," he said, turning her around in front of him as if she were an antique vase that he was considering buying. "This is Gobi all right."

He handed her back to me. "We tried our best to keep her safe for you, but she escaped. She's going to need a good fence when you get her home."

Our plan for getting Gobi back into the hotel was simple. We were going to put her in a bag and carry her in. The trouble was, like all hotels and public buildings in Urumqi, there was more to security than a guy with a bulletproof vest and an AK-47. There was an X-ray machine and a walk-through metal detector to negotiate.

It was up to me to play the fool and create a diversion. I had an

unzipped bag full of posters and snacks that I dropped on the floor near the scanner. I made a big fuss and apologized profusely as I crawled around the floor picking them up. Meanwhile, Richard—with Gobi sitting silently in a bag made of denim that looked a little like a coat—walked right through the metal detector, hoping he'd remembered to remove anything that would set off the alarm.

Back in my room, it was finally time to check out Gobi. The scar on the top of her head told the story of a nasty wound, and I wondered whether it had been inflicted by another dog or a human. It was thick, but the scab was well formed, and I didn't think I needed to worry about it too much.

Her hip, though, was a problem. She clearly had been in pain when the doctor had picked her up awkwardly the night before, and even when I put the lightest pressure on it, she twitched away. But it was when I put her down to walk that the problem was the most obvious. She could barely sustain any pressure on it at all.

Again I was left wondering what had happened to her.

I'd spoken to Kiki that morning about what needed to happen next. We knew Nurali hadn't made a start with any of the medical requirements that Gobi needed in order to fly, so the first priority was getting her to a vet. After that, it would be a question of waiting for the paperwork to be completed and the travel to Beijing to be authorized.

"How long will that take?" I asked.

"Maybe one week, maybe one month."

I felt a little of yesterday's depression return. "Are you sure we have to fly? Why don't we drive?"

"It's a thirty-hour drive, and no hotel will let you take her inside with you. Would you really want to leave her in the car?"

I wouldn't. We agreed that driving would be the back-up plan.

"Besides," she added, "I have a contact at an airline who says she might be able to get Gobi on the flight without any trace of Gobi being on it."

For the rest of the day, I did the only thing I could and looked after Gobi. I fed her when she was hungry, let her wrestle with my socks when she was bored, and snuck her down in the lift to the basement car park when she needed to do her business. She was the dream dog; she didn't bark in the room, and she didn't mind going back in the bag when I took her out of the room.

In a strange way the experience reminded me of the one time in my teenage years when I felt close to my mum. I was ill and needed taking care of, and for a while all that was toxic between us evaporated.

The illness flared up when I was thirteen, lying on the carpet at home, waiting for the biggest TV event of my lifetime to happen. The cute girl and cool boy in a popular Aussie soap opera called *Neighbors* were about to get married. It was all everyone could talk about—bigger even than Cliff Young's winning the Sydney to Melbourne run. I was in love with Charlene, the cute girl, and took my front-row space on the carpet as the opening music started. "Neighbors, everybody needs good neighbors . . ."

Just as Scott and Charlene were about to say "I do," I blacked out. That's all I remember.

When I woke up, I was in a hospital. I felt terrible, like everything inside me had been rearranged the wrong way. The doctors were using words I didn't understand, and I couldn't hold on to a single thought properly. A terrible feeling of nausea raged within me. For hours I felt as though I was about to explode, until I finally fell asleep and woke up twelve hours later.

I had had an epileptic fit, and Mum had to explain epilepsy to me.

I had seizures a few more times, and each one was followed by a period of a day or two when I'd feel terrible. I had to stay out of school, visit specialists, and deal with the prospect that this unexpected visitor to my life could return at any time, bringing chaos with it.

And then, less than a year after that first attack, I began to realize that months had passed since my last attack. The doctor appointments became less and less frequent, and life returned to normal.

The funny thing was, I almost missed having epilepsy. Not the attacks themselves but the way in which they turned the clock back on things with my mum. With each attack came a softening in her, a new kind of warmth. The harsh words disappeared, she cooked my favourite meals, and she even gave me cuddles. Having lost Garry the way she had, seeing me in the middle of an epileptic seizure must have been hard for her, but all I received from her was love and care. Those were precious times. Finally, I had my mum back. Sadly, that didn't last.

I tried to care for Gobi the way I remembered my mum caring for me. I tried to let go of the stress of the previous few weeks and just enjoy spending time with her. It helped that we were both exhausted, too, and spent a lot of that day dozing together.

The next morning I had a problem. Gobi had all the food she needed right there in the room, but I wanted something other than dog biscuits and tinned meat for breakfast. Because Gobi was sleeping, I decided to creep out and head down to the ground floor for a quick bite.

I pulled the door shut as silently as I could, hung the "Do Not Disturb" sign on the handle, and crept down the corridor to the lift. As I watched the doors shut in front of me, I wondered whether I would hear a dog bark.

I was back upstairs on my floor in less than fifteen minutes. Striding out of the lift, I passed a cleaning trolley, turned the corner, and saw immediately that the door to my room was open. I ran in. There was no sign of Gobi at all, not under the bed, in the closet, or behind the curtains.

"Gobi!" I was calling, trying to keep the panic out of my voice.

My brain searched through possible scenarios. The hotel manager must have arranged for her to be taken. I ran to the main door and was about to head back to the lifts when I noticed that my bathroom door was shut. I opened it, and there she was, sitting in the tub, head cocked inquisitively to one side, watching the housekeeper wipe down the counter. Gobi looked at me briefly, a kind of "Hey, Dad, what's up?" kind of look.

The housekeeper didn't seem too worried and said a few words as she continued working. I did the only thing I could think of and pulled out my wallet and handed her a 100-yuan note—about ten pounds. I mimed not saying anything about Gobi. She nodded, pocketed the money, and went back to cleaning.

Maybe she wasn't surprised to see the dog there, and maybe she thought the tip was to clean the bathroom extra well. I had no way of knowing. She stayed a long time, cleaning everything in sight. I didn't want to be out in the room since the door to the hallway was standing open, so I stayed in the bathroom, trying to keep out of the cleaner's way with Gobi on my lap. Every time she moved on to clean another part of the room, Gobi and I would have to find a new place to perch.

"Thank you," I said each time we shifted, hoping that she would get the message. "Goodbye. You can go now."

She never got the hint. Instead, she'd just nod, shooing me and Gobi to move from the edge of the tub to the toilet, or from the toilet to the corner behind the door, as she cleaned.

Gobi thought it was all great fun. She sat happily, her tail swatting the air, her eyes darting back and forth between me and the housekeeper.

This has to be the strangest scene ever, I thought.

18

I WEDGED THE DUVET AND PILLOWS FROM THE bed against the door, hoping that if Gobi did make a noise it wouldn't be audible out in the corridor. There was no way I was leaving the room again until I absolutely had to.

I spent the rest of the morning on my phone. I was sending messages to Richard, telling him about the incident with the housekeeper, and to Lu Xin, asking her to look into alternative accommodation options. I spoke to Paul de Souza, a literary agent and film producer in California. He had first heard about the story from his daughter, and he was helping me negotiate a possible book deal. I was amazed at how many publishers had contacted me, but Paul's wisdom and knowledge about the industry were second to none. In between all of that, I was doing Skype interviews with American and British media outlets.

The interviews were fun. Right from the start of the crowd-funding appeal, I knew people wanted to hear about the story because it seemed as though it was heading for a happy ending. Whenever I was interviewed while Gobi was missing, I struggled

to know how to adjust to the new questions: How did she go missing? Where did I think she was? Did I fear the worst? I couldn't be upbeat because I didn't have a feel-good story to share. And more importantly, I knew that Gobi's disappearance was shrouded in suspicion. I'd been convinced that something odd had taken place, though I wasn't sure exactly who had taken her. But I chose not to reveal any of this in the interviews. I didn't have all the facts, and it was still too early to be blaming people.

So up in the hotel room, with Gobi asleep on my lap, as I talked to journalists from the *Washington Post* and CBS, things felt right again. I could relax and smile and tell them that I was finally going to be able to repay Gobi's love and determination by giving her a forever home back in Scotland.

Midway through the morning, Gobi woke up, desperate to get outside to do her business. Even though I knew it would happen eventually, I still dreaded the moment when I would have to open the door and peer up and down the hallway to check that the coast was clear.

Thankfully, we had the lift to ourselves as we sank down to the basement level. Gobi trotted off to the same patch of bushes that stood at the car park exit, and I gave her some privacy and looked around.

There was nothing much to see, apart from two men in dark suits stepping out of the lift and walking over to a grey saloon parked nearby.

I was pleased to see that Gobi took a bit of care to kick the dirt back over after relieving herself, but by the time she was finished, the lift doors had opened and out stepped another man into the basement. This time it was a security guard.

It cost me another ten pounds to persuade him to let us

through. I wondered whether it was going to be enough to keep either him or the housekeeper quiet.

Two hours later I found out the answer.

The moment she heard the knock at the door, Gobi started barking. Through the spy hole I could see two men. I recognized one of them instantly—Nurali's husband.

I stalled. What to do? I couldn't pretend I wasn't there—Gobi had seen to that—but how did they find me? One of the hotel workers must have told them which room I was in, but how did they get up to my floor? The only way to operate the lift was by swiping a valid room key. But that seemed to me to be a lot effort on their part, and it did nothing to ease my paranoia.

I sent a message to Richard: *Come to my room immediately.*

"Hello," I said, as I opened the door, trying to crack a smile and appear relaxed and unthreatened. Nurali's husband stared impassively while his friend was trying to look past me into the room.

"Can we come in?" asked Nurali's husband.

I was surprised but curious, so I mumbled "okay" and stepped back from the open door to let them in.

I shut the door behind me and turned around to see them standing over Gobi, looking down. She didn't seem too worried about them, but I doubted they had come just to visit her. Were they here to take her back? Why had they come?

I was about to walk over and pick up Gobi when there was another knock at the door. I saw Richard standing in the corridor, so I opened the door and exhaled a little in relief.

"Hey, man, what do you need?"

"Um, yes, mate," I was terrible at bluffing like this. But I didn't mind. Richard was ex-Marines and having him in the room made me feel a lot safer. More important, he spoke Chinese and could

help me get to the bottom of all this. "Didn't you want to come and get some of those posters to take home as souvenirs?"

Richard stayed by the door as I picked up Gobi and waited for Nurali's husband to speak. He fired off a whole load of Chinese and waited for Richard to translate.

Nurali and her husband had seen all the press coverage about Gobi and were worried I would blame them for her escape.

"All I want to do is get Gobi out of here and back home. I'm not interested in trying to find out how she escaped, and I'm not interested in trying to find someone to blame. As far as I'm concerned, it was just an accident, and it's all fine now. It's in all our interests to keep it that way, isn't it?"

Nurali's husband nodded. There wasn't much more to say.

Later that night, after I'd taken Gobi back down to the basement for another ten-pound bathroom break, I watched her fall asleep, then tiptoed out of the room, closing the door silently behind me. I hung the "Do Not Disturb" sign up again and hoped that when I returned a couple of hours later, she would still be there.

It was time to visit the hotel restaurant for the thank-you dinner. I knew I had a lot to be thankful for, and for the next two hours, I was almost able to forget about the events of the day.

The search team had worked harder than I could have hoped for. They had put in long hours in scorching heat and walked mile after mile sticking up thousands of posters. They had been shouted at, ignored, and ridiculed, and they had done it all for a dog they had never even met. Their sacrifice, endurance, and love left me a little teary, and I was honoured to be able to stand up, offer them a toast, and tell them all how deeply grateful I was.

Mr Ma was there, too, with his wife and son. I handed over the reward money, and though he protested a bit at first and seemed slightly confused, after I insisted a few times, he eventually accepted the £1,000.

Midway through the evening I realized that even though I'd been in Urumqi for almost a week and had spent ten days in China for the race, this was my first time socializing with Chinese people. Many Westerners assume the Chinese are serious people, not given to acts of spontaneity. Looking around the restaurant and seeing it full of my new Chinese friends, all laughing, singing, taking selfies, and relaxing, I didn't see anyone who fitted that stereotype.

The doctor was laughing the loudest, Malan was right in the middle of the action, and Mae-Lin, the hairdresser, had turned full-on cougar and was trying her absolute best—but failing—to seduce Richard. I caught Lil and Lu Xin staring at them, and we all laughed even harder.

"I remember when I first heard about Gobi," said Lu Xin.

"When Chris called you?" I asked.

"No. When you were racing. There aren't many news stories about dogs, so whenever there is a story, I always follow it. I knew Gobi was special even then, but I never thought I'd get to meet her."

"You did a lot more than just get to meet her, Lu Xin," I said. "Without you we wouldn't have found her. You're the reason we're all celebrating tonight."

She blushed at the compliment, but I meant every word of it.

She looked up and pointed at the doctor, Mae-Lin, and the others. "Before Gobi, we were trying to care for stray dogs, but nobody listened to us. We were fighting but had no power and no influence. Finding Gobi has changed all that. It's given us a voice. You've helped show that it's right that people should care for animals."

I didn't want to leave, but the longer the night went on, the more I thought about Gobi. I hoped she was still okay in the hotel room on her own. Eventually worry got the better of me, and I headed back upstairs. Gobi was fine, and I did a brief interview with *The Times* before heading back out briefly to find Richard, who was leaving early the next morning.

I knew that having him join the search was going to be helpful, but I didn't know quite how much I was going to depend on him. He didn't just help me keep going when I was at my lowest point; he masterminded the plan to get Gobi into the hotel and gave me some convincing back-up when I thought she might be taken.

I'm a bit of a loner by nature—it's non-negotiable for someone who needs to log a hundred miles or more in training runs each week. But the irony is that some of the strongest friendships I've formed in my life have been formed with people I've competed alongside in ultras. We go through hell on our own out there on the course each day, but the bond that forms is powerfully strong.

When I flew out to Urumqi, I assumed the search was going to be just like another ultra. I thought I'd have to push myself hard, and I expected others to do the same. But in finding Gobi, I found out some valuable lessons for myself as well.

I discovered that working as a team—rather than as a bunch of individuals—wasn't nearly as bad as I used to think it would be. I found out that my areas of weakness were covered by other people's strengths. I didn't have to shoulder the work all on my own. I could lean on the others, and they could take it. They didn't let me down. And I didn't fail them either.

19

EVERY RADIO STATION AND TV NETWORK THAT I had spoken with while the search was in progress wanted a follow-up interview after Gobi was found. In the days immediately following Gobi's return, I gave a total of fifty interviews in person, over the phone, or on Skype. Being that busy suited me. It took my mind off the fear that was growing stronger within me with every hour that passed.

It wasn't just the visit from Nurali's husband or the encounter with the housekeeper that had me worried. In the hotel bar after my *Times* interview, Richard had been sharing his conspiracy theories with me, and all that night my mind had been filled with shady characters lurking in the shadows.

Richard's logic was admittedly compelling. He didn't think Gobi had ever escaped, at least not the way Nurali thought. He said that when the story first went global, someone could have figured out that there was some money to be made from the dog, and when the opportunity arose, they took her. They probably hung on to her so long because the interest kept increasing along with the chance of getting an even bigger payout. But my coming to Urumqi changed things. Suddenly the local press was looking into it, and then the

government started taking an interest, with local officials joining the WeChat group. After that, the whole thing became riskier.

"That's why Lu Xin got so many calls saying that Gobi was dead already or that she was going to be killed unless the reward money increased."

"Wait," I said. "What do you mean 'so many calls'? I thought there was just the one phone call. And nobody told me they were asking for more money."

"Yes," said Richard. "They had hundreds of them. They just didn't want to worry you."

I didn't know what to think. Part of me was grateful for their care. Had I known the full story, I couldn't have done anything to help, and I'd have been even more worried. But I didn't like the thought that I'd been scammed.

I was trying to wrap my mind around it all, but Richard hadn't quite finished.

"And don't you think it's weird that Gobi ended up with someone who knew Nurali?"

"So you think the Ma family took her?"

"No. They didn't need the money and wouldn't be interested in taking a dog. But it's quite a coincidence that Gobi was left where people who knew her story could find her. And in a city with mountains and open space nearby, how come Gobi decides to hide on a road near the most expensive gated community for miles? She's not accustomed to high-class living just yet, is she?" It's more likely that the dognappers planted her.

In between interviews the next morning, I messaged Lu Xin to say that I thought it would be best if Gobi and I found somewhere

else to stay. Apart from feeling vulnerable in the hotel room on my own, the fact that I couldn't take Gobi freely in and out of the hotel meant that I still hadn't taken her to a vet to get her checked out. If the hip was a problem, it didn't seem fair that she should have to wait. Kiki was still working to get Gobi to Beijing, and I was getting increasingly worried that someone else would try and kidnap Gobi in the hope of a decent reward payout. And besides, every day spent waiting was another day to wait until she could finally come home.

I'd just finished texting Lu Xin when there was a knock at the door. Gobi was in a deep sleep and didn't stir at all, but I still tiptoed across the carpet, my heart jumping and my head spinning.

As I looked through the peephole, I was half-expecting to see the hotel manager standing outside, or maybe a housekeeper who had ignored the "Do Not Disturb" sign. I hoped it wouldn't be Nurali's husband.

It was none of these people.

It was two men in dark suits. I recognized them instantly. They were the same two men I had seen in the basement the day before.

I stepped back from the door, pushing myself flat against the wall. A random movie scene, where a sharply dressed assassin shot the unsuspecting occupant through the peephole, flashed across my mind. I told myself that I was being ridiculous and stole another glance.

They were still there, staring impassively at me.

The door was locked and bolted, and the security chain thrown over, which is how I always have it whenever I'm in a hotel room. I wondered whether I should open it up and see what they wanted. Perhaps they had been sent from the government to make sure Gobi was safe. If that was the case, there was no risk in having a talk with them. But what if they were there to take Gobi, kick us

out of the hotel, or exact revenge on behalf of whoever took her in the first place? If any of those were correct, then opening the door was the last thing I should do.

I made up my mind and backed away, keeping close to the wall just in case my thoughts about gunmen and Hollywood movies were some kind of premonition. I hid around the wall by the bed and hoped that Gobi would stay asleep.

Another knock.

It wasn't loud or angry, but it made me hold my breath and freeze. What would I do if they forced the door? Would I pretend I'd been asleep and try and talk my way out of it? Or would I try to use the element of surprise and charge past them with Gobi under my arm and head for the fire exit?

The seconds crept by. There were no more knocks, and they didn't try the handle to see if the door was open. After five minutes I edged back to the door and looked out of the peephole, seeing nothing but an empty corridor. I strained from side to side to see if they might be hiding down low, out of normal sight, but after ten minutes I was convinced they had definitely gone. I carefully pulled away the bedding that covered the bottom of the door and eased the door open. Nothing left, nothing right. I quickly closed, locked, and bolted it again.

I found my phone and sent a message to Lu Xin: **Please, get us out of here! I'm really worried that someone's going to grab Gobi. I didn't sleep all night, and I am really scared for our safety.**

I wanted to get in a car and drive back to Beijing that afternoon, but between Kiki, Chris, and Lu Xin, they came up with a different plan. Kiki's contact said she could help get Gobi permission to

fly, and that all we'd need were the basic medical checks carried out by a vet. Once we'd done that, we could be in Beijing in four or five days.

Lu Xin found a flat that I could rent and assured me no one else knew where it was. I didn't want to take any chances. So the next morning I took Gobi down to the basement and handed her over to Lu Xin—the only person in the whole of Urumqi I trusted completely. I was on edge, scanning the parked cars for a grey saloon with two dark-suited males in it. I didn't see it, but that was little comfort to me.

I rushed back up to the lobby, settled my bill, and checked out.

The location of the flat was just as Lu Xin described. I'd not been in that part of the city before, and I was pleased to see that the streets and shops were busy enough to give me and Gobi some cover, without being so crowded that we'd get swamped.

The flat itself was clean and basic, and I felt myself exhale with relief as I said thank you and goodbye to Lu Xin and locked the door behind her.

After Gobi had a good sniff around the entire place, she sat in front of me and looked up into my eyes, just the way she had done on the second morning of the race. It was like she was telling me that she knew something was different but she was okay with it.

"It's quite an adventure we've got ourselves into, isn't it, Gobi?"

She stared back, gave my feet a quick sniff, then trotted over to the couch, jumped up, spun around four times, and curled up in a little ball of sandy-brown fluff.

Gobi wasn't so happy the next day when I took her to the vet. Kiki had arranged for her to be seen by one of the top guys in the city,

and I was excited. For the first time in this whole affair, Gobi and I were about to make some real progress towards getting her home.

Gobi didn't agree.

From the moment we got out of Lu Xin's car and walked into the vet's office, Gobi was on edge. She tucked in behind me at first; then as we walked into the examination room, she planted herself on the floor and refused to move.

I laughed it off at first, but once the vet picked her up and started to check her over, I wondered whether she'd sensed something about the place—or the vet himself—that I'd not picked up. He was about as rough and uncaring as any vet I'd ever seen in my life. He pushed and pulled and didn't show any sign of liking dogs in the least.

He told me her hip was displaced and he needed an X-ray to confirm how bad things were.

"Hold her down," he said to his two assistants as he wheeled a portable machine over. They positioned themselves at either end of the table, then grabbed her front and rear paws and pulled back. Gobi squealed, the whites of her eyes showing, her ears pinned back flat against her head. She was terrified and in obvious pain. I tried to protest, but the vet ignored me and carried on with the X-ray.

Gobi was still shaking an hour later as I carried her back into the flat. I was angry with the vet, especially when he showed me the image he'd taken. It was obvious why she had been limping; while her left femur was snug into the hip, her right femur was angled away from the socket, as if it had been bent away with great force. The vet hadn't bothered to explain what might have caused it but told me Gobi would need surgery to correct it. I didn't bother to ask whether it was a procedure he could perform. There was no way he was touching Gobi again.

After a short sleep, Gobi was up and trotting around again. I wondered—as I had a hundred times already—what had happened to her while I was away. Had she been hit by a car, or was it human hands (or feet) that injured her? Only she knew the answer.

Her fear was now clearly gone, and she was ready for some fun. Watching her hop about, keeping her weight off her right leg, as she had ever since I got her back, I was amazed all over again. She must have been in serious discomfort, yet she chose not to complain or let it spoil her pursuit of fun.

I decided to reward her with a little trip outside.

It was a beautiful late afternoon, and she found some good bushes to sniff around in. I wanted to explore the area and see where I might be able to eat later, so I picked her up and carried her as we set off towards the shops.

Within a few feet a couple of twentysomething girls stopped me. "Gobi?" they asked.

I told them yes and let them take a photo of all of us standing there together. Gobi stared right into the camera like a pro.

A few feet farther on, someone else asked for a photo. I didn't mind, and if Gobi wasn't stressed, I let people make as much of a fuss over her as they wanted. It was great to feel that we were free again.

But when we were twenty feet from the block of flats, I looked across the road and saw it—the grey saloon. It took a moment to sink in, but as soon as I saw the outline of two men in dark suits sitting in the front, I knew the men from the hotel had followed me.

I turned to walk back to the flat. I thought about walking past my block and trying to throw them off the scent, but that was pointless. They must have watched me walk out of the building a few minutes earlier. They had probably been watching me all day. Maybe they even followed me from the hotel.

As I stood in the lift, going up to the seventh floor, the flat didn't feel quite as safe as it had before. I was a little suspicious when the lift stopped on the fifth floor and a man got in. And I didn't think I could trust the woman who was struggling with the lock on her door at the other end of the corridor. Were they all in on it? Or was I just imagining things?

My phone rang as soon as I got back inside the flat, and I jumped at the noise. It was Wendy, an international freelance journalist living in Hong Kong, but it took me a few seconds to register who it was.

"Are you okay?" she asked. "You sound odd."

I told her about the men and the car and how I was getting freaked out by it all.

"That's actually why I'm calling," Wendy said. "It's not just the guys in the car. You've got some pretty big people watching this, Dion."

"What do you mean?" I said.

"Just that—you've got to be careful what you say. I've spoken to some colleagues, and they've heard there are some local government advisers who are watching the story and listening to everything you say. They're okay with what you've been doing so far, but if you criticize the state in any way, they're going to shut this whole thing down. You've got to make sure that anything you say about China is said in a positive way."

"You've talked to people about this? You mean someone's told you this? How could that even happen?"

"Don't worry about how, Dion. I just wanted to make sure you got the message"

"So you think these guys in the suits are from the state?"

"Well, they're not there to steal Gobi, are they?"

I thought about it. Wendy was right. If their intention was to snatch Gobi, they could have done it anytime, and they probably would have done a better job of keeping themselves hidden from me.

"They're here for my protection?"

"Kind of. As long as you do the right thing, you'll be fine. Just don't talk to CNN again."

"CNN? How do you know about CNN?" I'd already had one interview with that news network and was in the process of setting up a second.

"There's bad blood between CNN and the state. Just steer clear, okay?"

The call ended, and I sat on the floor stunned. I felt like I was in a bad spy movie. I didn't know whether I ought to be barricading myself in and sweeping the flat for listening devices or packing Gobi into a bag and climbing down the fire escape. From the way Wendy spoke, it was no big deal, but I found it hard to relax knowing I was being watched so closely.

I sent a message to CNN explaining as vaguely as possible that I had to pull out from the interview. Then I rejected every other interview request from overseas media in my inbox, and I told Lu Xin that I didn't want to speak to any of the Chinese media either. If there was a chance I could say the wrong thing and get myself thrown out of the country—and presumably lose Gobi forever—I wanted to eliminate that risk altogether.

I asked Wendy if she could help find out exactly who the guys in the suits were. I knew it was ridiculous to ask, but I had to know, not for my own safety but for Gobi's. If there was a chance I'd end up being whisked onto the next flight home, I needed to have somewhere to take her.

I spent the rest of the day in the flat. The sun dropped and the

room filled with shadows and street lights, but I didn't turn on any of the lights. It felt safer that way.

I ran through possible scenarios, and none of them made me feel any calmer. If someone broke in and tried to take Gobi, I didn't have a clue how to call the police. And if the guys in suits decided to take me, then I would have no choice but to give in and hope that Lu Xin would take good care of Gobi.

I was powerless. Even though the only thing that had changed about the team was Richard's departure, I suddenly felt alone again. I was back to being the one on whose shoulders everything rested, and, for once in my life, I didn't like it. It seemed too much for me to carry.

20

AT SOME POINT IN ALMOST EVERY RACE, I
question why I'm running in it. Sometimes it's during those early
miles when I'm cold, tired, and just plain grouchy because someone in the tent kept me awake with his snoring. Sometimes it's
when my mind drifts to the finish line that's seven or eight hours
away. Sometimes it's when I need to take on more water or knock
back another salt tablet.

But for every time I ask myself whether running a race is worth
all that discomfort, stress, or fear, a moment comes when I know
the answer is yes. Sometimes all it takes is to crack out a few more
miles and let my body settle into the run. Other times I need to
block out thoughts that aren't helpful. And sometimes I need to
swallow a salt tablet. In every situation the solution is far simpler
than the problem.

On the night before Gobi and I finally left Urumqi, I looked
about me and smiled. Even though I had not known any of them two
days earlier, I was surrounded by friends. As the laughter got louder
and the evening wore on, I knew how grateful I was for the simple
way in which their friendships came along at just the right time.

These friendships had started after my second night in the flat. I had spent most of the morning sitting around with Gobi, hoping the door wouldn't burst open and someone rush in to grab either one of us. Eventually Gobi had to get down to ground level and do her business, and we left the flat. As I waited by her favourite bush near the entrance, I watched people going in and out of a restaurant nearby. A guy was manning a barbecue out front, and the smells coming off it were incredible. So, because I'd had enough of eating instant noodles out of a plastic pot in the flat, I decided to take Gobi back up, make sure she was settled, and then come back down and get a quick meal.

That was one of the best decisions I've ever made. I'd eaten Xinjiang barbecue on the last day of the race, but this was even better. The waiter brought over great chunks of perfectly spiced mutton on foot-long metal skewers. I licked the grease from my fingers, sat back, and sighed.

I looked up and noticed a couple of people out on the street staring in at me, grinning from ear to ear. I smiled and waved, then mimed how full I was, and they laughed. It was a fun moment, and soon they came in, bringing a dozen others with them. They all were about my age or a little younger, and they introduced themselves to me, said something about Gobi, and invited me to have a drink and more food with them.

They knew the restaurant staff, and as we tried to communicate in broken English and with translation apps on our phones, they fed me some wickedly spicy noodles, put a shot glass of clear liquid in my hand, and invited me to knock it back with them. Whatever it was, I lost my voice for a few seconds after it went down. A lot more laughter followed, and the night ended with me

tripping over the doorstep on the way out, full of great food, a little too much booze, and the sound of new friends' laughter in my ears.

The next night was my last in Urumqi. Kiki had worked wonders and arranged for me and Gobi to fly to Beijing the following day. She'd even flown to Urumqi herself to make sure that everything went smoothly. She knew what a big deal it was, as well as the risks we were facing. Once Gobi was settled and I'd packed what little I'd brought with me, I walked back to the restaurant, hoping to meet my new friends again.

We had another great evening. A couple of shots kicked things off; then before I knew it, the table was filled with skewers and noodles and, eventually, the most amazing cast-iron structure— like the frame of a lampshade but with inch-long spikes sticking out—covered with wonderful-tasting lamb. We laughed about things I can't even remember, talked about nothing much, and when it came time to pay the bill, they insisted I put my cash away.

"Drink tea?" said the one guy who had a few words of English.

I'm more of a coffee guy, but almost two decades of living among the English has taught me to say yes anytime anyone offers tea. Not because I have grown to love the drink but because I know that the offer is actually an invitation to hang out.

So I said yes and followed them all as they walked up the road and walked through a low wooden door set back from the street. I'd assumed we were going to one of their homes, but once inside, it was obvious that this was no home. It looked more like a high-end jewellery store; only instead of display cases filled with rings and necklaces, there were glass-fronted cabinets containing metal tins as big as a pizza and four times as deep.

"I sell tea!" my new friend said. Then, guiding me to a mahogany table that ran almost the entire length of the room, he said, "Sit!"

I watched as he sat in a chair opposite me and arranged an assortment of earth-coloured teapots and delicate bowls, a wooden-handled knife, and a set of mats in front of him. The room fell silent, and everybody watched as his hands glided across his tools, first opening one of the metal tins and then prying a nugget of tea away from the disk inside. He poured water into bowls and swirled it around with all the precision and grace of a magician at a card table. And when, after a few minutes, he poured me a cup of pale amber tea and invited me to drink, I thought I'd never tasted anything quite as wonderful.

More cups of tea followed, all prepared and drunk in almost total silence. The experience wasn't awkward or weird; it was special. I'd never known anything quite like it.

Gradually the chatting and laughter returned. They passed their mobile phones and showed me clips of them dancing around a flat celebrating one of their birthdays. They showed me pictures of them hanging out in a park and of getting dressed up for some big night out. They were fun, and being with them reminded me of the way the search team knew how to laugh with one another. Nobody was trying to be cool, and nobody was trying to exclude other people from the group.

This kind of atmosphere was the exact opposite of what I'd experienced as a teenager in Warwick. Whether it was the tea or the company or the fact that finally, after so long, I was about to get Gobi one giant step closer to home, I started to feel a profound sense of peace about everything.

Eventually it was time to say goodbye. We hugged one another out in front of the shop, and I walked back to my flat holding two

beautifully presented bags of tea they had given me. Going up in the lift, I realized they'd paid the bill at the restaurant yet again. They'd never asked me to show them Gobi, even though when I showed them the WeChat group and some of the news coverage about her, their eyes lit up. They didn't want anything from me. They were just offering friendship with no strings attached.

I was nervous about saying goodbye to Gobi at the airport check-in desk, but Kiki had made it clear that there was no way for her to fly with me in the cabin. "Take care down there," I said through the bars of the crate we'd bought. Gobi had an old T-shirt of mine in there with her, and a cushion that was pure luxury. Even so, she knew something odd was happening, I could tell.

For almost all of the three-hour flight, I sat in the cabin fretting about Gobi. Could I trust that she'd made it onto the plane? Enough things had gone wrong already to make me nervous about that possibility. Then there was the experience of being in the hold. I knew she'd cope with the cold—her performance in the Tian Shan mountains proved that she was a rugged little pooch—but how would she manage with all those strange noises? The last time she was locked up was when she was with Nurali, and she had run away from there. I couldn't imagine how stressful she might be finding the experience of being locked up again.

I'd hoped that Gobi was going to take the flight in her stride and waited nervously near the baggage carousel. When her crate was finally wheeled out to me, the sense of relief I felt was so much greater than I imagined it would be. It didn't last. One look and I knew that Gobi had struggled on the flight: she had chewed through her leash, smashed the water bottle, and looked like she had gone

ten rounds with a boxer. She had obviously spent the journey feeling petrified, and seeing her in this state made me realize getting all the way to the UK was going to be really stressful for this pup.

Kiki took us straight to her kennels and outlined the plan on the way. Once Gobi had spent thirty days in Kiki's facility, she would be allowed to fly back to England, where she'd spend four months in quarantine. I didn't like the idea of Gobi spending so much time away from me, but it was by far the best option. I had some work commitments that I needed to get back to, and Kiki promised to send lots of photos and videos of our little girl, keeping me constantly updated about everything. Kiki clearly loved animals, and she seemed to forge an instant bond with Gobi. The feeling was mutual, and I knew they'd both get plenty of cuddles and kisses from each other in the month they would be together.

Even so, saying goodbye to Gobi the next morning was far harder than I anticipated. After all we'd been through, especially in the hotel, I knew she trusted me completely. I'd left her in the hotel or the flat but never for more than an hour or two. She had always greeted me with a massive shower of affection and excitement when I returned. But what would she think when it dawned on her that I wasn't coming back in a few minutes? What would it be like when I finally saw her again, a month down the line, and yet again I'd leave her in an unfamiliar place full of other animals? I feared it might wound her far more deeply than whatever had scarred her head or damaged her hip.

I'd stopped talking to journalists and TV producers almost as soon as I got to the flat, but that didn't mean that I had stopped talking with other people about how Gobi's story could help raise

awareness of the importance of looking after abandoned dogs. As well as helping us find a great publisher to work with, Paul de Souza had also introduced us to Jay Kramer, a lawyer who represented some of the biggest writers in the world. Jay knew exactly what he was doing and was helping us think through some of the other ways to share Gobi's story.

Jay and I had been talking for about a week. When he called later that evening, I assumed he wanted to fill me in on his latest conversations with partners. Instead, he had some unexpected—and unwelcome—news.

"Are you making plans for some kind of website?"

"No," I said. I had thought about it vaguely but had done nothing about it. "Why?"

"Someone's just registered at least two domain names that relate to Gobi. They've registered the trademark too."

I was stunned as Jay told me who it was, and I realized I knew the people who were responsible for this. I felt instantly sick and queasy, like I did after I helped Tommy that day. I was struggling to process this new information, and all I could think to say was, "Why?"

"Whoever's done it is trying to cash in. They know that Gobi's been found and that she's coming home, so the story's about to get even bigger."

"But nobody else has ever cared for Gobi. Nobody else owns her."

"Not yet, they don't."

My fears ran deep as though I were in a terrifying nightmare. I thought we'd left all the danger behind us in Urumqi, but was Gobi still at risk? If someone was making a play to claim Gobi on the Internet, wouldn't it make sense for them to try and get Gobi in the flesh? If they had the dog, they could control the story.

Was that why I was being followed by the men in suits and the grey saloon? I'd always thought they were from the government, but was it possible that they were actually reporting to someone else entirely?

These thoughts stayed with me like a mosquito bite. I couldn't stop returning to them long after my call with Jay ended. The more attention I paid them, the more inflamed and painful these dark fears became.

I spent the entire flight home going over the same thoughts. Images of Gobi getting stolen from Kiki's kennels flashed through my mind. Conspiracy theories about what might happen cast deep shadows over me. And a desperate desire to make sure that Gobi was okay left me feeling hollow inside.

Added to that, I was thinking about work.

I had been away from my job for almost two weeks, and I worried that I was pushing the limits of the company's generosity. Everyone had been supportive throughout, and there was never any pressure to return from Urumqi, but I knew my colleagues were working extra hard to cover my workload in my absence. I didn't want to abuse their kindness or take advantage of it.

But I knew that, yet again, I had a choice to make.

I could stick with the plan and leave Gobi in Kiki's care for the next twenty-nine days while we waited for the all-clear on her rabies blood test. I could get on with my work, get back to spending quality time with Lucja, and wait for Gobi to be flown back to the UK, where she'd then spend four months in a secure kennel quarantine. We'd be able to visit her if we wanted, but it was not recommended because the confusion it caused for dogs was frequently traumatic. So if she did ride out the quarantine in the UK, she'd have to do it alone.

The other option was for Gobi to wait the twenty-nine days for the all-clear on the rabies and then spend ninety days living a normal life in Beijing rather than four months locked in a UK facility. With the right tests and paperwork at the end of the ninety days, she could then fly back to the UK without having to set a paw in a quarantine facility.

I knew I could trust Kiki. She had been great right from the very first e-mails we exchanged. But was it fair to leave her the burden of looking after a dog for so long that—just maybe—someone was planning to steal from her? Could I be sure that every single visitor to the kennels would be legit? Could Kiki be asked to maintain that level of vigilance and still run her business at the same time?

I felt guilty leaving Gobi, and if something happened to her again as it did after the first time I said goodbye, I doubted I would have the strength to push through it. I had reached the edges of what I thought I could endure. All I wanted was for these problems to fade away, for the threats to stop, and for Lucja and me to get back to the job of bringing Gobi home.

I knew exactly what I had to do. After hours of thinking it through on my final flight back to the UK, I came up with a plan—the only solution that made any kind of sense.

The trouble was, I had absolutely no idea how I was going to explain it to Lucja or to my boss. They'd think I'd lost it completely.

PART 6

21

SAYING GOODBYE TO LUCJA WAS DIFFICULT. I
had been home only a week when, for the second time in less than
a month, I bought a last-minute plane ticket and made the twelve-
hour journey back to China. I've travelled a lot for work over the
years, but this was different. This time I'd be gone for four months.

I'd thought it through, and it all made perfect sense. I needed
to go back to Beijing and be with Gobi until her rabies results
came through. After that, I figured I might as well stay the following three months so we could live together. The alternative of
four months alone in quarantine outside Heathrow Airport simply
wasn't an option. I couldn't leave her alone again. A 120-day sentence would turn her into a different dog.

Just like Lucja, my bosses were wholly understanding and supportive. As soon as I returned from Beijing, I phoned and told them
I was worried about Gobi, even though we'd finally found her. I
mentioned that there were mysterious things going on behind the
scenes and that I had to go back to China and spend the duration
of the quarantine period with Gobi. I offered to resign, but they
refused. Instead, they rushed through approval for a six-month

sabbatical. That allowed me to leave the UK knowing I could focus fully on Gobi and have a job to come back to once the dust settled. In the eleven years I'd been working for them, I'd never known of anyone else taking a sabbatical for something like this, and I was staggered by their kindness.

They say it takes a village to raise a child. I think it takes almost half a planet to rescue a dog. At least, that's what it seemed like with Gobi. So many people had helped, from the thousands of supporters who had given money online to the search team who had pounded the streets and gone without sleep in Urumqi. My work colleagues had covered for me, and my bosses had given me generous time off. Kiki and her team had already done much more than I could have asked, and Lucja—who was also surrounded by an army of caring, supportive friends—never once wavered in her unrelenting support of my crazy mission. I could only do what I did because of the help of all those people.

I was looking forward to arriving back in Beijing and seeing Gobi again. I knew Kiki would take great care of her, but in the back of my mind was the thought that anything was possible. At times it seemed as though every other Facebook message I received was yet another warning not to trust anyone and not to let Gobi out of my sight.

Kiki met me at the airport. I climbed into the back of the van to have my face covered in doggie kisses as Gobi scrambled all over me, her tail going a million miles an hour. My reception was just like the night we were reunited back at the Ma family home. Gobi's joy was infectious, and the van was soon full of tears and laughter.

When she had finally calmed down enough for me to speak, I held her in the crook of my arm and said, "I guess this is where

you and I start our new life together." She stared back at me, those big eyes locked on mine, just as they had been during the race. My head told me that she couldn't understand what I was saying, but my heart said otherwise. This little dog knew exactly what I meant. And I was convinced that in her own way, she was telling me that whatever the next stage of the adventure held for us, she was all in.

Kiki had found us a place to stay for the first night, but the next day it was time to find a proper home for Gobi and me. With four months to wait until she had passed the strict UK requirements, I wanted to make sure we found a home where she would feel comfortable and safe.

So, like a couple of college graduates who had just moved to a new city, we went looking for a home.

The first place belonged to another pet owner, also one of Kiki's clients. The man was temporarily moving his family back to Mexico and had generously offered to let us stay free of charge while we were in Beijing.

It was a beautiful home in a gated community. High-end cars drove along pristine streets and parked in front of perfectly manicured lawns. The owner and his two dogs welcomed us warmly, and I was pleased to see Gobi trot up and give both the Labradors a friendly sniff and follow them around the den.

"Let me show you the rest of the house," said the owner as he stepped over a low wooden barrier at the bottom of the stairs.

Instinctively I picked up Gobi and lifted her over.

"Oh," he said. "No dogs upstairs. They stay down here."

Oh dear, I thought. "Okay," I said, putting Gobi back down on the other side of the barrier.

Before I'd taken my second step, Gobi was whimpering. By the time I'd gotten halfway up, she had pushed her way through

the barrier and was right beside me. I picked her up and followed the guy into an immaculate lounge area that looked as if it was prepped for a *Vogue* photo shoot.

Gobi was straining to get down, her tail shaking wildly. "I don't think this is going to work," I said. "You have such a lovely place. If we stay here, it'll end in tears."

The man smiled back. "I think you're probably right."

Only two months had passed since I first met Gobi, and even though we had been together for only a few days of the race and the week in Urumqi, the bond between us was strong. Now that we had been reunited for the second time, she seemed determined not to let me out of her sight.

The flat we looked at next was everything the previous house was not: it was small, was a little bit shabby, and contained almost no furniture. It was perfect.

I particularly liked the fact that it was up on the eleventh floor. Even though I didn't know how Gobi escaped from Nurali's home, or whether she had been taken, I didn't want to take any chances. After all, it had only taken a few seconds for Gobi to burst through the dog barrier that kept the Labradors out. If she did manage to find a way out of the flat door, surely she wouldn't be able to hack the lift.

Kiki's guys took us to the local Walmart equivalent—WuMart—and we returned to the flat with all the essentials for the next four months: bed linens, a toaster, a frying pan, and a monster bag of dog food.

I don't think I'll ever forget the moment I said goodbye to our helpers and closed the door behind them. I took a moment to look at Gobi, who stared, as she always did at times such as this, right back at me.

"This is it," I said. "Just you and me." I was excited but pretty daunted as well. I knew enough about China to know that I was helpless. I couldn't speak more than four words, and I couldn't read a single character.

If it was possible, Gobi's stare grew even deeper. She tilted her head to one side, trotted back into the flat, jumped up on the couch, curled herself into a ball, gave two heavy sighs, and closed her eyes.

"Fair enough," I said, sitting down beside her. "If you're not stressed, I guess I won't be either."

During the coming days, I got to know Gobi a whole lot better. I knew from the race and our time in Urumqi that she liked to sleep up against me, using me as her pillow, but in Beijing she took being affectionate and tactile to a whole new level.

As soon as I stepped out of the shower the following morning, she was licking my feet and shins as if they were covered in bacon. I just laughed and let her have at it. It was quite a change from the way I'd tried to avoid touching her when I first saw her in the desert. And even though I still didn't have any medical evidence that proved she didn't have rabies, she had charmed her way to my heart. I couldn't resist.

When the rest of me was dry, we went out to explore the local area. I'd seen a few shops at the bottom of the block of flats and a large shopping centre half a mile away. It was a beautiful summer's day with no pollution that I could see, and I fancied a stroll along the nearby canal and a decent cup of coffee.

The walk was easy enough. The coffee, however, was impossible.

I went into the first Starbucks I saw and waited my time in the queue.

I shuffled up to the counter and was just about to give my order when the server looked at Gobi in my arm and pointed to the door.

"No dogs!"

"Oh, it's okay," I said. "I'll just get a takeaway."

"No. Take dog outside." She waved her hands at me as if trying to flick off something unpleasant from her wrists.

I left the store and continued walking. No way was I going to tie Gobi up and leave her outside.

We got pretty much the same reaction at the next coffee place as well as the one after it, where we stopped and sat on the seats out front. I was giving Gobi some water from my hand, just as I did during the race, when a guy came out and told us to leave.

"It's only water!" I said, a bit annoyed by now.

"No!" he shouted. "Must not do. You go."

We walked home more than a little dejected. In a small way I felt that I knew what it was like for Gobi and the countless other stray dogs in China. Being treated like an outcast was no fun at all. Being judged and rejected like that was painful.

If Gobi was bothered by it, she didn't let on. In fact, she seemed happier than ever. She held her head high, and her eyes shone bright as we walked. In many ways it was impossible to tell that she'd been a stray dog on the city streets a couple of weeks earlier, and the deep scar on the top of her head was slowly healing. But the way she carefully held her right hind leg up, avoiding putting weight on it, made it perfectly clear that we needed to fast-track her operation.

Before that, however, I had another task to deal with. One that was even more urgent. I needed to register ownership of Gobi under my name. Chinese law states that every dog owner must

carry his licence whenever out in public with his dog. I'd heard that if I was caught without one, Gobi could be taken away that instant.

Kiki helped with the paperwork, and once it was done and I slipped the dog licence into my wallet, I felt a huge weight lift from my shoulders. Not only was I now legal, but I also had another line of defense against someone else trying to claim ownership of Gobi.

The more time I spent with Gobi, the more I learned about her. The more I learned about her, the more intrigued and amazed by her I became.

Every time we walked past a piece of rubbish on the pavement, she'd pull at the lead and drag me over to let her scavenge for food. It told me that her street days in Urumqi probably weren't her only experience of having to fend for herself, and I'd often watch her devour the leftover remnants inside a takeaway wrapper and wonder just how many secrets her life held.

In spite of being a connoisseur of street food, she had already shown me in Urumqi that she could adapt easily to a more sophisticated style of life. I guess not every dog is suited to flat living, but Gobi settled into it with ease. In many ways she never seemed happier than when she was curled up beside me, staring deep into my eyes as we hung out on the couch. She didn't bark when I was with her, she didn't attack what little furniture we had, and on the few occasions when she didn't manage to hold on until we'd got outside to do her business, I could see she felt guilty about it.

The first time Gobi had an accident was soon after we moved in. I'd decided to get my coffee fix in the flat that morning, and I didn't quite read her signs correctly. I thought Gobi was spinning

around and sniffing the door because she'd heard a dog barking in a nearby flat.

It was only when she disappeared into the bathroom for a minute and re-emerged, head down, walking sideways up to me, that I knew something was wrong. With her ears pinned down and head hung low, she wore a look of complete shame.

I checked the bathroom and found a small lake of dog pee on the floor. Poor thing. I apologized profusely, and as soon as I'd cleaned up, I took her downstairs to her preferred toilet stop in the bushes near the entrance.

The only thing Gobi didn't like was being left alone in the flat. I tried to leave her as little as possible, but there were times when I had no other choice. If I needed to go to the gym to run on the treadmill, or if we were out of food and I needed to go to the supermarket, she had to stay back. Almost every time we did go out together, we would be spotted at least once or twice and asked for a photo. Gobi's story had been a huge hit all over China, and leaving her tied up outside a supermarket or Starbucks while I went inside wasn't a risk I was prepared to take.

But leaving her was hard. I'd try to slip out the door as quickly as I could, often having to gently block her from following me. I'd always check and double-check that the door was locked, and as I walked away, I could hear her making the same noise that she did at the river crossing. That pained, high-pitched whimpering sound cut through me every time.

As tough as it was to leave her, whenever I returned, she was just as overjoyed as she had been at the Ma family house the night we were reunited. She'd spin and sprint and yelp with pure adrenaline-rush excitement. Eventually she'd calm down enough

for me to pick her up, and a deep sense of calm would fall over her, again just like at the river crossing. It's still the same today; whenever Gobi is in my arms, I'm convinced that she doesn't have a care in the world.

To be trusted so much by a living creature is a powerful thing, especially when you know it could choose to leave at any time. But Gobi never showed any signs of wanting to be anywhere other than right by my side.

Every morning I'd wake up and find her staring at me, her head so close to mine that I could feel her breath on my cheek. Most days, if I didn't start playing with her soon enough, she'd start licking my face. That was one sign of doggie affection that I didn't find quite so cute back in the early days, and it got me straight out of bed.

We'd get downstairs quickly so she could do her business, but it was always obvious to me that what Gobi wanted more than anything was to get back up to the flat and settle down for a good cuddle.

For me to be on the receiving end of that kind of love and devotion is a special thing. To be able to care for her, to be able to give her the kind of attention and affection she needs, touches something deep down in my heart.

Love. Devotion. Attention. Affection. In many ways I feel they all disappeared from my life when I hit ten. A whole decade would pass before I met Lucja and felt all that good stuff begin to flood back into my life.

What Gobi introduced to my life was the chance for me to treat someone young and vulnerable in the way I wanted to be treated when my life was shaken out of control. Gobi needed me. Even though I'm still not sure I can adequately put words to the

feelings, I know that rescuing her has healed wounds I didn't know were within me.

Not that it was perfect. The TV, for example, was terrible.

I expected there to be at least a basic range of channels. Maybe a little BBC or some Fox News from time to time. No chance. All I could get were two channels: a Chinese news service that looped an hour-long summary of the previous day's events and a movie channel with the occasional Hollywood offering presented with Chinese subtitles. I got my hopes up when I discovered this second one, but it turned out that most of your favourite B-list movie stars have an awfully long catalogue of films that are so bad they've never made it to our Western screens. I watched some truly terrible movies in those early days. I eventually got bored and gave up trying. I was fed up with nothing to do.

The Internet was a problem too. It took me a week to work out how to get around the extensive filters the Chinese authorities put on the web, but my hack made streaming any video content almost impossible.

Gobi and I tried to spend more time outside. The mile-long footpath along the canal was always a good place to walk, especially when the construction workers were on their breaks. They ignored us as they gathered around the food vendors on the street, who had a great trade going among them. Gobi and I soon learned that the best stalls of all were the ones serving jianbing—what I called a Beijing burrito. Think of a thin crepe with an egg cooked inside it and a load of crushed, crispy fried wonton, delicious spices, and chilli. Gobi and I couldn't get enough of those.

We had got thrown out of almost all of the coffee shops we

tried, but, thankfully, we found a Starbucks that was happy to break the rules and let us sit outside. Best of all was a little independent café where the staff not only allowed us inside but even ignored me when I put Gobi on the seat and fed her a bit of my pastry.

For a city that doesn't allow dogs in taxis or buses, and has only recently passed a law allowing guide dogs to travel on subways, this was a major success. We made sure we supported them well throughout our stay.

As fun as it was to learn about this new life together, one thing continually worried me—Gobi's damaged hip. She did her best to hide it and had learned how to skip along without putting too much weight on it. But if I ever picked her up the wrong way or tried to hold her on my left side instead of my right, she'd let out a little cry of pain.

In addition, the injury on her head hadn't healed as well as Kiki or I had hoped.

So after a week in the flat, I broke the bad news to Gobi.

"No café for you and me today, little one. We're going to see the vet."

22

I COULDN'T STAND THE NOISE. I STOOD IN THE corridor and tried to block out the sound of Gobi gripped by pain and fear, but it was no use. Those squeals and cries were the most horrible noise I'd ever heard in my whole life.

I'd read somewhere that to prevent dogs from associating deep pain and fear with their owners, you shouldn't be in the same room with them when they're given an injection. Even without that advice, I don't think I would have been able to be by her side.

When the anaesthetic kicked in and she finally grew quiet, one of the nurses came and found me.

"She's fine. Do you want to come in?"

Thanks to Kiki, Gobi was about to be operated on in one of the top veterinary hospitals in the city. And thanks to the Chinese media, all of the nurses and doctors had already heard of Gobi. That (plus a good word from Kiki) meant Gobi had the most experienced surgical team and both Kiki and I were allowed to wash up, put on the blue scrubs, and join the team in the operating theatre.

After numerous scans and extensive consultations, the staff unanimously confirmed what I'd been told in Urumqi—that the cause of Gobi's pain and strange hopping was an injury to her right hip. Whether she had been hit by a car or a human, it was impossible to say, but sometime during her runabout in Urumqi, she'd picked up the injury, which had forced her hip out of the pelvis.

The staff recommended Gobi have a femoral head ostectomy: a form of hip surgery where the top of the femur is removed but not replaced with anything, leaving the body to heal itself and the joint to reform with scar tissue.

I'd been reassured a dozen times that this was a standard procedure that could yield excellent results. I was confident in the team and felt we were in safe hands. But as I stood and watched them about to begin the hour-long operation, I was still a nervous wreck.

Again, it was the noises that got me, though this time Gobi was too heavily drugged to make a sound. She was lying with her tongue hanging out like an old sock, breathing steadily into the mask placed over her mouth, while the nurses shaved away all the fur from her right hip. What bothered me this time was the sound of the machines that were monitoring her heart rate and oxygen levels. Ever since Garry's death, I have always hated hearing the sound of those machines on TV. They remind me of the night I stood in my sister's room and listened to the medics try to save him, and whenever I hear the steady beeps, I ask myself the same, simple question: *If I'd got out of bed sooner, would I have been able to save him?*

A conversation broke out among the doctors, their voices slightly raised. Kiki must have sensed my concern because she tapped me

on the shoulder and spoke softly. She told me they were trying to decide how much of the drug to give her to prevent a heart attack without going too far and inducing one.

"I hope they know what they're doing," I muttered. I felt physically sick inside.

Eventually, when the room quietened down and they started to operate, I told Kiki I had to go. "Come and get me as soon as it's all done," I said. "I can't be in here."

The hour felt more like a month, but when it was finally over, the head surgeon came to reassure me that the surgery had gone well and Gobi would soon be coming around. I sat beside her in the recovery room and watched her gradually wake up.

There was a moment when she looked at me, and everything was just as it was every morning, her big eyes locked on mine. But a second later the pain must have kicked in, for her high-pitched whimpering started up again. Looking at her, listening to her, I understood clearly that she was in a world of pain. Nothing I could do seemed to help.

Within less than a day, Gobi's true spirit was shining through again. She was in pain from the operation, and I knew her hip would take weeks to fully repair itself, but by the time I got her back to the flat, she was back to her old tail-wagging, face-licking self.

I, on the other hand, was feeling unsettled. I couldn't be sure whether it was seeing Gobi in pain that had bothered me or the memories of Garry's death, but I knew for certain that in the days and weeks that followed, I was still worried about Gobi's safety.

Right from the start of our time in Beijing, I'd felt a little

nervous about the number of people who recognized Gobi. But as we spent more and more time in the flat during her recovery, I grew a little paranoid. If I was down in the lobby waiting for a lift and someone else joined me—especially if the person wasn't Chinese—I'd make a point of getting out at either the tenth or the twelfth floor and using the stairs to reach the eleventh, looking over my shoulder as I went. I knew it was silly, and I knew that if someone did want to snatch Gobi, it would take a lot more than my amateur spy impression to keep us safe. But the instinct to be suspicious about strangers was too strong to resist.

It didn't help that the rest of the flats on my floor were also short-term rentals. That meant there was a constant turnover of people. Remembering the visit from the guys in suits in Urumqi, I eyed all residents carefully.

"It's okay to go out and live a normal life," said Kiki after I shared my fears one day.

A normal life? I wasn't even sure I knew what that meant anymore. Four months earlier I'd been working sixty-hour weeks, away three nights out of seven, fitting in my training at nine or ten at night while others were watching TV. I was filling my time with work, training, and trying to live life with Lucja in our home in Edinburgh. Now I was on long-term leave, living thousands of miles away, barely running, trying to keep safe a little dog who seemed at times to be the most famous pup in the whole world. Normal was a lifetime away.

I was also concerned about the number of photo requests Gobi got whenever we went out. Most people were great, and I liked that Gobi made people happy, but I knew, for some, she was just a cute photo opportunity.

Part of the stray dog problem in China stems from people's buying pedigree dogs, bringing them back to their flats, and then getting annoyed when the dogs make a mess on the floor or trash the furniture. In a country where there's so much wealth, dogs are sometimes treated as a fashion accessory—temporary and disposable.

Gobi deserved better than that.

A month into my stay in Beijing, the result of the rabies test was due.

All throughout the twenty-nine days we'd spent waiting, my instincts had told me Gobi would be fine. I knew the test would come back clear and we could move on to the next phase of waiting the ninety days for the second round of tests. But as much as I believed this, a part of me had started to wonder. What if Gobi did have rabies after all? What then? If we couldn't bring Gobi back to the UK, would we move to China to live together? Instead of bringing Gobi home, would we have to bring home to Gobi?

The result was as we expected. Gobi didn't have rabies. I exhaled a huge sigh of relief, cheered with Lucja, and shared the news with the rest of the world via our growing social media accounts. The reaction brought a tear to my eye.

So many strangers were heavily invested in Gobi's story, and it still amazes me to read of the ways in which she has touched people's lives. For instance, one woman who has cancer told me that she looks at our Facebook, Twitter, and Instagram pages every day to see what Gobi and I are up to. "I've been with you from the start," she told me.

I love that the story isn't just about Gobi and me trying to

get home. Whether people have lost their jobs, are suffering with depression, or are going through marriage troubles, this little dog has put a smile on so many people's faces.

In the end, it was the running that helped ease my fears. Soon after Gobi's operation, I was invited by someone I'd met in Urumqi to take part in a single-stage race in a different part of the Gobi Desert. The organizers had gathered fifty of the world's best sixty-mile specialists for the race in Gansu Province, next to Xinjiang. It's not a distance I usually run—at least, not as a one-day, point-to-point race—but somehow I was still in pretty good shape from the training I'd managed to put in for the Atacama race I'd skipped.

But now the Gansu race organizers were offering free lodging and free return flights home to Edinburgh in exchange for me taking part in the sixty-mile run and giving them a PR boost by meeting with journalists. I had quite a few requests for interviews and photo shoots, all of them from journalists interested in getting an update on Gobi and capturing me in action. The thought of being able to use the ticket to fly back and see Lucja again was too tempting to resist.

Just four days before the race, I received even better news from the race organizers. They had a few spaces still available and were willing to pay to fly in any other elite runners who might want to compete. I called Lucja right away. It was a crazy idea to come all the way to China and run so far at such short notice, especially as six weeks earlier she'd completed a brutal five-day, 300-mile challenge across Holland. But as well as being a world-class runner, who finished thirteenth among the women in the 2016 Marathon

des Sables, Lucja's a tough lady who loves an adventure. She said yes immediately. Forty-eight hours later she was on a plane heading east.

I was a little worried about Gobi. But Kiki had promised to take good care of her, and I could trust her. Besides, I had the feeling that Gobi wouldn't mind a few days of serious pampering in Kiki's recovery pool and grooming parlour.

As soon as I knew Lucja was coming, I was all in. Running has played a special part in our relationship, and the race coincided with our eleventh wedding anniversary. I couldn't think of a better way to celebrate how far we'd come together.

One of my favourite memories of running with Lucja comes from the first Marathon des Sables we competed in together. As with most multi-stage ultras, you get your finisher's medal at the end of the long stage (usually the penultimate stage of the race). I was surprised how well I was doing, and as the long stage came to a close, I knew I had secured my finisher's spot just outside the top one hundred. For a first-time runner—who almost quit on day one—among thirteen hundred other runners, it wasn't too bad a result.

I cleared the final ridge that hid the finish line from view and saw the crowds up ahead, cheering the runners home. And there, a few hundred feet back from the finish, was Lucja. She'd started earlier than me that day, and I hadn't expected to see her on the course. But there she was, her hand shielding her eyes from the sun as she looked back in my direction.

"What are you doing here?" I said when I finally reached her. "I thought you'd have finished an hour ago."

"I could have," she said. "But I wanted to finish with you, so I waited."

We crossed the line hand in hand. She could have finished so much higher up, but she chose to wait for me.

I still think about that when I run today.

It was good to get back to the desert, good to be able to run without traffic or pollution, and most of all, great to see Lucja. We'd been apart for almost six weeks, and I wanted to spend every minute I could with her. So even though I thought I could have placed fairly well, I was far happier to hang back and run the race together with her.

The route led us twice around a thirty-mile loop. It was a hot day, easily in the 110s, and as we completed the first lap, we saw that the medical tent was already doing good business. And a bunch of people had decided to throw in the towel and quit. They had started the race far too quickly, had pushed too hard, had struggled in the conditions, and didn't want to keep pushing through a second loop. I've bailed on more than my fair share of training runs, though never because of the heat. It's the Scottish mud, wind, and rain that send me back to the car.

We ran the first thirty miles a bit slower than I'd planned, but I figured we still had a good eight hours to get around the rest of the course before the fourteen-hour cut-off.

As we started the second loop, Lucja had second thoughts.

"You go, Dion. I don't have it in me," she said.

Lucja and I have run enough races to know when it's time to throw in the towel and when it's time to grit it out. I took a long look at her. She was tired, but she was still fighting. This was no time for towels.

"We can do this," I said. "I've got a television crew following

me, and the organizers have really looked after us; we owe it to them. I'll get you round it. Just stick with me."

She did what she does so well and dug in. We kept going, running from marker to marker, ticking the miles off as we went.

Things got worse, with eighteen miles to go, when a sandstorm struck up. Visibility was cut to less than one hundred feet, and it was getting hard to see the markers. I thought back to the huge sandstorm at the end of the long day when Tommy nearly died. I didn't have Gobi to look after, but I had Lucja to protect. With no sign of any race officials around us, I started to formulate an emergency plan if the sandstorm got any worse or if Lucja started to tank.

She didn't, and the storm eventually lifted, but the winds were still strong. They had blown our hats off, and our eyes stung with sand. Debris was flying everywhere. We pushed on, though we were making slow progress between markers, only moving on to the next one if and when we could see it. Lucja tried taking a gel to give her some energy, but every time she did, she threw it back up again.

When we reached the next checkpoint, it was a mess, everything blown away and the volunteers looking shell-shocked. We pressed on, though, despite the fact that we were running slower than ever. I thought it was odd that nobody was passing us, but I put all my effort into encouraging Lucja to block out the pain and keep going.

We passed another half-destroyed checkpoint and kept going, knowing that we had eight miles left to run.

It was dark by now, and when a car approached with its headlights on full, the whole sky lit up. "What are you doing?" the driver asked.

"We're racing," I said, too tired to try and be funny.

"But a lot of people have been pulled already because of the sandstorm."

"Nobody told us at the checkpoint. We've only a few miles left, and we're not stopping now."

"Okay then," he said, before driving off.

Those last few miles were some of the hardest I've ever seen Lucja complete. Amid tears, shouts, and serious pain, she held on to an unshakable determination to finish.

As we crossed the line, I held her hand.

"Happy anniversary," I said. "I'm so proud of you."

We got to spend one night together back in Beijing before Lucja had to fly home for work. Kiki met us outside the airport, and yet again Gobi was a hurricane of excitement in the back of the van. This time, though, it wasn't just me she was licking. Gobi seemed to know instantly that Lucja was special and gave her the full welcoming experience.

Gobi showed Lucja her affection all night. I crashed soon after we made it back to the flat, but Lucja didn't get any sleep at all because Gobi decided that an even longer bonding session was required. By the time I woke up, they were inseparable.

I made some big decisions after the race.

First, I decided I was going to say no to all interview requests for the rest of my time in Beijing. Some journalists had contacted me during the race, telling me they needed to get a photo of Gobi and asking if they could visit her at Kiki's place while I was out of town. They'd even gone to the point of directly contacting Kiki, who of course said no. I didn't like this, as I'd tried hard to keep our location secret.

Being with Lucja had made me think about what life might be like when Gobi and I finally got home. I was sure there would be some press interest for a week or two, but I knew I'd want life to return to normal as quickly as possible—whatever the new normal would look like. So I made the choice to stop doing interviews. It was time for Gobi and me to go dark.

The second decision I made was about running.

The sixty-miler had been a piece of cake. I looked at the times of the different finishers and worked out that I could have made it into the top ten—not a bad possible result given that the elite field included some 2:05 marathon runners from Kenya. A couple of weeks later I had a conversation with the organizers of an upcoming 104-mile ultra-race, the Mt Gaoligong Ultra. As part of the invitation to run, we talked about my doing a few interviews with UK running magazines. The opportunity to travel to another part of China, to the city of Tengchong in Yunnan Province, close to Myanmar, was a great drawcard for me. I'd never done a non-stop hundred-miler before, so I certainly wasn't signing up to compete with the idea of winning.

It was a brutal race in the mountains. Climbing 29,000 feet altogether, I was pushed to my limits and was close to pulling out at one point during the race. My fitness wasn't as good as it should have been, but seeing the finish line after thirty-two-non-stop hours, I was stoked to complete it. I received my medal—styled in the form of a sheep bell to remind runners of the local herders we ran past in the mountains—finishing a respectable fourteenth out of fifty-seven hard-core endurance athletes.

23

ONE DAY GOBI AND I WERE SHIVERING, TRYING
to wrap up against the winter wind that whipped through the
ageing flat windows; the next we were unable to sleep, fighting for
air as the sweltering heat sapped the life out of us.

15 November was the day the government turned on the heat
nationwide. It was the start of our toughest times in Beijing.

Almost as soon as the heating went on, the pollution increased.
Like everyone in Beijing, I'd learned to monitor the air quality
and tailor my day accordingly. If the index was below 100, I'd
take Gobi out without any worry at all. Above 200, and I'd keep
our walks short. Above 400, and even the fifty-foot walk from the
bottom of the block of flats to my favourite Japanese restaurant was
enough to leave my eyes stinging.

I'd heard that when the levels are between 100 and 200 and you're
outside, it's like smoking a pack of cigarettes a day. Two hundred is
two packs, 300 is three, and anything above that is like a whole carton.

With the coal-fired power stations spewing their heavy smoke,
the sky was so full of toxic filth that you didn't dare open the windows in the flat.

Trying to avoid the pollution led to a sense that our freedom had been cut. We were not able to go for walks or out for coffee. Everything stopped. We felt as though we'd been cut off from the world.

The change was not good for Gobi. After just a few days of shutting ourselves away in the flat, I could tell she was struggling. She stopped eating, barely drank anything, and lay about with the saddest look on her face I had ever seen. About the only thing I could do to get her up and moving was to take her out into the corridor and throw a tennis ball for her to chase and bring back. It was the kind of game she would have played for hours had we been out by the canal, but up in the flat block, with the security lights continually switching themselves off and plunging us into darkness, she'd want to play for only thirty minutes.

Thinking the problem with the corridor might be too many distracting smells wafting out from under our neighbours' doors, I took Gobi down to the basement car park one day. I knew it was usually empty during the day, so there would be plenty of space for her to run and chase the ball, just like she used to.

As soon as the lift doors opened on the cavernous car park, Gobi planted her feet as if she were a hundred-year-old oak tree and refused to move.

"Really?" I said. "You're definitely not going in?"

She stared ahead into the darkness. She would not be moved.

On the night that I came back from my evening sushi and she didn't get up to greet me, I knew we were in trouble.

The next day the vet took a good look at her and diagnosed

kennel cough. The remedy was a course of medication and a week locked up in the flat.

With Lucja not due to come back to Beijing until Christmas, no media duties to fulfil, and no way of getting out, the days dragged by. Twice each day we'd take the tennis ball out to the corridor, and every evening I'd squint my eyes up tight against the pollution and hurry over to the Japanese restaurant. The flat was a furnace, but I dared not open the windows and let more pollution in. So every morning I'd wake up feeling hungover, regardless of whether I'd drunk three beers the night before or none at all.

I'd go to the gym from time to time, but I could stream only an hour's worth of video before my Internet account dropped out. Without a screen to distract me, I'd soon lose interest.

I tried to work on my strength and conditioning in the flat, but it was hopeless. The pollution was everywhere. Even though I washed the floor and wiped the surfaces regularly, every time I did push-ups, my hands would be covered in black grime, which must have crept in through invisible cracks in the windows.

Just as I was starting to slip into the darkness, Gobi recovered. Her timing was perfect. I'd wake up to see her staring at me, I'd receive the customary lick, and my day would be off to the best of starts. How could I be depressed when I had Gobi all to myself?

Gobi grew in confidence every day. Once she bounced back from the kennel cough, her old self re-emerged. Even when we were going outside so she could do her business, she'd walk with her head up, her feet light, and her eyes bright. I loved seeing her look so confident and self-assured.

Yet again Gobi got me through. I thought about how she had put herself through so much, from the run to the time on the streets in Urumqi, just so she could find a forever home with

people who would love and care for her. If she could tough it out, then so could I.

During those long days, I had a lot of time to think and a lot of things to think about.

I thought about coming home and how, even though I compete wearing the Aussie flag and would never support any sporting nation other than Australia, the UK is now my home. I've lived here for fifteen years and seen so many of the good things in my life flourish here. My running, my career, my marriage—all these things have taken off in the UK. I couldn't think of anywhere else I'd rather take Gobi back to.

I thought about my dad too. I was in my early twenties when my real father made contact and came into my life. Things were complicated, and it wasn't possible for us to have a lasting relationship.

Even though I never had that father–son experience that many of my friends have, I am grateful to him for one thing. He was born in Birmingham, England, but as a child his family emigrated to Australia. My dad didn't give me any money, and he didn't give me any support when I needed it most. But when I was an adult and ready to make a fresh start thousands of miles away from home, my dad's nationality meant that I was eligible for a UK passport.

I thought about my mum too. Around the same time my dad reappeared in my life, my mum became sick. She phoned me one day before Lucja and I met. I was surprised to hear her voice, given that we'd spoken only on Christmas Day in the years before that.

When she told me that she was seriously ill, I was stunned.

As I watched her go through treatment and saw her get danger-ously close to death, it pulled us closer. She wanted to make things better, and that was exactly what we vowed to do. We built the relationship back up from there. We took our steps slowly, but over the years we've at least grown to become friends.

Waiting around in the flat, counting down the days until I'd see Lucja again, I also thought about why finding Gobi had been so significant for me. It wasn't hard to figure it out.

It was about keeping my promise.

I'd vowed to bring Gobi back, no matter what it took. Finding her, keeping her safe, and making it possible to fly back home meant that I had kept my word. After all the ups and downs, I'd been able to rescue her. I'd given her the safety and security I had been so desperate for when my life went wrong as a kid.

The day Gobi stood by my side and looked up from my yellow gaiters and stared into my eyes, she had a look about her that I'd never seen. She trusted me from the outset. She even put her life in my hands. To have a complete stranger do that to you, even if it is a four-legged stray, is a powerful, powerful thing.

Did Gobi save me? I don't think I was lost, but I know for sure that she has changed me. I've become more patient, and I've had to deal with the demons of the past. She has added to the good things in my life that started when Lucja and I met and then continued when I discovered running. Maybe I'll no longer feel the need to run long-distance races to sort out the problems from my past. In many ways, by finding Gobi, I've found more of myself.

When Christmas was finally a few days away and I stood in the airport and watched Lucja walk through the arrival door, I

couldn't help crying. It was just like the day she waited for me at the Marathon des Sables: the longest, toughest, most gruelling part of the challenge was behind us. We'd made it. Soon we'd be going home.

24

SOMETIMES, IF I CLOSE MY EYES AND CONCENTRATE
hard enough, I can remember all the times I've been told that I was
going to fail. I still can picture my junior high school headmaster
holding out his hand for me to shake, a fake smile stuck on his face
as he whispered that one day I'd end up in prison.

I can see countless sports coaches, teachers, and parents of
people I thought were my friends, all looking at me with disapproval
or disappointment, telling me that I'd wasted whatever talent I had
and was nothing but a bad influence.

I remember my mum at the lowest points of her grief and how
helpless I felt.

For a long time I tried to block out those memories. I got
pretty good at it. I needed to, for whenever I let down my guard
and gave those dark memories some room to move, I instantly
regretted it.

Like the very first time I ran an ultra-marathon. I was nervous right from the start, but as the miles inched by and the hours
stretched out, I started to doubt myself.

Who am I to line up alongside all these other runners who know what they were doing?

What was I thinking, to try and run thirty miles with barely any training?

Was I really a fool to think that I could do it?

As these grew louder within me, the answers soon came.

You're nothing.

You're no good.

You're never going to finish.

Four miles from the finish, I proved those voices right. I quit.

This was a few weeks before my first multi-stage ultra, the 155-mile Kalahari race that Lucja had first spotted in the book I'd bought for her previous birthday. In the days after I bailed on my first ever ultra-marathon, the doubting voices within me grew louder and louder. When friends asked whether I really thought I was capable of running so far, given that I'd not managed a measly thirty-miler, I was almost convinced they were right.

Who am I to think I could do it?

I'm nothing.

I'm no good.

I'm never going to succeed.

But something happened between bailing on the thirty and starting the Kalahari. I wish I could say that I had a flash of light or a great training sequence, like in my all-time favourite movie, *Rocky*.

I didn't.

I just decided to try my best to ignore the voices that told me I was a failure.

Whenever those toxic whispers started up within me, I chose to tell myself a better story.

I can do it.
I'm not a failure.
I'm going to prove everyone wrong.

Our flight out of Beijing was late on New Year's Eve. I spent the day cleaning the flat, walking Gobi, and saying goodbye to the guys in the Japanese restaurant who had served up kimchi hot pot, sushi, salad, and friendship on an almost daily basis. They even gave me a bottle of the secret salad dressing that I had come to crave.

As we waited for Kiki to pick us up at the flat that evening, Gobi knew something was up. She was wired about as tight as I'd ever seen her, sprinting around the empty flat. When we finally walked out of the block of flats for the last time ever, Gobi raced towards Kiki's car as if it was made out of bacon.

I was a little calmer.

I sat and watched the street lights pass by, thinking about the people and places that had become important to us during the four months and four days we had spent in Beijing.

We passed the hotel gym where I had tried so hard to keep up my training. I thought back to all those times when the Internet had dropped out and I had to quit after just one hour on the tread-mill. I'd found the whole thing frustrating but nothing more. A mark of how much had changed in my life was that I'd been able to let go of it so easily.

There was the Little Adoption Shop, where Chris worked, and where we donated £10,000 from the donations left over from the Bring Gobi Home fund. Without Chris and his careful advice to Lu Xin about how to conduct the search for Gobi, I knew we never

would have found her. Without Chris, who knew where Gobi would be by now?

I thought about all the other people I'd met in Beijing, as well as those back in Urumqi. It was hard to leave so many great people behind, especially since my time in China had completely changed my view on the country and its people.

If I'm honest, when I arrived in China for the Gobi race, my view of the Chinese was a bit clichéd. I thought they were closed-off and serious, rude and uncaring. In that first journey from Urumqi to the race start, I saw in the people only what I expected to see. No wonder I didn't think much of the place.

But everything that happened with Gobi changed my perspective. Now I know the Chinese are lovely, genuine, hospitable people. Once they let you into their hearts and homes, they're incredibly generous and unfailingly kind. One family I'd never met but who had followed the story loaned me a £1,000 electric bike for the duration of my stay. They didn't ask for anything in return, not even a selfie with Gobi.

People were the same in Urumqi. The city itself might be full of closed-circuit TV cameras and security guards outside public parks, but the people are some of the friendliest, most generous, and most kind-hearted I've ever met. I'm pleased to have a connection with them and know that it won't be long before I return.

And then there's Kiki. She agreed to help us when everybody else was saying no. She came to Urumqi to make sure Gobi got out safely, and she spent the whole four months that we were in Beijing in a state of nervous tension, feeling responsible not just for Gobi's well-being but also for my welfare. I called her 24/7 with all sorts of questions (How do I pay for more electricity? Gobi's not feeling well. What do I do? Where do I go to buy

pollution masks?). She was never too busy or too tired to help, and she never once complained when I asked if she could take Gobi for a few days while I went out of town. She even sent video updates every couple of hours to me, and I was kept fully up-to-date with all the ways her staff pampered Gobi. Kiki made her team available to me as well. Her drivers ferried us everywhere, dropped off supplies to me in the flat, took care of the paperwork, and tended to countless details. They did more than I could have ever asked.

We pulled up outside the airport, unloaded the bags, and let Gobi take one last potty break before zipping her into the special doggie carrier that she'd be in for most of the journey.

UK law prohibits dogs from being in the cabin for any flights, in or out of the country. After she'd been so traumatized by travelling in the cargo hold when we left Urumqi, I vowed never to stow her away down there again. That meant our journey home was going to be long and complicated: a ten-hour flight to Paris, a five-hour drive to Amsterdam, a twelve-hour overnight ferry crossing to Newcastle in northern England, and a two-and-a-half-hour drive back home to Edinburgh. With all the waiting around added on, the whole thing was going to take forty-one hours.

We'd purposely paid extra for business class to make sure Gobi was comfortable and able to be next to me in the cabin. I felt pretty good as I walked up to the counter and was seen straightaway. I handed over my passport to the woman at the desk, stepped back, and thought about how much life had changed for Gobi. Six months earlier she'd been living on the edge of the Gobi Desert, desperate enough for survival to run three marathons alongside a

total stranger. Now she was about to fly business class to the chic city of Paris, of all places.

I was pulled out of my daydream by the sound of Kiki having an increasingly loud conversation with the Chinese check-in lady. During my time in China, I'd come to understand that anytime the volume rises in a conversation, trouble is brewing. I closed my eyes, listening as whatever issue Kiki had encountered grew bigger and bigger.

"What's going on, Kiki?"

"Did you book Gobi on to the flight?"

It was as if all the air around me suddenly turned stale.

"I didn't do it," I said. "I thought you were doing it."

Kiki shook her head. "Lucja supposed to do it."

Kiki turned back to the clerk, and the conversation continued. I dialled Lucja.

"Did you book Gobi on?"

"No," she said. "Kiki was supposed to do it."

It was obvious that this was just a simple misunderstanding between the two of them. They'd both been so busy organizing so much from other ends of the world that this little detail had been missed. And I was sure it was going to be relatively simple to fix. Maybe a little expensive but simple enough.

"Kiki," I said, tapping her on the shoulder. "Just get them to tell me how much it's going to cost, and we can get on with it."

She shook her head. "She say she can't. No way to put Gobi on system now. It's impossible."

I closed my eyes and tried to take control of my breathing. Steady in, steady out. Keep calm, Dion. Keep calm.

Another check-in clerk came over and joined the conversation, pushing the volume up another couple of levels. By now Kiki was

in full flow, pointing at Gobi and me in turn. I could do nothing but stand there and panic in silence.

All the paperwork we had to allow Gobi into the UK was tailored to our journey. That meant that if we arrived at Newcastle any later than midnight on 2 January, it would all be invalid, and I'd have to get Gobi seen and signed off by another vet. At the very best, that would add another day or two to the journey. At worst, it could take another week.

A third official joined the two behind the desk, and as he did, the atmosphere changed. The volume dropped, and he listened while Kiki talked.

After a few words from the boss, Kiki turned to me. "Gobi not booked on this flight," she said. I knew what was coming next, how we would have to book her onto the next flight out, but that would cost us an extra—

"Go to that counter there," Kiki said, pointing to another Air France desk nearby, "pay two hundred pounds, and he say they will get her on board."

I was stunned. "On board *this* flight?"

"Yes."

I didn't waste any time. I paid the fee at the other counter and came back to get my boarding pass.

"I told them Gobi a famous dog," said Kiki, and she smiled as I waited. "They know story and wanted to make it happen for you."

As soon as I had my passport and my boarding pass in my pocket, it was Gobi selfies and smiles all around for the check-in staff.

I finally said goodbye to Kiki at passport control, then drifted through security, exhaling a ton of stress as I went.

"Wait one moment," said a woman as I started putting my shoes back on. "You go with him."

I looked up to see a serious-looking man staring at me from the side of the scanners. I grabbed Gobi—still in her carry-on bag—and my luggage and followed him down a narrow corridor. He showed me into a sparse, windowless room that had nothing much more than a desk, two chairs, and a large bin full of confiscated lighters and water bottles.

Keep calm, Dion. Keep calm.

The guy stared at my passport and boarding pass and started typing at the computer. Minutes passed, and still he didn't speak. I wondered what it was that I'd done or said that could have landed me in trouble. I knew I hadn't outstayed my visa, and it had been weeks since I'd last given an interview. Could it be the pills that Lucja had given me to help keep Gobi calm during the flight?

More typing. More silence. Then, suddenly, he spoke. "We check dog."

My heart sank. I knew two hundred was far too cheap a price to pay to sort things out. And I knew that by now Kiki would be gone, and even though I had a file stuffed with paperwork from the vet, including proof that Gobi's vaccinations were up-to-date and that she'd passed the ninety-day assessment required before she could be brought into the UK, I'd have absolutely no chance of explaining anything to anyone. Without Kiki, I'd be at the mercy of Chinese bureaucracy.

The guy stopped typing, picked up the phone, and spoke for a moment.

"You wait minute," he said, once he had hung up and turned back to his keyboard.

Gobi was still in her bag, which I was clutching on my lap.

Through the mesh I could see her looking up at me. I wanted to tell her that it was going to be okay, to get her out and give her a cuddle to reassure her—as well as myself—but doing so wasn't worth the risk.

So I waited. It was the longest minute of my life.

The phone rang. I listened to one half of the conversation, clueless about what was being said or what the outcome might be.

"Okay," he said eventually. "Dog cleared to fly. You go."

"Where?" I asked.

"Fly."

I hurried back down the corridor, past the scanning machines, and eventually to the terminal. I found an empty gate and took Gobi out to give her a drink. I heard some French people nearby count down and burst into cheers. I checked my watch. It was midnight. The most remarkable year of my life was over. The next adventure was about to begin.

"Listen, Gobi," I said to her. "You hear that? It means we bloody well did it! We made it here, and we're about to go. It's going to be a long journey, but trust me that it'll all be worth it. When we get to Edinburgh, you'll see; life is going to be amazing."

Air France made sure that the seat next to mine was empty, so even though Gobi had to stay in her carry-on bag for the duration, we travelled in style. She was a little unsettled as we took off, but as soon as I could put her bag on my lap, she calmed again.

I watched the in-flight map and waited until we flew over the Gobi Desert. It put a smile on my face to see Urumqi flash up and think about the way a city I'd never heard of a year earlier had become so significant to me now.

The cabin lights were dimmed, and my fellow passengers went to sleep. I turned the seat into a bed and quietly took Gobi out of the bag. She had started to get a little restless again, but as soon as she curled up in my arm, she fell into a deep, deep sleep.

I closed my eyes and remembered what it felt like to run on the long day. I could feel the heat all over again, the way the air was so hot it threatened to scorch my lungs. I saw Tommy struggling to stand and remembered the desperate search for shade. I also remembered that even though I was faint and queasy and worried that I might not make it out alive, I knew that if I did, I would do everything I could to make sure that Gobi and I spent the rest of our lives together.

I couldn't hold back the tears when I saw Lucja at Charles de Gaulle Airport. Gobi, on the other hand, couldn't hold back the fourteen hours of pee that her little bladder had stored up. I'd taken puppy pads with me and tried to get her to do her business on the plane, but she had refused. Only when she stood on the highly polished floor right in the middle of the concourse did she finally feel ready to let go.

I was sure that the rest of the journey home was going to be a simple affair, and we even made a detour into the city to show Gobi the Eiffel Tower and the Arc de Triomphe. After that we headed north to Belgium first, and then on to Amsterdam and the home of Lucja's uncle, aunt, and cousins.

Seeing their excitement at meeting Gobi for the first time reminded me of the way people had responded to Gobi's story in 2016. The year had been full of sad news, from celebrity deaths to terrorist attacks. Much of the world had been divided by politics, but I'd read many comments from people who felt Gobi was one of the few good news stories that restored their faith in human nature. In a year marked by grief and fear, Gobi's story was a beacon of light.

After a shower and a rest, Lucja, Gobi, and I said goodbye to the family and made our way to the ferry terminal that was just around the corner from the house. Lucja had spent weeks persuading the ferry company to bend the rule that forced dog owners to leave their pets in their cars or keep the dogs in the kennels provided on board. There was no way that was going to work for Gobi, and the company had finally agreed that we could take her with us in a cabin.

So I thought boarding would be easy and we were going to be fine. Nothing could go wrong, could it?

Well, yes, it could. And it did. Almost.

The moment we handed over Gobi's pet passport at the check-in desk, the air changed. The woman behind the counter was flicking manically back and forth across the pages, a look of total confusion on her face.

"Do you need some help?" said Lucja in Dutch. "What are you looking for?"

"I can't read it," she said. "It's all in Chinese. If I can't read it, I can't let you on."

She called her superior over, and the two of them riffled through the pages all over again.

"We can't read it," said the boss. "You can't come on board."

Lucja had spent weeks learning about all the various requirements for moving a dog across borders, and she knew the rules inside out. She carefully and calmly showed both of them which stamp related to which vaccination, but it was no use. They weren't changing their minds, and until they did, Gobi was stuck in Holland.

Then I remembered the stack of paperwork that Kiki had given me for when we reached UK border control. It was all the same information but in English. I handed it all over, watched them look

through it all carefully, and listened to them finally make some encouraging noises.

Eventually, with just a few minutes to spare, we got a smile and a stamp in Gobi's pet passport. We were good to go.

The next morning, driving off the ferry, Lucja and I looked at each other nervously. Would we get stopped by UK border control? Would they find some flaw in the paperwork and send Gobi to London for an extra quarantine period? We approached the booth, held hands, and were surprisingly waved straight through. No checks. No hassle. No delay. Gobi was in the UK.

The drive north to Scotland was slow and easy, and as we passed low-slung hills and wide-open moors, I let my mind drift. I thought about the promise I had made to Gobi and the six months it took to make it happen. I thought back to all the people who donated money to help, the volunteers who spent day and night searching, and all the people worldwide who sent support messages and prayed for us. It wasn't just me who made this happen; it was the collective power of generous, loving people.

These thoughts brought a tear to my eye. The world was still a loving, kind place.

As the long journey home drew to a close, we drove over the hill and stared at the view. All of Edinburgh was laid out before us: Arthur's Seat—the mountain that stands guard over the city—the beach to the east, the Pentland Hills to the west. It was a beautiful day, not just because of the clear sky and clean air, and not even because it was my forty-second birthday.

It was perfect because of one simple, single reason.

We were together.

We made our way into the city, the car silent but our heads and hearts full. Turning onto our street, I realized I'd never thought about what it would feel like to walk through my front door, this remarkable little dog tucked under my arm.

I'd never thought about it because I'd never allowed myself to believe it would happen. All the deceit, all the fear, all the worry had weighed heavily on me. I'd never allowed myself the luxury of believing we'd finally do it.

But as the door opened and I saw good friends and loved ones inside, heard the popping of champagne corks and the cheers of people who were there to celebrate with us, I knew exactly what it felt like.

It felt like the beginning of a wonderful new adventure.

The hours and days that followed were busy in ways that reminded me of Urumqi. A TV crew had flown all the way from Australia to capture our return home and interview me. We received calls from journalists all over the world—some I knew well; others I had never spoken to before. They all wanted to know how Gobi had coped with the journey and what life held in store for her now.

I told them all how quickly she was adjusting to this new life, and how she and Lara the cat had already teamed up and taken joint ownership of the couch in our living room. I said that Gobi was an inspiration because she had dealt with the journey as she had dealt with every challenge thrown at her since we met. I told them I was proud of her.

But that was only part of the story. More than a handful of answers would be needed to say everything I wanted to say about Gobi. And sharing the ways in which finding Gobi had changed

me would take even longer—especially as I was aware that this new life had only just begun.

Only Gobi knows the answer to many of the questions: Why was she wandering in the Tian Shan? Why did she pick me? What happened when she went missing?

What mattered most then and what still matters most today is this: from the moment I said yes to Gobi, my life has been different. Gobi has turned up the contrast. She has added to all the good things in my life and brought healing to some of the bad.

Gobi's hip has healed, and the hair has grown back where she had to be shaved for the operation. She doesn't squeal in pain if the site is inadvertently touched. When walking on soft ground, she will sometimes lift her leg slightly. The vet in Edinburgh says that's likely a memory habit because placing weight on that hip used to be painful. When Gobi and I now run the hills and trails, her stride is perfect, and keeping up with her is just as difficult as it was in the Gobi Desert.

That first night when we all were finally together, Gobi and Lara took up residence at the foot of the bed, and I heard again the familiar silence of home. Lucja turned to me and quietly asked what I wanted to do the next morning. We had nothing planned, and the first few hours of the day were ours.

I knew exactly what I wanted. I looked at Gobi and then back at Lucja.

"Let's all go for a run."

Acknowledgements

CHINA HAS BROUGHT SO MUCH GOOD TO MY life, and I am grateful to have spent so long a time there. In a country of more than one billion souls, I have met some of the most generous, thoughtful, and kind people I could ever hope to meet.

Kiki Chen was the one person who stuck with us from the start and made getting Gobi out of China actually happen. Chris Barden was a genuine "dog whisperer" who set up our search team and was instrumental in finding Gobi. To Lu Xin, I owe so much. She never stopped looking for Gobi and showed me what true generosity looks like. Jiuyen (Lil) was more than a translator, and her words helped me every day in the toughest of circumstances. I am profoundly grateful to all the volunteers who searched day and night for a dog they had never seen, to help a guy they had never met. I can never thank them enough but hope they know how important they are to this story.

To the Ma family, I owe great thanks for finding Gobi. WorldCare Pet's support and guidance was second to none, and the WorldCare Pet team in Beijing showed unconditional love, care, and dedication to Gobi around the clock.

I still smile when I think of the times I spent with the Urumqi boys from Lvbaihui Tribes Barbecue restaurant (especially when I remember the firewater they gave me. *Ganbei Maotai!*).

I miss my Beijing brothers from Ebisu Sushi and am proud to be able to call the city of Urumqi my home city in China. I do not know a more supportive, kind, and generous city on earth.

The Chinese media showed support and dedication for our story and the love within.

Back home in the UK, reuniting with Gobi could not have happened without Lisa Anderson, who looked after Lara and kept our house a home. Iona, Kris, Tony, and Gill are just a few of the wonderful people who supported Lucja throughout it all. And Ross Lawrie, I just have one thing to say to you: bobby-dazzler!

The media has played such an important part in this story. Jonathan Brown from the *Daily Mirror* was the first reporter to bring the story to press, Judy Tait brought the story to BBC Radio 5 Live, and host Phil Williams supported us from the start. They saw the story in ways that I did not, and they led the way in sharing it with others.

Invaluable support also has come from the BBC UK and World Services, Christian DuChateau at CNN, Amy Wang at the *Washington Post*, Deborah Hastings at *Inside Edition*, Oliver Thring at *The Times*, Victor Ferreira at the *Canadian Post*, Nick Farrow and Steve Pennels at Channel 7 Australia, Pip Tomson at ITV's *Good Morning Britain*, and the *Eric Zane Show* podcast.

To all the many other journalists and radio and television hosts

who covered the story, I am thankful for your help in sharing our journey.

So many people have donated money, sent messages of love and support, or prayed every day for us. They didn't just believe in us—they made this whole thing possible.

I also want to thank Winston Chao; Mark Webber, for the tweet (Aussie Grit!); and Dr Chris Brown for his help, knowledge, and guidance. Richard Henson, who was an absolute legend, coming all the way to Urumqi to help. Tommy Chen, for being a great competitor and ambassador for Taiwan. Running coach Donnie Campbell, "one-two-three-one-two-three"; WAA Ultra Equipment, for standing by me; and William Grant and Sons, the kindest employers a man could wish for. Thanks are also due to DFDS Seaways and Air China.

Lastly, I am thankful for Team Dion and Gobi. Thanks to his daughter, Quinn, Paul de Souza made all of this a reality. Jay Kramer offered invaluable support, advice, and experience. Matt Baugher backed us and believed in us, and we owe him and all of the team at W Publishing, Thomas Nelson, and HarperCollins immense thanks for working so hard against such a tight deadline. Craig Borlase's vision, guidance, and patience putting this book together were incredible.

About the Author

DION LEONARD, a forty-two-year-old Australian, lives in Edinburgh, Scotland, with his wife, Lucja. Dion has not only completed but also competed for the top prize in some of the toughest ultra-marathons across the planet's most inhospitable landscapes: the brutal Moroccan Sahara Desert, twice in the 155-mile Marathon des Sables, and twice across South Africa's Kalahari Desert, also 155 miles.

During Dion's 155-mile race across the Gobi Desert in China, he fell in love with a stray dog (later named Gobi) who followed him during the week and changed both of their lives forever.

In the best books, the ending often comes as a shock.
Not just because of that one last twist in the tale,
but because you have been so absorbed in their world,
that coming back to the harsh light of reality is a jolt.

If that describes you now, then perhaps you should track down
some new leads, and find new suspense in other worlds.

Join us at www.hodder.co.uk, or follow us on
Twitter @hodderbooks, and you can tap in to a
community of fellow thrill-seekers.

Whether you want to find out more about this book,
or a particular author, watch trailers and interviews, have
the chance to win early limited editions, or simply browse
our expert readers' selection of the very best books,
we think you'll find what you're looking for.

And if you don't, that's the place to tell us what's missing.

We love what we do, and we'd love you to be part of it.

www.hodder.co.uk

@hodderbooks

HodderBooks

HodderBooks